REBIRTHING INTO ANDROGYNY

* * * * * *

REBIRTHING INTO ANDROGYNY

YOUR QUEST FOR WHOLENESS
AND AFTERWARD

*   *   *   *   *   *   *

A Textbook for Soul Searchers

BERENICE ANDREWS

BALBOA
PRESS
A DIVISION OF HAY HOUSE

Balboa Press books may be ordered through booksellers or by contacting:

Balboa Press
A Division of Hay House
1663 Liberty Drive
Bloomington, IN 47403
www.balboapress.com
1-(877) 407-4847

ISBN: 978-1-4525-5946-9 (sc)
ISBN: 978-1-4525-5947-6 (e)

Library of Congress Control Number: 2012918866

Because of the dynamic nature of the Internet, any web addresses or links contained in this book may have changed since publication and may no longer be valid. The views expressed in this work are solely those of the author and do not necessarily reflect the views of the publisher, and the publisher hereby disclaims any responsibility for them.

The author of this book does not dispense medical advice or prescribe the use of any technique as a form of treatment for physical, emotional, or medical problems without the advice of a physician, either directly or indirectly. The intent of the author is only to offer information of a general nature to help you in your quest for emotional and spiritual well-being. In the event you use any of the information in this book for yourself, which is your constitutional right, the author and the publisher assume no responsibility for your actions.

Any people depicted in stock imagery provided by Thinkstock are models, and such images are being used for illustrative purposes only.

Certain stock imagery © Thinkstock.

Printed in the United States of America

Balboa Press rev. date: 1/18/2013

Acknowledgment is made to the following for permission to reprint copyrighted material.

Minx Boren, Soul Notes Too, Four-Fold Path, Inc., 2003.

Joseph Campbell Foundation, Joseph Campbell, The Hero With a Thousand Faces, 3rd edition, Novato, California, New World Library, 2008.

From AGELESS BODY, TIMELESS MIND by Deepak Chopra, copyright © 1993 by Deepak Chopra. Used by permission of Harmony Books, a division of Random House, Inc.

Alan Cohen, The Peace You Seek, Alan Cohen Publications, 1991.

Cyndi Dale, New Chakra Healing: The Revolutionary 32-CenterEnergy System, Llewellyn Publications, 1997.

From WELLSPRINGS; A BOOK OF SPIRITUAL EXERCISES by Anthony de Mello, copyright © 1984 by Anthony de Mello, S.J. Used by permission of Doubleday, a division of Random House, Inc.

Prayer [p.41] "Abwoon (Father-Mother of the Cosmos)" from PRAYERS OF THE COSMOS; MEDITATIONS ON THE ARAMAIC WORDS OF JESUS by NEIL DOUGLAS-KLOTZ. Copyright © 1990 by Neil Douglas-Klotz. Forward © 1990 by Matthew Fox. Reprinted by permission of HarperCollins Publishers.

Golden Sufi Center for excerpt of quote by Al-Hakim at-Tirmidhi from The Taste of Hidden Things: Insights on the Sufi Path by Sara Sviri, © 1997/2002. The Golden Sufi Center (www.goldensufi.org).

Chris Griscom, Feminine Fusion, The Light Institute, 1991.

HarperCollins, Publishers: Lynne McTaggart, The Field: The Quest for the Secret Force of the Universe, 2002; Carol Pearson, Awakening the Hero Within: Twelve Archetypes to Help Us Find Ourselves and Transform Our World, 1991.

Valerie Hunt, Infinite Mind: Science of the Human Vibration of Consciousness, Malibu Publishing Company, 1996. (Used with the author's permission.)

Inner Traditions Publishing: Julius Evola and the UR Group, Introduction to Magic: Rituals and Practical Techniques for the Magus, 2001; Ervin Laszlo, Science and the Akashic Field: An Integral Theory of Everything, 2004; Jean LeLoup (trans.) The Gospel of Philip: Jesus, Mary Magdalene and the Gnosis of Sacred Union, 2003.

From the Penguin anthology, Love Poems from God, copyright 2002 Daniel Ladinsky and used with his permission: "The Chance of Humming," by Rumi, "The Spirit's Hands," by Meister Eckhart, and "I Have Come Into This World to See This," by Hafiz.

Bruce Lipton, The Biology of Belief: Unleashing the Power of Consciousness, Matter and Miracles, Hay House, 2005.

Littlefield Publishers: Jean Piaget, The Child's Conception of the World, 1951.

From PATHWORK OF SELF TRANSFORMATION by Eva Pierrakos, edited and compiled by Judith Saly, copyright © 1990 by The Pathwork Foundation. Used by permission of Bantam Books, a division of Random House, Inc.

Princeton University Press: Jolande Jacobi, Complex, Archetype, Symbol in the Psychology of C.G. Jung, 1959.

Rupa Books: Rabindranath Tagore, The Later Poems of Rabindranath Tagore, 2002.

Sounds True, wwwsoundstrue.com; an interview with Michael Beckwith, Spring, 2008.

Si Aurobindo Ashram: Sri Aurobindo, The Life Divine, 1990.

Mark Stavish, The Path of Alchemy: Energetic Healing and the World of Natural Magic, Llewellyn Publications, 2007.

John Wiley and Sons, Inc., Cynthia Bourgeault, The Wisdom Way of Knowing: Reclaiming An Ancient Tradition to Awaken the Heart, 2003.

From Maryann Zapalac for use of the drawings in Anodea Judith, Wheels of Life: A User's Guide to the Chakra System, Llewellyn Publications, 2000.

This book is dedicated with love to Marj, who has gently helped me to follow my bliss; and to Jack, who taught me that it's all a grand adventure.

ACKNOWLEDGMENTS

I pay special homage to the thousands of (mainly) unnamed and unknown people throughout the ages, who have contributed directly and indirectly to the creation of this book. It could not have been written without the paths they followed and the teachings they gave to the world.

I pay homage to my beloved teachers; the spirit guides, who provided the direction and the insights. I pay homage also to the human guides, who provided their wisdom, knowledge and practical expertise.

I am indebted beyond words to my students and clients, who have given me the experiences that I needed in order to "grow" into the depths of awareness required for generating this book. Although I cherish all these experiences, I make special mention of those I shared with my first great student, Rev. Temple Hayes.

I express my deep appreciation to Karen Blanden, whose financial assistance made this publication possible; to Nancy Devlin, who helped me to deal with the mysteries of computer technology throughout the writing and publishing process; to Sonam Palmo, Kay Warring, Dr. Sandy Sela-Smith, Judith Ando, Cate Alam, Rev. Alice Anderson and Rev. Russell Heiland, who read all or parts of the evolving manuscript and provided helpful comments and suggestions; to Denise Taylor, who made the inner illustrations dance on the page; to Paula Kozak, who created the wonderful cover design, to Mike Bowen, who designed the splendid web site "classroom" where this textbook will be used, and to my daughters, Diana and Carolyn, whose unfailing love and encouragement carried me through many moments of discouragement.

Finally, I say "thank you" to the publishers' representatives and to the authors, whose friendly advise helped to guide me along the new (to me) paths of obtaining copyright permissions and the other intricacies of publishing. And my special "thank you" goes to the consultants at Balboa Press, who helped me clear the last hurdles. It has been a grand adventure!

CONTENTS

PROLOGUE

Hello: thank you for dipping into this book. Are you resonating with any part of it . . . the title, perhaps? If you are, that deep-within vibration might be signaling something important. After focusing your attention into it and quietly waiting, you might detect a feeling/tone[1] of profound readiness: somehow you **know** that you have arrived at a crucial moment in your life.[2]

That insight could come as quite a surprise! And there might be more surprises in store. After further introspection, you might also realize that you have been getting a "readiness message," perhaps for a long time. It could even be "saying" something like this:

"Although I have been a 'success' for a number of years,
I have never really felt like one, or anything else."

"My recurrent thought ever since childhood has been that
life is okay and there's really nothing to it."

"For a very long time, I have known that as I got older I was not getting wiser
and that I was stuck in a lifestyle I despised."

"Although I've done exactly what I wanted to do most of my life,
I have always felt discontented and frustrated."

"While the years have drifted by, I have studied and thought
and yearned to be . . . what?"

"From a very early age, I have felt a terrible sense of loss and grief
when I encountered someone who seemed to glow with an inner light."

"I have *known* for years that something big
was missing in my life and I have felt lonely."

"I'm a stranger and afraid

---

[1] This metaphor was borrowed from many sermons recorded at Agape by Rev. Michael Bernard Beckwith.
[2] This inner state could be compared to "critical mass;" a physics term adopted into metaphysics. It means that concentrated and accumulated energies have reached a point of major and irreversible change.

1

in a world I never made."

"After some wasted years, too tiresome to count, my life's a complete mess:
I'm a mess, my relationships are a mess and my world is a mess . . .
dammit."

"Looking out at this world and in at myself,
I can see nothing but the desolation left by years of rage and conflict."

"Now that I've hit rock bottom,
where do I go?"

"God (or something) help me:
what meaning is there in my life?"

Do any of those examples of unutterable feeling and thought seem familiar, or trigger your own? If so, you might be a "soul searcher"[3] . . . in readiness. With readiness, there is something within that is "calling" insistently to you. It is inviting you to stop, now, and undertake a fundamental inner and outer change. The invitation is sublime, but you must be aware of this: if you **choose** to accept it, you will be embarking on a "journey;" a lifetime commitment that is both immensely difficult and immensely fulfilling.[4]

If you are a soul searcher in readiness (or suspect that you might be), this book is intended for you and you are invited to read on.

About the Title

"Rebirthing" — a fundamental reformulating of a person's inner beingness — has long been promised and promoted by many of mankind's spiritual traditions.[5] Modern spirituality, having inherited this wisdom teaching, seeks to expand its meaning in the light of present theories and knowledge about the living Cosmos. Within that context and understanding, an important re-configuring of the ancient wisdom can be given in a "rebirthing" teaching of the 21st century: that there is within each human being a power of creativity and renewal; that this power is both spiritual and "material;" that this power is inherent in the energies of human consciousness; that this power can be developed intentionally through a "rebirthing"

---

[3] I am indebted to Teresa de Bertodano, whose book bears this title. A "soul searcher" is defined herein as someone who has chosen to follow a "way" of life that is centered in an awareness of and obedience to a Spirit-guided inner evolutionary development.

[4] The "call" has been described many times in the world's spiritual teachings and myths. It is a summons, both ancient and forever new.

[5] In shamanism, the world's oldest spiritual tradition, rebirthing has always been part of soul retrieval practices. In the "mystery" tradition including the Greek, there were (and still are) intense rebirthing practices designed to bring about the healing of human bodies and minds. Also, a "rebirth" into higher consciousness was included in the teachings given in *The Hermetica* and in *The Upanishads*.

process, and that this power can be utilized for generating a more abundant inner and outer human life.

In the Christian spiritual tradition, there is a "rebirthing" story that can be re-told within that modern context. It is the story of Jesus, the Teacher and Nicodemus, the Pharisee.[6] It is a story about an encounter between a man who was truly en-lightened and a man who was reaching out for a more abundant inner life. On the one hand there is Jesus, whose "miraculous" powers clearly indicated that he was "from God" and that he was "with God" in an unusual way; on the other hand, there is Nicodemus, whose theological knowledge had not given him this God-connection and who sought to understand and (if possible) to acquire it. If we regard the Pharisee as a soul searcher in readiness, we can see that he was spiritually ignorant, for we are told that he came "in the night"[7] to meet with the Teacher. Continuing in that vein, we can also see that the Pharisee was probably expecting an intellectual discussion (perhaps even a debate). Instead, he met up with a man who wasted no time with superficialities, but went straight to the truths that he knew the other man was seeking. Indeed, Jesus was thoroughly aware that he was both an emissary and an exemplar "sent"[8] by and from the Spirit. In the context of modern spirituality, he was completely in-formed by the One Consciousness.[9] And he could speak about the Father/God and the inner Kingdom from that illumined **knowing** and **being**.[10]

Thus, in a modern re-telling of the story, the Teacher informs the Pharisee that those who seek to "see the Kingdom of God" (to have God-consciousness), i.e., to develop their sacred power of creativity and renewal, must be "born again." With that stunning announcement, Jesus launches Nicodemus (and us) into a profound teaching.

In the beginning, your rebirthing into God-consciousness comes "of water."[11] With this imagery, you the soul searcher are directed to plunge deeply into your own murky inner depths,

---

[6] *The Gospel of John*, 3: 1-12.

[7] These words, which are deeply meaningful, could also indicate that Nicodemus, who had a high social standing, feared for his reputation and came under the cover of darkness.

[8] Throughout the Gospels, Jesus repeatedly declared this about himself. He knew that he was both the messenger and the message.

[9] The One Consciousness is a modern phrase used throughout this book to indicate the All-Encompassing (omnipotent, omniscient, omnipresent) Power that is transcendent Spirit. Other words, used throughout history, have been Atum, Jehovah, Brahma, the Tao, Allah, the Ein Sof, the Cosmic Consciousness, God, Father, Mother, Wakan Tanka, the Source, Universe, Unity and others. Jesus, who knew that he was "one" with the Father (the One Consciousness), was completely aware of that Presence functioning within him. See *The Gospel of John* 10: 30.

[10] The word **knowing** is synonymous with **"gnosis,"** which is an awareness that is more than intellectual, although the intellect is included. The greater awareness that is gnosis is an all-encompassing and informed "knowing" in which there is no separation between the "knower" and the "known." Thus, **knowing** and **being** become one and the same. The seeds of this insight are to be found in *The Gospel of Philip*: "The truth is not realized like truth in the world; those who see the sun do not become the sun: […] But when you see something in this other space, you become it […] and in that All-Other you become all things, and never cease to be yourself." Jean-Yves LeLoup (translator), *The Gospel of Philip*, Verse 44. pp. 75-76.

[11] The word "of" given in Verses 5 and 6 of this account is herein taken to mean "part of" and "out of."

commonly referred to as your "unconscious mind."[12] By exploring within those "waters," you are seeking to become aware of all the hidden truths about you.[13] First you discover who you **believe** you are, physically, emotionally, mentally and spiritually. Then, while probing deeper into your obscurities and undergoing a radical inner re-formation, you slowly come into **knowing** who you **really** are. Thus, rebirthing "of water" is an intense experience of consciousness-raising and inner change. But it cannot be done by you, alone.

Then, the Teacher immediately states that those who seek to "enter into the Kingdom of God" (actualize their God-consciousness) must also be born again "*of* the Spirit." In other words, because you are "born of flesh" (an incarnation), you cannot attain your sacred creative power unless/until you surrender into a re-generative process that is wholly spiritual. When you do, your inner probing "work" will succeed because your deep "waters" can be stirred by the indwelling Spirit. It guides the process by sending Its messages into your depths and then assists you to emerge. [14] [15] And who will you be?

Jesus clearly indicates that "that which is born *of* the Spirit is spirit." By these words, he reveals the very "modern" awareness that whatever is *out* of and *part of* the Spirit, (the One Consciousness) **is** that consciousness and that by undergoing the "rebirthing" process you are becoming the God-consciousness.[16] In other words, during your "rebirthing," you become increasingly aware of who and what **you** are as **spirit**; a microcosmic consciousness which is a **knowing** creative power.[17] Then Jesus provides the final "piece" of the lesson.

---

[12] Carl Jung, who explored deeply into the human "unconscious," regarded it as having its own consciousness and carrying "knowledge" (revealed in dreams) that often exceeded that of the ordinary "conscious" mind. See Jolande Jacobi, *Complex/Archetype/Symbol in the Psychology of C.G. Jung*, pp. 190-198. Please note that the "conscious mind" is inferior to gnosis but is changed during rebirthing. The "unconscious mind," referred to herein as a person's "unknowing dimensions," is the opposite of "gnosis" (see Note #10 above). The "unconscious mind" is also changed during rebirthing.

[13] In Jungian psychology, "water" is a symbol of the "unconscious mind." For example, see C.G. Jung, *Four Archetypes: Mother/Rebirth/Spirit/Trickster*, p. 100. The "water" into which people are plunged during emotional distress and out of which healing and restoration can emerge has been a mythological symbol since ancient times. Note the reference to "deep waters where the floods overflow me" in Psalm 69: 1-3. In Jesus' day, the Pool of Bethesda was water that carried immense healing power. See *The Gospel of John* 5: 1-9. In the ancient Middle Eastern wisdom teachings, the "waters" are those of the Cosmic Womb out of which God called all creation. See Neil Douglas-Klotz, *Desert Wisdom: Sacred Middle Eastern Writings from the Goddess Through the Sufis*, pp. 4-38. Finally, water has been revealed by modern scientists to be an essential creative energy in the human body. See Massimo Citro, *The Basic Code of the Universe: The Science of the Invisible in Physics, Medicine and Spirituality*. Please note that all of those images of "water" are applicable while dealing with this "rebirthing" story.

[14] This is also an insight from Jungian psychology.

[15] The idea of Spirit as midwife is found in the sermons of Meister Eckhart. See Matthew Fox, *Passion for Creation*, p. 101.

[16] As already indicated, the One Consciousness has been referred to with many terms throughout the ages. Another modern designation used throughout this book and implied in the re-telling of the "rebirthing" story is "Creative Energy." Thus, the "rebirthing" process can be regarded as a change brought about by spiritual energies.

[17] The Spirit (the One Consciousness, Creative Energy) has also been referred to as the macrocosm, which has created out of Itself Its multivariate, living expressions, referred to as the microcosm. And people are microcosmic expressions of the One Consciousness, Creative Energy. After being reborn into sacred spiritual

He informs Nicodemus (and us) that a person reborn *of* the Spirit is analogous to the "wind;" creative energies that can be heard but not seen and are perfectly free and empowered to go wherever they choose. In the present re-telling, you who are reborn *of* the Spirit are in truth a multidimensional consciousness energy being[18] that can expand to fill the universe. Thus, there is brought about in you, as there was in the psalmist, an exaltation of awareness: you **know** that you are a god.[19]

To re-phrase the story and the teaching: rebirthing is an intense inner and outer experience; a process chosen by you, the soul searcher, and guided by the indwelling Spirit. It is simultaneously a "gestation" and a "labor," during which you create (generate inwardly) and bring forth (manifest outwardly) what you truly are. While rebirthing, you go through several necessary stages of trans-formation and re-formation; fundamental changes and re-shaping which include those of your self-identification and of your relationships. During that process, you slowly evolve into God-consciousness — your creative power — and your sacred human **beingness**. Thereafter, you live with and by this reality.

Thus, it can be said that the "rebirthing" story of Jesus, the Teacher and Nicodemus, the Pharisee is a timeless wisdom teaching, applicable as much today as it was that long-ago night in Jerusalem.

Continuing with the title . . .

"Androgyny" indicates an immense possibility, for androgyny is "a potential of beingness for every person who undertakes the quest of bringing it into realization."[20] In other words, being androgynous is not a special state reserved for certain types of people. But the process of becoming androgynous requires the unshakeable commitment and the courage to undergo a rebirthing journey. In the quest for wholeness, the person becomes increasingly aware that he or she "is a contrasexual person, looking to join within himself or herself the energies of both

---

humanness, they are fully aware of their creative power, unlike those who are not reborn but who have the creative power without realizing it or using it wisely.

[18] The microcosmic, multidimensional person as a consciousness energy being is dealt with throughout this book. In preparation, please note that "consciousness" is the microcosmic expression of the macrocosmic One Consciousness. In further preparation, please note that "energy" is the microcosmic expression of the macrocosmic Creative Energy, which is also the One Consciousness. In this context, the microcosmic energy is a **living, constantly changing, intangible and creative power** that is known in quantum physics as both "particle" and "wave." For more detail, see Barbara Brennan, *Hands of Light*, pp. 24-28 and Fritjof Capra, *The Tao of Physics*, pp. 189-283. Thus, "consciousness energy" can be defined as **the creative, living vibration of knowing and being**, the microcosmic expression of the macrocosmic Spirit (the One Consciousness, Creative Energy). And you are the human "consciousness energy being." (See Note #38 below.)

[19] See *Psalm 82*: "I said, 'you are "gods:" you are all sons of the Most High'." See also the *Gospel of John* 10: 35-36. Please note that the "knowing" that is "gnosis" is **the fully developed human consciousness**.

[20] June Singer, *Androgyny: The Opposites Within*, p. 236.

the feminine and the masculine modes of being human."[21] Those "modes" are the archetypal[22] "opposites within."[23] In a human being, androgyny is an inherent and harmonious interaction of those inner opposites. In turn, the inner opposites are in-formed by the Cosmic Feminine and Masculine Principles, the archetypes-as-such, differentiated in a "primordial cosmic unity."[24] Since this is a "unity" of opposites, being androgynous means living a paradox. As such, it eliminates inner duality, because androgyny is **both** masculine (andro-) **and** feminine (gyne), "the One that contains the Two."[25]

Echoing Hindu teachings, to rebirth into androgyny, the wondrous paradox, is to learn how to "dance," metaphorically, the Dance of Shiva and Shakti; Cosmic Energies that come together but never merge. In their configurations and excitations, they always move in mutual vibration.[26] It is an oscillating (and, as you will discover), a multidimensional "dance" that becomes more and more dynamic and balanced as the soul searcher continues the quest. And while all this happens, there is an increasing awareness that the dance is a response to an "inner guiding mechanism that senses what is needed at any particular moment."[27]

---

[21] Ann and Barry Ulanov, *Transforming Sexuality: The Archetypal World of Anima and Animus*, p.4. Please note that the masculine and feminine "modes" are not the same as male and female. Thus, being contrasexual is not the same as being hermaphrodite or being bisexual. The latter are states of physicality. To elaborate further, in *The Myth of the Goddess: Evolution of an Image*, page 444, Anne Baring and Jules Cashford note that " [...] from our knowledge of other cultures we can say that the *relation* of masculine and feminine [...] was always the culmination of religious ritual. And this must tell us something about a universal need to reconcile these two polarities of human existence."

[22] The teachings about archetypes, while ancient in origin, have been made familiar by Jungian psychology. In preparation for the lessons to follow, please note that while "archetypes" have been defined and described in many ways, the idea used throughout this book is that **archetypes are "active, living dispositions" that are the "basis of all the usual phenomena of life."** Archetypes not only "transcend culture, race and time" but also reach "back into the primordial mists of evolutionary time." (Quoted from Anthony Stevens, *Archetypes: A Natural History of the Self*, p. 39.) In other words, archetypes are expressed in, as and through the human beings who invoke them. The Archetypes-as-Such are manifested in the world's religions, mythologies, fairy tales and art. Humans experience the archetypes as **images** in the individual "unconscious." The symbolism of those images, often given in dreams, requires not only intuitive and insightful but also intellectual understanding. See Jolande Jacobi, *Complex/Archetypes/Symbol in the Psychology of C. G. Jung*, p. 101.

[23] Singer, *Androgyny: The Opposites Within*, p. x. Those forces are also carried within the archetypal human energy system presented later herein.

[24] The universal Feminine and Masculine are the differentiated archetypal energies symbolized by the gods and goddesses of the world's myths. See Singer, *Androgyny: The Opposites Within*, p. 5.

[25] *Ibid*, p. 5.

[26] The Dance of Shiva as the "endless rhythm of the universe" is found in Hindu teachings. See Fritjof Capra, *The Tao of Physics*, p. 90. An early 20th century Hindu sage and scholar, Sri Aurobindo, has dealt with the "mystery of the masculine and feminine cosmic Principles whose play and interaction are necessary for all creation.". For more detail, see Sri Aurobindo, *The Life Divine*, pp. 373-377. The dance of Shiva and Shakti is found in the teachings of Kashmir Shaivism, as a "pulsing union" that merges and separates the divine pair and brings about the "emission of cosmic manifestation." See Mark S. G. Dyczkowski, *The Doctrine of Vibration: An Analysis of the Doctrines and Practices of Kashmir Shaivism*, p. 100.

[27] Singer, *The Opposites Within*, p. 10. In the present context, that "inner guiding mechanism" is the indwelling Spirit, the inner guidance system.

In other words, to rebirth into androgyny is to transition into the highest level of consciousness possible for a human being. Jesus of Nazareth was androgynous.[28] In the "rebirthing" story, Jesus taught Nicodemus (and us) how this could be achieved. Continuing with the title . . .

A "quest" is a prolonged and dedicated search; one that has been part of the human experience for untold centuries. Often symbolically presented in myths, legends and fairy tales, a quest can be both a heroic journey and a pilgrimage. As such, it is an arduous and sacred adventure, usually begun at the behest of an "inner compulsion."[29] And this adventure, which involves both inner and outer searching, is a "work" motivated by only one desire; the achievement of an inner transformation, liberation and regeneration; the prelude to wholeness.

Clarifying that last statement . . .

Although the descriptive images vary, inner "transformation" is always a fundamental change; the re-forming of soul" structures.[30] Although the traditional teachings can vary, inner "liberation" is essentially a relinquishing of the destructive, fear-based beliefs, attitudes and values with which the ego/self[31] is predominantly identified. And while there are other words to describe it, inner "regeneration" is the experience of a new and authentic integration; both a fullness and an emptiness of being.[32] And all the while, the quest is taking the soul searcher **toward** the indwelling Spirit.

Continuing with the title . . .

"Wholeness" has long been the ultimate goal of an inner quest; the attainment of self-realization and a sense of oneness with the Divine.[33] In Christianity, wholeness and holiness are the same; the awareness of having become purified, through divine grace ("salvation" through Christ), good works and a life devoted to maintaining that awareness. In the Hindu tradition, "the [sage] who is settled in this final union [. . .] realizes that God has become his nature, his little self, as well as all other selves."[34] In Jungian psychology, wholeness is "individuation,"[35] which brings into harmony the archetypal masculine and feminine forces, and actualizes the androgynous Self in a human being. In the Diamond Approach, wholeness

---

[28] I am indebted to Dr. Anthony Stevens, whose insights about Jesus led me to this conclusion. See Stevens, *Archetypes: A Natural History of the Self,* pp. 207-209.

[29] *Ibid.* p.134.

[30] The concept of soul structures is thoroughly explained later herein. Please note at this point that they are your embodiments of consciousness energy.

[31] This term is also thoroughly explained later. Please note at this point that the ego/self is a very complex and necessary soul structure that, like all the others, undergoes a developmental process and like the others, can be healed.

[32] It is what the Apostle Paul might have meant by his words "seeing through a glass darkly, then face-to-face."

[33] There are many spiritual/psychological paths that serve Life and are, therefore, oriented towards wholeness. Basically, it is our eventual realization of oneness with the immanent and transcendent Spirit (the One Consciousness, Creative Energy), in whatever words we use.

[34] Paramahansa Yogananda, *The Bhagavad Gita,* Verse 54, pp. 296-297.

[35] Anthony Stevens, *Archetypes,* p. 34. "Individuation is the process of responding to a basic motive of human psychology—the quest for wholeness."

is the realization of the Personal Essence.[36] In "New Thought," wholeness is the achievement of the Authentic Self,[37] (in some teachings referred to as the Christ Consciousness). And in shamanism, to have wholeness is to have the capacity to embrace one's own infinity.

"And Afterward" . . . beckoning to the newborn androgyny, there awaits the awakened capacity to explore life's deepest mysteries, to live **with** the indwelling Spirit. And this is done by **knowing** your own spiritual humanness and living as a **real** human being, on this Earth plane. And while the "afterward" continues, there will be yet more awakening, for human beings carry the capacity to live **in** the Spirit and, thereby, to **know** their totality of Being.

Having looked into the title, you might be interested in finding out how it will be developed in this book.

Purpose, Contents and Format

The purpose of this book is two-fold: first; to teach you about "you" as a multidimensional soul; an intensely **human** energy being,[38] whose embodiments are generated by your archetypal human energy system[39] and shaped by your inner and outer environments, and, second; to guide you through a rebirthing process of transformation, liberation and regeneration into your wholeness of being.

In these pages, you are given lessons drawn from many sources, including the world's wisdom teachings, along with history, metaphysics, physics, philosophy and psychology; all presented within the context of evolutionary spirituality.[40] The instruction is enriched by the inclusion of the imaginal realm, indicated by shamanic practices,[41] myths, fairy tales, poetry and dreams.[42] Also included are ongoing practices that are developmental disciples and self-

---

[36] This is the message of A. H. Almaas, a great modern wisdom teacher.

[37] See, for example, Robert Brumet, *The Quest for Wholeness: Healing Ourselves, Healing Our World.*

[38] The ideas about a human "consciousness energy being" presented throughout this book have emerged out of my study of the theories presented by the authors cited in the "Bibliography," my learning sessions with my teachers and my many healing encounters with my clients. A human energy being is defined herein as **a microcosmic consciousness manifesting and expressing as a four-fold embodiment that has evolved over millions of Earth years into a person, with the potential for transcendent awareness; a "work" that is still in progress**.

[39] Please recall Note #22 above. In addition, note that archetypes are expressed **in**, **as** and **through** the people who invoke them. These ideas are presented in several lessons. An introduction to the human energy system, which is fundamental to the rebirthing process, is given in the first lesson of this book and elaborated upon in all the remaining lessons. In preparation, please recall Notes #17 and #18 above.

[40] The term "evolutionary spirituality" was used by Ken Wilber in an audio taped interview with Bill Moyers. The message was two-fold: that human spirituality has evolved and will continue to do so, unless human beings prevent it from happening; and that in this 21st century, a transformative, regenerative spiritual undertaking requires that people use all the life-enhancing ideas and insights that are available to them from the great thinkers of the past and the present.

[41] The shamanic practices are both traditional and modern. They reflect the orientation of both tribal and 21st century urban shamans. The latter differ from the former in that their practices include the knowledge of modern metaphysics, psychology and quantum physics.

[42] The "imaginal realm" has been described as "a world as ontologically real as the world of the senses and the world of the intellect." See Mary Pat Mann, "The Door to the Imaginal Realm," in *Mytholog*, Vol. 4, Number 3, p. 2, (internet web site).

healing therapies that are also disciplines, plus homework assignments; all designed to raise your vibratory frequency and, thereby, to promote your rebirthing process. In sum, this book is both a manual to instruct you and a map to guide you, while you make your journey and move through your quest.

Emulating the spiraling, cyclical "paths" of the Celtic shaman,[43] each part of this book takes you to a higher level of "knowing." At each level you, the knower and you, the known, become increasingly inseparable. Finally, you arrive at self-awareness well beyond the intellectual. It is the illumined **knowing** (the "gnosis"")[44] that has become your true **being**.

In Part One, you start your journey on the path of the East ("Opening the Way"). Two lessons give you the Big Picture; the historical, metaphysical, scientific and theoretical context which is both a framework and a foundation (the "grounding") for your quest. In the first lesson you are given ancient and modern wisdom teachings about your energies of consciousness. Then, you receive basic instruction about your human energy system. Still within the Big Picture, you continue into the second lesson with more teachings; those about your energies of soul. Finally, in the culmination of "opening the way," you learn how your energies of consciousness and your energies of soul are linked with each other and with your human energy system. Meanwhile, you have undertaken your first practices and healing therapies. By being "grounded" in the Big Picture, you are being strengthened for the remaining paths of your quest and you are experiencing the first stages of your rebirthing.

The three lessons of Part Two, the path of the South ("Coming into Being") teach you that **what** you are as consciousness energies[45] is **who** you are as soul. You learn that since your conception, you have carried the power to generate out of your soul substance, the soul structures that are the components of "you." You also learn why and how your ego/self,[46] a necessary aspect of you, has developed in relation to the "dancing" masculine and feminine energies that are inherent in your soul substance and intrinsic to your energy system.

In these lessons, your quest for wholeness involves getting to know and expand into your own interactive multidimensionality. You do this by tuning into and healing your three "lower" centers of consciousness[47] along with your very complex "animal" soul structures. In this ongoing process of transmutation and transformation,[48] you add new practices and healing therapies, while you maintain the old ones. And as you proceed, you are not only gestating the second stage of your rebirthing, but you are also promoting a new sense of inner

---

[43] I am indebted to R. J. Stewart for the seed ideas. See *The Way of Merlin*, pp. 18-19.

[44] See Note #10 above.

[45] The term "energy" is usually conjoined herein with the term "consciousness." See Note #18 above.

[46] The terms "soul," "soul substance," "soul structures," "soul field" along with "ego/self" are defined and presented later. In preparation please note that all of these terms are indicative of consciousness energies.

[47] The centers of consciousness are the vital components of the human energy system. They are also defined and presented later.

[48] Although there is a tendency to make "transmutation" and "transformation" synonymous, there is an important difference. To transmute is to change the energies from **one nature, condition and/or state** into another. To transform (which includes re-form) is to change the energies from **one form, appearance and/or structure** into another.

empowerment. It is emerging from your increasing certainty about the ways in which you are "coming into being" in this lifetime.

In the one lesson of Part Three, the path of the West ("Entering Within"), your quest takes you into your heart center and into your first direct contact, through your heart archetypes, with your "higher" centers of consciousness. You enter into your "heart awareness." While continuing your established/practices, you add the heart disciplines and more healing therapies. You repair your damaged heart "bridge" and discover the great alchemical powers of your heart "crucible." Thereby, you enhance the healing of both your heart center of consciousness and your "lower" centers. During this transmutation and transformation, you recognize and harmonize your seemingly opposing masculine and feminine inner forces, continue to heal your "animal" soul structures including your ego/self and welcome in your "shadows;" your disowned and rejected "selves." And, in this "work" you are entering into and emerging from your third rebirthing stage.

Then, in the one lesson of Part Four on the culminating path of the North ("Finding Wisdom"), you remain in your new heart awareness, while you probe into your "higher" centers of consciousness. You discover the full meaning of "upward" and "downward" causation. This you do by perceiving and understanding the creative power of those centers in relation to the "lower" ones. While maintaining all the practices and healing therapies and adding to them, you bring about more healing of those centers of consciousness, Thereby, you are culminating the journey and the transformative "work" involving your "animal" soul structures. And you realize that all this time you have been developing spiritual humanness; the indicator of your God-consciousness, which is your creative power and the essential context of both androgyny and wisdom. During this final stage, when all is in readiness, you complete your rebirthing.

But, although your quest for wholeness is over, your journey is not.

While on your paths, you are taking an "inner journey home."[49] With all your steps you are journeying *toward* the indwelling Spirit. Yet, when you arrive at your anticipated "destination," you discover that there is yet more for you to experience. In other words, although you have achieved the wholeness of androgyny, you have barely begun to actualize all that you are.

At your new level of awareness, your next journey involves all your paths; in particular the path of "Finding Wisdom." In the "Afterward," you embrace the adventure of living as an androgynous human being, with the possibility of becoming *moshel meshalim*; a "Master of Wisdom." You explore what that might be like, while you live and function "*in* this world but not *of* it;" in other words, while you live an ordinary life in an extraordinary way. You discover that this way of living involves a heart awareness that includes, above all else, your relationships; with this Earth, with yourself, with intimate others and with the rest of the world. You go yet more deeply into the **knowing**, which is becoming your **being**.[50] And you continue your journey until you are walking *with* the indwelling Spirit.

---

[49] This is the title of the splendid book by A.H. Almaas.
[50] See Note #10 above.

Finally, in the "Epilogue" you go farther. Having attained spiritual humanness, you grow higher and higher, deeper and deeper, until you come to realize your completion; that of **knowing** and of **being** *in* the Spirit. Having achieved that oneness, you may, if you choose, develop these lessons into their next level.

If you are interested in knowing why this book was written, please read on.

A Personal Account

It was at the gloaming[51] of a beautiful day in May, when my friend brought me to the circle of stones on the moors in northern England. There stood "Long Meg," the enormous stone "head" outside the circle.[52] With her back to the north, she faced inward toward her "Daughters."[53] Approaching with a sense of awe, I walked up the incline, between the entrance stones and onto the grassy center.

I had greatly anticipated this moment and felt confident that I was adequately prepared. On the preceding day, we had gone to the Castlerigg stone circle, where I had tried an experiment. Having spent years working with the human energy system as a shamanic healer, I felt a deep need to explore the energies of the stones. When I placed my hands on *any of those that were still standing*, I discovered that *each stone carried either a predominant masculine or feminine energy*.[54] Although I had known about stone energies, I had never before heard of such specificity. I was both amazed and delighted.

Made bold (and somewhat careless) by my success, I did the same thing in the Long Meg stone circle. I had exactly the same results. Then I unthinkingly placed my hands on Long Meg. Immediately, they were punched by a jolt of energy so strong that it pushed them away. In tears, I was almost overwhelmed by the realization that this stone "head" embodied a living consciousness energy just as real as mine.

I have never forgotten that experience. The encounter with Long Meg, an androgynous presence (if there ever was one!),[55] triggered the writing of this book. Long Meg and her Daughters (and Sons) became a metaphor, on two levels:

First, the stone circle was a place where ancient pilgrims, questing for divine help, came to participate in communal ceremony and ritual. It was a sacred space where transcendent

---

[51] This word, meaning the twilight of the day, also carries the special, other-worldly and magical energies that can be present in the evening.

[52] The stone stands twelve feet high and weighs approximately seven tons.

[53] The name was given to the stone circle in the Middle Ages. The story is that Long Meg and her daughters were witches, who were turned into stone by a Christian monk after they had refused to mend their wicked ways. The circle itself pre-dates Christianity by several thousand years.

[54] These are not male and female biological designations. They are the masculine yang and feminine yin forces already mentioned and clearly discernable to shamans (and other energy-oriented people) in humans, other mammals, reptiles, plants and (obviously) stones.

[55] Although I have not again had the opportunity to touch Long Meg, I have studied for many hours the photograph taken by my friend that day. The always-present inner resonance is that of a mother's tenderness toward her young children, a brooding like that of a brood hen (or "broodingmale") and a fierce warrior energy; a watchfulness that is totally focused, always gentle and completely ruthless.

Spirit dwelt and in-formed those who were ready to receive Its messages.[56] In the lessons that follow, you will come repeatedly, in an act of imagination, to the Long Meg Stone Circle, as a hallowed place of teaching, learning and healing.

Second, the circle of stones is analogous to the circular **chakras** that are the "wheels of light;"[57] the centers of consciousness of the archetypal human energy system. While you make your quest, you will probe deeply into those indwelling sacred centers. And you will reverently come to acknowledge — while at the same time you will utilize — their great creative power.

And afterward . . . Long Meg with her Children will be there to help you continue to explore and to expand all that you are. What a grand adventure is awaiting you!

Now, Soul Searcher, if you are ready . . . and willing . . . we shall proceed.

---

[56] The circle, being a symbol of unity, has always been integral to shamanic work. Shamans, who refer to the entire cosmos as "sacred space," enclose a portion of it here on Earth, for the purposes of ritual and ceremony, by "casting the circle." Thus, the Long Meg Stone Circle is a shamanic sacred enclosure.

[57] The word "chakra" (shaw-cra) is Sanskrit, meaning "wheel." The teachings about the centers of consciousness hat are wheels of light (color and sound) are derived from the ancient Hindu yogic tradition.

PART ONE

THE PATH OF THE EAST:

"OPENING THE WAY"

FIRST INTRODUCTION

Shamans know that the infinite and continually-expanding Cosmos is "sacred space." It is an eternality filled with the living Power and Presence of the Spirit.[58] [59] [60] Shamans know that wherever they stand on Earth, they are at the center of sacred space. From this vantage point, they travel into that space in order to obtain and to return with spiritual knowledge. Shamans also know that spiritual knowledge is available not only to them, but also to anyone earnestly seeking and diligently working to acquire it.

The cosmic spiritual knowledge includes the wisdom teachings. They are the timeless writings and interpretations that constitute your spiritual inheritance.[61] The wisdom teachings undergird your humanity and provide both the foundation and framework for your rebirthing quest. Thus, it is necessary that you receive your sacred legacy.

If you are starting to feel a little lost, help is at hand.

When shamans travel ("spirit journey") into and back from sacred space (the "spirit world") in order to acquire spiritual knowledge ("power"), they use as their points of reference the four directions of Earth.[62] Those directions are the names of the parts of the spirit world (the "realms")[63] into which shamans journey. Each realm carries its

---

[58] The word "shamans" used throughout this book refers to both traditional tribal and modern urban shamanism. (See Note #41 in the "Prologue").

[59] As already indicated in the "Prologue," the word **knowing** refers to a microcosmic consciousness, a **gnosis** that goes well beyond any intellectual, conceptual awareness. The phrase "shamans know" indicates that **knowing.**

[60] Please recall that the Spirit is the One Consciousness, omnipotent, omniscient and omnipresent, and that Spirit is also the Creative Energy. (See the "Prologue" Notes #17 and #18.)

[61] Those teachings were probably first "located" in the Akashic Field about which you will soon learn more.

[62] In Celtic shamanism and others, these are the cardinal points of the compass: East, South, West and North. In some shamanic traditions that use the "medicine wheel", the ordinal points are also included.

[63] For further information about the shaman's "spirit world," see Michael Harner, *The Way of the Shaman.* See also John Matthews, *The Celtic Shaman,* Tom Cowan, S*hamanism as a Spiritual Path for Everyday Life* and

own immense power.[64] Each is traveled by its own "path." On your quest for wholeness, you will be invited to journey on the paths in the four realms of the spirit world. You will do this so that you, like the shamans, can acquire your spiritual knowledge, i.e., your power.

You begin your rebirthing quest by surrendering to the power of the East. It is the cosmic realm of beginning and renewal. The East contains the power that invariably expresses in this third dimension as the energies of a new day dawning and the seasonal energies of springtime with its freshness and vigor. The East also contains the power that invariably expresses in Earth's living things, including people, as the energies of "gestation," newness and earliest development. In addition to those immense powers, the East contains the power of "letting go." But this power, unlike the others that are freely bestowed by the cycles of "nature," is only a possibility that must be actualized. Because beginning and renewing often require the letting go of the old so that the new can be generated, actualizing this power is essential for your journey.

Embracing the power of the East, you set your feet on the path of **opening the way** and you plunge into the "Big Picture." In that total immersion, you receive your first wisdom teachings — those about consciousness and soul. And you receive the preliminary instruction about their connection with you. In these beginnings while you open the way, you start to generate a new knowing with its potential of new being.

Shamans know that in the East, the macrocosmic energy of Life-as-Such is paramount. Eternally unchanged and unchanging Life is an aspect of the Spirit. Shamans also know that, at the same time, the microcosmic life energy is constantly beginning and constantly renewing itself. Thus it is that life energy is vibrating as every particle/

Mircea Eliade, *Shamanism: Archaic Techniques of Ecstasy.*

[64] The word "power" in the shamanic context, throughout this book has several meanings that can be understood within the context itself. When capitalized, the word "Power" refers to the transcendent macrocosmic **Energy** of the One Consciousness, Creative Energy that is the Spirit. When spelled with lower case, the word "power" means the immanent microcosmic **energy** of the Spirit expressing Itself in two ways. First; the energy is carried by and contained in the symbolic imagery that appears in each of the spirit world realms as particular "forms" of **instruction.** Second; the spiritual knowledge that is imparted by connecting with and intuiting the meaning of this imagery, then evolves into the "power" (the "medicine") that in-forms shamans. Another word for this power is **knowing,** i.e., "gnosis," out of which **being** develops.

wave of all creation (the manifested cosmos), including you. An awareness of that energy is what you require now. Beginning and renewing mean accepting and allowing Life/life.

Now let us go to the stone circle.

Lesson One

THE "BIG PICTURE:" YOUR ENERGIES OF CONSCIOUSNESS

Hello: welcome to the stone circle. This enclosure is truly a sacred space, hallowed by centuries of use.[65] It is a place where pilgrims gathered to worship their divinities and to participate in special spiritual practices. Like you today, the pilgrims often came at this season of the year, when an eagerly-anticipated springtime had finally arrived and new growth was bursting forth on the moors. As you are today, those ancient ones were also soul searchers. Some had traveled for a long time, over great distances. Many had undergone considerable hardships. How glad and relieved they were to enter, finally, into the welcoming embrace of Long Meg and her Children! Come . . . sit here in the center . . . . Earth is warm. The air is sweet. The tender, fresh grass is soft. Spread this ground sheet and make yourself comfortable. Just by coming to this place today, you have already taken your first steps on your path of "Opening the Way."

It is a path whose milestones are those of "letting go." While you sit here at the center of this sacred enclosure, start now to enter into the Big Picture. You do this by releasing all outside distractions and focusing on the patch of Earth beneath you. In this first step on your quest for wholeness, you are invited into a new awareness. It is this: you are *of* the Earth. Beneath you is energy;[66] energy that is also consciousness.[67] Now, "tune into" that living consciousness energy by putting your attention into it. Feel it, as it vibrates with your energies, with your consciousness.

---

[65] The circle itself is a remarkable structure that was "geometrically planned and cosmically oriented." See Joscelyn Godwin, *The Golden Thread: The Ageless Wisdom of the Western Mystery Traditions*, p. 27, 33.

[66] In preparation for what is to follow, please recall Notes #17 and #18 in the "Prologue." To add to this information, the energy of Earth is more than physical, although the physicality of kinetic and potential energy is contained therein. **Earth energy is part of the cosmic energy**, described by Ervin Laszlo as the "quantum vacuum" of the Akashic Field, by A. H. Almaas as the "vital energy field", and by Barbara Brennan as "the Universal Energy Field". See Ervin Laszlo, *Science and the Akashic Field: An Integral Theory of Everything*, p. 47, A. H. Almaas, *The Inner Journey Home: Soul's Realization of the Unity of Reality*, p. 445, and Barbara Brennan, *Hands of Light,* pp 31, and 39-40.

[67] In further preparation, please again recall Note #18 in the "Prologue." To add to this information: consciousness is energy "that infuses all things in space and time." See Ervin Laszlo, *Science and the Akashic Field*, p. 156. Consciousness, as the term is used herein, has been demonstrated in quantum experiments. See *Ibid*, pp. 102-103. In this context, consciousness is infinite mind. For more detail, see Valerie Hunt, *Infinite Mind*, pp. 80-110.). Consciousness is also a quantum field, a field of excitation, See A. H. Almaas, *The Inner Journey Home*, pp. 30-31.

Focus . . . Feel it . . . Focus . . . . Feel it . . . Just by sitting here at the center of sacred space and realizing your connection to Earth, you have already begun your rebirthing.

Now, take in a shaman's story,[68] about your connection to Earth's energy that is consciousness.

Before the beginning there is the Mystery;
The eternal "now"
Out of which all beginnings come.

In the beginning there was the One Consciousness,
The Creative Energy.
And the One Consciousness, Creative Energy was *with* the Spirit,
And the One Consciousness, Creative Energy *was* the Spirit,
The same was in the beginning.

And there was nothing that was made
***Except* that it was created *of* and *by* the Spirit.**

And there was created the entire Cosmos,
And within that Cosmos, were manifested all the universes,
Including this universe,
Wherein exists the Milky Way Galaxy.
In that galaxy were manifested all that astronomers have seen
And all that astronomers have not yet seen.

And the planets were formed.
And Earth began to journey around the Sun.

And on Earth there gradually came the oceans and the seas
The lakes and rivers; all the waters were formed.

And Earth continued to journey around the Sun.

And on Earth there gradually came the mountains
And the valleys,
The deserts and the plains; all the lands were formed.

And Earth continued to journey around the Sun.

And on Earth there slowly incarnated the creatures

---

[68] By "taking in" you are doing more than merely listening: you are paying attention in a special way because you are **absorbing** and **assimilating** the images and insights that you are being given. Throughout the coming lessons, you will be asked frequently to "take in." In that request, there is the undertone of accepting a life-giving and life-enhancing nourishment.

Who lived in the waters, the scaly creatures of the deep,
And out of those waters, there slowly emerged
The creatures that formed feathers and wings
And began to fly.

And still Earth continued to journey around the Sun.

And on the land there slowly incarnated the scaly, crawling creatures,
There also incarnated the four-footed creatures,
Those that were furry and those that had scales.

And Earth continued to journey around the Sun.

Then there slowly incarnated on Earth those creatures
Whose destiny was to become human beings.

And still Earth continued to journey around the Sun.

For billions of years that journey has been made.
And for millions of those years people have also made the journey
As an intrinsic part of living Earth.

The consciousness energies of Earth have been shaped by that journey.
And those consciousness energies have shaped and formed the people
Who were your ancestors.
You, too, have been shaped and formed by that journey.

This Earth has evolved as a living expression and manifestation
***Of* the Spirit,**
The One Consciousness, Creative Energy.
You, too, have evolved as a living expression and manifestation
***Of* the Spirit,**
The One Consciousness, Creative Energy that made you.

Earth, you and all of Creation are living embodiments . . .
The images and likenesses . . .
***Of* the Spirit,**
The One Consciousness, Creative Energy.

That ends the shaman's story.[69] It teaches you many things, as shamans' stories always do. You are learning that both you and Earth are living manifestations *of* (out *of* and part

---

[69] I am indebted to Dr. Ervin Laszlo. His formulation of the "Metaverse" and insights into the energies of consciousness, based on scientific research all relating to the Akashic Field contributed to the creation of this shaman's story. See Ervin Laszlo, *Science and the Akashic Field,* Chapters Seven, Eight and Nine. See also

of) the Spirit (the One Consciousness, Creative Energy). You are also learning that Earth's energies are consciousness[70] and that your energies, which constantly require nourishment from Earth, are also consciousness. Soon you will learn about the many dimensions of your consciousness energies and the great creative power that you truly are. You will also learn how to maintain your connection with Earth's nourishing consciousness energies. And during all of this learning, you will remember the shaman's story about how and why you and Earth have an indissoluble relationship with the Spirit.

*   *   *

After getting your first glimpse, you are again invited to experience the Big Picture. But now you will immerse yourself in it. It is the necessary context — the framework and the foundation — for the entire journey to come. In that context, you will receive ancient wisdom teachings about your Spirit-generated consciousness energies and about your human energy system. Going deeper into the Big Picture, you will explore modern metaphysical and scientific theories, derived from both Eastern and Western thought, about that archetypal system. Going deeper still, you will receive the guidelines necessary to help you to nourish and protect it. Finally, you will be given homework to help you to connect with your own consciousness energies. And you will start to experience what you are as an energy being

Come; on the path of "Opening the Way," let us plunge into the Big Picture.

Ancient Wisdom Teachings about Consciousness

The great spiritual teachers of the past gave you a sacred legacy; the "wisdom teachings." You will explore these teachings because they connect you to the deep **knowing** that is carried by the "collective unconscious;" a source that can also be referred to as the "Akashic Field," the "Akashic Records"[71] and the "informed universe."[72] While opening the way, you can expect to learn from and to interact with your wondrous legacy. The wisdom teachings about human consciousness energies began with the shamans. Twenty thousand years ago, they

---

The Gospel of John, 1: 1-4. My heartfelt thanks go to Matthew Fox, who reframed the Biblical "Word" of John's Gospel into "Creative Energy." See Matthew Fox, *Original Blessings*, p.40. See also the biblical account of creation in *Genesis* 1: 1-31 and *Genesis* 2: 7.

[70] That the Earth's energies are consciousness has been hypothesized by J. Lovelock in *Gaia: A New Look at Life on Earth*. Also, the "intelligent" energies of many crystals produced by the earth and used by healers and by scientists would support this idea. Healers also utilize Earth's energies directly by **grounding** into them and transmitting a consciousness energy that interacts with that of their clients. The energies carried by the plant and animal food eaten by humans and produced out of the earth are also consciousness that the human body utilizes.

[71] Ervin Laszlo states in *Science and the Akashic Field*, p.150. "Generation after generation of humans have left their holographic traces in the Akashic Field … This is the collective information pool of humankind." See also Kevin Todeschi, *Edgar Cayce on the Akashic Records*, p.xii. "The Akashic Records contain the history of every soul since the dawn of creation." See also Ervin Laszlo, *The Akashic Experience: Science and the Cosmic Memory Field*, various paging, including p. 22: "The Akashic Records […] are intrinsic to the oneness of infinite consciousness."

[72] For more detail, see Ervin Laszlo, *Science and the Akashic Field*, pp 116-120.

spirit journeyed into dimensions other than this one.[73] They entered the spirit world, where they obtained, with the help of the spirit beings, the knowledge they required for story-telling, teaching, counseling and especially for healing. Working on and with the consciousness energies (the "spirit") of their patients, those ancient shamans knew that **there was no distinction to be made between matter and spirit**. Everything was formed out of immortal spirit.[74] Thus, all of Earth's living things were "embodiments" of spirit. Shamans still **know** this; they still work with the consciousness energies of their clients, human and non-human.

Eight thousand years ago, the Egyptians were very aware of the spirit realms and of an immortal human consciousness energy called the "Ba."[75] The wisdom teachings stated that the Ba energy, believed to be housed in the physical heart, could continue to be immortal and even reincarnate. But, this could happen only if after death the person was able to present to the "savior god," Osiris, in the Hall of Judgment adequate proof of having lived a virtuous life.[76] These teachings were passed on for hundreds of years in the temples and schools of the Egyptian mystery tradition.

Throughout that period, the belief about immortal spirit energy and about "savior gods" would be repeated in the many other mystery religions of the Fertile Crescent. One of them was Christianity.[77] In the Christian wisdom teachings the immortal consciousness energy, referred to as the "soul," was believed to be completely separate from human physicality. After the death of the physical body, if the "soul" had been "saved" it would enter into the heavenly kingdom of God. Otherwise, that immortal consciousness energy would be cast into everlasting torment. There was no teaching about reincarnation.

Meanwhile, other mystery religions had been established in many of the Mediterranean countries. An important part of the tradition involved the healing temples in "classical" Greece [500-400 B.C.E.]. There the healer priests and priestesses worked on and with the consciousness energies of those who went there seeking help. During the course of the healing treatments, the patients would receive not only physical healing modalities such as baths, massage and herbal drinks but also psycho/spiritual help in the form of dance, drama, dream analysis and rituals of worship.[78]

---

[73] The Lascaux Caves at Dordogne, France have been dated at c.15, 000 B.C. See Marija Gimbutas, *The Language of the Goddess*, p. 178. There is evidence that the shamans of Siberia were practicing *before* that date. See *Mircea* Eliade, *Shamanism: Archaic Techniques of Ecstasy*, p. 6. For a description of spirit journeying, see Tom Cowan, *Shamanism as a Spiritual Practice for Daily Life*, Chapter Three.

[74] Paleolithic graves have yielded up evidence of a belief in the immortality of the 'soul'. The dying were arranged in a fetal position, indicating a rebirth into the afterlife. Some graves contained pottery "breasts", indicating a belief that the newly reborn would be suckled by the goddess. See Marija Gimbutas, *The Language of the Goddess*, pp.149 and 198.

[75] Anthony Mercatante, *The Facts on File Encyclopedia of World Mythology and Legend*, p. 133.

[76] At that time, the heart of the deceased would be weighed in the balance scales against the Feather of Truth. If the heart failed the test, it would be thrown to a nearby crocodile and the immortal energies would be extinguished. Thus, in this teaching, at least part of the physicality carried the immortal Ba.

[77] For further information, please consult *The Ancient Mysteries*, edited by Marvin W. Meyer, pp. 223-254. Joscelyn Godwin in *The Golden Thread: The Ageless Wisdom of the Western Mystery Tradition* in Chapter Six provides an intriguing discussion about the immortal and powerful consciousness energies of the city of Rome. See "The Power of the Egregore," pp. 47-54.

[78] For more detail, see Jean Houston, *The Search for the Beloved: Journeys in Mythology and Sacred Psychology*, pp. 3-9.

The Greeks believed in the continuity of the consciousness energies after physical death (the myths told of the "shades" in Hades), but by this time the shamanic awareness that matter and spirit were synonymous had drastically changed. Scientific thought had begun and with it the idea that spirit and matter were separate. Only in shamanic societies such as those of the Celts[79] did the old belief continue.

At the time of the Greek healing temples, the Chinese had already developed Taoism. This religion taught that the universe existed as a unified whole, symbolized by a circle and that an all-pervasive consciousness energy called "chi" was the life force that powered that unity. Chi suffused every living thing, even non-organic matter. But chi was believed to be separate from matter.

In the Taoist teaching, chi was composed of two creative forces, the yin (feminine) energy and the yang (masculine) energy. Those consciousness energies were mutually interdependent and constantly in motion. Within the unity, the human body was viewed as **the universe in microcosm.** In that microcosmic universe, there was the constant interplay of feminine and masculine consciousness energies in the chi, which affected every stage of growth and development, from conception until death. Then the chi would dissipate. Although the chi was seen to be immortal, there was no belief in a personal immortality.[80] Later, the concept of chi was borrowed by the Japanese who labeled it "ki."

But the chi awareness had been there long before Taoism. The masculine/yang forces symbolized by the sun and its rays and the feminine/yin forces symbolized by the moon had been painted on the walls of tombs in ancient Egypt. The same symbols were part of the writings of Hinduism, concurrent with the ancient Egyptian teachings. Later, the symbols are also to be found in the writings of the ancient Greeks and of the medieval European alchemists, whose symbolism revealed an ancient esoteric knowledge.[81]

When you follow the thread of the wisdom teachings for the many centuries through early shamanism, the mystery tradition, Hinduism, Judaism, Christianity, Sufism and Gnosticism, you learn about another (related) area of thought. This deals with the conflicts between feminine forces of "darkness" and masculine forces of "light," startlingly similar to the yin and yang energies of the Taoist teachings. The antagonistic forces, described as archons, demons and devils ranged against angels and other light beings were believed to be living things. In some parts of the modern world, that belief continues. And reflecting the ancient beliefs are the wisdom teachings about human nature to be found in all those religions. Now, as you shall soon be made aware, those antagonistic forces and the mythological beings can also be regarded as consciousness energies.[82]

---

[79] For more detail, see Tom Cowan, *Fire in the Head: Shamanism and the Celtic Spirit*, pp 4-7.

[80] For more detail, see Jacqueline Young, *The Healing Path*, pp. 90-97.

[81] For more detail, see Julius Evola, *The Hermetic Tradition: Symbols and Teachings of the Royal Art*.

[82] All of these "living things" have appeared in the world's myths, indicating the presence of opposites, analogous to the masculine and feminine forces, within the universe. In the ancient teachings, the masculine was equated with light and the feminine with darkness. See See June Singer, *Androgyny: The Opposites Within*, p. 139. All of those forces are the archetypal energies of Jungian psychology already referred to in. the "Prologue." They are present in the "collective unconscious," that is, the Akashic Field, and are invoked into the individual "unconscious." They provide the foundation for understanding the teachings about "human nature."

Berenice Andrews

Modern Wisdom Teachings about Consciousness Energies

Please pause to consider the extent of the Big Picture you have already explored and the immense antiquity of the lore about both energies and consciousness. Note that your legacy reveals a complex inter-connectedness of thought. This, in turn, reveals that human energies of consciousness have spanned huge geographic distances and united widely disparate people. Your legacy also reveals the deep concern that people have had for millennia about their place in a living Cosmos. This concern (and curiosity) has continued into modern times. Let us turn now to the modern teachings.

Actually the term "modern" is a misnomer, because what we have in the Western world is essentially a rephrasing of many of the ancient wisdom teachings, especially those of Christianity. This religion, as already noted, has derived some of its concepts from the mystery tradition and some from Judaism. The Christian teachings were also enriched by those from paganism[83] and from the "heretical" writings of Gnosticism.[84] And all of those traditions carried an awareness of human consciousness energies.[85]

Although Christianity has obviously in-formed the Western "collective unconscious," that is, the Akashic Field, other spiritual traditions have also contributed. Modern accounts and studies of near-death experiences, for example, all bear a startling resemblance to descriptions of the after-death experiences of human consciousness energies described in the *Tibetan Book of the Dead* set down thirteen hundred years ago.[86]

What makes modern wisdom teachings "modern" is that they add science to the ancient wisdom. For example, the thought described as "new" borrows from the past while describing humanity as a microcosm of a macrocosmic universe. This is a restatement of the ancient Orphic mysteries, and the Platonic, the Hermetic and Kabbalistic traditions[87] as well as those of Taoism. But the ideas have been enriched by the inclusion of holographic theory and the findings of quantum physics; both necessary to evolutionary spirituality.

Within the holographic framework, the microcosmic human being, a micro-consciousness, is analogous to the portion of a hologram which re-presents the information found in the entire hologram. The entirety is analogous to the macro-consciousness, that is, the macrocosmic universe.[88] The latter has been described by Barbara Brennan as "the universal energy field,"

---

[83] The Trinity is a concept borrowed from the pagan Celts. The holy trinity of the Mother/Goddess was Maiden, Mother and Crone.
[84] Timothy Freke and Peter Gandy, *The Jesus Mysteries: Was the "Original Jesus" a Pagan God?* See also Joscelyn Godwin, *The Golden Thread: The Ageless Wisdom of the Western Mystery Traditions*, various paging.
[85] This is implied in the many references to creative "thoughts," and "feelings," to "being possessed by the gods" and to having "godlike powers" to mention a few.
[86] For more detail, see Sogyal Rinpoche, *The Tibetan Book of Living and Dying*, pp. 319-336. These experiences include seeing light at or near the end of a tunnel, encounters with spirit beings and feelings of either bliss or terror.
[87] For more detail, see Joscelyn Godwin, *The Golden Thread*, pp 11, 13, 14 and 45.
[88] For more detail, see Barbara Brennan, *Hands of Light: A Guide to Healing through the Human Energy Field*, pp. 25-26. See also Anodea Judith, *Wheels of Life*, pp. 292-296. For further information, see Michael Talbot *The Holographic Universe* Chapter Two, "The Cosmos as Hologram," pp. 32-55.

24

in which the human beings and all the other created things of Earth (including stones) live, move and have their being.

Embedded in these ideas, the "new thought" teachings relate neatly to modern quantum physics, which is finally replacing the old Newtonian ideas of a mechanistic universe. Quantum physics is making us more and more aware of a quantum energy field in which there exist elementary particles thousands of times smaller than electrons. As the experiments continue, the notion of the separation of spirit and matter is becoming increasingly tenuous. More and more it would appear that matter is spirit, i.e., energy.[89] The quantum energy field is emerging as a macrocosmic consciousness energy field which actually *responds* to and *changes* when impacted upon by the energies of human thought. Thus, the quantum field (the hologram) exists as a creative energy out of which form (matter) is generated. And the microcosmic human being (as part of the hologram) is also an energy field which is a living creative power.[90]

Deriving from Taoism, Christianity, holographic theory and quantum physics, a modern "new thought" wisdom teaching about your consciousness energies involves the following: positive thoughts, beliefs, attitudes and values rooted in love, compassion and self-esteem create one form of reality for an individual, group and the world, while negative thoughts, beliefs, attitudes and values rooted in fear, hatred, anger, etc. create another form of reality; since an infinite Universe implies infinite potentiality, your consciousness can take you individually and collectively to unlimited development; since your consciousness extends to infinity and you are connected to everything, your **attention** and your **intent** create an energy flow which can change your individual, collective and earth reality; since you can create your reality, that reality is the direct reflection of your consciousness (individual and collective) in this **moment** and the power to change is **now**; since you, individually and collectively, are the microcosm of the macrocosmic consciousness, your power to effect change "now" comes from within yourselves. Therefore, you must assume responsibility for becoming aware of and using this power.

*   *   *

Having come thus far, let us pause to reflect: from antiquity until the present, people have pondered on and probed into the mysteries of the Cosmos, while they sought to **know** their relationship with It. Reflect also on the fact that from very early in mankind's development there have been those who were aware that the living consciousness energies of the cosmos and the living consciousness energies of people were (somehow) connected. After taking sufficient time for reflection, let us turn to the body of thought that indicates this connection. That body constitutes the teachings and theories dealing with the human energy system.

---

[89] Barbara Brennan, *Hands of Light*, p.24.
[90] More detail about holographic and quantum theories is provided in the next lesson.

Ancient Thought about the Human Energy System

Your immersion in the Big Picture now takes you into the following instruction about the human energy system and presents ancient Eastern wisdom teachings that have been "westernized."

Thirteen hundred years ago in India, a description of the human energy system was first set down in writing. Yet knowledge about that system, integral to an ancient yogic tradition, had existed for thousands of years prior to the written records.

Within that tradition, the *Bhagavad-Gita,* a Hindu sacred text, contains the epic tale of the spiritual/psychological warfare that goes on in every human being until there is enlightenment and triumph over the "material" body. Enlightenment is achieved through using the life energies, the "prana," in breath work and in meditation; yogic practices to cleanse and clear the human energy system, specifically the centers of consciousness. After much practice, the yogi merges with the Brahma and reaches the spiritual goal.[91]

In the yogic tradition, as you have already learned, those inner centers of consciousness are referred to as the ***chakras***, the Sanskrit word for "wheel." They are wheels of light; energies that are both sound and color. The primary chakras are depicted as lotus flowers arranged in a sequence in the human body from the tailbone up a central column, to the crown of the head. The lotus flower, sacred in India, symbolizes the "opened" chakra. Growing up from the mud, the sequence of lotuses depicts a path of development from a primitive first chakra being to a fully developed consciousness, free from the entrapment of physical needs. Like lotus flowers, the chakras have petals which, to our Western eyes, indicate the different vibratory frequencies of the energies carried by these centers of consciousness.[92]

Modern Theories about the Human Energy System

Borrowing from the ancient yogic tradition, Western teachers and healers such as Rosalyn Bruyere and Barbara Brennan have written extensively about the seven primary chakras. Their writings (and other sources) provide many indicators that these human centers of consciousness **generate** the human "bodies" of consciousness.[93] These "bodies," which you will later learn are multidimensional structures of soul, are indicated by an "aura." The human aura is an electromagnetic field surrounding each living human being. (Actually, there is an aura surrounding every living thing on Earth.) The chakras and the aura constitute the human energy system.

---

[91] Although there are many translations and interpretations of this classic available, please see Paramahansa Yogananda, *The Bhagavad Gita: The Immortal Dialog Between Soul and Spirit,* Volumes One and Two.

[92] Anodea Judith, *Wheels of Life: A User's Guide to the Chakra System*, p. 16.

[93] The seeds of this insight (and hypothesis) were provided by the wisdom teachings and the scientific theories about consciousness energies already described, by years of working with the human energy system of hundreds of clients, by Rosalyn Bruyere, who wrote about the "bodies" of consciousness and by Barbara Brennan, who wrote about the "metabolic action" of the chakras. See Rosalyn Bruyere, *Wheels of Light*, pp. 44-47 and Barbara Brennan, *Hands of Light*, pp. 61-68. This insight and hypothesis has been corroborated by my shamanic spirit guides, who provided the supporting details given in the pages that follow.

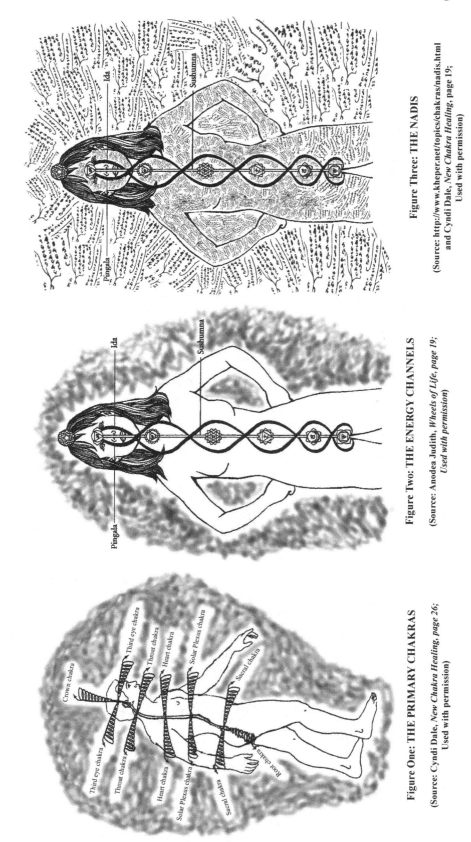

Figure Three: THE NADIS

(Source: http://www.kheper.net/topics/chakras/nadis.html
and Cyndi Dale, *New Chakra Healing*, page 19;
Used with permission)

Figure Two: THE ENERGY CHANNELS

(Source: Anodea Judith, *Wheels of Life, page 19*;
Used with permission)

Figure One: THE PRIMARY CHAKRAS

(Source: Cyndi Dale, *New Chakra Healing, page 26*;
Used with permission)

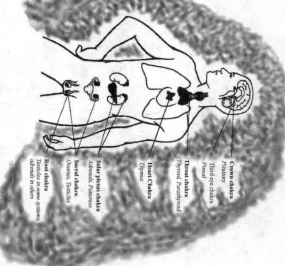

Figure Four: THE NERVE GANGLIA

(Source: Anodea Judith, *Wheel of Life*, page 12;
Used with permission)

	Crown chakra
Cerebral cortex
C1–2	Third eye chakra
Carotid plexus
C3–7	Throat chakra
Pharyngeal plexus
T1–5	Heart chakra
*Pulmonary and
Cardiac Plexi*
T5–9	Solar plexus chakra
Solar plexus
T9–12	Sacral chakra
Sacral plexus
L1–5	Root chakra
Coccygeal plexus
S1–5	Root and
Sacral chakras

Figure Five: THE ENDOCRINE GLANDS

(Source: Anodea Judith, *Wheel of Life*, page 22 (corrected);
Used with permission)

Crown chakra
Pituitary

Third eye chakra
Pineal

Throat chakra
Thyroid, Parathyroid

Heart Chakra
Thymus

Solar plexus chakra
Adrenals, Pancreas

Sacral chakra
Ovaries, Testicles

Root chakra
*Testicles in some systems,
adrenals in others*

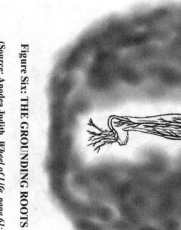

Figure Six: THE GROUNDING ROOTS

(Source: Anodea Judith, *Wheel of Life*, page 61;
Used with permission)

[See Figure One: "The Primary Chakras"]

In describing the "workings" of the human energy system, there is need for additional borrowing from the Eastern yogic tradition: the central energy channel, which is called the "sushumma," is the conduit for the prana, that is, the Life Force energy. The energies travel up the sushumma and feed each chakra. In addition to the sushumma, there are two major channels, each originating on opposite sides of the root chakra. On the left is the "ida" which carries feminine energy and on the right is the "pingala" which carries masculine energy. They carry the energies around the chakras in a spiral motion. Breath work often utilizes the sushumma, the ida and the pingala to bring balance and healing into the system. (There is greater detail about the feminine and masculine energies of the human energy system in a moment.)

[See Figure Two: "The Energy Channels"][94]

In the yogic tradition there are many more of the energy channels . . . thousands that carry energy throughout the system. These channels are called the "nadis" and are analogous to the meridians that are used in acupuncture. Barbara Brennan, a modern Western teacher and healer, describes the nadis as "rivers of light."[95]

[See Figure Three: "The Nadis"]

When the energy channels are primed, deliberately or accidentally, there are Life Force energies present that can trigger what has been referred to as a "kundalini awakening." In the yogic tradition, the kundalini has been depicted as a snake coiled at the tailbone in the root chakra. The kundalini awakening can be an intense experience resulting in profound changes in consciousness.[96]

Now, take in some scientific theory about the chakras.

Referring to modern physiology, Rosalyn Bruyere and others describe the chakras as being located near the seven major nerve ganglia that emanate from the spinal column. In this theory, the chakras form an elegant system that maps logically onto the physical body through the nerve ganglia, yet connects to the non-physical dimensions.

[See Figure Four: "The Nerve Ganglia"]

Again, in theories involving human physiology, each chakra is also relating to an endocrine gland. This connection has been emphasized by both Bruyere and Brennan. Just what the relationship is has not yet been clearly established medically, but many healers have noted how the interaction between an endocrine gland and its chakra is implicated in physical disease. For example, a thyroid malfunction can indicate an inability to express oneself; the result of a malfunctioning throat chakra. Adrenal malfunction can indicate deep fears around physical and financial security, an indication of a malfunctioning root chakra.

[See Figure Five: "The Endocrine Glands"]

---

[94] Please note that the Ida and Pingala channels actually curve around the third eye chakra and face each other above it, like snake heads.

[95] Barbara Brennan, *Ibid,* p.48.

[96] There will be much more detail provided in Lesson Three.

Despite the theories, there is no direct scientific proof of the existence of the chakras. No amount of surgical exploration indicates their presence. Yet, throughout the last three decades, both Bruyere and Brennan have developed some pretty convincing proof that the human chakras do exist and can be described clearly. The following is a distillation of their observations:

According to Bruyere, each chakra is the center of consciousness of a specific "body" of consciousness. Each chakra is driven by its own purpose; its "prime directive." (For example, the prime directive of the root chakra is the generation and maintenance of your physicality, in this third dimension.) Yet, with each chakra there is more than a prime directive, which might suggest a separate functioning. It is important to realize that the human energy system is **holistic**. As such, each chakra interpenetrates the other chakras. Thus, the chakras can and do interact with and fundamentally affect each other. They cannot stand alone, although they each serve a particular purpose. Brennan concurs with this last point.

Both Bruyere and Brennan postulate that each chakra functions within a particular range of vibratory frequencies that are indicated by its color and sound. As living, creative "wheels of light," they embody both color and sound.

Both teacher/healers suggest that the health of a chakra can be determined by its direction of rotation, its shape and its diameter (as indicated by a pendulum).

Bruyere states that the primary chakras each carry a plus or minus polarity and corresponding masculine, feminine or androgynous energies. Each chakra also carries an element that constitutes its "quality." (The elements in chakras are not chemical but are those described in ancient teachings about the fundamental constituents of the universe.) Brennan is silent on these matters.

Bruyere and Brennan have developed very different theories about the relationship between the chakras and the electromagnetic field: Bruyere postulates that the path of prana coming in from the universe/cosmos via the earth, travels up the system and goes outward, thereby creating the aura; Brennan postulates that the prana, coming in from the aura, goes into the chakras, which in turn produce outgoing secondary energies which travel through the nadis, the nervous system, the endocrine system and through the blood stream. It is quite possible that both these theorists are correct, for other healers have observed that energies travel in both directions.

Another noted modern healer, Cyndi Dale, has provided detailed descriptions of the functions of the chakras.[97] In addition to this information, Dale has provided invaluable insights about each chakra's prime directive and its reinforcing "i-am" statement of consciousness. Both the prime directive and the statement of consciousness are expressed by the person's ego/self. For example, the root chakra's "i-am" statement of consciousness that reflects and reinforces its prime directive is: "I sense (that is, I have sensations), therefore, I am." And the ego/self states: "My i-am-ness is my physicality." Dale's work also implies that the chakras

---

[97] Cyndi Dale, *New Chakra Healing: The Revolutionary 32-Center Energy System.* Her insights have been cited extensively throughout these lessons to support the thesis of chakra generativity (the archetypal imperative).

do not exist in this third dimension, although they can be sensed by someone "tuned into" them. Her observations of their functions and power provide a clear indication of human multidimensionality; the microcosmic beingness that is inseparable from the macrocosm out of which people emerged.

Thus, it can herein be suggested (and later demonstrated) that the human energy system is the microcosmic ***creative*** power (the holographic re-presentation of the macrocosmic hologram) intrinsic to people. In other words, the human energy system is the microcosmic "expression" *of* (out of and part of) the macrocosmic One Consciousness, Creative Energy

As such, the human energy system can be regarded as "a living disposition that is the basis of all the usual phenomena of life;" i.e., the human energy system is archetypal.

The Archetypal Human Energy System: The Chakras[98]

Within the metaphysical and scientific context presented in this lesson, the Jungian insights about archetypal energies can find a safe berth. That the Akashic Records described by Edgar Cayce and the Akashic Field postulated by Ervin Laszlo and others are analogous to the Jungian "collective unconscious," which contains the "Archetypes-as-Such,"[99] is likely quite clear.[100] The combination of metaphysics and science in Jungian thought can be found even in the use of the word "archetype," which Jung borrowed from *The Hermetica* and from the mystical writings of Dionysius the Areopagite.[101] While exploring the human psyche, Jung developed the three following hypotheses that are the "ground" of his theories and of the ideas to be presented herein: 1) "the psyche [soul/self] is a primary datum – not only of psychology but of our lives; 2) [. . .] the psyche exists *a priori,* a product of nature or evolution, and 3) the basic unit of the psyche is the archetype."[102]

In the Jungian theory about archetypes, there are two key ideas[103] that can readily be applied to the human energy system and to the chakras in particular. Those key ideas present the "archetypal endowment" and the "archetypal imperative."

In the context of these lessons, the first idea, that of the archetypal endowment, means that every person born has been endowed by the Spirit (the One Consciousness, Creative Energy) with a microcosmic creative power, a human energy system, which is constituted of centers of consciousness (chakras) that can, *when they are understood and properly nurtured*, "guide

---

[98] This awareness has evolved out of many years of dealing directly with the human energy system.

[99] Jolande Jacobi, *Complex/Archetype/Symbol in the Psychology of C. G. Jung*, pp.32 and 35.

[100] Jacobi points out that the collective unconscious comprises all the contents of the psychic experience of mankind. See *Ibid* p. 60. Kevin Todeschi in *Edgar Cayce and the Akashic Record*, p.xii and Ervin Laszlo in *Science and the Akashic Field*, p.150 each indicate the same function for the Akashic Record and the Akashic Field respectively.

[101] Jolande Jacobi, *Complex/Archetype/Symbol*, p. 34

[102] Anthony Stevens, *The Two Million Year Old Self*, p. 10. Although Jung used the word "psyche" meaning "soul/self" in a different sense than the words are used later in these lessons, the **basic** meaning, that of a creative consciousness; the underlying theme in his writings, is the meaning taken herein.

[103] These ideas are explored throughout Anthony Stevens, *The Two Million Year Old Self* and are presented in Jung's words in Jolande Jacobi, *Complex/Archetype/Symbol in the Psychology of C.G. Jung*, pp. 31-73.

and control every aspect of the life cycle."[104] The Jungian ideas that can support this thesis are as follows:

"Archetypes exist preconsciously and . . . Empirically considered . . . the archetype did not ever come into existence as a phenomenon of organic life, but entered into the picture with life itself."[105] At conception, the human energy system, containing all the centers of consciousness, the chàkras, enters immediately into guiding the fetal gestation while expressing the Life aspect of the Spirit.

. . . there are present in every psyche forms which are unconscious but nonetheless active, living dispositions . . . that preform and continually influence our thoughts and feelings and actions."[106] The human energy system, with its generative centers of consciousness, the chakras, each one with its own prime directive and "i-am" statement of consciousness, is the power that acts upon the "active, living dispositions" and *makes possible* the preforming and influencing of human thoughts feelings and actions.

"Psychologically . . . the archetype as an image of instinct is a spiritual goal toward which the whole nature of man strives . . . ."[107] The human energy system shapes "animal soul" and tirelessly promotes its evolution into the awakened self awareness of a self-actualized human being, if the proper conditions prevail.[108]

". . . the archetypes . . . have a meaningful character related to consciousness and are capable of manifesting themselves in all psychic as well as spiritual domains."[109] In the **holistic** human energy system, the chakras generate the physical, emotional, mental and spiritual "bodies" of consciousness, i.e., structures of soul, that are the manifestations of the archetypal endowment.

"Thus the archetypes are nothing other than typical forms of apprehension and perception, of experience and reaction, of active and passive behavior, *images of life itself* [emphasis added], which takes pleasure in creating forms, in dissolving them and in creating them anew . . . a process that takes place in the material, the psychic and the spiritual realm as well."[110] The human energy system as the microcosmic expression of the One Consciousness, Creative Energy is the archetypal endowment that creates the forms. Another Jungian idea that supports this theory states: **". . . a principle of form has always been inherent in the psyche . . . the structure of the psyche . . . embodies a universally human heritage and bears within it the faculty of manifesting itself in definite and specific forms."**[111] Again, it is the chakras of the human energy system that interact with the

---

[104] *Ibid.*, p.16. Although Stevens refers to the life cycle of the species, it is with each individual energy system that the species is maintained.

[105] Jolande Jacobi, *Complex/Archetype/Symbol*, pp. 31 and 32. This quote is taken from Jung's essay "A Psychological Approach to the Dogma of the Trinity."

[106] *Ibid.* p. 36. This quote is taken from Jung's essay "Psychological Aspects of the Mother Archetype."

[107] *Ibid.* p. 38. This quote was taken from Jung's essay "On the Nature of the Psyche."

[108] These ideas are further elaborated in Lesson Three.

[109] Jolande Jacobi, *Complex/Archetypes/Symbols,* p. 45. The teaching about soul is in the next lesson.

[110] *Ibid,* p.51.

[111] *Ibid.,* pp. 51-52.

"principle of form" inherent in the soul substance and, within that context, shape the forms that are soul structures.[112]

In the context of these lessons, the second key idea, that of the archetypal imperative, means that in the human energy system of the microcosmic energy being that is a person the generative power of each chakra during each stage of that person's necessary physical, emotional, mental and spiritual development is "mediated by a new set of [. . .] imperatives."[113]. The fullest realization of these stages is the "intent" of life.[114] In the context of these lessons, that intent is wholeness, i.e., true humanness. The Jungian ideas that can support that thesis are as follows:

"The primordial, essentially unchanging needs, the typical, eternally recurrent, basic experiences of mankind perpetuate the archetypes, and at the same time create those "magnetic tensions" within the psyche which cause them to be manifested, forever anew, in the most diverse variations and guises."[115] Thus have the chakras of the human energy system been "eternally recurrent" while continually shaping human soul substance into the varieties of soul structures characterizing human beings. Yet another Jungian idea that adds weight to that archetypal imperative is as follows: **"but not only do the archetypes form the "primordial pattern" for personification of partial aspects of the psyche, and hence for figures of all kinds: they can also represent the "basic principle" for abstract relationships and laws."[116]** The human energy system, re-presenting the macrocosmic creative, generative power in the microcosm, carries and exhibits in its functions the basic principles that shape human existence. And another Jungian idea that emphasizes the archetypal imperative of the human being is as follows: **"the fact that the psyche of every individual in the course of his natural growth, develops into a totality comprising such different components as the ego, the unconscious, the persona, the shadow, etc., is an archetypal phenomenon."[117]** All of these and more are the soul structures generated out of soul substance by the chakras of the human energy system.[118]

Finally, **". . . the archetypes, as the voice of the human species, are the great ordering factors, disregard or violation of which brings with it confusion and destruction . . . they have an ordering effect on the psychic process and on the contents of consciousness, leading them by labyrinthine ways toward a possible totality, since they determine the nature of the configurational process and the course it will follow,** *with seemingly foreknowledge,* **[emphasis added] or as though they were already in possession of the goal to be circumscribed by the centering process."[119]** As you will soon learn, the centers of consciousness, the chakras, in the human energy system, are the microcosmic constituents

---

[112] The lessons that follow will support this idea.

[113] Stevens, *The Two Million Year Old Self*, p.67.

[114] *Ibid.*, p.68.

[115] Jacobi, *Complex/Archetype/Symbol*, p. 57.

[116] *Ibid.* p. 58.

[117] *Ibid.* p. 58.

[118] The lessons that follow will clarify this statement.

[119] Jolande Jacobi, *Complex/Archetype/Symbol*, p. 72.

of the "centering process," that has an "ordering effect" on the soul substance. They are also the "ordering factors" that are the "voice" of human beings.

Having learned about the archetypal nature of the chakras, you are ready to turn to the other component of the human energy system; the aura.

The Archetypal Human Energy System: The Aura

As already noted, your aura is the electromagnetic field that surrounds your physical body. Unlike the theorists dealing with the chakras, scientists had known about electromagnetic phenomena since the 1700's. But "field" theory was not known until the work of Michael Faraday and James Clerk Maxwell in the mid-1800's. A "field" was thereafter defined as a "condition in space which has the potential of producing a force, i.e., energy."[120] Since then, there have been many scientists and others who have probed into the mysteries of the human aura.[121] It has been found to be much more complex than at first described.

Your aura, as part of your energy system, (your archetypal endowment) is a field that is composed of many dimensions of energy. From a scientific perspective, how that aura is generated is not entirely known, and even Brennan and Bruyere, who have studied it closely, have contrary views.

What everyone can agree on, however, is that every component of your auric field is constantly moving in a "cosmic dance."[122] It is that dance that makes the human aura archetypal, for it, like the chakras, "entered into the picture with life itself." Life is movement: your aura is a metaphor for life.[123] Life is energy dancing. As such, your electromagnetic energy field constantly moves and constantly changes. In your cosmic dance, some dimensions of your aura vibrate at the high frequencies required by spirituality. Others vibrate at the low frequencies required by physicality. Your aura is, therefore, an expression of you as an energy being. As life energies, your aura can indicate to a healer the well-being of your physical, emotional, mental and/or spiritual "bodies."[124] Thus, your auric field is expressing the "workings" of your archetypal centers of consciousness, your chakras. It is the **measurable** and **observable** indicator of unseen archetypal phenomena. And it is an archetypal phenomenon in its own right. Indeed, it is an indicator of your multidimensionality. So, you can safely conclude that your aura is much more than you might have imagined.[125] (Indeed, at this point, your archetypal endowment is likely more than you could ever have imagined!)

---

[120] Barbara Brennan, *Hands of Light*, p. 22.
[121] For an account of "The Rolf Study" that established the function of the centers of human consciousness and led to the conclusion that the human aura was "infinite mind", unlimited consciousness, see Valerie Hunt, *Infinite Mind*, pp. 315-337. See also Rosalyn Bruyere, *Wheels of Light: Chakras, Auras and the Healing Energy of the Body*, pp. 219-233 and various other paging.
[122] Please recall the cosmic Dance of Shiva which has been described in the "Prologue."
[123] Rosalyn Bruyere, *Wheels of Light*, p. 73.
[124] *Ibid.*, p. 19.
[125] For more information, see Michael Talbot, *The Holographic Universe*, Chapter Six, "Seeing Holographically," pp. 162-193.

Now there can be added the essential information about the feminine and masculine forces that you have already learned suffuse the macrocosm and all living things. Those forces are also present in the human energy system. Let us turn to them now with this necessary proviso.

Although you require and you will receive much more detail about your archetypal masculine and feminine energies in later lessons, what you require at this moment is the beginning awareness of their ancient lineage and of humankind's knowledge of them. You also require a general description of their characteristics. (While you receive this description, please keep in mind that your masculine and feminine energies are **not** your sex or gender.[126] They are archetypal principles inherent in all living things, including the centers of consciousness, the chakras, of your human energy system.

The Archetypal Human Energy System: The Masculine Force [127]

The masculine (yang) energy inherent in soul substance is also a force in the human energy system, an energy that pushes out or through. This force is carried by three of the chakras (the root, solar plexus and throat) and by the pingala channel. Healers "see" the masculine energy on the right side of the physical body.

Masculine energies are active and out-going. They are oriented toward the five senses and what they apparently perceive. Masculine energies are competitive and aggressive, results oriented, dominating and controlling, oriented towards needs satisfaction, personal survival and almost exclusively towards matter.

Masculine energies are analytical in nature. They process all incoming information sequentially and are oriented towards "facts" and historical precedent.

Masculine energies primarily see life as a solo performance. They demand that you are always in control, over everything in your life.

Masculine energies are reluctant to change. They prefer that you stay with the familiar (beliefs, behavior, attitudes, values, etc.) rather than create new ways of being.

Masculine energies provide the fortitude and determination needed to survive in all types of threatening situations. The wisdom of the masculine force reveals itself in relation to the outer "material" world.

It is essential that both sexes of people realize that they carry the masculine energies (force).

---

[126] In this context, sex is the biology, while gender is part of the personality of a person.

[127] This description has been compiled from many sources and all have reflected the cultural "awareness" of the authors. Whether or not the archetypal "image" provided herein actually reflects the Archetype-as-Such cannot be stated with certainty. This is the best description that is currently available.

The Archetypal Human Energy System: The Feminine Force [128]

The feminine (yin) energy inherent in soul substance is also a force in the human energy system, an energy that pulls in or attracts. This force is carried by three of the chakras (the sacral, heart and third eye) and by the ida channel. Healers "see" the feminine energy on the left side of the physical body.

Feminine energies are receptive. They are inwardly oriented toward the unknown and to the changes necessary for life to move forward.

Feminine energies are oriented toward relationship, partnership and co-operation. They trust instinctive and intuitive insights.

Feminine energies are oriented toward the non-material qualities of life and toward supportive, nurturing activities. They are process-oriented.

Feminine energies are persistent, yet non-controlling strength.

The feminine force gently encourages you to let go of old patterns; beliefs, behaviors, attitudes, values, etc., that need changing. The wisdom of the feminine force reveals itself in relation to the inner emotional world.

It is essential that both sexes of people realize that they carry the feminine energies

Your human energy system truly is amazing! Thus, as part of the Big Picture, on these beginning steps on your quest for wholeness, it is necessary for you to learn how to protect and maintain this precious system.

Protecting and Maintaining Your Energy System

You protect your energy system by realizing that you are much more than mere physicality (although you require a lot more instruction for a more comprehensive understanding!). When you are immersed in the world's energies which are often damaging, you can "shield" your energy system in the following manner:

Your Energy Shield

Tuning into Earth's energies, breathe up an imagined white "light" and let it pour out of the top of your head as an enveloping light that completely encloses you. The shield will, in your mind's eye, look like an egg. The light will automatically enclose your aura. You can relate to all that is in your environment from within this shield and, with practice, deflect the "slings and arrows" that might come your way.

Essentially the maintenance of your energy system involves the following guidelines.[129] Please note that in these guidelines there is no separation between "matter" and spirit: both are energy.

---

[128] See Note #127 above.

[129] These guidelines were distilled from those presented by Barbara Brennan in *Hands of Light*, pp. 265-268.

Your "Maintenance" Guidelines

Maintain a deep connection to yourself and your purpose in this lifetime, both on the personal and the interpersonal level. Do that by meditating and learning to be in the "now;" loving who you are right now and doing the same for others; connecting with your spiritual source in whatever spiritual practices you are guided to undertake and by allowing trust and faith in the universal energies to energize and carry you forward.

Nourish your physicality: by eating food that carries the energies of life; practicing good hygiene; resting when your system tells you; wearing clothing made of natural fibers (wear colors that energize you and wear styles that express who you are); surrounding yourself in your home and other environments with healing energies, e.g., living plants, ionizers, incandescent lights.

Nourish your emotionality: by cultivating loving friendships and healthy intimate relationships.

Nourish your mentality: by reading, by recreational and intellectual activities and with creative ventures, that align you with life.

Nourish your spirituality: by continually opening to a deep and abiding connection with your indwelling Spirit. If, at this point, that idea is unfamiliar to you, start simply by inwardly hearing and speaking prayers that come from your heart and require no special words or postures. Those prayers are already there and awaiting your attention! Included in your prayers, your words and thoughts of gratitude will provide additional spiritual nourishment. Begin a daily meditation practice that takes you deeply within. Your meditation practice[130] which is also a discipline will be hugely sustaining throughout the journey ahead.

*   *   *

On your path of "Opening the Way," your immersion in the Big Picture thus far has brought you into a beginning awareness of two important ideas. They constitute a major portion of the foundation and framework that you require for your rebirthing quest. Based on your legacy of ancient and modern wisdom teachings and on the findings of modern science, these concepts reveal that for thousands of years people have sought to **know** who they are and how they relate to an all-encompassing Cosmic Power that they (somehow) know exists.

The first important idea refers to that Cosmic Power and indicates that across the span of many millennia, the wisdom teachers from all parts of the world have postulated the existence of that Power as One Consciousness, a Creative Energy omnipotent, omnipresent and omniscient, that they have named the Spirit, Jehovah, Atum, God, Brahma and many other sacred names. Although the concept underwent considerable modification, because most thinkers (religions and non-religious) have focused on the duality of spirit and "matter," the wondrous thread of seeking to understand and connect with the One Consciousness has

---

[130] There are many forms of meditation in the world's spiritual traditions. Find the one that you resonate with.

persisted into the 21st century. During many of the intervening centuries, an undercurrent of gnostic thought has evolved in this world's unfolding "story." The gnostic **knowing** has brought people closer to the edge of that understanding and connection. Gradually, there has come about the awareness that the One Consciousness is infinite and ever-expanding **Knowing** (sometimes referred to as Mind) into which people can enter and which can enter into them. Developing out of that realization, a new awareness based on gnostic metaphysics and quantum science, has arisen in this 21st century. It is this: both spirit and "matter" are energy and this energy is both macrocosmic Consciousness and microcosmic consciousness; a unity that is Creative/creative. That awareness has further broadened to encompass an ancient idea that has been modernized by science; that the One Consciousness, Creative Energy can be regarded as a macrocosm analogous to a hologram, while people can be regarded as the microcosmic portion (re-presentation) of the hologram that quantum physics calls a "particle/wave." Thus, people are starting to **know** that they are (somehow) consciousness that is living creative energy. These are exciting times! Now more than ever before, people are seeking to understand their connection with the Spirit that is the One Consciousness, Creative Energy; an understanding so much yearned after for so many centuries.

For the second important idea, the ancient Eastern wisdom teachings and the findings of Western science have provided the clues. The human energy system, known in the East for thousands of years, and now revealing itself as an archetypal system that (somehow) utilizes the vital Masculine and Feminine Principles as the "dancing" masculine and feminine archetypal energies, can be regarded as a means of understanding (and realizing) the connection of people (the microcosm) with the One Consciousness, Creative Energy (the macrocosm). So far in these lessons there has been only a brief (but tantalizing) description of the metaphysics, psychology and science that can support such a connection. You have been given the basic ideas: that the human energy system is constituted of centers of consciousness (chakras) that are energies; that these centers carry masculine and feminine forces; and, that these centers seem to be a creative power that (somehow) generates the "bodies" of consciousness indicated by the human electromagnetic auric field.

With this summation, your immersion in the Big Picture is finished, for the moment. Before you depart, please look around you and experience the timelessness of this circle of stones. In sacred space, it is shamanic time that prevails and shamanic time is always "now." Thus, the time when you began this lesson is the time that it is now. And your rebirthing journey, no matter how long it takes, will always be happening now. (As you expand your **knowing**, you will better understand what this means) . . . .

You may leave the stone circle.

* * *

Soul Searcher, you are well started on your path of "Opening the Way." Please take time to ponder on all the parts of this lesson. And you ponder, not so much by "thinking" and "analyzing," but by focusing inwardly and allowing the resultant images and responses to arise.[131] Please do not reject anything; just quietly observe whatever comes, including new insights. Foster a balanced combination of intuition and reason. Keep a journal, if doing so appeals to you. Meanwhile, start recognizing your consciousness energies and start maintaining your energy system, (although at this point you might have some doubts about its existence!).

Homework: Experiencing Your Energy System

In order for you to be able to **know** your own consciousness energies and energy system, you must learn how to connect with the living energies of Earth, the prime source of all your human nourishment. This connection to Earth involves breath work called "grounding." For experiencing your energy system, you will prepare first with some deep **grounding** breaths. That preparation will be necessary before you do this homework. The connection to Earth will also be the unvarying prelude to all of your later work of self-discovery. At this beginning point, you can start a practice of sensing the energies that surround you, wherever you are. That, in itself, is very grounding. No matter what sort of energies are there, even if you require an energy "shield," remember that, like the shamans, you are in sacred space. And no matter what your geographic location is, if you are sitting, standing, walking or lying down, you can be **grounded** by breathing as follows:

Begin by inhaling deeply, preferably through your nose. Breathe into your belly, while dropping your diaphragm. If you want to do so, count slowly to eight.

Then exhale through your mouth, while emptying your belly and raising your diaphragm. If you are counting, count to eight.

Repeat at least five times.

[See Figure Six: "The Grounding Roots"]

Now focus your attention on the arches of your feet and sense your connection to Earth's energies. You will do your **grounding** breath work as follows:

"See" (i.e., imaginatively) on each arch a portal that looks like a closed "eye."

Now, "open" that portal and see within your arch some tightly coiled thread-like rootlets.

See those rootlets emerge from the portal and go straight down into Earth.

See the rootlets get thicker and stronger as they move downward.

See in Earth a round ball of light or a pool of light energies.

See the rootlets attach themselves to that energy source.

Now, continue to inhale deeply and as you do see the energies (like translucent "air" or "water") rise up the "roots," up your legs and into your body.

With each exhalation, "hold" the energies.

On each inhalation, draw up the energies higher and higher into your body.

"Fill" all your body, including your legs and arms.

---

[131] This type of focusing has sometimes been called "willed introversion" and it produces remarkable results.

When you sense fullness, gently disconnect your "roots" from the energy source.

Retract them and as they re-enter your feet, see them become thread-like rootlets again.

This exercise can be done in "lotus" position, if you prefer. Sense your connection with Earth. The rootlets can also be sent into Earth from your ankles, knees or the bottom of your tail bone. But note that your **grounding** can be done at any time in any place. It is fundamental to all the work you will do with your energy system. Now, try out these "experiences" to familiarize yourself with your own aura and that of others.

Experience #1: Your Aura Beach Ball

Either sitting or standing, cup your hands 12 inches apart.

Take several deep **grounding** breaths.

Focus your attention on the space between your hands.

Move your cupped hands slowly towards each other.

Feel the pressure. That is your electromagnetic energy field.

Feel the response in the rest of your physical body.

Experience #2: Making a Big Aura Beach Ball

While you are seated, take deep **grounding** breaths.

Repeat Experience #1.

Focus on the thought; "I am expanding my aura," and sense that expansion out from your physical body.

Now repeat Experience #1 . . . note the size of the energy "ball" this time between your hands.

Experience #3: An Aura "Taffy Pull"

While you are seated, take several deep **grounding** breaths.

Focus again on the thought; "I am expanding my aura," and sense that expansion out from your physical body.

Make a big aura beach ball.

Now, focusing on your fingers, pull the energies like taffy from your fingertips.

Feel the resistance like an elastic piece of sticky taffy

Experience #4: "Scanning" Your Aura

While you are seated, take several deep **grounding** breaths.

Focus on the thought: "I am expanding my aura," and sense that expansion out from your physical body.

Reach down to your foot with both hands cupped about one inch from either side.

While focusing intently on your cupped hands, slowly move them up your leg within your aura.

Feel it as you move your hands up your leg to your groin.

Sense the dips and bumps in your aura.

Note the physical and emotional energies generated in your body as you do this

Repeat with the other foot.

Note any differences with this leg in the dips and bumps in your aura.

Note the physical and emotional energies generated in your body.

Experience #5: Scanning the Aura of Plants and /or Pets

You might want to investigate the aura of plants and/or pets.

Again, start with several deep **grounding** breaths.

Cup your hands as indicated above about one inch from the plant or pet.

While focusing intently on your hands, move them and make note of the energies that are impacting on them.

On plants you will note that the dips in en indicate where damage has been done or even where parts of the plant are missing.

On dogs, cats, rabbits, ducks and guinea pigs, move your hands slowly from the head to the base of the tail.[132]

Note the dips and bumps in the aura.

Pay attention to your physical and emotional responses and to those from the pet.

Experience #6: Scanning Another Person's Aura

(Please do not attempt this until you have thoroughly practiced all the experiences already given.)

While the person to be scanned is standing at ease, take several deep **grounding** breaths, while you increase your energy flow by briskly rubbing your hands together.

In the back, starting at their ankles and holding your cupped hands about one inch away, focus intently on your hands and scan their aura slowly up both legs.

Note the dips and bumps.

In the back, starting just below their tailbone, gently "sweep" their aura from the outer limits of both sides of their physical body. Note the dips and bumps.

In the back, starting just below the tailbone, slowly move your cupped hand up their spine and note any dips and bumps in the aura.

Now, go further.

At each chakra, "tune into" the size, shape, rotation and direction of the "spin."

Do not try to "interpret" anything.

Then move to the front and do the same scan.

Now, go further.

Experience #7: Detecting Masculine and Feminine Energies

With deep focusing, you might want to note the masculine and feminine energies present in all living things.

Start with something big, for example, a tree.

Scan as you have already learned.

Focus intently on the "incoming" (feminine) and the "outgoing" (masculine) energies.

Where are they located? How strong are they? How do they impact on you? How do you relate with them?

---

[132] Your pets also have an electromagnetic aura that you might want to scan. See Margrit Coates, *Hands-On Healing for Pets: The Animal Lover's Essential Guide to Using Healing Energy.*

Then go to other forms of plants, then animals, then people.

Finally, scan Earth formations, such as rocks.

There are great benefits to be gained from all these experiences. Primarily, they will help you to become aware of living, consciousness energies. While you do this work, the physical and emotional vibrations you experience will gradually open you to experiencing your chakras; your centers of consciousness. And as you continue working with these "experiences," you will become increasingly aware of the energies of the living things around you and how deeply you are connected with them. Thereby, your **knowing** and your **being** will be enhanced.

Your practice of **grounding** will eventually become a habit. Although there are other exercises that you will undertake in order to experience and **know** the "workings" of your energy system, the grounding practice is essential for all of them.

In this first part of your quest, on your path of "Opening the Way," please stay with this lesson until you start to feel comfortable with the Big Picture. Stay with it and with your beginning awareness of your own and others' consciousness energies and human energy system. And be assured that there are more awareness experiences in store!

Peace and blessings

Lesson Two

THE "BIG PICTURE:" YOUR ENERGIES OF SOUL

Hello: welcome again to the stone circle. Come over here to the center. Now, stand very still. Slowly, take a few deep **grounding** breaths and really connect to this wonderful place! Breathe and focus . . . Breathe and focus . . . Do you notice how the consciousness energies of this sacred space enfold you? Do you sense how Long Meg and her Children are sharing their vibrations with you? Here in the center, the fresh, green grass is soft. Basking in the sunlight of this springtime, Earth is warm and still a little damp. (The moors get a lot of rain!) Here, spread this ground sheet again. Now, sit very still and immerse yourself in all the energies of this enclosure.

In this place, you are connecting with the immense nurturing consciousness energies of Earth. You are also connecting with the soul searchers who came here before you. This space is permeated with their consciousness energies, with **who they were as souls**. They came, singly and in groups, during all the centuries that this stone circle has existed. They came and they departed. Every one of them had been incarnated for the sojourn in this dimension. Every one of them was a soul whose energies made an impact on this place. That's what soul searchers have done in the past and that's what they still do. So, if you sense the presence of invisible others, do not be surprised. They are here. If you wish to tune into those living energies, generate an energy shield around you (as you would in any situation involving a variety of energies) and make the connection . . . .

While you continue on your path of "Opening the Way," you will immerse again in the Big Picture. Remaining here for one more lesson, you will venture further on your rebirthing quest and begin the discovery of **who you are as soul**.

Now, take in a shaman's story about why and how you came to be incarnated for your sojourn in this dimension, on this Earth plane. It is the story of Little Soul.

In a time beyond time
You had your being with and in the Spirit;
The One Consciousness, Creative Energy,
And you lived and moved in

The Rapture.

You were Little Soul.
You were your original Wholeness.
And you vibrated in synchronicity with the light and the sound
Of the One Consciousness, Creative Energy,
For you were an expression *of* (out of and part of)
The Divine.

One day, you chose to leave that state of bliss,
And venture into the third dimension,
To incarnate as a human being on planet Earth.

There was a grand adventure awaiting you
And you, Little Soul, were ready.

You contacted Soul Keeper
And that all-wise Being placed you in the care and keeping of
Your Celestial Guides,
Who proceeded to help you draw up
Your Life Plan for living as a person on Earth.

First, you chose your parents . . . carefully,
For they would give you
Your human genetic coding
And they would give you
Your Sacred Wound:
Both gifts would be necessary
For your forthcoming sojourn.

You also chose your immediate and extended family members.
And with each and every one of your immediate relatives
You drew up your Sacred Contracts;
Mutual agreements applicable only on planet Earth.

Then you drew up contracts with everyone else you would meet
On your grand adventure.
You chose your long—and short-term relationships:
You chose those people who would bring you joy
And you chose those who would make you miserable.
You chose them all in order to provide your life's lessons
To promote your further evolution.

You also chose your date of birth, the time and location.
You chose your ethnicity, your ancestry, your sex, your gender,

Your sexual orientation and the states of your health.
You chose your social position and your life's work.
You chose the length of your days.
And you chose the date, the time and the manner of your "death."

Your Celestial Guides helped you to read your Akashic Record
In which all your lifetimes were set down and
Your karma was awaiting your attention.
And you, Little Soul, chose the soul searcher's challenging path
Whereby you could clear your karma
And achieve an advanced stage of evolution.
And you received your Creative Spaces;
Those crucial opportunities in life
To choose a different way.

After much joyful labor, your Life Plan was complete
And your Celestial Guides were satisfied.

Then off you went to the Council of Ascended Earth Masters,
Who carefully perused your work and queried you
On a number of points.
Then, after further deliberation, the Masters approved your Plan.

For final preparation, you eagerly approached Soul Conductor,
Who lovingly ensured that a portion of your original vibratory
frequency
Was encased permanently within you.
It was a nucleus of divinity that would be
The indwelling Spirit
And the inner guidance system
Of your human incarnation.

Then Soul Conductor also ensured that you had brought along
An essential prerequisite to be actualized *en route*.
It was your archetypal endowment:
All the centers of consciousness, creative energy;
Those microcosmic wheels of light that would be
Your human energy system.

Finally, Soul Conductor led you to the "Earthbound" departure gate,
And gave you a drink of the water of forgetfulness,
For your Earthly sojourn would involve forgetting your origins
And who you truly were.
And your human adventure would include getting to *know*
Those things about you

While you, Little Soul, made your inner journey home,
Back to Wholeness . . . but as a human being . . . on planet Earth.

With a final loving look at what you were leaving behind,
You stepped out of the departure gate and onto a ribbon of light.
Down, down, down, down you traveled through all the dimensions
And as you journeyed, you decreased your vibratory frequency
(Except for your nucleus).
And as you journeyed, you actualized your archetypal endowment.
Down through the celestial and the etheric dimensions you sped.
Down into the astral realm;
All the dimensions of emotional vibrations,
Down, down through their murkier depths,
Down into this third dimension.

It all happened in a nanosecond and there you were
In a huge, wet, red chamber.
At that moment of conception, when sperm and egg fused,
You, Little Soul, merged with them
And triggered your protoplasmic process;
Your incarnation on planet Earth.

How interesting it was to gestate in a human uterus
Inside a blue etheric womb!
You experienced many feelings and thoughts
While your fetal development progressed.
It seemed to take a very long time
And the chamber got very small.
But, finally, there came the birthing pulsations
And you emerged.

Then gentle hands held your tiny embodiment.
You drew your first breath
And uttered your first cry.
You, Little Soul, had arrived.
You had birthed your human incarnation
Here in this third dimension, on planet Earth
And your grand adventure was well underway.

That ends the shaman's story.[133] It teaches that you are no "accident" (despite what you or your mother might have thought!). You are on this Earth plane because you **chose** to be here in

---

[133] I am indebted to many mystery traditions for providing the important parts of this story. For example, see *The Book of Jeremiah*, 1:5: "Before I formed you in the womb I knew you and before you were born I consecrated you." See also Carolyn Myss, *Sacred Contracts: Awakening Your Divine Potential*, pp. 1-105.

order to carry out a Life Plan crafted by you to promote your physical, emotional, mental and spiritual evolution, as a soul searcher. The shaman's story continues your rebirthing process by opening ways for you to become aware of that purpose and, thereby, to become aware of your energies of soul.

* * *

Regarding the latter . . . once again you will tap into your sacred legacy of wisdom teachings; this time, those focused on "soul." In-formed by ancient and modern thought, you will progress into awareness of soul; as consciousness energy, as a holographic field that is constituted of "soul substance." You will receive the key descriptors of that consciousness energy and experience your own. During this time, you will also be made aware of the agonies of soul wounding and soul fragmentation. After receiving those insights, you will learn more about the archetypal, microcosmic masculine and feminine energies; forces that are inherent in soul substance. Still on the path of "Opening the Way," you will be introduced to soul "structures;" the constituent "parts" of the "bodies" of consciousness. You will be given preliminary information about those structures, including the egoic structures. Finally, you will be provided with the essential linkages connecting consciousness, soul substance and soul structures with the archetypal human energy system. There are many exciting moments ahead!

Come; let us continue on your path of "Opening the Way" and plunge again into the Big Picture . . .

Ancient and Modern Wisdom Teachings about Soul

We start with the ancient Egyptian wisdom teachings; those partially incorporated into the *Hermetica*.[134] This text indicates that Atum, the All and One Creative Power is Primal Mind in which everything exists; that the Cosmos which embodies Atum, flows out of Primal Mind; that the Cosmos is saturated with Soul; the Light and Life that emanates out of Atum. The teachings also reveal that all souls, human and non-human, are parts of Soul; that like Atum, people can also create with "mind;" and that a human soul that has come to **know** Atum will become Atum.

There is a strong flavor of the Egyptian teachings in those of the later Greek and Roman philosophers, whose insights heavily influenced Western ideas about "soul."[135] The Greek philosopher, Socrates [470-399 B.C.E.] postulated that a human being was his soul. "The soul,

---

[134] Timothy Freke and Robert Gandy, *The Hermetica: The Lost Wisdom of the Pharaoh,* pp. 37-63. In these lessons "Primal Mind" is defined as the One Consciousness, the Creative Energy. Although the hermetic writings were set down about 1,000 C.E., the teachings had entered into the Greek "classical world" by the 4th century B.C E. See Godwin, *The Golden Thread,* pp. 9, 11. The teachings were also reflected in the *Upanishads* that have been dated starting at the sixth century B. C.E. See Robert Hume, *The Thirteen Principal Upanishads,* pp 22-27. It was an amazing cross-fertilization of ideas.

[135] For more detail about the Western, Eastern and Sufi concepts of soul, see A.H. Almaas, *The Inner Journey Home,* pp. 483-527.

for Socrates was identified with [. . .] consciousness [. . .]. In short, for Socrates soul is the conscious self, it is intellectual and moral personhood."[136] After Socrates, his student Plato [428-348 B.C.E.] taught that soul was eternal, originating from a spiritual dimension and "akin to the eternal Forms, changeless, simple, without parts, ever the same."[137]

The Egyptian flavor was still present centuries later when the philosopher Plotinus [205-270 C.E.][138] was formulating a system of thought around the One, Mind and Soul: the One was the absolute Source of all manifestation; Mind was the first and universal manifestation of the One, and Soul, which was a creative and ordering force behind the universe, was the manifestation of Mind. Each human soul was an individualization of Soul and inseparable from It, although not often aware of this fact.[139]

Meanwhile, the biblical writings arising out of Judaism[140] taught that God had made a deliberate choice to create humanity: "in his own image, in the image of God created he him; male and female created he them." The writings also stated that God breathed "the breath of life" into the nostrils of the clay He had shaped into a human form and "man became a living soul."[141] Moreover, God was pleased with His handiwork.[142] In the Judaic wisdom teachings, humans are a "blend of dust and divinity;"[143] living souls who are commanded to "bless the Lord,"[144] the Master of all creation (the manifested cosmos).

Having borrowed a portion of that teaching from Judaism, the Christian teachings about soul changed throughout the centuries. Starting with the early idea that the "soul was eternal and had divine origins,"[145] the teachings went through various stages during which the soul gradually lost its inherent divinity. Finally, the Council of Nicaea [325 C.E.] declared that the soul had "no divine origin."[146] As that doctrinal development unfolded, soul was assumed to lose its original connection with the transcendent Spirit and to become a receptacle of the God Presence. Thus, the human soul was a container for the inner divinity but not integral with

---

[136] Quoted in *Ibid*, p. 484 from Giovanni Reale, *A History of Ancient Philosophy.* Vol. 1: *From the Origins to Socrates*, p. 202.

[137] Quoted in *Ibid* p. 486 from G. M. A. Grube, *Plato's Thought*, p. 129. Plato's "Forms" bear a startling resemblance to the "archetypes" postulated by Jung.

[138] Plotinus has been variously described as Greek and Roman. He was born in Egypt and received the ideas that he later incorporated into his philosophic system in Alexandria. Note the similarity with the ideas in the *Hermetica*. In these teachings, Plotinus was also echoing the Greek mystery teachings incorporated into the teachings of the Pythagoreans. For more detail, see Joscelyn Godwin, *The Golden Thread: The Ageless Wisdom of the Western Mystery Traditions*, 31-37.

[139] Quoted in A.H. Almaas, *The Inner Journey Home,* p. 489 from Giovanni Reale, *A History of Ancient Philosophy*, Vol. 4, *The Schools of the Imperial Age*, p. 380 and 544.

[140] The concept of a monotheistic god was likely taken from the Egyptian teachings.

[141] In these writings, it appears that the Divinity is understood as being Consciousness Creative Energy acting with intent. See *Genesis* 1: 27 and 2: 7.

[142] *Genesis* 1: 31.

[143] Huston Smith, *The World's Religions,* p. 280.

[144] *Psalms* 104: 1.In its entirety, this passage is a powerful expression of worship and praise.

[145] A. H. Almaas, *The Inner Journey Home*, p. 490.

[146] *Ibid*, p. 492.

it. In the teaching that still prevails, this soul was separated from the divine and in a state of impurity because of original sin. Even after purification it could not regain its divinity.

In past and present Christian theology, within the context of "impure" human soul, there is the related teaching indicating a primitive soul, which is the "sensual" soul. This soul can attain spiritual purity ("salvation") upon baptism or by believing in and opening to the Christ as the Word made flesh.[147]

In the Kabbalistic writings deriving from Judaism and owing much to the Hermetic tradition, there was also the idea of a primitive soul. In this teaching, the human soul was described as comprising five levels, starting with the most primitive. This primitive, "irrational" soul was the primary barrier to spiritual development because of its drives and instinctual appetites. Therefore, the Kabbalistic teaching advocated disciplines and ascetic practices to purify this soul level. Lack of purification meant that the person would not be able to access his/her divine nature and the irrational soul would prevail.

In Sufism, sometimes referred to as the mystical branch of Islam, there was much concern with soul and its stages of development. Echoing the Kabbalistic teachings, the Sufis regarded the first level of soul as a primitive, "animal soul," ruled by the instinctual animal passions. The transformation of soul involved a process of seven stages (some versions indicated five) with the final stage being the pure and complete self. This process of refinement has been described as a "marriage" between the soul, the changeable, formative substance, and the unchangeable "Essence."[148] The transformative process ended with the soul's becoming one with the Divine from whence it had come.

Meanwhile, within both mystical Judaism and Christianity, the Gnostics had taught that a human being could have a direct **knowing** of the inner divinity. For example, Clement of Alexandria [150-215 C. E.], who was an early Christian bishop and (to modern eyes) a gnostic, instructed children with these words: "The greatest of all lessons is to know yourself, for when a man knows himself, he knows God."[149] In short, the self and the soul consciousness energies of a human being were one and the same, and that, in their purest state, they were a divine wholeness.

Throughout the centuries since Clement, there has been a conflict between those in the Christian Church who were gnostic soul searchers and those who followed the theology. Eventually the theology prevailed and any form of gnosticism was declared to be heresy and severely punished. Even today, Christian concepts about soul are informed by "original sin," mankind's separation from the Divine and the need for "salvation."

---

[147] For more detail, see A. H. Almaas, *The Inner Journey Home: Soul's Realization of the Unity of Reality*, Chapter One, "Soul or Self," pp. 3-14 and Note #1, on page 583. In very early Christian writings, that of the *Gospel of Philip*, translated by Jean – Yves LeLoup, there is reference to animal soul. In verse 84, page 115 you read: "There is no lack of animal-humans, they are many and they revere each other."

[148] For more detail, see A. H. Almaas, *The Inner Journey Home*, p. 517-527. In this context "Essence" is pure Being. Regarding the "formative substance" that is soul, Ernest Holmes in *The Science of Mind*, page 600 has described soul as the "matter of Spirit, the substance of Spirit."

[149] See foodwhichendures.com. On this web site the information is taken from William Jurgens, *Faith of the Early Fathers*, Volume One, p. 189.

Yet, a Christian mystic of the 13th century, Meister Eckhart [1260-1327 C.E.], a Dominican preacher, another apparent gnostic and a declared heretic, could speak these words: "God is in everything, but God is nowhere as much as he is in the soul. There where time never penetrates, where no image shines in, in the innermost and the highest aspect of the soul God creates the entire cosmos."[150] Thus, those with a mystic's orientation knew that the macrocosmic Creative Energy was always at work in the microcosm; the human energy being, the expression *of* the One Consciousness, Creative Energy.

A later Christian poet, mystic and obvious gnostic, William Blake [1757-1827 C.E.], wrote an "Everlasting Gospel" in which he had God speak to Jesus, the evolved human being:

> "If Thou humblest Thyself,
> Thou humblest Me,
> Thou also dwellest in eternity,
> Thou art a man. 'God' is no more.
> Thine own humanity learn to adore,
> For that is My spirit of Life."[151]

With those words, Blake revealed that he clearly understood the connection between the microcosmic "self" and macrocosmic "Self;" that human beings were essentially divine.

Returning to the early years of the Common Era, you learn that the world's third great monotheistic religion, Islam, owed much to both Judaism and to Christianity. (The sacred book of Islam, *The Koran*, stated; "We made a covenant of old with the Children of Israel [and] you have nothing of guidance until you observe the Torah and the Gospel.")[152] But note the difference in the teaching about soul: the human soul in the tradition of Islam is the human "self." In this teaching, God is an individual and so is the human soul, whose individuality is everlasting, "for once it is created, it never dies."[153]

Evolving through centuries and concurrent with those of the Egyptians and Judaism, the teachings of Hinduism, contained in many sources including the *Rig Veda* and the *Upanishads*, have indicated that the individual human self or "i" was made up of both matter and consciousness, that consciousness was hidden in matter. Consciousness was associated with the Soul or Self, referred to as the "Atman." There was also the "stuff" of consciousness, referred to as the "chitta," energy which could flow outward toward the world and inward toward the Atman; it being a non-dimensional point of light and consciousness residing in the deepest level of the chitta. The relationship between the Atman and the chitta was that between an unchanging divine center core and a changeable soul "substance." [154]

---

[150] Matthew Fox, *Passion for Creation: Honoring Spirituality of Meister Eckhart*, "Sermon Two," p.65.
[151] Quoted in Tobias Churton, *The Gnostics*, p. 145.
[152] Quoted in Huston Smith, *The World's Religions*, p. 233.
[153] *Ibid*. p. 240.
[154] For more detail, see A. H. Almaas, *The Inner Journey Home*, p. 495-500.

The concept of a divine center was also carried in the teachings of Kashmir Shaivism in which Shiva, the ultimate Reality, the Consciousness that manifested this world, was the Self. In degrees of delimitation, the individual self was considered to be an expression of Shiva, concealed within the human being. In an echoing of Sufism, the spiritual path in Shaivism was one of recognizing one's original primitive nature and, through successive stages of refinement of consciousness, progressively realizing oneself as Shiva.[155]

Throughout the thousands of years that your sacred legacy of wisdom teachings about soul has existed, there has been, despite many seeming differences, a noteworthy sameness in the mystical awareness. That sameness can be summarized as follows:

Human soul is created by and out of the One Consciousness, Creative Energy referred to as Atum, Yahweh, Brahma, God, the Tao, Allah, Spirit, Siva, Ein Sof, Cosmic Consciousness, Mind etc. Human soul is imbued with this energy and eventually must become aware of it, for the soul is a creative power that can change its inner and outer environments. But, at birth, human soul is primitive and sensuous; in short, it is animal soul. However, because it is alive and teachable, primitive human soul (if properly taught) can change from its initial animal state into an enlightened awareness of its true nature. Human soul is consciousness and self which can merge into and become Consciousness and Self. This spiritual development is accomplished by undergoing a process of transformation and integration, resulting in a restoration into wholeness; the realization of soul's original divinity.

What an immense energy you carried when you chose to incarnate on this planet Earth! Of course, you do not have to believe any of it, but keep an open mind. On your path of "Opening the Way," please remain aware of your sacred legacy of wisdom teachings, while you begin to explore both the theories about and the realities of your consciousness energies of soul. Your quest is proceeding nicely!

Some Modern Theories Relevant to Soul Energies

As you have already learned from the wisdom teachings and from modern theories, you are endowed with an archetypal human energy system; an awareness that is part of an immense "picture" making you aware of both macrocosmic and microcosmic creative consciousness energies. At this juncture, more wisdom teachings, those dealing with "soul" energies have been added to the "picture" and to your awareness. Now, pursue these ideas further by again shifting your attention to scientific theories.

Please recall from the previous lesson that quantum physicists have been exploring the invisible world of quanta for about one hundred years. These researchers were often puzzled by what they were finding. As they moved away from the concepts of Newtonian physics, they became increasingly aware that they were encountering "matter" that was conscious and that could (and did) respond to the focused thought of the scientists performing the experiments. In short, human consciousness energies could change the energies of "matter" and in so doing

---

[155] For more detail, see *Ibid.* pp. 500-505. See also, Mark S. G. Dyczkowski, *The Doctrine of Vibration*, pp. 139-162.

be creative energy! To continue into this lesson . . . as the scientists delved ever more deeply into the invisible world of quanta, they slowly began to formulate theories about a "Zero Point Field" (ZPF) and the human relationship with it.

The ZPF has been described as "an ocean of microscopic vibrations in the space between things [. . .]. **the very underpinning of our universe** [emphasis added], a heaving sea of energy, one vast quantum field. [. . .] On our most fundamental level, living beings, including human beings, [are] packets of quantum energy constantly exchanging information with this inexhaustible energy sea.**"[Emphasis added][156] (As a brief aside . . . please note that the Akashic Field is likely part of the ZPF and that Barbara Brennan's "universal energy field" is likely also part or all of it.)

Now, while remembering that science is necessary to evolutionary spirituality, let us explore ZPF theories as being relevant to soul energies . . .

Turning to modern scientific minds, you again encounter Brennan and Rosalyn Bruyere, healers, along with Valerie Hunt, and Karl Pribram, neuroscientists. They have spent decades probing into the energies of human consciousness and studying it in the context of holographic theory.[157] Out of their work and that of others have come tantalizing clues that can be related to ZPF theories. Hence, it could be suggested that the (fundamental level) human "packets of quantum energy constantly exchanging information" with the ZPF could be regarded as the living holographic re-presentations of a quantum field, i.e., a ZPF, which is an immense living hologram. In other words, a person could be regarded as a holographic part/portion, i.e., a **microfield**, of a quantum energy field; a hologram which is a **macrofield**. (Please recall the holographic theory relating to micro consciousness and macro consciousness already mentioned in Lesson One.)

At this point, recall your legacy of wisdom teachings about soul and note that throughout the many centuries that people have pondered that subject, they have all (except the shamans) either implied or clearly stated that somehow "soul" was part of the duality of "matter" and spirit. In other words, the mortal physicality that was a person "had" a soul that was immortal. **Yet, the One Consciousness, Creative Energy is a macrocosmic Unity that is an All-Encompassing Power. Thus, there is no possibility of duality.** Please remember this while you explore further into ZPF theories as being relevant to soul energies . . .

The question arises: is the ZPF quantum energy field analogous to that macrocosmic Unity? The answer involves asking you to make a "quantum leap." It brings you into the framework of scientific and philosophical theories relating to holarchy. A holarchy has been described as "the self-organization of fields within fields within fields [. . .].[158] It is an "evolutionary emergence [that] takes us from the most fundamental fractals ["the patterns of nature that reveal to us that . . . all matter is fundamentally connected, unified at its

---

[156] Lynne McTaggart, *The Field: The Quest for the Secret Force of the Universe*, p. xvii. For further exploration, see Ervin Laszlo, *Science and the Akashic Field*, p. 47-50. Please note that humans **exchange** information with the ZPF.

[157] Please refer to the "Bibliography" for their writings.

[158] Ken Wilber, *The Eye of the Spirit*, p. 43.

source"][159]of existence to the entirety of the universe. Each [. . .] level is both a whole in itself and a subset [holon] of the next level of complexity."[160] From this idea, it could follow that there are holographic quantum fields (holons) within holographic quantum fields (holons) within holographic quantum fields (holons) that probably stretch into infinity and re-present, with greater and greater complexity and detail, the macrocosmic Unity. And it could be suggested that the people in this third dimension, on this planet Earth, are the microcosmic re-presentations of a greatly reduced and simplified version (a holographic quantum field, the ZPF) of that macrocosmic Unity.

It is within that context that the ZPF quantum energy field (a vastly simplified **macrofield**) could be regarded as analogous to the macrocosmic Unity and that you (a **microfield**) could be regarded as a microcosmic re-presentation (a holon) of that Unity. There is your "quantum leap;" feasible, but subject to much scientific verification. Please ponder those ideas, while you remember that there is no duality between matter and spirit: it is all spirit, i.e., energy.

Now, stretch your capacity yet further and "open the way" to explore this idea: the uncreated Spirit (the One Consciousness, Creative Energy also referred to as Atum, Yahweh, Brahma, God, Allah, Shiva, Ein Sof, Mind, etc.), in other words, the macrocosmic Unity, is a **macrofield; a** multidimensional, ever-expanding, eternally creative energy field. And the **microfield** is your individual consciousness, a multidimensional energy field, whose existence has been demonstrated in the work of the scientists already mentioned and implied, for centuries, in the wisdom tradition. So, let us postulate with some assurance that a human being is a living embodiment of consciousness energy functioning as a multidimensional and holographic field; a creative energy field which is a **microcosmic** re-presentation of the **macrocosmic** One Consciousness, Creative Energy. In short, a human being is an energy being who is a creative consciousness[161] analogous to a particle/wave in the ZPF quantum sea. Please ponder that idea.

Now, recalling again the wisdom teachings, stretch further and explore this related idea: since the macrocosmic, omnipresent Spirit (the One Consciousness, Creative Energy) created the manifested cosmos and illuminated (i.e., energized) it with macrocosmic Soul, it would follow that the microcosmic human energy being, who is a holographic re-presentation of the macrocosmic One Consciousness, Creative Energy is also a holographic re-presentation (a manifested and energized ("particle/wave") of the macrocosmic Soul. (Please recall the shaman's story of Little Soul!) And you are a **holographic soul field,** (hereafter referred to as a soul field). To round out the idea: when you focus your attention on Soul as macrocosmic energies, you are focusing on manifested macrocosmic One Consciousness, Creative Energy and when you focus your attention on human soul as microcosmic energies, you are focusing on manifested microcosmic human creative consciousness energies. In this unity, no matter where you focus your attention, your consciousness energies cannot be separated from soul,

---

[159] Robin Kelly, *The Human Hologram*, p. 14.
[160] Ervin Laszlo and Jude Currivan, *CosMos: A Co-creator's Guide to the Whole-world,* p.34.
[161] This idea and the idea in the following paragraph are the essential insights of these lessons. They constitute the foundation for the later ideas about a generative human energy system already mentioned in Lesson One.

for **they are one and the same microfield**. And you come to realize that as a soul searcher, what you are looking **for** is what you are looking **with** and what you are looking **at**. It is soul/creative consciousness energy and there is no duality of "matter" and spirit. You are a consciousness energy being, a soul field. You are involved in an incredible evolutionary process that includes other lifetimes, this lifetime and many more to come. And **who you are, and always have been, is soul.**

Having been given this insight, you might welcome the opportunity to test it while on your path of "Opening the Way," by exploring "you" as an energy being, a soul field. In order for you to do this, you must be introduced to the Observer.

The Observer

The Observer is a unique energy, a **presence** that you can sense as somehow being part of who you are. But it is an energy detached from all your sometimes noisy and jostling "selves." It has long been referred to as the Watcher and as the Witness. It is a gentle and loving discernment and detachment that is there in your field.[162] You can summon the Observer to assist you on your rebirthing journey. Indeed, the Observer is essential, for it enormously enhances your capacity for inner self-exploration. With the Observer, you are capable of tuning into your consciousness energies, because the Observer is "an objective other who lives in the midst of [your] subjectivity."[163] It will not advise, console or criticize you. It will simply be there to assist you while you undertake all the experiences, the probing inner explorations, the healing therapies (disciplines) and the disciples/practices that are required for your journey. The Observer will be there to **observe, without judgment** all that is going on. And while your quest for wholeness progresses, your connection with that presence will slowly bring about a change in your awareness. As you continue to enlist its assistance, you will become more and more aware that you know the truth about yourself, about others and about your situation. And you have acquired this truth in such a way that you can (and do) have compassion for yourself and for others. You will have entered into a new "reality." Your quest for wholeness cannot succeed until you have entered into that reality, because it will indicate that you no longer reject who you are. It is important to realize that "we cannot be real while we reject ourselves. It's as simple as that. It doesn't matter what comes up; we cannot reject anything that arises in ourselves and be real."[164] The Observer will ensure that while you are rebirthing you are becoming "real."

Now, here at the beginning, you do what you will do countless times; call in the Observer to help you. This time it will be there to assist you to experience your soul field.

---

[162] The Observer in your soul field seems to be standing outside of your physical body.
[163] Ann and Barry Ulanov, *Transforming Sexuality: The Archetypal World of Anima and Animus*, p. 21.
[164] A. H. Almaas, *The Unfolding Now*, p. 92.

Experiencing Your Soul Field

Prepare by setting aside a quiet space and a period of undisturbed time.

Sit or lie down. When all is in readiness, silently state your intent to experience your soul field. Then begin with many deep **grounding** breaths. Take your time. As you continue your breathing, gradually focus all your attention inwardly. While continuing to breathe deeply, "call" in the Observer. You will soon sense that energy, perhaps beside or behind you. Let it be wherever it is. Ask the Observer to assist you to experience your soul field.

Stay focused . . . . Allow a deepening of what is happening. Slowly, you will get the sense of being completely immersed in a tangible "something." (For some people it seems to be liquid. For some people it is colors. For others it is fragrance. For yet others it is sound.) Do not anticipate or try to make things happen. Just **go** with it and **experience** whatever unfolds. That is the practice which you will undertake again and again. Always with the Observer, you will be experiencing your own soul field.

As you explore and become increasingly familiar with that consciousness energy, you will realize that "the field of the soul is related to [your] awareness and consciousness" and that with this awareness, "[you] can begin to experience [your soul field] assuming all kinds of shapes and forms."[165] You can do that because you can be conscious of your consciousness "aware of itself as a field."[166]

After you have become somewhat comfortable with experiencing your soul field, you may continue by exploring how it can be said that your soul field can assume shapes and forms. You do that by experiencing your soul substance.[167] And you can do that because your soul field is consciousness and the "substance" of soul is also consciousness. In other words, your soul field and soul substance constitute a unity.[168]

Experiencing Your Soul Substance

Proceed as you have done already while experiencing your soul field and enlist the help of the Observer. This time your silently stated intent will be to experience your soul substance. Allow yourself to enter into the state of altered awareness . . . .

Since soul energies are a holographic field, your first few experiences of **knowing** soul substance directly will be indefinite and somewhat ambiguous. Persist, and focus on getting the sense of a totality.[169] You will realize that soul substance is dynamic. Those energies are constantly moving, shifting and changing. In short, they are dancing the cosmic Dance of

---

[165] A. H. Almaas, *The Inner Journey Home*, p. 28. This idea is an exact description of the shapeshifting that shamans do.

[166] *Ibid.* p. 30.

[167] Although all of the discussion that follows is based on modern theory, it likely has its roots, in part, in the Pythagorean ideas about "soul stuff" that was immortal. After being released at death, it could animate other bodies, human or animal. See Joscelyn Godwin, *The Golden Thread: The Ageless Wisdom of the Western Mystery Traditions*, Note #8, p. 160.

[168] This unity is analogous to the ocean (soul field) and the drops of water in it (soul substance).

[169] For more detail, see A.H. Almaas, *The Inner Journey Home*, pp. 76-112 and 200-217.

Shiva and Shakti. That dance is changeable, active, interactive, responsive and adaptive. The dance is happening in your soul field where all of your experiences of everything and on all levels, is happening. All that you are as a doer and a knower and all that you are as the action and the known, is inherent in your soul substance. Inherent also are the believer and the belief, the chooser and the choice, the perceiver and the perception, the thought and the thinker, the sufferer and the suffering . . . you get the picture. It's all part of the "dance," Please allow the experience.

And there's more. Inherent also in that soul substance is the **information** that can be shaped into the belief, the choice, the perception, the reasoning, the insights, the feeling, etc. All of this dynamic change is happening in your soul field as an ever-changing "dance."[170]

Take your time with this. Until you can comfortably experience your soul field and soul substance, please remain with this part of the lesson. And be aware that with this "work" you will immensely expand your **knowing** of you as a soul field. You will thereby expand your **being**.

Soul Wounding and Fragmentation

Then, Soul Searcher, you must learn that while your soul substance consciousness energies can change themselves, they can also be changed. You as a soul field are changed by your external and internal environments; energies that are crucial in your development. How and why? Soul substance is malleable, like silly putty. How easily soul can be manipulated! This is what makes it possible to train children to a particular cultural framework. Soul substance is impressionable, a necessary quality for learning and social conditioning. Moreover, these impressions can reinforce and build on each other. This can create a particular individual or national "character." Soul substance is receptive and easily responds to repeated stimuli. If the stimuli are those of love or those of fear, soul energies will be changed accordingly. Above all else, soul substance is vulnerable. People can be traumatized in a multitude of ways, including the savagery of warfare. In sum, "malleability, impressionability, receptivity and vulnerability" are the key descriptors of soul substance. The implications for the soul field are immense.

The indescribable suffering that has afflicted humankind for all its existence is grounded in the malleability, impressionability, receptivity and vulnerability of soul substance. Those agonies have been produced by soul wounding, an idea very familiar to healers, shamans and to other people conversant with human consciousness energies. Soul wounds can lead to soul fragmentation, referred to by shamans as soul "loss,"[171] which means that the soul substance and even the forms that have been shaped out of it cannot maintain their integrity and parts of the soul field go missing. The wounding is brought about by physical, emotional, mental and/or spiritual trauma (sometimes referred to as "post traumatic stress disorder") and can happen

---

[170] See the description of the Dance of Shiva (and Shakti) in the "Prologue."

[171] This is a term used by shamans, part of whose work involves retrieving the "lost" soul fragments.

even in the uterus.[172] Because so much of your quest for wholeness involves dealing with and healing your woundedness, there will be more to learn in all the lessons to come.

To anticipate what comes later in the lesson . . . when you become familiar with your soul field, you will be able to discern the forms, i.e., the structures that soul substance assumes. While you do this, you will become increasingly aware of how soul substance has been shaped, (one could even say "in-formed") and made into "you." And you will already be comfortably aware of the help that is always there in the presence that is the Observer.

It will be a very important ally in a discipline/practice that will actually continue throughout the better part of your journey. This discipline/practice involves a "letting go" of many of the forms that constitute your deeply buried beliefs and preconceived notions. Herein lies the most challenging part of your path of "Opening the Way." As this journey unfolds, you will be tuning ever more deeply into your own consciousness energies and becoming increasingly aware that your in-formed beliefs, along with your values, habits and attitudes sometimes do not tell the truth about you and/or the world. The discipline/practice will be one of "letting go" and replacing those forms with the truth. Very soon you will be required to call in the Observer and establish that discipline/practice. To anticipate what is coming . . . it will relate closely to detachment and discernment.

Meanwhile, let us continue with the lesson by providing additional information about the masculine (yang) and feminine (yin) forces as they relate to both to soul field/substance and to soul wounding.

The Masculine and Feminine Energies of Soul

Because you, the microcosm, are a holographic field, a soul field, the Masculine and Feminine Principles in the macrocosmic One Consciousness, Creative Energy/Soul are inherent in your microcosmic soul field/soul substance consciousness energies.[173] As you have already been made aware, there is within the world's spiritual teachings a thread carrying humankind's knowledge of the presence of those archetypal masculine and feminine energies that suffuse the entire cosmos and all living things. Thus, there probably resides deep within you the awareness that out of the Unity, your original fundamental Wholeness, there are in you, the microcosm, the archetypal two (the "andro" and "gyne") that are inseparably "attached," yet always apart.

To illustrate on a lighter note, please take in the re-telling of a tale given to us by Plato, whose character, Aristophanes, speaks of man's original nature and of what happened to transform him into his present state.[174]

---

[172] There is more detail given in the next lesson.
[173] Anthony Stevens, *Archetypes: A Natural History of the Self*, p. 29. These Principles are a "precondition and coexistent of life itself."
[174] Paraphrased and distilled from June Singer, *Androgyny: The Opposites Within*, pp. 81-82.

In the beginning, human nature was different from what it is now. There were three sexes, not two; man, woman and a union of the two, a double nature, termed "androgynous." These primeval humans were round and made up of sun and earth. Their backs and sides formed a circle; one head and two faces looking in opposite ways, four ears, two sets of genitals and other parts to correspond. The androgynies could walk upright, backwards or forwards and they could also roll over and over at a great pace. Terrible were the might and strength of these creatures. They eventually dared to aspire to the heavens and to attack the gods therein.

Zeus, father of the gods, took counsel and the decision was made to continue to allow the existence of these presumptuous beings but to put them into their proper place. He thereupon cut them in two, "like a crab-apple which is halved for pickling."

After the surgery, the two parts of the androgynies diligently sought to come together and lived entwined in each others' arms. In time, they were on the point of dying from hunger and self-neglect. When Zeus saw that they were being destroyed, he pitied them and devised a new plan. He turned their genitalia to the front (this had not heretofore been their position) and henceforth they sowed the seed, no longer as they had done, like grasshoppers on the ground, but in each other. After the transposition, the "man" generated in the "woman" in order that in mutual embraces they might breed and the race would continue. So ancient is the desire of one another which is implanted in us, reuniting our original nature, that we will eagerly look for our other half and when we find it, get lost in an amazement of love and friendship and intimacy.

That ends the story from the Greek teacher; on the surface a rather credulous tale about sex and gender. Yet it reveals a **knowing** about the nature and function of the archetypes-as-such: the Masculine and Feminine Principles; the macrocosmic originals of the microcosmic androgyny.

Having received that instruction (with more to come), you are ready to learn about the embodiments that your soul substance (with its inherent masculine and feminine forces) can assume. These are the soul structures that in-form your "bodies" of consciousness. (But, because these embodiments and soul structures are dealt with throughout the remaining lessons, they are only briefly introduced here.)

Your "Bodies" of Consciousness as Soul Structures

As you have already learned in the previous lesson, you, a multidimensional, microcosmic, energy being, a soul field, are a collectivity of four "bodies" of consciousness energies. Learn now that these bodies "are held together by the magnetic force of the universal field which

[. . .] interpenetrates them, [. . .] and connects them to it."[175] Getting to **know** and learning how to heal the often misunderstood soul structures of your "bodies" is a fundamental part of your quest for wholeness.

Your most obvious embodiment is your physical body, also referred to, in many texts, as your "gross" (meaning "material") body of consciousness. Although it looks pretty solid and vibrates at a very low frequency, your physical body is actually "an organized and self-organizing field of protoplasm,"[176] ultimately reducible to pure consciousness energies.[177] Your physicality is structured out of soul substance in accordance with an inherent, biological "plan;" part of the information carried by your soul field. This physical embodiment of consciousness is referred to throughout these lessons as your "soul structures of physicality." They include the egoic structures. (The details about your physical embodiment, including those of the ego, as soul structures of physicality will be explored in the next lesson.)

Visible in your aura to those with higher sensory perception,[178] your three other "bodies" are predominantly invisible in this third dimension and are described in many texts as your "subtle" bodies of consciousness.[179] Those three embodiments, as their constituent soul structures, will be explored in later lessons, in which each collectivity is referred to respectively as your "soul structures of emotionality, of mentality and of spirituality." Each subtle "body" of consciousness also includes the egoic structures. The "subtle" consciousness energies constantly interact ("dance") with each other and with your protoplasmic consciousness energies to express all that you are.

And all of the soul structures that constitute your embodiments of consciousness relate intimately with the centers of consciousness, the chakras, of your human energy system, your archetypal endowment.

Now you are ready to finalize your immersion in the Big Picture by looking at the linkages connecting your soul substance, your soul structures and your human energy system.

The Linkages

As already briefly indicated, while you, an energy being, a soul field; were involved in the cosmic "dance," your soul substance was also being shaped by the energies present in your internal and external environments. Bit by bit, your "gross" and "subtle" soul structures were in-formed. Many of those structures in turn, impacted upon soul substance and, as a result, continued to be shaped and reinforced. Thereby, your embodiments of consciousness were developed.

---

[175] Keith Sherwood, *Chakra Therapy: For Personal Growth and Healing*, p. 103.

[176] A. H. Almaas, *The Inner Journey Home*, p. 37.

[177] For more detail, see *Ibid*, pp. 610-611.

[178] Barbara Brennan, *Hands of Light*, p.7.

[179] These "bodies" were known in the "primordial philosophy" starting with the Chaldean and Orphic mysteries, then going into the "classical period" of Pythagoras and Plato, then into the Common Era with the Muslim Suhrawardi, the Byzantine Plethon, then into Renaissance Italy and into the present. For more detail, see Joscelyn Godwin, *The Golden Thread*, pp. 2-8.

In time, the reinforced soul structures became crystallized and seemingly unchangeable. Those crystallized structures were of immense complexity and durability. They have appeared to be what you have "become." They have often been the result of soul wounding and even of soul fragmentation and loss. Consequently, many of those soul structures have been "crippled" and have required transformative healing.

Now, having stretched your capacity to "open the way" in order to encompass the teaching thus far, please expand further and note the linkage with your human energy system, about whose archetypal nature and androgynous forces you have already learned.

How that structuring came about from the moment of your conception can be understood only by reference to the generative capacity of your human energy system.[180] **Fed by the living energies of the Cosmos via Earth and guided by the indwelling Spirit (the nucleus of divinity), your archetypal energy system — the microcosmic re-presentation *of* (out of and part of) the Unity; the One Consciousness that includes Creative Energy, Soul and Masculine and Feminine Principles — has been the creative power that has formed, out of your microcosmic consciousness energies that are your soul field/substance, the soul structures that constitute you as a multidimensional and (potentially) androgynous energy being; a soul that expresses as and through your "bodies" of consciousness.**[181] (The remainder of the lessons in the stone circle will demonstrate that linkage.)

The shaman's story about your incarnation into this dimension described you as Little Soul, an "expression *of* the Divine." How you continued to develop thereafter was directly related to your human energy system, your archetypal endowment, and its connection with your nucleus of divinity. If you are still uncertain about that idea, the wisdom teachings, right up to the present time, and modern scientific discoveries could help you considerably in your ponderings. Here you may begin your discipline/practice of "letting go" (if you have not already started!) and with the help of the Observer examine your present beliefs. There is an immense new **knowing** that you are being asked to acquire.

And now a parting thought to summarize the new instruction you have received in the Big Picture: you rebirth into androgyny by exploring and working with who you truly are; a holographic, microcosmic re-presentation, a microfield (a holon) of the macrocosmic Unity, the macrofield. You are an energy being, a soul field whose "structures" are self-generated out of its "substance" by the microcosmic creative energies you can **know** as your human energy system, your archetypal endowment. You are an energy being, a soul field carrying the archetypal, microcosmic re-presentation of the Masculine and Feminine Principles. Those energies are not only inherent in soul substance but are also the "forces" within that energy system. As such, the masculine and feminine energies are carried by your "soul structures." You are an energy being, a soul field whose soul structures include those of the ego/self. You are an energy being,

---

[180] Please recall Note #93 in Lesson One. This idea undergirds the teachings presented throughout all the lessons.

[181] Lorin Roche, *The Radiance Sutras: Tantra Yoga Teachings for Opening to the Divine in Everyday Life,* p. 21.

a soul field that the shaman's story tells you starts as Little Soul, an expression *of* (out of and part of) the Divine and chooses to incarnate as a human being in this third dimension.

That ends your immersion in the Big Picture and this lesson on your energies of soul. There is much for you to ponder and to experience. Before you leave this enclosure, look around you and, again, take in the timelessness of this place. In this sacred space you are in shamanic time, in the "now." Are you beginning to understand what your own timelessness entails?

When you are ready, you may leave the stone circle.

*   *   *

Soul Searcher, you have done well on your rebirthing journey and you have traveled far on your path of "Opening the Way!" Here in the East the journey can be strenuous while you are "letting go" of long-cherished beliefs and other notions. Please stay with this lesson until you feel comfortable with it. In particular, cultivate your relationship with the Observer in all the ways you have already learned. Then rest briefly before you attempt the "Interlude."

Peace and blessings

FIRST INTERLUDE

Here in the East, let us pause together to remember and recognize: remember what launched you on this rebirthing journey; recognize the amazing insights you have already acquired. After your rest period, you are invited to undertake a deeper work of "opening the way." In this you will return to your first two lessons. There are profound experiences in store that are more than "study" or "review." **They are an assimilation of the teachings; an internalization so complete that they become part of you as a soul field.**

In order for this to happen, you may choose to return to the sacred space of the stone circle, or you may choose to create your own shamanic "sacred space." You do this by "casting the circle:" after putting your "roots" into Earth and taking a few deep **grounding** breaths, you face in the direction of the East and, in your own words, "call in" the healing and supporting powers of the East. Then, in succession, you face the South, the West, and the North, while you "call in" their powers. (You do not have to know or name them. You are already gaining enough awareness about you as a microcosmic energy being to allow for the existence of macrocosmic healing and supportive powers and to accept the idea that you, the microcosm, can "call" them in. Shamans have tapped into them for centuries. They are there for you.)

To inspire and support your "work" in your sacred space, here are the thoughts of a great wisdom teacher of the early twentieth century:[182]

> "The earliest preoccupation of man in his awakened thought and as it seems,
> his inevitable and ultimate preoccupation – for it survives the longest periods
> of skepticism and returns after every banishment – is also the highest which
> his thought can envisage. It manifests itself in the divination of Godhead, the
> impulse toward perfection, the search after pure truth and unmixed Bliss, the
> sense of a secret immortality."

Soul Searcher, you probably resonate with those words! They indicate a profound awareness of you and what has been "calling" to you. For the work of assimilation, which is analogous to the absorption of nourishment, here are a few suggestions that you might want to follow or improve upon:

After you have "digested" the contents of your first two lessons, you are invited to expand your capacity to take in by delving directly into the wisdom teachings and the theories of those

---

[182] Sri Aurobindo, *The Life Divine*, p. 5.

63

teachers you have already encountered. They are great souls awaiting your attention! If you are led to more, then add them to your intake. In all of this you will be strengthening your foundations and, thereby, enhancing your capabilities as a soul searcher. Excellent!

Meanwhile, continue the **grounding** breath work and 'experiences" that have connected you directly to your own energy system (chakras and auric field) and indirectly to that of others. And be diligent in cultivating your relationship with the Observer. This relationship is especially important when you are experiencing your soul field/soul substance, i.e., when you are in a state of altered awareness and sense that you are a consciousness conscious of itself. In all of this commitment to disciplines and practices you are fostering the inner growth that is expanding and deepening you as an energy being, a soul field. In these beginnings, while you are opening the way be assured that you are on your journey and that your transformation, liberation and regeneration are happening.

And you will be transforming and re-shaping your soul structures, even those of which you are unaware. While you go through this first interlude, please be aware that as a soul searcher with "the sense of a secret immortality," you are opening the way to some intense moments of "letting go." During and after that discipline/practice, you will likely experience the resultant feelings of uncomfortable nakedness. Be assured that the letting go of old ways (mainly patterns of **belief**) is the way of the pilgrim. Each letting go constitutes a "milestone" of the journey; each letting go is usually uncomfortable.

And while you stay with this first interlude, you will increasingly become aware that "letting go" does **not** mean discarding, obliterating or rejecting your old ways. With the slowly developing capacity for detachment and discernment which your connection with the Observer is teaching you, you are realizing that the "letting go" involves the deep change of transformation.[183] This is to be expected: the journey involves the "work" of becoming "real." You do this by being in your truth. Thus, the letting go at a deeper level of meaning can also mean "letting be," which is "acceptance."[184] In other words, with your discipline/practice you gradually release your need to manage your situation and circumstances and you just let them "be" what they are. Meanwhile, you are opening the way into accepting and doing what serves your life, as an increasingly aware expression *of* the Spirit. In the disciplines/ practices of "letting go" and "letting be," you will undergo many beginnings. You will be "stretched." Let it happen! While you let the old ways "be" with the help of the Observer you will be opening into new ways (mainly patterns of belief). Here, at the beginning, while you are being "stretched," these new ways will be tentative and unfamiliar ventures into the "real:" into the truth of relationships with you, with others and with the world; relationships without judgment and without control. You will be going into the deeper places of **knowing** things differently. In other words, you will be developing the immense energies of discernment and detachment.

---

[183] Please recall Note #48 in the "Prologue."

[184] For a splendid description of a "true letting be," see Matthew Fox, *Passion for Creation: The Earth-Honoring Spirituality of Meister Eckhart*, pp. 213-225. See also A. H. Almaas, *The Unfolding Now*, "True Acceptance," pp. 94-97.

And while you continue with a deeper "opening the way" into the internalization, which requires even more letting go/letting be, you will gradually experience a gentle undercurrent that is sustaining you.

The undercurrent is this . . .

In the East as shamans know it, the Life aspect of the indwelling Spirit (your nucleus of divinity) is always present. As you journey on this path and endure its rigors, the Life undercurrent will be giving you its qualities of strength and courage to persist. They will be your powers that carry the confidence synonymous with "faith," a masculine quality of the highest spiritual order.[185] As you further internalize these first two lessons, you will experience other wonderful Life qualities; vigor, confidence, self-esteem, optimism and openness, to mention a few. Please do the work of assimilation and let it start to in-form what you are as an energy being, a soul field. And, while you explore and "work" with the new patterns, you will be opening the way into a sense of freedom. It is the Life undercurrent fostering a deepening sense of inner empowerment. It is the wonderful beginning of your rebirthing.

Herein lies the power of the East as shamans know it. Stay here for as long as it takes you to progress into a new sense of readiness, even an eagerness, to continue on your quest for wholeness.

Peace and blessings

---

[185] Faith is described by Paul, the Apostle, as being the "evidence of things not seen." This statement implies the focus of an outward oriented, i.e., masculine, energy.

PART TWO

THE PATH OF THE SOUTH:

"COMING INTO BEING"

SECOND INTRODUCTION

Shamans know that the multidimensional spirit world is populated by innumerable forms and types of "spirit beings." While shamans walk "between the worlds," in other words, while they spirit journey, they meet up with many different spirit beings and learn from them. Then, here on Earth, those beings often become the archetypal "characters" of shamans' stories, some of which are referred to as "myths" and "fairy tales." [186] While rebirthing into androgyny, you will be in-formed by many spirit beings. Some will come to you in your dreaming state. Others will be the archetypal characters found in myths and fairy tales.

Having traveled in the cosmic realm of the East on the path of "Opening the Way," you have received the necessary foundation and framework for your quest. Quite likely, you have also undergone some strenuous moments while you acquired the necessary power of "letting go." Those moments were intense because they often involved not only the "letting go" of old patterns of beliefs and perceptions but also the "letting be" of some situations and circumstances that required further questing. While you continue, you will gain more power of letting go/letting be. Yet, you are already in-formed by a fresh (an embryonic) **knowing** that is quietly suggesting your emerging **being**. Thus, you are ready to enter upon your next stage of rebirthing and of your quest.

You continue by surrendering to the power of the South. It is the cosmic realm of growth and expansion. The South contains the power that invariably expresses in this third dimension as the energies of the day's high noon and as the seasonal energies of summer, with

---

[186] Those who first told the myths and fairy tales were shamans in orientation if not in practice. All those stories are derived from the "spirit world." They provide profound lessons in the workings of the Spirit. See Marie-Louise Von Franz, *Archetypal Patterns in Fairy Tales*, p. 17.

its enveloping, sensuous heat. The South also contains the power that invariably expresses in Earth's living things, including people, as the energies of development and growth into adulthood. In addition to those immense powers that are freely given by the cycles of "nature," the South contains the power of "balancing." Because your continuing journey requires the equilibrium of your inner forces, this power of the South is essential. Yet it is only a possibility that must be actualized. While you continue to develop more power of letting go/letting be, you will have a greater capacity to develop the power of balancing.

Embracing the power of the South, you set your feet on the path of **coming into being**. On this path you explore and start to heal your "lower" centers of consciousness[187] and their multidimensional soul structures. During this "work," you develop yet more **knowing** while your **being** undergoes a corresponding growth and expansion.

Shamans know that in the South, the **macrocosmic** energy of **Light-as-Such** is paramount. Eternally unchanged and unchanging Light is an aspect of the Spirit. Shamans also know that at the same time the **microcosmic** light energy is constantly beginning and constantly renewing itself. Thus it is that light energy vibrates as every particle/wave of all creation (the manifested cosmos), including you. An awareness of that energy is what you require now. Growing and expanding mean accepting and allowing Light/light.

Now let us go to the stone circle.

---

[187] The word "lower" refers only to the vibratory frequency of these centers of consciousness.

Lesson Three

YOUR ROOT CHAKRA AND SOUL STRUCTURES OF PHYSICALITY

Hello: welcome to the stone circle on this glorious early summer day. Before you enter this sacred enclosure, please pause to observe and absorb your surroundings. Beyond this grassy incline, in all directions you can see rolling hills patterned by lush green pasture land enclosed by miles of low stone fences. And to the North behind Long Meg, you can discern the misty outline of the mountains. Now look up and really see the blue sky and clean, white clouds. Listen to the 'voices" in the wind. Do you hear the curlews calling? Those little birds have been braving the winds on these moors for many centuries. Now inhale and taste the freshness of the air and the aromas of fertile Earth. Stand here beside Long Meg and tune into her massive presence. Now take several deep **grounding** breaths and scan her aura. Be respectful; she punches! . . . Do you sense her energies of consciousness? She is alive and you are sharing your aliveness with her.

Come, walk inside the circle. Touch her Children, the standing stones. Feel their texture and temperature. Take in their size, mass and color. Gently scan their auras and tune into their energies of consciousness.[188] Now see, touch and inhale the scents of the grasses and Earth. Move slowly and care-fully. Do you hear the humming insects and the gentle rustling breeze in the grass? Absorb the energies of the living things all around you. Feel your connection with the totality. What a glorious display of physicality and sensuality has been given to you!

Now, come here into the grassy center. Standing with your feet apart and your face uplifted, raise your arms high. Take several deep **grounding** breaths. Feel all of you balancing between and connecting to both Earth and Sky. You are an intrinsic part of the Cosmos and of this place. You throb with those vibrations. Feel them . . . . Feel them . . . . Here is your ground sheet. Be seated please . . . .

---

[188] If you are interested in scientific verification, the "Dragon Project," which was started in the late 1970's and continued for more than a decade involved measuring the electromagnetic energies in the megalithic sites of Great Britain and other parts of the world. It was discovered that the stone circles were located on spots that "emitted strong radiations." Because it was people who **knew** this and built and used these circles, there can be implied a "link [...] between the field of earth energy and human psychology." For more detail, see John Michell, *Secrets of the Stones: New Revelations of Astro-archaeology and the Mystical Sciences of Antiquity,* pp 116-120.

Soul Searcher; after completing your immersion in the Big Picture, your rebirthing journey is progressing nicely . . . at its necessary speed. Throughout your sojourn in the East, you probably experienced some dramatic changes of awareness. Excellent! Here in the South there are more awaiting you.

Here is the first one: while you were letting go/letting be on your path in the East, the path of "Opening the Way," you were often **already** journeying along your next path; the path of the South, of "Coming into Being." That experience was possible because the path was "next," not in the sense of a linear progression, but as one **parallel** to and **contiguous** with the old path. Here in the South, as you move along this new path, there will be times when you are seemingly on both paths at the same time. In actuality, you will often be experiencing an opening of the way and a coming into being **simultaneously**. Be prepared for this to happen and be prepared to feel "larger" when it does. As your quest continues, more and more you will experience those moments of simultaneity. More and more you will enjoy getting to **know** your own amazing multidimensionality.

The feast of the senses that you have just received is a gift from this third dimension "reality." It is here that you obtain all your feasts of physicality, as you fully experience your involvement with Earth's splendid "materiality." You do this through your **intent** and your **attention**.[189] Those energies of materiality impact upon your receptive soul substance. Then they are shaped into your soul structures of physicality by and through the generative power of your **root chakra**. Having experienced many such feasts in this lifetime, you have already repeatedly experienced those generative. Soon they will become real to you and you will truly **know** what they are.

Come; step forward on your path of "Coming into Being."

* * *

Enriched by Celtic mythology and by references to human biology, modern psychology and fairy tales, this lesson will continue your rebirthing quest by presenting you with paradox, the first of many such experiences. After this initial preparation, you will learn about your root chakra. And you will do this within the context of the **holistic** energy system which is your archetypal endowment. Your root chakra, your first primary center of consciousness is the creative energy that has shaped your soul substance into the soul structures of physicality that are your "gross" embodiment. You will learn about the root chakra's qualities and function, which are intrinsic to its generative power. It is a power manifesting the chakra's prime directive, the archetypal imperative, and "i-am" statement of consciousness. Within this framework, you will also learn how your physical structuring came about, during your gestation and after your birth, in interaction with your inner and outer environments. After that, you will receive preliminary instruction about the vitally necessary discipline/practice

---

[189] Although you have already been doing this, you now receive the deeper purpose. It is this: by focusing your intent and attention, you call into action the creative power of your indwelling Spirit and tap into the macrocosmic Creative Energy.

of "balancing" and begin that practice. Then you will start to learn about your ego/self: why it exists; how the archetypal masculine and feminine forces[190] were implicated in its initial formation and function; how and why you first experienced and expressed it as your physicality. While this lesson unfolds, you will be required to start probing into what you are as an energy being, a soul field, and pondering on what you discover, including your own soul structures of physicality. Finally, after learning about root chakra malfunction, you will be given some self-healing therapies (disciplines) which will, of course, constitute your "homework." This lesson is very full!

*   *   *

First, please recall the shaman's story of Little Soul, about how and why you incarnated in this third dimension. Your recollection will be a reminder that you, who are an expression *of* (out of and part of) the Divine; you, who are a microcosmic re-presentation of the One Consciousness, Creative Energy, came from the Spirit and that you must not (again!) forget your origins or your true being. Very soon, you will be delving into the complexities and crudities of your initial postnatal beingness. In that exploration, awareness of your origins and of your original wholeness will be the gentle light illuminating your path. Pause now and recall the story . . .

Then, take in these words from a modern soul searcher:[191]

"The Advent"

"The events of history were controlled
for my coming into the world
no less than for the coming of [the] Christ.
The time had to be ripe,
the circumstances ready,
before I could be born.
[. . . .]
The Christ Child comes, like every other child,
to give the world a message.
What message have I come to give?
I seek guidance from the [Spirit] to express it
in a word or image.
[. . . .]

---

[190] Please recall the teachings in the "Prologue" about the archetypal "dancing" masculine and feminine energies. Also recall the description of those forces presented in Lesson One.
[191] Anthony De Mello, *Wellsprings,* pp.21-22.

**I look with expectation
and surrender
at all that is to come
and, like [the] Christ,
I say: "Yes. Let it be done."**

**Finally, I recall the song the angels sang
when [the] Christ was born.
They sang of the peace and joy
that give God glory.**

**Have I ever heard the song the angels sang
when I was born?**

**I see with joy what has been done through me
to make the world a better place
and I join those angels
in the song they sang
to celebrate my birth."**

That ends the reminder. Know that you, too, are entitled to celebrate your advent, for you carried into this incarnation your nucleus of divinity (the indwelling Spirit). Within that sacred core, you brought your potential to "make the world a better place." You were a "god" in the flesh who had chosen to come here in order to further your evolution. But there was a huge **paradox** involved in your becoming flesh. At this juncture, you might want to heed the words of an insightful woman, who said:[192]

"We must always keep in mind the opposite of what we believe in, the opposite of our highest ideals, even of our most serious and holiest convictions, for all of these have another side. We should always be able to think in terms of paradoxes and opposites."

The paradox to be kept in mind is this: although you originated in and with the Spirit, your human incarnation required that you descend through many cosmic dimensions, while you decreased your original vibratory frequency, except for your nucleus of divinity. Thus, after your conception on this Earth, you could develop and experience what you were only at a very low vibration. In other words, in your very beginnings, in your first phase as a human energy being,[193] you vibrated as animal soul. And immediately after your advent, you

---

[192] Marie-Louise Von Franz, *Archetypal Patterns in Fairy Tales*, p. 178.
[193] Please recall from Lesson Two your legacy of wisdom teachings about the phases of human spiritual development. The first phase, as described in many wisdom teachings, is analogous to animal soul.

continued your evolutionary development, which was expressing as primitive, instinctual drives, needs, appetites and urges, all of which were present as a demanding physicality. At this stage you were, in many respects, the energy equivalent of the first hominid.[194] Yet you were also "containing all possibilities,"[195] for you carried your nucleus of divinity (the indwelling Spirit).

As animal soul, you could be described in these words from Sri Aurobindo:

> "Animal being is mentally aware of existence, its own and others, puts forth a higher and subtler grade of activities, receives a wider range of contacts, mental, vital, physical, from forms other than its own, takes up the physical and vital existence and turns all it can get from them into sense values and vital-mind values. It senses body, it senses life, but it senses also mind, for it has not only blind nervous reactions, but conscious sensations, memories, impulses, volitions, emotions, mental associations, the stuff of feeling and thought and will. It has even a practical intelligence, founded on memory, association, stimulating need, observation, a power of device; it is capable of cunning, strategy, planning; it can invent, adapt to some extent its inventions, meet in this or that detail the demand of new circumstances. All is not in it a half-conscious instinct; the animal prepares human intelligence."[196]

Please be aware of this: in your third dimension incarnation, you were no different from the Babe of Bethlehem, whose story, **when understood symbolically**, indicates that in his human beginnings he, too, was animal soul. Herein lies the immense paradox that all human beings embody. (This shall become clearer as the lessons progress, with the final understanding at their ending.) Beginning here, your path of "Coming into Being" takes you further into your rebirthing by making you fully aware of your animal soul consciousness energies.

Come; let us continue to embrace paradox, while exploring your human beginnings.

Your Root Chakra

How helpless you were when you emerged into this world! At your first birthing, your tiny embodiment started its next stage of development by being washed, dressed and fed. But there was more to you than the obvious. "Normal" delivery or not, "normal" physicality or not, no matter how you made your debut into this dimension, you arrived enclosed in a blue light. Present from your conception,[197] the blue light remained until you were about one month of age. Then it slowly disappeared. It was a last vestige of the etheric womb that had

---

[194] For an interesting description, see *The National Geographic*, "Origin of Childhood," November, 2006, pp. 148-159.
[195] A. H. Almaas, *The Inner Journey Home*, p. 71.
[196] Sri Aurobindo, *The Life Divine*, p. 743.
[197] For more detail, see Barbara Brennan, *Hands of Light*, p. 62-65.

enclosed the human uterus in which you had gestated.[198] Yet, the blueness in your auric field also indicated the presence of a "spiritual blueprint;" part of an etheric matrix that came with you into your incarnation and is still here. It is linked not only to your inner guidance system (your nucleus of divinity) but also to your root chakra. In that linkage, the "blueprint" is an always-present spiritual component of an animal soul's root center of consciousness. That is the second paradox! There are more to come.

But now you must learn the "basics" about your root chakra. (See Figure One for its location.) You can sense that chakra hanging from your tailbone. Please do that now. Focus inwardly and tune into its presence. Take your time . . . .

Next, you will learn about the power of that center of consciousness, beginning with its prime directive (its purpose, the archetypal imperative). It is this: from the moment of your conception, your root chakra's prime directive has been to generate and maintain your physicality, including your physical survival. Focused in this manner, that chakra is "rooted" in the evolutionary physicality of this third dimension.[199] And the reason is this: your root chakra is the microcosmic re-presentation of a macrocosmic Consciousness, Creative Energy that has generated and continues to generate your physical evolution. In other words, the archetypal imperative of your root chakra is your physicality. Moreover, because your root center of consciousness has been involved in that evolution for many lifetimes, its imperative involves generating and maintaining not only your basic physical existence but also your "safety" and "security;" in your initial stages as you instinctively perceive them and later, as you intellectually define them according to your culture and social position.

In addition to all of this, your root chakra's involvement with your physicality is indicated clearly by your initial self-identification. This phase of your ego/self not only reveals the chakra's prime directive, but also reproduces its reinforcing "i-am" statement of consciousness, which is: "I sense (that is, I have sensations), therefore I am." In other words your initial ego/self is, "I am my physicality." Now, please pause for a moment or two and ponder on these "basics" of your root chakra.

To illustrate, we will now turn to mythology – but first, here are the reasons for doing so:

Dealing with archetypal characters that have included gods, goddesses, heroes, lovers, warriors, kings, magicians and fools, the myths of humankind have revealed how people have evolved emotionally, mentally and spiritually.[200] And their myths have helped them for

---

[198] Please recall the story of Little Soul. Where that etheric womb originated cannot be told with certainty. You might have "picked it up" during your descent though the etheric dimensions and/or it might have been from your mother. In Lesson Seven you will learn in detail about the etheric energies.

[199] For more detail, see Rosalyn Bruyere, *Wheels of Light*, pp. 50-53.

[200] See Anne Baring and Jules Cashford, *The Myth of the Goddess: Evolution of an Image*, pp. 443-444. In *The Hero With a Thousand Faces*, page 3, Joseph Campbell notes: "It would not be too much to say that myth is the secret opening through which the inexhaustible energies of the cosmos pour into human cultural manifestation." In some of the myths, for example "Sir Gawain and the Green Knight," there is also an indication of the spiritual **potentiality** of people. For more detail about the function of mythology in all the times and places of human history, see Joseph Campbell, *Myths to Live By*, pp. 214-215.

many millennia to connect with their own self-awareness and with the natural world. This interaction of a slowly evolving humanity with its mythology has taken place, in part, because people have, somehow, discovered a way to "be" both in this dimension and in the "imaginal realm."[201] Quite possibly, their shamans were the first to venture there and to tell them about it in breathtaking stories.[202] But, increasingly, that realm became accessible to others. It was (and still is) a multidimensional energy field filled with images and other information, whose source has always been the transcendent Spirit that has created and maintained the Cosmos. Human mythology was, in other words, the ongoing verbal (and later, written) presentation of a slowly growing awareness (expressed as metaphors) of the One Consciousness, Creative Energy and of human relationships both with It, and with Its manifestations on Earth.

Now, take in a Celtic (Irish) myth about Cuchulain (coo-hoo-lin), an archetypal warrior/ hero, who vividly symbolizes the root chakra's prime directive and "i-am" consciousness, along with the ego/self of physicality. As background to this story, please note that Cuchulain was semi-divine; a son of the god Lugh (loo) and a human. At his birth, the child was given away by his mother as a gift to the people of Ulster County in Ireland. He was provided with a portion of that territory as his inheritance. The boy was raised by a group of warriors in a cultural environment of lovelessness and brutality. Although small in stature and mild in demeanor (when not "provoked"), he became a mighty warrior, whose entire attention was focused on his physical prowess. When Maev, the unscrupulous Queen of Connacht County, sought to add Ulster to her territory, Cuchulain became her implacable foe. The myth continues . . . [203]

After slaying thousands of the enemy, Cuchulain harried the forces of Queen Maev. By this constant harassment and terrorist tactics, he effectively prevented them from advancing into Ulster. While the battles continued, Cuchulain's wrath grew in intensity. Upon whole companies of the enemy he descended like a whirl-wind, wielding his mighty weapon, which had magical powers. As he whirled faster and faster, his battle frenzy consumed him. His body distorted into fearsome shapes. He became swollen and grotesque. "All over him, from his crown to the ground, his flesh and every limb and joint and point and articulation of him quivered."

With the ghastly, whirling weapon, Cuchulain slew dozens in one swoop and many dozens more died of horror. Greater and greater his battle frenzy grew and faster and faster he whirled amongst the enemy. "His mouth was twisted awry until it met his ears . . . flakes of fire streamed from it. [. . .] Among the aerial clouds over his head were visible the

---

[201] As already indicated in the "Prologue," this realm is as ontologically real as that of this dimension. It is the world of shamanic spirit journeys and dreaming, of spirit guides and angelic encounters and of romps with fairy folk. It is the world where you can do things but not control them. It is the world without space and time.

[202] This idea was also suggested by Joseph Campbell in *The Power of Myth*, p. 107.

[203] The sources for this myth about Cuchulain are T. W. Rolleston, *Celtic Myths and Legends*, pp. 182-233, and Joseph Campbell, *The Hero with a Thousand Faces*, 3rd Edition, pp. 284-287.

virulent pouring showers and sparks of ruddy fire which the seething of his savage wrath caused to mount up above him. [. . .] taller, thicker, more rigid, longer than the mast of a great ship was the perpendicular jet of dusky blood which out of his scalp's very central point shot upwards and then was scattered to the four cardinal points; whereby was formed a magic mist of gloom [. . .]."[204]

You shall continue your forays into the imaginal realm with Cuchulain in later lessons. At this point, the warrior/hero can be regarded as the "archetypal motif,"[205] and symbol of a root chakra's consciousness energy at its most instinctual; a physical survival-oriented generative power identifying with and furiously maintaining its safety and security.

Having illustrated the root chakra's prime directive and "i-am" consciousness, the myth graphically introduces the two root chakra qualities intrinsic to that power; the color red and the element of fire. The myth also suggests how these qualities are essential in shaping your soul substance and, thence, your soul structures of physicality, including your ego/self. Let us turn next to those qualities

Your Root Chakra's Qualities

Please recall from the previous lesson the instruction about the Observer and its importance in helping you to tune into your consciousness energies. Now, summon the Observer and prepare to explore the root chakra hanging from your tailbone. Your intent is to learn about this center of consciousness not only through attention to the instruction but also through **experience**. You begin by focusing on the chakra's qualities: the color of red, and the element of fire. Again, there is paradox.

In the wheel of light that is the root chakra, the predominant color and sound is red; the lowest vibrational "band" of light. The red frequency is related to basic instinctual energies.[206] Traditionally, red has been associated with the sun, masculinity, passion and war. Symbolically, blood is the red stream of life that courses throughout the physical body. Rosalyn Bruyere has described the root chakra red in this way:[207]

> "It is the red quality . . . that sets all of the power in one's life. The red quality, the quality of our blood, the quality of our sexuality, the quality of our drive, the quality of our financial substance or prosperity all reside in the [root] chakra."

---

[204] The quotes are from a copy of Eleanor Hull's *The Cuchulain Saga in Irish Literature* pp.154 and 174-176, downloaded off the Internet at www.archive.com.

[205] This is an established literary metaphor and symbol. There are entire dictionaries of motifs for both myths and fairy tales. To start your exploration, see Marie-Louise von Franz, *The Interpretation of Fairy Tales*, "Index," p. 206.

[206] Rosalyn Bruyere, *Wheels of Light*, pp. 224-225.

[207] *Ibid*, pp.161-162.

Conjoined with the color red in the root chakra is the element of fire.[208] It is the fiery power that enhances the red quality. Paradoxically, this power can be both a brutally destructive energy (as demonstrated by Cuchulain), and a passionately creative energy that propels you into all the great achievements of your life. It is the fiery power of your root chakra that drives your inventive genius, your creative artistry and your dreams of glory (whatever they are). In the heat of your sexual passions new life is generated. It is in that heat that you fuse your relationship with your mate. It is through that same center of consciousness that the crucial bonding with your family (both biological and cultural) takes place. Indeed, your root chakra would not be a generative power and neither you nor humankind would exist without the red and the fire. Yet that same red and fire, while being part of a generative process that shapes your soul structures of physicality, can be the means of destroying both you and (by extension) all of humankind! It is a frightening paradox, is it not? (After taking several **grounding** breaths, focus on your own root chakra's red and fire. Do you "see" them? Ponder on the power that those wonderful, primitive energies have represented in your life. By going into altered awareness, start to see the forms that these energies seem to be generating in your soul field.)

It is within that context of paradox that you will encounter the archetypal masculine force inherent in this chakra. (Please recall the description of that force given in Lesson One and maintain your focus.)

Your Root Chakra's Masculine Force

As suggested in the myth of the aggressive Cuchulain, your root chakra's red and fire energies have traditionally been expressions of the archetypal masculine principle. Yet, even the predatory Maev, although female, clearly revealed the masculine force that in-formed her. **Thus, in both sexes of human beings, the archetypal masculine energies are required to focus the generative power of a survival-oriented root chakra**. Those energies were vitally necessary from the moment of your conception. Your physicality and physical survival, including both safety and security, have been rooted in them and will continue to be throughout your life. (Take some time to ponder on this: to what degree have those masculine root chakra energies in-formed you in the unfolding of your life?)

To enhance your pondering . . . an **excessive** amount of archetypal masculine energies in the root chakra is one likely reason for the development of "root chakra people;" male and female, who are "(in)famous for their qualities of dominance, conquest, power, ambition, and a driving need to express their vitality and prove their virility."[209] In many instances, these root

---

[208] In this context, the elements of the chakras are those of the hermetic, alchemical tradition. The ancients believed that the material universe was made out of the basic elements of air, water, earth and fire, the macrocosmic "stuff" of creation. According to a modern alchemist, "the four elements are the foundation for all experiences, expressions of consciousness, and material manifestation. They exist on several levels, giving personal and impersonal expressions of their nature." See Mark Stavish, *The Path of Alchemy: Energetic Healing and the World of Natural Magic*, p. 19.

[209] Rosalyn Bruyere, *Wheels of Light*, p. 41.

chakra energy beings express what can be described as a "wild man." This is an archetypal motif found in many familiar fairy tales, for example, "Little Red Riding Hood," and "The Three Little Pigs," in which a powerful, predatory animal, usually a "wolf," seeks to "eat" the more "civilized" beings that he encounters. In other words, he is ingesting their consciousness energies. In these stories, the "wolf" has to be killed. In a person, male or female, the "wild man" is a huge egoic structure that can and must be transformed (not "killed"), if the person is to be more than animal soul..[210]

Continuing the enhancement . . .

There are also many people who have been described psychologically as being "red" personalities.[211] Although most cannot be defined as "pure types," they are readily recognizable from the following attributes: they are "masters at managing the everyday realities of life;" they are "rapid-fire thinkers and become impatient with too much planning;" they have a need to control . . . both their environment and the people in it;" they are "fiercely competitive;" they are "driven by the need for completion;" they are "hard workers [who] expect the same of others;" they "see what they do for a living as the means of identifying who they are;" they "want to belong and serve;" they are "physical people;" at their best they are "production machines;" at their worst they are "indecisive, overly cautious, abrupt and argumentative."

Human history and human relationships are replete with root chakra people, wild men and red personalities! (Please take time here to ponder on your involvement with them. Perhaps you will recognize yourself as one of them. Call on the Observer to help you and remain detached.)

Then note an important idea that you will encounter many times in this and in succeeding lessons. Those root chakra "types" indicate that in some people their holistic energy system's root chakra masculine energies have become extremely unbalanced. This imbalance has been revealed by the words and actions that indicate their ego/self. Paradoxically, feminine energies have been required. Without them (or enough of them) the imbalance would impact on all the other "bodies" of consciousness. Thus, from the beginning there has been an immense need for **balance** in your **holistic** human energy system. The symbolism of Cuchulain is an apt reminder. (This theme will receive further attention later in this lesson, with more to come in the next two lessons.) Now it suffices to note that on your path of "Coming into Being," you will acquire the necessary "balancing."

Continuing with the root chakra, please recall again its prime directive and "i-am" statement of consciousness; both focused on your physicality; its embodiment and its survival, safety and security. Keeping that archetypal imperative in mind, let us turn to an essential constituent of your human energy system. Please maintain your focus on your chakra and prepare for yet more paradox.

---

[210] See Robert Bly, *Iron John*, for a wonderful modern tale about the "wild man" and his/her redemption.
[211] Carol Ritberger, *Your Personality, Your Health*, pp. 121-127.

Your Root Chakra's Life Force aka the "Kundalini"

Known in Eastern spiritual teachings as the "kundalini," the Life Force is depicted in the sacred writings as a snake tightly coiled in your root chakra. (Focus . . . Do you sense it?) Snake symbolism and power have been present for millennia in the myths and the religious traditions of many of the world's civilizations.[212] Represented by the caduceus of modern Western medicine (a depiction of the ida and pingala energy channels), the kundalini manifests the powers of "generation and regeneration"[213] that enable all your chakras to function. That is how your root chakra ensures your physical survival, in a **holistic** system.

In the midst of your instinctual, animalistic root chakra the paradox is this; the kundalini is a **spiritual** force of great intensity. This is possible because it is an expression of "the inhabitant and all-containing Spirit."[214] Within the red, fiery and masculine force of your root center of consciousness, the kundalini energies are instrumental in promoting a creative, generative process that is incredible in its scope. ***Connecting with both your inner guidance system (your nucleus of divinity), and your etheric matrix, the kundalini (Life Force) of your holistic energy system triggers . . . out of your soul substance . . . the formation and the re-formation of all your structures of soul; your "bodies" of consciousness.***

On your quest for wholeness, you will directly experience the kundalini energies in the "shifts" that will accompany your healing process. In this "shift," often indicated by a sensation of warmth rising in your physical body, the energies of your soul structures will be raised to a higher frequency (transformed), because the center of consciousness has been healed (the energies have been transmuted). (There is more detail later in this lesson.)

In yogic practice, the ultimate experience of the kundalini shift, described as an "awakening," can happen this way: after proper preparation, often involving years of concentrated spiritual and physical practice, the Life Force energies in the root chakra are activated by a message from the *brahma randhra* in your crown chakra. Then, the energies quickly move up the ida and pingala channels, like undulating twin serpents, whose heads touch in your crown chakra. In this kundalini awakening, the resultant energy flow is described as ecstatic, blissful and "alive." It is the wonderful physical, emotional, mental and spiritual experience of a properly prepared and aware human energy being.

The kundalini awakening can also be triggered accidentally by intense emotions and/or by the use of certain drugs.[215] The resultant energy flow has been described as frightening and debilitating.[216] It is an experience often conducive to deep depression and emotional instability that can last for years. What has happened is that the whole energy system has

---

[212] For more detail, see Rosalyn Bruyere, *Wheels of Light*, pp. 107-142.

[213] *Ibid.* p. 125.

[214] Sri Aurobindo, *The Life Divine*, p. 735.

[215] Yvonne Kason, *Farther Shores: Exploring How Near Death, Kundalini and Mystical Experiences Can Transform Ordinary Lives*, p. 156.

[216] My observation has been that yogic meditation that becomes an obsessive practice can be harmful. Without preparation guided by a trained practitioner and without **grounding**, the kundalini energies can rip through energy channels unable to deal with them.

become dangerously out of balance. In a **holistic** system, this has occurred because there has been no preparation for the awakening and no curbing of the volatile root chakra energies. And/or the energies have been malfunctioning, likely for years, and require healing. (In this culture, there are some adventurous souls who actively seek to have a kundalini awakening as yet another exciting "experience," usually sexual. They have apparently failed to understand the real purpose and meaning of the kundalini.)

Your Root Chakra's Function and Generative Power

To comprehend your root chakra's generative power in relation to the indwelling Spirit (the inner guidance system), the etheric matrix and the kundalini, please continue to focus your attention and intent on that chakra, while you receive instruction on its function, front and back.[217] Note also that the root chakra's prime directive, "i-am" consciousness, masculine force and qualities are revealed in its function and that all are intrinsic to its generative power.

Functioning in your energy system from the instant of your conception, your root chakra has assiduously continued its "work" after your advent. With the generation and the maintenance of your physicality as its only purpose (the archetypal imperative), your root center of consciousness has shaped your animal soul substance in an on-going process of amazing complexity. Now, enhance your capacity for detachment and discernment by summoning in the Observer to help you delve into that complexity.

In the front side, opening to this dimension and connecting with your outer environment, your root chakra's consciousness energies have generated your soul structures that are the primal **instincts**. Those, in turn, have in-formed your physicality with your drives, needs and appetites for food, air, water, warmth, comfort and sexual stimulation. (With the Observer to assist you, focus into the deep physical regions of your root chakra. Your gonads have, from early in this lifetime, registered your sexual drive. Remaining detached, do you sense it? Do you sense the others? Do they come to you as forms?) Later, the needs and appetites might have expanded to include more elaborate clothing and shelter, money, and more mature sex. Later still, the needs and appetites might have further expanded to encompass immense amounts of money, material goods and services. (In this culture, that is how the "wheels of commerce" have been maintained! Please note the masculine force at work.)

In the root chakra, within the context of your needs and drives, any perceived or real threat to your physical survival has triggered fight or flight responses, likely from before your birth. After your advent, these threats became more and more complex while your soul structures of physicality continued to develop. All this time, "learning" was taking place through your perceptual filtering system (there is more about that later in this lesson) and you

---

[217] I am indebted to Cyndi Dale for much of the information in this part of the lesson. See *New Chakra Healing: The Revolutionary 32-Center Energy System*, pp. 32-33, 96-97, 117-118, 137-140 and 242-243. I have modified the information that she gives about the DNA: although the root chakra is closely connected with the DNA information, the information itself is in the soul substance and (as coding) in the protoplasmic consciousness of the parental egg and sperm, rather than in the chakra, as Dale suggests.

learned to interpret certain events and situations as "threats." Meanwhile the development of your soul structures of physicality went on because your root chakra had carried your DNA information connection since your conception.[218] All the while guiding, sustaining and triggering transformation, there was your nucleus of divinity, the inner guidance system (the indwelling Spirit) empowering the spiritual blueprint in your etheric matrix and guiding the kundalini. How very complicated and how wonderful the process was (and continues to be), as your soul substance has undergone its protoplasmic shaping and forming! (Ponder on this soul-shaping "work" as it must have proceeded in you. While pondering, continue to sense and "see" the forms that were generated. Do not try to "make" anything specific. You are simply tuning into and, with the help of the Observer getting a sense of the protoplasmic consciousness energies.)

Continuing with the front side; please recall that your root chakra is part of a **holistic** system. As such it is an amazing paradox that exhibits a very strong emotional component in its function. Your rage and fear reactions have been and continue to be triggered here. Conversely, intense feelings of sexual pleasure are stimulated here. (While staying detached with the help of the Observer, focus again on that deep "area" and tune into those emotions. Do they assume forms?) As your root chakra took you along in life, it could also register physical and feeling-based sensations from sources perceived as not there. These sensations could include the physical pain and illness belonging to someone else or they could include odors, and touch vibrations that seem to come from nowhere. An example of the latter would be the "touch" sensations that sometimes come to a person who has lost a beloved person or even a pet, who still seems to be there with them. (In the root chakra there can be those huge energies of intense emotions. While remaining focused, ponder on your own emotional root chakra experiences.)

In addition, in this paradoxical **holistic** system, there is a mental component of your root chakra. This component was developed through your root chakra's DNA information connection and the activity of your perceptual filtering system, (described later in this lesson), in interaction with your inner and outer environments. Herein were the first primitive beginnings of your soul structures of mentality. As your root chakra accompanied you through life, it could convey information regarding your mental needs through the physical. For example, while hungrily imagining your favorite food, you can often "taste" it. For another example, in

---

[218] Although the quantum physics research has barely begun, there are some indications that the DNA acts as an "antenna receiving and sending signals to turn on or off the expressions of the genes" and that it is not the "master key" but actually "mediates our intentions, volitions and beliefs." Ervin Laszlo and Jude Currivan, *CosMos*, p. 116. Other researchers have indicated that the DNA receives, processes and projects light (biophotons), that is a measurable auric field and that the "waves" of light display the characteristics of sound. See Robin Kelly, *The Human Hologram: Living Your Life in Harmony with the Unified Field*, pp. 78-82. Earlier research had indicated that the biophotons seemed to function as a regulator of the energy processes and communication both within and between cells. Recent research has sought to make the connection between the biophotonic biofield and consciousness. Laszlo and Currivan, pp. 124-126. Because the root chakra is a center of light and sound, it could be suggested that what research is revealing is the DNA information connection with that center of consciousness.

the initial stages of a creative endeavor, you can sometimes "see" the end product and become sexually excited, although the endeavor does not seem to relate to sex. (Do you resonate with that? Recall an experience and explore those energies while you remain detached yet focused on your root center of consciousness.)

Finally, since this is a **holistic** system, there is in your root chakra front a spiritual component carried by the kundalini energies, expressing as a passion for life. Because life is **movement**, that passion revealed itself very early as a physical drive to be moving; to walk, talk and to be "independent." The same passion for life also triggered the creative labors that you might later have undertaken. Many are the accounts of the incredible physical hardships people have endured for the sake of their creative 'Muse"[219] (and that can include developing a business enterprise or undertaking scientific research.) Finally, the **grounding**, life energies of Earth are spiritual. They were first brought into your soul structures of physicality through your root chakra. (You have already connected with those **grounding** energies while you experienced your auric field. Practice that breathing now and go into the passionate kundalini energies of your root chakra.)

Amazing as all of this is, there are still more discoveries to be made about the function and generative power of your root chakra. Please continue your inner focus.

In the back of the chakra, opening to other dimensions, the physical component, sustained and guided by the indwelling Spirit expressing through your etheric matrix, has in-formed your DNA soul substance (protoplasmic consciousness) and connected you to your genetic ancestry. In addition, this component has regulated your chemical balance in a connection with your **beliefs** about your life and how it is to be maintained. (There is more later in the lesson.) And your root chakra's back physical component has also connected you to the web of human life and to humanity's need for survival. The latter connection has become increasingly manifest, as people throughout the world have communicated with each other on the internet. They have started to recognize, at last, that humans cannot continue with impunity to ravage this Earth and each other. (As you are **grounding,** "see" all of those connections until you make yourself part of a web of life by "seeing" your aura expanding and connecting to that of other people.)

Continuing with the chakra back, your root chakra's emotional component has allowed for the entrance of universal, high frequency love energies into your field. These are the loving, nurturing energies that you required, from the moment of conception, because they have shaped your malleable, receptive, impressionable and vulnerable soul substance. In many instances, however, that love influx has been prevented by primordial feelings of rage and fear. The myth of the archetypal Cuchulain would suggest that the conditions conducive to the negation of the love energies have been part of the "collective unconscious" for a very long time! In other words, the lovelessness that has been conducive to so much agony throughout the history of mankind has been thoroughly recorded in the Akashic Field and brought into the

---

[219] Michelangelo's painting of the Sistine Chapel ceiling, a four-year labor involving intense physical discomfort, is one example.

generation of soul structures. (Focus on your own. Ponder on how they were shaped and sense their forms. Then, while remaining detached, note the implications for your own relationships and for the web of life.)

In the root chakra back, the mental component has carried your perceptual filtering system. (That system requires much more detail, which will be presented very soon.) It is sufficient now to note that in the workings of your perceptual filtering system you will encounter the key to your **beliefs** about **deserving** physical life and wellbeing and about everything else that somehow can be connected to your physical survival. Those beliefs have been generated since your infancy and become part of your soul structures of physicality, as you will soon be made aware. Later, you will return to a deep focus on them. Meanwhile, keep in mind the importance of the disciplines/practices of "letting go/letting be."

Finally, in your root chakra back, the spiritual component has served as the physical "ground" of your sacredness. There, as you open to the awareness of your creative, generative power, you can realize that all of life, including your soul structures of physicality, is sacred. **The Earth ground and the Spirit ground are identical**. Out of this realization can come the practices of sacred sexuality, known for centuries to the few who have not chosen to believe in the duality of matter and spirit. In sacred sex you experience the most profound paradox inherent in your root chakra.[220] (Ponder on the implications of spiritual sexuality, if it has been present in your life. If not, what has been? Are you now realizing something different?)

Truly, the workings of that root wheel of light are amazing! (After focusing on them, you probably agree with that statement. And, have you noticed how much your awareness has been enhanced because you were tuning in with the help of the Observer? Ponder for a few moments on this form of assistance that enables you to discern so deeply into your soul field and to do so with detachment.) Yet, what you have been given thus far is but preliminary to the realization of the astounding generative powers of this center of consciousness.

As you have already been made aware (it bears repeating!), your root chakra, guided by the indwelling Spirit (your nucleus of divinity) through the etheric matrix and the DNA information while carrying the kundalini has been driven by its archetypal imperative and "i-am" consciousness, both focused on your physicality; its survival, safety and security. In that context, the red, fire and masculine energies have been involved with shaping your soul substance into your soul structures of physicality. In the creative, generative process, ongoing since the instant of your conception, the prana carried by your breath and the other energies that Earth provided in food, air and water have been crucial. Those energies were constituent parts of your inner and outer environments. Those essential energies, along with all the environmental energies that humans and Nature can generate, have in-formed you by impacting upon both your soul field/soul substance and your root center of consciousness. We will deal in detail with those energies now.

---

[220] For a splendid introduction to sacred sex, see Margot Anand, *The Art of Sexual Ecstasy.*

The Environmental Impact

When you made your advent into this dimension, you had already experienced intense environmental energies that had shaped your soul structures of physicality. While your fetal development had proceeded according to your root chakra's DNA information connection and your spiritual blueprint (etheric matrix), always guided and sustained by your nucleus of divinity, you had been in-formed by many other influences. Linked by your umbilical cord to your mother, you had ingested whatever nourishment she had made available. You had also ingested her emotional energies, crucial in your fetal development, plus many of the manmade energies in her outer environment.[221]

After your advent, with your root chakra working full force, you continued to develop your physicality within your inner and outer environments. If your outer environment was **nourishing**, you would receive and utilize the energies of good food, of comfortable housing and of wholesome sensory stimulation. If your outer environment was **nurturing**, you would receive the energies of love in all the ways that love could be expressed to you by adoring parents and other loving people. You, as a developing energy being, could thrive in that type of environment. Meanwhile, your root chakra would function healthily. With soul substance so malleable, impressionable, receptive and vulnerable, you would be off to an excellent start. If that type of environment continued, your formation would be ideal. As your soul structures of physicality developed, your inner environment would become a reflection of the outer. You, as animal soul, would be "doing" well.

But as you are likely aware, those ideal environmental conditions do not occur very often. Indeed, there are many people who congratulate themselves on having survived their childhood! But they have not survived unscathed. Impacted upon by an unhealthy environment, present (in all likelihood) from before birth, their root chakra would have started early to malfunction. Meanwhile, soul substance would have been wounded, with, perhaps, a resulting soul field fragmentation or loss. These conditions, in turn, would have resulted in soul structures of physicality that were unhealthy, perhaps even crippled, at several levels of consciousness. (There will be more detail later in this lesson.) But first, we must pause.

In order to understand all those dynamic interactions, let us turn now to the "workings" of a fundamental part of your root chakra and of your human energy system.

---

[221] Age regression studies by Stanislav Grof and later researchers have established this fact.

The Perceptual Filtering System

Please take in these words from a modern spiritual leader:[222]

> "... physical senses are extensions of a spiritual sense. You do not see because you have eyes; you have eyes because you can see. *Form follows consciousness* [emphasis added]. There had to be something within us as spiritual beings that sees and hears which then produced the mechanism in the Body Temple called the eyes and the ears."

That "something within us as spiritual beings that sees and hears" is your perceptual filtering system.[223] It is the expression of a fundamental quality of your human energy system that is described by Rosalyn Bruyere in this manner: "In the root chakra, to be aware . . . is to be tactile. Nothing happens until we sense it, until it "touches" us. [. . .] A complete view of the physical body must include everything we sense about ourselves."[224] So you see that you carry an incredible archetypal "biology." But it is more than that. It is also an energy that in-forms all the chakras and keeps your soul field "in touch" with its environments. Let us explore that "tactile" power; your perceptual filtering system.

After your advent, while your root chakra worked continuously to ensure your survival, the energies of your immediate outer environment were seeking entrance into that center of consciousness. While all this was going on, the chakra was continuing a process, ongoing since your conception; the generating and maintaining of your soul structures of physicality. With nothing to protect your aura, your tiny embodiment was likely undergoing great stresses. And the energies seeking entrance were unremitting.

Into your root chakra's perceptual filtering system went all the consciousness energies of Earth that your physicality required; the food, air and water. Into that filtering system went the sight, sound, smell, taste and touch vibrations of your care-givers, your pets and any other living things that were in your immediate surroundings. Into that same system went the stimuli of the wider environment, brought in by television and other household technologies and by Nature, with light and dark, heat and cold and pleasant and unpleasant sounds. Your root chakra's filtering system had to deal with it all. For a new human energy being, it was an immense challenge. (Please note, however, that the lack of adequate sensory input can also create serious dysfunction. Thus, the challenge has to be undergone, but with reasonable limits placed on the amounts of environmental stimuli.) While you, the human infant, were "coming into being," there was an ongoing, internal struggle for balance. During the onslaught, you

---

[222] This idea was presented by Rev. Michael Bernard Beckwith in an interview in *Sounds True Catalog*, Spring 2008, p. 5. Sri Aurobindo put it this way: "...the physical sense-organs are not the creators of sense-perceptions, but themselves the creation, the instruments and here a necessary convenience of the cosmic sense; the nervous system and vital organs are not the creators of life's action and reaction, but are themselves the creation, the instruments and here a necessary convenience of the cosmic Life-Force;...". See *The Life Divine*, p. 271.

[223] This idea was developed with the assistance of my spirit guides, after many years of working with clients.

[224] Rosalyn Bruyere, *Wheels of Light*, p. 145.

often sought to escape into the arms of your care-givers, if they were available. You did not understand, because you were precognitive and preverbal. You were wide open, while your malleable, impressionable, receptive and vulnerable animal soul substance was being shaped into your soul structures of physicality. And what was occurring was quite remarkable. In the creative, generative process taking place, many of the filtered energies were changing, not only into soul structures of solid ("gross") physicality but also into the "immaterial" structures of attitudes, values and, above all, **beliefs**.

A Dramatic Presentation

To enhance your understanding of the human perceptual filtering system, here is a dramatic presentation. It could be entitled "The Turning Point" or "The Hand That Rocks the Cradle (Probably) Rules the World."

The action takes place in a sparkling clean kitchen. The players are an infant able to sit up and just beginning to crawl, its mother and a beetle. As the curtain opens, the infant, clad in diaper, is seated in a patch of sunlight on the floor. There is no sign of the mother. Suddenly, crawling across the patch of sunlight, the iridescent beetle appears. The movement catches the infant's attention. The child watches the beetle intently. When the insect gets within arm's reach, the infant stretches out a hand and . . . the mother appears.

Now comes the turning point, a moment of soul substance shaping. The mother has a choice to make. The choice will impact permanently on the child because soul structures of physicality will be formed.

In choice #1, the scene unfolds in this manner: The mother sees the infant reaching out. She utters a loud shriek, leaps forward and stomps on the beetle. The infant, frightened into a startle response, catches its breath and then starts to scream. It falls over on the floor and rapidly turns red. The mother, shaking and tearful, snatches up the child and cuddles the little body. She frantically kisses the little face and head. In words colored by emotional intensity she gasps: "You must never, ever, touch one of those horrid things. It is bad. It could hurt you." Slowly the child stops sobbing and snuggles into its mother's embrace.

Although both mother and child remembered nothing about the incident, the child grew into an adult revolted by natural phenomena, including physical body secretions. The **attitude** was one of aversion. The child also developed, as part of its **values**, a tendency to kill any "lower life forms" that it encountered. (Please note how these values are expressions of lovelessness.) The powerful **belief**, engendered by this and many similar incidents, was that these creatures were "bad", that is, dangerous to survival. Fostered over years, out of these attitudes, values and beliefs there developed a lack of concern about life. (We shall return to this situation in the next lesson.)

In choice #2, the scene unfolds in this manner: The mother quickly takes in the situation and calmly kneels down beside the child. She gently moves the beetle out of reach and, placing her hand across the child's shoulders, she lovingly says: "How beautiful that little bug is and

I'm glad it came to visit. But you must not grab it. It might get hurt." The child coos happily and falls over into her lap. She chuckles softly and cuddles the little body. She kisses its head and back. The baby lies contentedly in her embrace.

Although neither mother nor child remembered the incident, the child grew into an adult "at home" in the natural world. The **attitude** was one of confidence and trust in the natural order. The child developed as part of its **values**, a sense of connection to the web of life that included all living things. The powerful **belief** engendered by this and many similar incidents was that all living things were here for a purpose and required safeguarding in order to maintain Earth. Fostered over years out of these attitudes, values and beliefs there developed a deep concern for life in all its forms. (We shall return to this situation in the next lesson.)

While the drama just presented is over-simplified,[225] the message is clear; many are the turning points that occur in human infancy and that impact hugely on later development. Many, too, are the ways by which care givers, as archetypal figures, have shaped children throughout all the generations of humanity. The turning points arise out of the choices initially made, knowingly or unknowingly, by those who parent children.

In your infancy, every one of the choices made for you shaped your malleable, impressionable, receptive and vulnerable animal soul substance. Having ingested the energies of those choices, you would reinforce them by slowly creating inner patterns based upon them. In your preverbal and precognitive state, the parental energies would be shaping you. With this ongoing reinforcement and emerging patterns, there would be two important results:

First, the material of your organism would gradually and inexorably be formed into your cellular "biology of belief" which includes your chemical "molecules of emotion."[226] Those beliefs and emotions, tightly linked together, would very early in your life become the **invisible** patterns expressing your soul structures of physicality. In short, those energies would have disappeared into the great depths of your "unconscious," along with their accompanying attitudes, values and habits.

Second, the immensely powerful energies represented by those **beliefs** and emotions would begin very early to impact upon your perceptual filtering system and, thereby, determine your choices. As your physical development continued, your filtering system would become "selective." Those patterns of learning would become crystallized. Hence, there would be a loop that was set up through your root chakra and its perceptual filtering system: the environmental energies of parents and later those people who reinforced those energies, into the patterns of beliefs and emotions and, into your choices and, into remembered environmental energies

---

[225] Although there is no mention made of the genetic information also at work in the child, it is implied in the "built-in" responses of both infants to the beetle and to the mothering.

[226] In *The Biology of Belief*, on p. 137 Bruce Lipton states that "... our perceptions, whether they are accurate or inaccurate, equally impact our behavior and our bodies." On page 143, he notes:" Your beliefs act like filters on a camera changing how you see the world. And your biology adapts to those beliefs." See also Ervin Laszlo and Jude Currivan, *CosMos: A Co-creator's Guide to the Whole-World*, pp. 138 and 142 for a discussion of the work with the molecules of emotion by Candace Pert.

and, into more patterns, etc. To illustrate; an account attributed to Deepak Chopra tells of a dramatic physical change effected by belief and the accompanying emotions:

There was a man almost dead from the ravages of cancer, who appealed to his doctors for any help they could give him. One of them reluctantly mentioned a new, experimental drug. With the man pleading desperately for his life, the doctor agreed to give him a "trial" dosage. Within hours the tumors were subsiding and in two days the cancer had totally disappeared. Happily, the man went about his normal life.

After about one year, he happened to be in his dentist's office. While awaiting treatment, he picked up a magazine and came upon an article that stated that the drug he had received had been proven to be totally ineffective against the type of cancer that he had had. Within two days the cancer had returned in the advanced stage. He died shortly thereafter.

What had happened?

By means of his root chakra's perceptual filtering system that man's biology of beliefs and emotions had developed. They had structured his physicality and they had killed him. The generative power of the root chakra is mighty in its scope. That story could be told about other human beings thousands of times.

Beliefs carried in the body's cells are only part of the picture. Humans store all their memories in their physical body's tissues. Many "body workers" have reported the sudden appearance of stored pain, and other sensory memories, while clients were being massaged or rolfed. Up would come traumatic memories with the accompanying emotions, and up would also come pleasurable memories involving all the physical senses. In other words, your soul structures of physicality "remember" all your experiences. This memory can assume some interesting guises. To illustrate, there is an experiment that has been replicated many times. This example involves a male college student "subject," the centerfold of a "Playboy" Magazine (a photograph of a nude Bo Derek) and a lie detector.[227]

A white cell culture taken from the mouth of the subject, was placed in a test tube and transported several miles away to a separate location, where the test tube was attached to a lie detector. The subject, who had been told to await further instructions, was placed in a room and observed. While he waited, the young man idly leafed through a "Playboy" magazine, he found on a table. Nothing observable happened until he came to the centerfold that revealed the beautiful, nude woman. "At that moment, the needle of the lie detector attached to the test tube containing the distant cell culture began to swing and kept fluctuating as long as the subject was looking at the picture." Then the needle stopped and remained unmoving . . . until the young man took another look at the centerfold.

(Please ponder on the implications of this experimental finding. It involves the activity of the consciousness energies of an energy being whose physicality extends well beyond the confines of his skin. Does it not indicate a consciousness that is a multidimensional consciousness that is a vibrating energy field?)

---

[227] Excerpted from Ervin Laszlo, *Science and the Akashic Field: An Integral Theory of Everything*, pp.102-103.

To complete this part of the lesson, please note that as your life has unfolded according to your Life Plan and purpose (recall the shaman's story about Little Soul!), the workings of your root chakra's perceptual filtering system have unfolded with it. They have probably followed a path similar to the one presented in the little drama. The details would be different but the basic patterns would be much the same. (Ponder on some experiences of dramatic intensity you have had. Ponder on the environmental impacts during your unfolding life. Get the sense of the inner patterns of beliefs, values, habits and attitudes that you have likely generated. As the years went by, your soul structures of physicality were being built. All of them were generated and shaped out of your soul substance by your root center of consciousness.)

Let us turn now to those soul structures.

Your Soul Structures of Physicality

Your soul structures of physicality (your "gross" body) are the **protoplasmic** forms generated in the amazing process that will end only at your physical "death." (Please recall from the shaman's story about your incarnation that your protoplasmic **possibilities** were those carried by your parental egg and sperm that fused at the precise moment that you, Little Soul, merged with them.) That life-long generative process can be described in this way: your human energy system — your archetypal endowment — the microcosmic expression *of* the One Consciousness Creative Energy, has included your root chakra, whose prime directive has been the embodiment, survival, safety and security of your physicality and whose "i-am" consciousness reflects that archetypal imperative. In the generative process your root chakra, sustained and guided by your inner guidance system (nucleus of divinity) and connected with your etheric matrix, with your DNA information and with the kundalini, while being impacted upon by its own perceptual filtering system, has generated, your soul structures of physicality out of your soul substance; your protoplasmic consciousness energies. Constituting your trillions of cells, your protoplasm is intelligent "living matter," forming soul structures that orchestrate all the incredibly complex physical processes that keep you "alive."[228] That orchestration is continually directed by the cellular DNA, whose coding is, as already indicated, triggered and controlled by your root center of consciousness. (Focus deeply and see your physical body as organic protoplasmic soul structures of physicality.[229]

---

[228] This description of protoplasm was found in the Internet "Wikipedia" on Sunday, March 23, 2008. Please recall the experiment involving the college student's cell culture and the "Playboy Magazine." The cells were in-formed by protoplasmic consciousness energies. At its highest vibratory frequency, that protoplasmic consciousness can also be light energies; the pure consciousness energies that have been described as the "radiant body." As such, the physicality does not experience "death" as it is commonly perceived. See the *Gospels of Mark* 16: 9, *Matthew* 28: 8-15, *Luke* 24: 9-51, *John* 21: 1-24 and *Acts* 1: 6-26, regarding the many interactions of people with the "radiant body" of Jesus after His crucifixion. See also the accounts about the "Body of Light" by Chogyal Namkhai Norbu, *The Crystal and the Way of Light: Sutra, Tantra and Dzogchen*, pp. 161-167 and the alchemical teachings from Julius Evola and the UR Group in *Magic: Rituals and Practical Techniques for the Magus*, pp. 196-202, "The Doctrine of the 'Immortal Body'."

[229] To reinforce your explorations, you can directly study your own live blood cells. With a live blood analysis, you can observe the intelligent and purposeful actions indicating the protoplasmic consciousness of these soul

Know that they have been and will continue to be generated out of your soul substance. Please recall your explorations of soul substance and go to that level of awareness. With the help of the Observer, take a lot of time to explore and experience your essential physicality.)

Now, let us deal with your soul structures of physicality, but with a necessary limitation. Please note that as **processes** your physical and physiological development since conception have been described thoroughly in many sources. Only in relation to you as a soul field with a human energy system will you encounter those processes in this series of lessons. Herein, it is sufficient to point to two relevant facts: first, that every one of your physical systems and every component of each of them vibrate within a particular range of **measurable** frequencies; second, that the systems **communicate** with each other by exchanging information in order to maintain balance (stasis). Thus, from the outset, the balancing that you require on the path of "Coming into Being" is reflected in the "workings" of your root chakra and in the integrity of your physical organism. Quite clearly, **form follows consciousness!**

And in that balancing: there is the "cosmic dance" that you have already encountered. It is the dynamic balance of the archetypal opposites, the masculine and the feminine forces that are everywhere in the cosmos. They are, not surprisingly, an essential constituent of your soul structures of physicality.

Your Soul Structures of Physicality: The Masculine and Feminine Forces

According to the ancient precepts of traditional Chinese medicine (TCM), derived from the Taoist wisdom teachings, the microcosmic masculine (yang) and the feminine (yin) energies are incorporated into your entire physicality.[230] In the present context, it can be suggested that this occurs because those archetypal energies, inherent in soul substance and intrinsic to your human energy system, are shaped by the complex process involving your root chakra's generative power into your soul structures of physicality. They constitute your physical "body," its vital, internal organs and its physiological functions.

According to TCM, the yin and yang exist as unitive phenomena in every tissue and structure of your physicality. In that "body," the upper part is yang, the lower part yin; the exterior is yang, while the interior is yin; the back is yang and the abdomen is yin. The "dance" is expressed in your internal organs: the heart, liver, spleen, lungs and kidneys (the viscera) are yin (feminine), because their functions tend to be stable and they contain their substances, while the uterus and ovaries are also yin because they are interior. The gallbladder, stomach, large intestine and small intestine (the bowel organs) are yang (masculine) because their functions tend to be active and they release their substances, while the testicles and penis are yang because they are exterior. If you relate the location of those organs to the suggested location of the chakras, the yin organs are within the parameters of the heart and sacral

---

structures of physicality.

[230] Jacqueline Young, *The Healing Path: The Practical Guide to the Holistic Traditions of China, India, Tibet and Japan*, pp.92-95.

chakras (predominant feminine power) while the yang organs are within the parameters of the solar plexus and root chakras (predominant masculine power).

In dealing with the physiological functions, TCM suggests that the health of your physicality can be maintained when the "dance" between yang (function) and yin (substance) is in balance. Because physiological function requires substance, without that (the chi and body fluids) there would be no functions; on the other hand, the metabolism of substance depends on proper function. Thus, if yin and yang separate from each other and cannot "dance," the physical "body" will die.

Ponder on these ideas that are thousands of years old and not well known in Western culture. They speak about you as an energy being, whose protoplasmic consciousness energies carry the archetypal and microcosmic masculine and feminine forces and express them in an organism that is splendidly and wonderfully made. Quite clearly, there is an immense, creative intelligence at work here. At this point, you may start your discipline/practice of "balancing," (if you have not already done so!) by delving into the ancient knowledge that is available about the feminine (yin) and masculine (yang) energies of food. From this ancient lore, you will learn about the foods required to maintain and/or achieve balance within your physicality.

Your Soul Structures of Physicality: The Hidden Ones

Now this lesson will take you into a different set of ideas. They will focus on your hidden soul structures of physicality; those laid down as beliefs, attitudes and values. As you have already learned, this structuring has been accomplished by your perceptual filtering system through the generative power of your root chakra. And, as already noted these energies can drastically impact upon and change your physical and physiological development. Already, you have likely encountered their "forms." You are dealing with them now as an essential precursor to your first experience of your ego/self

You continue with the Observer to explore and experience your soul structures of physicality by focusing on a recent frontal photograph of yourself.[231] While looking at your photograph, ask the Observer to help you "tune into" your hidden soul structures of physicality. Take a few **grounding** breaths. Then, slowly and methodically do an inner "scan" and focus on those "parts" of you that you sense are expressing old patterns of beliefs, attitudes and values. You will be able to recognize them because they carry an emotional "charge." Be patient and take your time with this. There might be internal organs involved and even heavy tissues.

After that preparation, go to the next level of awareness . . . that those soul structure "patterns" have also constituted your "psychological" development. They accomplished this, in an ongoing creative and generative process, because you i**dentified** with them. They were not just beliefs, attitudes and values; they were **your** beliefs, attitudes and values. Pause here

---

[231] A photograph can be used for tuning into your physicality because the pixels of your auric field can register on photographic film. There is a vibratory connection between you and your photo. This also applies to photos of other people.

and focus on what you can sense are those "psychological" patterns. As you do this, note that they have become enmeshed in your sense of "self." In other words, your patterns of belief attitudes and values have become part of your egoic structures of animal soul. Again, be patient and take your time with this.

Your Ego/Self and Your Root Chakra's "i-am-ness"

We have arrived at another crucial concept – your ego/self — only briefly mentioned earlier. After this point, it will be paramount throughout the remaining lessons.

Please recall that your ego/self had its beginnings in the work of your root chakra, the center of consciousness of your physical "body." As has already been stated: **this development was possible because your root chakra has carried, since your conception, its own "i-am" statement about what you are as an energy being, a soul field.**[232] **It is a self-identification inherent in the chakra's prime directive and generative power, which are focused on your physicality; its embodiment and its physical survival – the archetypal imperative.**

That statement of consciousness indicating your primitive first stage of ego/self, has been the constant underlying theme in your root chakra's functioning and in all the shaping of your soul structures of physicality. In order to **know** your beginning ego/self and to recognize its immense physicality, we must look in greater detail at your root chakra's "i-amness."

As you have already learned, at your advent, you were immediately enveloped in sensory stimuli. Feeding your root chakra's "i-am" energies, they were necessary for your physical survival. Through your root chakra, your animal consciousness demanded nourishment and nurturing and made its connection to your environment. You, as ("gross") soul structures of physicality, grew rapidly. While your (visible) physical development progressed, your other (invisible) process of differentiation was also underway. At first, you had no "me" and you were symbiotically attached to your mother.[233] This was a critical time in your life, because the archetypal parental energies of love, or otherwise, were impacting on your root chakra's "i-am-ness" and becoming part of an emerging you.[234] Then, later in your first year, you began to sense a "self" in you. In other words and to re-phrase some Jungian concepts; it was your ego/self developing under the guidance of the indwelling Spirit (the "I-AM"/Self) working to "form, further broaden and maintain the ego."[235] It was your "self" developing in response

---

[232] As already indicated in the previous lessons, I am indebted to Cyndi Dale for this essential insight.

[233] The work by Margaret Mahler in the mid-twentieth century has provided essential insights into that symbiotic relationship. For an insightful discussion, see *The Eye of the Spirit: An Integral Vision for a World Gone Slightly Mad*, Note #11 on pages 365-377.

[234] The influence of the biological parents or their surrogates on early and later childhood has been given much attention in the last sixty years. For example, see Anthony Stevens, *Archetypes: A Natural History of the Self*, pp. 79-109.

[235] Marie-Louise Von Franz, *Archetypal Dimensions of the Psyche*, p. 175. I have added to the Jungian concept of a Self that "individuates." In the context of these lessons, the indwelling Spirit, which is your nucleus of divinity, is the macrocosmic Self, the eternal and unchangeable "I-AM" which could be regarded as a hologram. And your "self," which starts off as an animal soul structure of physicality is the microcosmic re-presentation of the divine macrocosmic hologram and has to evolve as part of a Spirit-guided process involving a microcosmic

to the environmental energies (both inner and outer), the stimuli that were not only feeding your root chakra's "i-am" energies but were also filtering through its perceptual filtering system and thereby, shaping your malleable, impressionable, receptive and vulnerable soul substance. As demonstrated in the myth of Cuchulain and in the dramatic presentation, there were thousands of encounters between you, a soul field, and your outer world. And there were countless more that were produced in your "inner" world. And all of these "encounters" were acted upon by your root chakra expressing its survival-driven "i-am-ness." Within a constant process of development sustained and guided by the indwelling "I-AM", there was emerging the "me" that "you" were becoming. More and more ego/self was differentiating; more and more your egoic structures of soul were manifesting. Let us now focus on those immensely important energies.

Your Ego/Self: Why It Exists

Let us begin with a brief review: you have already learned that in some of the wisdom teachings "soul" was synonymous with "self."[236] While the teachings implied that the soul/self was something a person **had**, there is a different understanding that has been suggested in these lessons. It is as follows: the human "soul" can be perceived as microcosmic, creative energy field (the microfield) that is the expression/manifestation *of* (out of and part of) the macrofield; the Unity which is One Consciousness, Creative Energy, which emanated the Cosmos and energized it with Soul. Moreover, the microfield (the soul field) is the "stuff" out of which all the human "bodies" of consciousness (the structures of soul) are generated. The generative power is the microcosmic human energy system, the archetypal endowment, which has already been established as an expression *of* the One Consciousness, Creative Energy.

To continue . . .

As you have also already learned, the human energy system, consisting of wheels of light (chakras/centers of consciousness) that are both color and sound, carries within each of the chakras the "i-am," which is the microcosmic expression *of* the macrocosmic "I-AM." Now, take in an additional (and related) teaching: the consciousness energies of your ego/self are an intrinsic part of the soul field. And the "bodies" of consciousness, constituted of soul structures generated by the centers of consciousness out of soul "substance" each contain egoic structures. They, too, develop and evolve during the rebirthing journey, while **knowing** becomes **being**. Herein you encounter another archetypal imperative. Receiving this teaching on your path of "Coming into Being," please take in an idea about why your ego exits.

Its purpose is this: within the context of you as a soul field, **your initial ego/self was a clear indication of the presence of the indwelling Spirit (the nucleus of divinity); the Being/Self, the "I-AM" in you. Indeed, from the moment of your conception, your ego/self was expressing all that it was capable of being as you, i.e., as incarnated Little Soul,**

---

human energy system that is also a re-presentation of the holographic Spirit (the One Consciousness, Creative Energy).

[236] That idea undergirds the teachings found in the *Bhagavad Gita* and in other wisdom traditions.

an expression *of* the Divine, which in this dimension expresses in, as, and through your archetypal self.[237] And paradoxically, it is the Self which "depends for its realization on human consciousness and its decisions."[238] Self-Realization is what this quest is all about.

Although your first egoic structures were pretty primitive, they were the necessary foundation for and prelude to your development into the awareness of your incalculable possibilities. This is the way spiritual evolution happens! That little ego/self was your first inkling of what you **are** as an energy being, a soul field; your first nebulous notion of your immense multidimensionality.

Emanating out of your root chakra's "i-amness," your initial egoic structures were expressing your physical body consciousness. That was all that the little ego "knew." While the root chakra's perceptual filtering system did its amazing work, your soul substance was being shaped into the precognitive, preverbal structures all humans require. As has already been noted, many of those structures were the beliefs, attitudes, values and habits that had disappeared into the deep dimensions of your "unconscious." (Please keep in mind the incalculable importance in this process of the nurturing energies of love.) As those soul structures continued to be reinforced, they became inextricably part of your "ego/self." Thus, even from the beginning, your ego was an amazingly complex soul structure. (While looking at your photograph, take time now to tune into those energies.) Then, one more complexity has to be noted.

Your Ego/Self: The Masculine and Feminine Forces

From the moment of your advent into this dimension, your emerging ego/self was continually in-formed not only by the archetypal masculine and feminine principles inherent in your soul substance but also by those energies as "forces," particularly in your root and sacral chakras. (You shall deal extensively with the latter in the next lesson.) How these masculine and feminine energies were revealed has been described by Chris Griscom in this manner:[239]

> "It is fascinating to perceive even in the newborn baby, the most basic
> components of [the masculine and feminine energies] as they are uniquely
> combined from the beginning . . . . For example, a male baby may demonstrate
> sensitivity, passivity, an expression or attitude that is very feminine. A small
> girl baby may be very active and express her will through her body, exemplary

---

[237] Please note what A. H. Almaas has written in *The Pearl Beyond Price*, p. 154. "It is more correct to consider ego development and spiritual transformation as forming one unified process of human evolution." And on page 161 "[...] it is one process of evolution from the beginning of ego development to the final stages of spiritual enlightenment." This insight is shared by Sri Aurobindo and others. Wilber accurately suggests that "if self development and spiritual development are part of the same spectrum of consciousness, and not simply antagonists, then early damage to the former can cripple the emergence of the latter." See *The Eye of Spirit*, p. 367.

[238] Marie-Louise von Franz, *Archetypal Dimensions of the Psyche*, p. 310.

[239] Chris Griscom, *Feminine Fusion*, p. 22.

of masculine force. These early patternings do continue and amplify themselves as the child grows. That quiet and passive little boy infant may become a sensitive five-year-old who likes to draw and to paint and is very careful in using his body to touch plants or animals; the very active girl baby may become the proverbial tomboy who wants to climb and swing and jockey for center position as king of the mountain. These two children will seek out models of behavior that confirm and increase their capacity to express the basic mixtures of energy within them."

Those children are revealing the archetypal "intent"[240] that they carry. And it would appear that their archetypal intent is to be **androgynous;** the "natural" state of a human energy being. Their ego/self will develop healthily if they receive the role modeling and other nurturing that they require. In many cultures, including this one, however, there is a tendency to socialize children in response to their biological "maleness" or "femaleness." This socialization into a "boy" or a "girl" according to cultural ideas about "masculinity" and "femininity" begins, in many instances, from before birth. After advent, the archetypal masculine and feminine energies inherent in the soul substance are rigorously shaped in the root chakra's interaction with the archetypal parenting energies present in the outer environment. Thus, the archetypal intention is overwhelmed and the "ego/self" that emerges cannot be said to be the "true" one.

Relating this teaching to you as a soul field, it must be stated that all the environmental energies (both inner and outer) that went into shaping your soul structures of physicality were essential in shaping your beginning ego/self. A description of the process would involve the following: from the moment of your conception, your malleable, impressionable, receptive and vulnerable soul substance, impacted upon by your uterine environment and by your root chakra's prime directive, "i-am" consciousness, masculine force and embryonic perceptual filtering system, was being shaped. Meanwhile, the archetypal masculine and feminine energies inherent in your soul substance had been crucially affected by all of those factors plus the genetic information held by the DNA connection carried by your root chakra. After your advent, those masculine and feminine energies derived their "meaning" from the cultural milieu surrounding your male or female genitalia. In this fashion, your masculine and/or feminine energies were made part of your egoic structures. They were disproportionately shaped by the cultural beliefs, attitudes, values and habits you ingested around "gender." (Even when the archetypal intent was clearly not in accord with the culture's preconceptions, as indicated by Griscom, your ego/self was likely going to be forced to fit the pattern.) In a patriarchal society, in which the Feminine Principle has been lost and/or negated,[241] there are innumerable ways in which that shaping could have occurred. (While studying your

---

[240] Anthony Stevens, *Archetypes: A Natural History of the Self*, p. 110. See also *The Two Million Year Old Self*, p. 68. The archetypal intent is another way of referring to the archetypal imperative.
[241] Marie-Louise Von Franz, *Archetypal Dimensions of the Psyche*, p. 151.

photograph, ponder for a while on the gender training that you received and how you were required to identify who you were with a preconceived cultural pattern.)

Now, let us focus on your initial ego/self and how masculine and feminine energies have been crucial in its shaping.

Your Ego/Self as "Normal" or "Abnormal" Sexual and/or Gender "Identity"

It is yet another paradox that although human wholeness has always involved androgyny, the psychological health of men and women has apparently required that they first experience their gender "identity;" the expression in "living reality [of] the principle appropriate to their sex."[242] Any other configuration has been considered to be "abnormal" and often judged harshly. For almost half a century, human sexual and gender "identity" has been the subject of intense debate and thousands of publications, as the feminist movement has called into question many hallowed notions around that entire subject. Within this lesson, there will be no attempt to define how the masculine and feminine energies are to be expressed "appropriately" in relation to biological sex or if, indeed, that expression is the basis of sound psychological health. Instead, let us examine that part of human self-identification which is unchanged and unchanging.

Although much has changed as the result of the feminist movement, it is safe to assume that the one thing that has remained constant is the sexual desire that people have for each other. Heterosexual and/or homosexual interactions are a very powerful part of most people's self-identification. Given the intensity of the drive to procreate and the passion for life contained in the root chakra, the shaping of soul substance with its inherent archetypal masculine and feminine energies would naturally find expression in sexuality. Within that exciting milieu, the sexual "i-am" of the ego/self would be formed. (Take time now to ponder on the huge involvement of sexual energies in many of the industries, for example, the entertainment industry, in North America. Then, with the Observer and your photograph to assist you, ponder on how this environmental sexuality has impacted upon your sexual "identity." After that, ponder on the huge involvement of your own sexual energies in that identity and, thus, your life.)

In the context of your human energy system and your spiritual journey, you will deal with your sexual ego/self by first recalling the story of Little Soul, and the Life Plan, which included sex, gender, sexual orientation and the Sacred Contracts. If your Life Plan included the choice of parents who would provide the genetic inheritance and the uterine environment necessary for a "normal" sexuality and gender "identity," nothing would have likely changed your soul structures of sex and gender, generated by your root chakra and in-formed by your brain sex, during your fetal developmental,[243] After your advent into a cultural milieu which

---

[242] For more detail, see Anthony Stevens, *Archetypes: A Natural History of the Self*, pp. 176-177. See also Ann and Barry Ulanov, *Transforming Sexuality*, p. 10.
[243] These structures have been "mapped" in the human brain for several decades and have been the subject of many publications, including *Brain Sex: The Real Difference Between Men and Women*, by Anne Moir and

lovingly nurtured "normal" sex and gender, your ego/self would have been "satisfied." You as a little boy or girl would have "known" who you "were" in the context of that patterning. Although there might have been other environmental energies adversely impacting on your soul substance and on your chakras and, thereby, promoting damage to other of your egoic structures, your structures of hetero-sexuality and gender "identity" would have remained intact.

If, on the other hand, your Life Plan and Sacred Contract with your biological parents included a "genetically predisposed" homosexual or any other "abnormal" sexuality and/ or gender "identity," your incarnation would have been quite different. And you could have accomplished this quite easily during your fetal development. In this instance, the genetic and brain sex information for homosexuality — a parental gift — and the energies of the etheric womb and of the uterine environment would have been compatible. Your malleable, impressionable, receptive and vulnerable soul substance, with its inherent archetypal masculine and feminine energies would have been in-formed and shaped accordingly into the soul structures of homosexuality and/or transsexuality and/or transvestitism.

In another type of Life Plan that included a genetically predisposed homosexuality or any other "abnormal" sexuality and/or gender "identity," your Sacred Contract with your biological mother would have involved you in intense physical and emotional experiences before you were born. In other words, there would be trauma causing damage to your etheric matrix and to your root chakra's connection with the (including brain sex) information. Then the wounding would be extended into your fetal gestation involving your soul substance with the inherent archetypal masculine and feminine energies. The result would be a shaping of soul substance into a genetically determined sexual and gender homosexuality, either separate or combined with another "abnormality." Now, for more detail . . .

In a genetically predisposed homosexuality, one of two things can happen: either the DNA information connection first carried in the etheric matrix and replicated by the root chakra is for homosexuality, or the information is for a particular sexual orientation gets "switched" into homosexuality during fetal development.[244] Within the first context, the gestation that proceeds is perfectly natural and quite possibly in keeping with an evolutionary purpose that is being served.[245] Within the second context, there is the strong likelihood of pre-birth trauma. The brain sex switch is made as the result of damage, first to the etheric matrix and thence to the root chakra's connection with the genetic information for sex and gender. In

---

David Jessel.

[244] The subject of "brain sex" has received much attention especially in the last two decades. It seems certain that DNA information for sexuality (the brain centers for sex and/or gender, which are different and are developed in different phases of gestation) can be switched during fetal development, with resultant changes in brain architecture, due to the activation of certain "sex" hormones. Then, the patterns of connectivity in the brain of a homosexual man are those of a heterosexual woman and vice versa. See articles cited in various web sites under "neuroanatomy, human sexual orientation." See also Anne Moir and David Jessel, *Brain Sex: The Real Difference Between Men and Women.*

[245] Since homosexuality has been part of humanity for thousands of years, and shows no signs of disappearing, it is reasonable to assume that human evolution, both physical and spiritual, is involved.

both contexts, there is a shaping of soul substance, with the inherent masculine and feminine energies, into the soul structures of homosexuality; the physicality, the emotionality and the ego/self "identity."

In both instances of genetically predisposed homosexuality, either alone or combined with another "abnormal" sexual and/or gender orientation, there is in the soul substance of the female fetus, a change and a re-shaping involving a portion of her archetypal feminine energies, with a corresponding re-shaping and changing of a portion of her archetypal masculine energies. In some instances, this might happen several times during fetal development. In other words, there is a re-arrangement of those "dancing" energies. As a result, her soul structures of brain gender are shaped, with the feminine becoming predominant, **in some cases**, and the masculine becoming predominant, in others. Nevertheless, according to recent research, her soul structures of brain sex are male.[246] She will then seek to connect physically, and often emotionally, mentally and spiritually with the feminine and/or the masculine energies in another woman. The opposite situation occurs with a homosexual male's soul substance. (Ponder on this: if a homosexual person is looking for his/her inner opposite in a same-sex person, is that "abnormal" behavior?)

When homosexuality, either alone or combined with another "abnormal" sexual orientation does not appear to be a genetic predisposition,[247] there is a different situation to consider. Again, there could have been a Life Plan choice. Or the choice might have been made in a "creative space" after birth. But, whatever the choice, what might have happened is the loss in early and/or later childhood of a portion of the soul field along with the inherent energies relating to one's own sex. This has been the result of intense physical and emotional trauma, especially sexual abuse. In those cases, the root chakra could be horribly injured and the functioning seriously jeopardized. In many cases, sexually abused children have adopted homosexuality and other forms of "abnormal" sexual orientation. (Ponder on this: some psychologists teach that in heterosexual relationships the partners have sought and found their own "disowned selves" to love in the other person.[248] It would appear that with the loss of all or a portion of the archetypal energies of one's own sex, homosexuality would involve the same process, but only with a same-sex person. Again, would this be "abnormal" behavior?)

Homosexuality, either alone or combined with another other "abnormal" sexual and/or gender orientation, could also be the result of early childhood wounding that has not resulted in soul loss. That wounding could manifest as a rejection of that portion of one's sexuality that desires its outer opposite. As one researcher has indicated: "there is a strong desire to unload [the sexual] identity, thereby achieving a sense of identity relief and to reorganize the sense of self."[249] Then, the homosexual orientation appears to unfold in stages. Highly "sensitive" children are the most vulnerable. In an early childhood environment of physical and/or emotional

---

[246] For example, see Andy Coghlan, "Gay Brains Structured Like Those of the Opposite Sex," in *New Scientist*, June 2008.

[247] With higher sensory perception, the energy field can be seen to be different.

[248] For more detail, see Hal Stone and Sidra L. Stone, *Partnering: A New Kind of Relationship*, pp 45-55.

[249] Richard F. Docter, *Transvestites and Transsexuals: Toward a Theory of Cross-Gender Behavior*, p. 32.

abuse, substance addictions, household violence, uncaring, absent, obsessively controlling and/or codependent parents, the loss of childhood through the premature assumption of adult roles and other unhealthy energies, soul wounding can occur. When homosexuality is the result, wounded soul substance has been shaped into an "identity" which is primarily a statement of the root chakra's prime directive, transformed into a belief: "my survival requires that I desire sex only with me either in transvestite 'fetishism' or in the guise of another same-sex person."

(Finally, ponder on this: given what you have learned thus far about Life Plan choices, sacred contracts, soul substance, environmental influences, the human energy system, in particular the root chakra, and soul structures of physicality, what (if any) difference does homosexuality and/or other "abnormal" sex and gender self-identification[250] make in a quest involving evolutionary spirituality?)

To sum up this lesson: your soul structures of physicality are generated by a safety-, security—and (above all) survival-oriented root center of consciousness, whose qualities and function are intrinsic to its generative power and whose purpose and "i-amness" are expressing as protoplasmic physicality. The generating of the protoplasmic structures of soul out of your soul substance, with its inherent archetypal masculine and feminine energies, is a complex process undertaken by your root chakra linked with your etheric matrix, in accord with the terms of your Life Plan under the guidance of your nucleus of divinity, and crucially influenced before and after your birth by an immense variety of environmental stimuli. Some of your soul structures of physicality disappear into your "unconscious" depths and constitute the beliefs, attitudes, values and habits that you regard as "yours." Thus, they become part of your beginning egoic structures. These include your soul structures of physicality (in-formed by your brain sex and gender) that become your sexuality and gender "identity." Within that context, your soul substance with its inherent masculine and feminine archetypal energies is shaped and can sometimes be changed before and/or after your birth. Thus, your sexuality and gender "identity" as an animal soul can be what has been described as "normal" or "abnormal." Whichever it is, your egoic structures of soul, the primitive precursor to your androgynous, realized Self, begin their/your life journey from the moment of your conception, when the root chakra starts to express its archetypal imperative.

That center of consciousness accomplishes an incredible, creative task. Your etheric matrix, your root chakra's DNA connection, masculine energies, perceptual filtering system and the kundalini energies are instrumental in the work. And guiding and sustaining all of it is the indwelling Spirit (your inner guidance system, your nucleus of divinity). Truly, your root chakra has been an awe-inspiring part of your human energy system. But, as has already been noted, it can malfunction.

---

[250] Although people labeled as "transvestite" and/or "transsexual" are not directly included in these lessons, the awareness and understanding that can be applied to homosexuality is applicable to them, but with certain qualifications. These are based upon the variety of sexual and/or gender orientations that prevail among them and are partly related to their beliefs, attitudes and values. After you have completed the lessons and developed a full awareness of the masculine and feminine energies, you might want to add your informed insights to the discussion.

Your Root Chakra's Malfunction

Your animal soul structures of physicality, emotionality and mentality are developing as infancy merges into early childhood and then into later childhood and then into early adulthood. (This will be made clear in succeeding lessons.) Your human energy system itself has also been unfolding in what appears to be a prescribed sequence, as one-by-one your chakras add their power to your process and continue to shape and re-shape your soul substance into greater and greater complexities. Yet, while all this happens, there are malfunctions that can occur, first of all, in your root chakra. As you have already learned, root chakra malfunction impacts upon you physically, often after prolonged environmental abuses. In addition to those already noted, the abuses could include both the toxic outer energies produced by modern technology and the toxic inner energies of "junk" food and other substances. The abuses could also involve the energies of toxic emotions and thoughts. (These will be dealt with thoroughly in the next two lessons.)

Your physical diseases all stem from root chakra malfunction.[251] Most of them are generated in some way by damaged and dysfunctional red and fire energies; rage and/or fear that directly attack the cells and/or attack the immune system.

The root chakra's malfunctions can also manifest themselves psychologically. As the little drama presented earlier would suggest, the beliefs, attitudes, values, habits and (later) thoughts initially shaped out of soul substance are reinforced and strengthened throughout life. They all become part of your egoic structures, whether or not you are aware of them and part of your soul structures of emotionality. As such, many will indicate root chakra damage. Psychological problems that indicate a malfunctioning root chakra will be dealt with in a moment.

Both the physical and psychological problems connected with the root chakra indicate some long-standing energy imbalances. Although they can get underway in very early childhood, or perhaps even before birth, there is hope for healing most of them.

Self-Healing Therapies for Your Root Chakra

Before undertaking any self-healing, please pay careful attention to these words: first, the healing modalities suggested for your malfunctioning root chakra and for all your other chakras include the **consistent** practice of the guidelines for maintaining your energy system as indicated in Lesson One; second, the self-healing suggestions given to you in all these lessons are **not** a substitute for therapies provided by caring, competent professionals. The self-healing is required so that you can learn to go **inward** and change the unhealthy energies of your centers of consciousness. Since you are the creative, generative power, you are also the healing power. As already indicated, there is a **transmutation** involving a "shift" of energies that signals the activity of your kundalini. With that transmutation, you change (transform) the consciousness energies of your crystallized soul structures. Always remember that **form**

---

[251] They originate, however, in the etheric matrix that has been damaged either before or after birth. Again, you see the impact of an inner and/or outer environment.

follows consciousness! By focusing inward and slowly bringing about that kundalini shift, you will splendidly augment the good work done by others; finally, the most important self-healing you can undertake is **discipline**, which has been described as "a doing that is an undoing of our resistance to awareness."[252] (And in that discipline, never fail to include your daily meditation.)

When self-healing therapy (discipline) for the root chakra is undertaken, it is necessary to remember that in a **holistic** system the healing energies for root chakra malfunction can be delivered into other chakras. Hence, if there is disease in the root chakra area that precludes direct involvement, other chakras are available.

Usually, the psychological problems indicate the **loss or great diminution** of the red and fire energies. When there is a combination of physical disease and psychological problems, the root chakra is seriously malfunctioning and requires intervention by an energy healer.

Essentially, self-healing involves introducing energies that vibrate synchronistically with the chakra's **healthy** consciousness energies. In this way, the chakra's unhealthy energies will be transmuted, as you have already learned. And, as the unhealthy energies are transmuted, balance will start to return to the system. (Please remember that in the **holistic** human energy system each of the chakras vibrates within a particular range of frequencies and this will change when the root chakra has been damaged. You do not have to "know" the ranges. Just work to restore the root chakra's healthy frequency and the entire system will undergo positive change.) By tuning into your soul structures of physicality throughout this lesson, you have already been made aware of your root chakra's state of health. After practicing the healing modalities you are about to receive, you will be able to "track" the healing process by calling in the Observer and by experiencing the kundalini shift. That is, you will feel a difference deep within you because a releasing energy change has occurred and balance is happening. Meanwhile, the physical disease and/or the psychological problem might have been ameliorated or have even disappeared. Thus, throughout all this "work," you will be involved with the discipline/practice of "balancing."

Yet, **your focus will be on healing the center of consciousness**. The physical and/or psychological malfunctions are transformed by the chakra's newly-restored generative power. Be patient and trust the process!

The consciousness energies that vibrate in "sync" with a healthy root chakra are those generated by your connection with Earth, by Earth itself and by those emanating from your indwelling Spirit, the nucleus of divinity. The energies produced by your connection with Earth will come from your own "body work," including toning, breath work and visualization. The Earth energies you will use are manifested as air, crystals and plants. The energies connecting with your indwelling Spirit you will receive through meditation and other spiritual practices. Those indwelling Spirit energies you will also receive when you do nothing at all; when you simply **allow**. This will happen gradually as you continue your quest and as you allow yourself to be still and **know** the Spirit within.

---

[252] A. H. Almaas, *The Unfolding Now*, p. 19.

Self-Healing Therapies: After Too Much Red and Fire Energies

The "rage" diseases of the soul structures of physicality indicate an **excess** of red and fire (masculine) energies in the initial stages and even throughout the disease. In the end, however, there would be no more energy either for rage or for recovery. Those diseases are cancers, diseases of the immune system, circulatory system diseases, blood diseases, inflammatory diseases and migraine headaches. Add to that arthritis, lupus and fibromyalgia. Diseases of the bowel, rectum and colon, prostate disease in men and uterine diseases in women[253] are generated by a malfunctioning root chakra. In addition to rage, some of the latter could be the result of impaired DNA information but that, too, indicates a malfunctioning root chakra. (Ponder on the physical implications of root chakra malfunction in your life.)

Psychological problems related to rage are substance and other addictions, attitudes of lack and limitation, issues around childhood abuse and (as you have already learned) gender confusion. The psychological problems can also be traced to a defective perceptual filtering system, the result of an unhealthy environment, and/or to a compromised DNA connection in the root chakra.

If physical disease and/or psychological malfunction have already resulted from the production of too much red and fire energies, your main challenge will be to heal the damage that has created this problem in the generative power of your root chakra itself. It will, thereby, be restored to its proper functioning. (Please recall that this functioning involves a physical emotional, mental and spiritual component. All four will likely require healing.) Although you will take in the medical treatments you require, your main focus will be on raising the vibration and, thereby, transforming the malfunctioning energies in your root chakra. If physical disease has not yet manifested but you realize that (like Cuchulain) you are expressing too much red and fire energies, you will benefit from root chakra therapy.

Body Work

There are two important practices for dealing with your electromagnetic energy field; your aura. First you must learn how to remove the excess energies that are either "stuck" to it on the outside or producing imbalances on the inside. The practice that you will do will become standard daily "body work." It is called "Scraping." You proceed as follows:

While you sit or stand, align the fingers of each hand, cup each slightly and, while using a gentle "sweeping" motion, use alternate hands to "pull" off the energies, starting at the top of your head.

Work your way methodically from your head to your feet.

---

[253] Please note that the rage itself is generated by the emotional component of the root chakra, in close interaction with the sacral. Thus the rage diseases also indicate the energies of a malfunctioning sacral chakra. The red and fire energies generate the frequencies of color and heat that damage the soul structures.

After each "pulling" motion, discard the energies into Earth.

While you "scrape" your aura, "see" murky, thick, sticky energies being removed and placed into Earth for cleansing.

Say "thank you" to Earth.

Second, you tap into the protoplasmic consciousness of your soul structures of physicality and thereby ascertain what foods, medicines, other substances and even clothing your physicality will accept. This practice is called "Muscle Testing." You do it as follows:

Stand comfortably with your feet shoulder-width apart.

Hold the item in your cupped hands at your heart.

Or write the word on a piece of paper and hold this at your heart.

Lower your eyes.

State firmly out loud or silently: "My body requires this [name it]."

Allow the energies to connect.

If you sway **forward**, the answer is "yes."

If you sway **backward**, the answer is "no."

If there is no response, wait for a moment and repeat your statement.

If there still is no response, add to the quantity of what you are testing.

If there is a strong "yes" response, you can safely ingest that product.

Test further to determine how often you require the product.

If there is a strong "no" response, reduce the quantity and test again.

If there is a "yes" response for the lower amount, test further to determine how often you require it.

If there is a "no" response, do not ingest the product.

With muscle testing, you have a direct awareness of your physical requirements and if you do not interfere with the test, you can, with practice, determine most of them.

With muscle testing you also have a means of identifying your physical ailments.

Proceed as already indicated but while holding your cupped hands to your heart, state firmly out loud or silently: "My [name the body system or organ] is healthy"

Proceed systematically through all your physicality.

When the response indicates "no," use further statements to delimit the condition.

In addition to these practices, your **grounding** breaths and connectedness to Earth will gradually bring healing into your energy system. When you focus your attention and intent on this breath work, you will reduce and eventually eliminate the excessive rage and fear emotions that accompany these red surges. When you realize that what is triggering this excess is a fear-based **belief** that is somehow linked to your survival, your work will also involve probing into this belief and healing it. (This probing work will be described thoroughly in the next lesson.)

Since "stress" is also an indication of excessive red energy, you require relaxation breath work. Again, there will be revealed a fear-based, survival-oriented belief. "Stress-Discharging Relaxation" breath work is described as follows:

Sit in a comfortable position with your back straight.

Take several deep **grounding** breaths.

Focus your attention on your feet.

Inhale your breath deeply and tense your feet while you count to five.

Hold your breath to a count of five while you continue to tense your feet.

Then exhale through your mouth while you relax your feet and silently say: I bless my feet."

Take several deep **grounding** breaths.

Focus your attention on your calves.

Inhale deeply and tense your calves while you count to five.

Hold your breath to a count of five while you tense your calves.

Exhale through your mouth while you relax your calves and silently say: "I bless my calves."

[Repeat the sequence for each area of your physical body; feet, calves, thighs, buttocks, abdomen, shoulders, and head. With the head, work with your jaw, mouth, nose and brow by making "funny" faces.]

For a "Quick Relaxation" breath work therapy in a "tight" situation, you can do the following:

Take several deep **grounding** breaths.

With each exhalation pucker your mouth as though you were blowing out a candle. "Blow" out your breath slowly.

As you do this, drop your chin to your chest and droop your shoulders. Think of you as a tire deflating all its air. Very quickly your physical body will relax and you will feel calm.

When your breath work is combined with **visualization**, your healing is enhanced. To **neutralize** red (the color of rage and inflammation), you require blue (the color of coolness).

Start by taking several **grounding** breaths. With your "roots" firmly connected to your energy source, breathe in a "colorless" energy.

"Pull" it up your roots and into your root chakra.

While puckering your mouth, exhale while "blowing out" "black" energies, which are indicating both physical and emotional toxicities.

After repeating this several times, "see" a clear cobalt blue color.

With each inhalation breathe in "blue" and with each exhalation, pucker your mouth and blow out "black."

Continue until you feel calm.

Practice this breath work as often as you need it.

Then add this **balancing** breath work and visualization. To "balance" the red energies, you require green (the energies of the heart chakra).

Start, as always, with several **grounding** breaths.

Then proceed as you did in the last exercise by "seeing" colorless energy, "pulling" it up into your root chakra on your inhalation and "blowing out" the "black" energies of toxicities.

After repeating this several times, "see" a clear green color.

With each inhalation, breathe in "green" and with each exhalation, pucker your mouth and blow out "black."

Continue until you sense a cleaner energy. The Observer can assist you in tuning into it.

Practice this balancing breath work as often as you need.

When you are physically able to undertake the next body work, it will speedily release excessive red and fire energies by "driving" them into Earth. This practice, referred to as "Kicks and Yells," is very effective for eliminating the symptoms of migraine headaches. You proceed as follows:

Stand with your feet at shoulder width apart, knees bent and back straight.

Take several deep **grounding** breaths and concentrate on building energies in your root chakra area.

When you get a sense of "fullness," slowly bend your right knee and lift your right leg as high as you can without losing your balance. At the same time, lift both your arms straight up above your lifted leg.

With a loud yell, kick your leg straight down, toes pointing toward the floor, while you vigorously thrust down your arms parallel to your leg.

Then shake your entire body vigorously, like a dog shaking off water.

Repeat with the other leg.

As you drive the red and fire energies into Earth by kicking, thrusting and yelling, you will feel a slow diminution of the intensity in stages down your back.

Repeat this "body work" until the energies have been released.

Then drink a large glass of pure water.

Earth Energies

The energies of **crystals** have been used for centuries to restore the consciousness energies of people. Crystals "work" on your centers of consciousness with varying electromagnetic frequencies. Within each chakra, the specific crystal will affect all four components. You will require a little practice in preparing, programming and using your crystals, but your efforts will be greatly rewarded. With diligent use, your crystals could become an important aspect of your healing process.[254]

When there has been too much red energy, the **crystals** that are needed to balance and restore the root chakra functioning and, thereby, the soul structures of physicality are as follows:

Smoky Quartz promotes calmness, centeredness and groundedness. It helps to reduce fear, panic or shock.

---

[254] If the use of crystals interests you, please acquire *Love is in the Earth: A Kaleidoscope of Crystals; Updated* by Melody, *Crystal Awareness* by Catherine Bowman and *Healing Stones for the Vital Organs: 83 Crystals with Traditional Chinese Medicine*, by Michael Gienger and Wolfgang Maier.

Erythrite provides a strong and flowing connection between all of the chakras and allows you to assimilate knowledge coming in from many sources of help.

Blue Lazurite promotes tranquility and allows you to probe your inner depths with patience and insight.

Melanite produces calm, mellow energies and softens your harsh attributes, while it augments the power of other healing crystals.

The plants of Earth have also had a long history in healing. Foremost are the **herbs,** whose use can be traced back to the early shamans.[255] Later in time, aromatherapies have used essential oils, which are pure plant and flower **extracts** to quieten or stimulate energies.[256]

Herbs are prepared in various ways, including teas, tinctures, compresses, baths and poultices. You will require practice in preparing herbs but the results will be well worth your efforts.

Herbs that can bring calm are *hawthorn* and *mistletoe* (for anxiety).

Herbs that can relieve insomnia and help your physical body achieve calm are *anise seed*, *celery seed*, *cowslip*, **hops**, *lovage*, and *sage*.

Aromas to bring a reduction of root chakra red energies are

Cedar wood is a fragrance that brings a feeling of calmness about your outer environment, your physicality and your path.

Patchouli is a fragrance that also brings calmness and can be used combined with cedar wood.

It is necessary that you use aromas with a clear **intent** to bring about a particular outcome, for they can be used for different purposes with different chakras. Use the aromas by putting a few drops into your bath, by putting a few drops into a diffuser (use one that contains water), or by sniffing a few drops from a cloth, or by putting a few drops into a non-fragranced "carrying oil" and massaging the afflicted area. Firm body massage (except when cancer is present) is very helpful for healing the root chakra.

Spirit Energies

Keeping in mind that there is in reality no separation between matter and spirit, that it is all consciousness energy, you can know that all the "body work" you have undertaken is "spiritual work." But there are special exercises to promote the renewed functioning of the spiritual components of all your chakras, including your root chakra. To enhance your spiritual practices, there are available, from a wide variety of sources, such practices as rituals and ceremonies, "mantras" and affirmations that you can learn. Please undertake only those that "call" to you. Meanwhile, these lessons in the stone circle will focus on the spiritual energies of prayer, that includes gratitude, and meditation.

---

[255] My favorite books about healing herbs are *Health from God's Garden* by Maria Treben and *Dr Stuart's Encyclopedia of Herbs and Herbalism* by Malcolm Stuart.

[256] My favorite book about aromatherapy is *The Encyclopedia of Essential Oils: The Complete Guide to the Use of Aromatics in Aromatherapy, Herbalism and Well-Being*, by Julia Lawless.

There are immense healing benefits to be derived from "sitting" meditation. If you have not already started a daily practice, you are encouraged to start now. Your choice of the practice is based on how it resonates with you. There will be at least one that calls to you. Please note that it is not the "position" that really matters.

In addition, in this and in the forthcoming lessons, you will be given guided meditations, which have been designed to help you augment the healing power of your own practice. With each one, you will be asked to "journal" your experiences, as a means of focusing. Then, you will summon the Observer and ponder on all the images and other messages you have received. Because you will acquire more capacity for detachment and discernment, the time you spend on this "work" will be well spent. The meditating and the pondering are also powerful means to achieve balancing, because they are a means of transmuting unhealthy energies. So, too, are those times (which shall occur with increasing frequency) when you simply "do" nothing except stay in the stillness within.

A guided meditation that helps you deal with too much red and fire energy is entitled the "Seeker's Lamp." Its purpose is to bring you into increasing awareness of the life experiences that triggered your fear-based, survival-oriented **beliefs**. With that awareness, you can then undertake the discipline/practices of "letting go/letting be." You proceed in this way:

Prepare a sacred space of uninterrupted quiet. Wear loose clothing. Set aside a large glass of pure water. Keep a writing pad and pen nearby. Call in the Observer. Carefully state your **intent** to discover the beliefs that are creating your root chakra malfunction.

Either sitting or lying down, start your deep **grounding** breaths.

As you do so, "see" in your hand a portable light, such as a lit candle, lantern, torch, flashlight, etc. It is your "Seeker's Lamp."

Continue your **grounding** breaths and as you do, focus your attention inward.

"See" an "elevator shaft" starting at your throat and extending downward indefinitely.

See yourself carrying your portable light step into the shaft. Keep breathing deeply. With each breath, go downward in the shaft.

You will eventually stop. At that point, the "elevator" door will open.

Without hesitation, step forward carrying your lamp.

If you step into "darkness," wait until something happens.

You will be given an image and/or a memory and/or a distinct spoken message and/or something symbolic from your depths of the "unconscious." Hold your lamp as you receive.

When the experience is over (usually nothing else happens) turn around and go back to the "elevator."

Carrying your lamp, ascend the shaft. When you stop "moving," find yourself back in this dimension. Slowly return to your accustomed awareness.

Drink the water.

Journal your experience.

In your pondering, do not try to analyze your experience or "explain" the images and messages. Simply wait for insights to surface, while you focus on the particular part of your experience that you **know** requires your attention because your belief is rooted there. Let more insights arise, this time into the belief. Take whatever time is needed. Make no judgments or decisions to "do better." In the meantime, you will start replacing your old patterns of fear-based, survival oriented beliefs with those based on trust in the creative energies of a macrocosmic universe that will allow you, the microcosm, to create "good" things for your life. It will be **your** responsibility to discover what those good things are. In this manner you will be generating new beliefs that are true. And you will be experiencing the kundalini shifts indicating that the old patterns are being transformed.

Please be aware that in this process your soul structures of ego/self connected with your root chakra will also be transforming, albeit imperceptibly. Your root center of consciousness has become healthier and that change will impact on all the other chakras. As a result, you will slowly start to love yourself and to become "real". (Please recall the teachings you have received about the Observer.) As for your ego/self as sexual identity, the real "you" as a sexual being will start to be expressed.

In addition to the "Seeker's Lamp" meditation, you might wish to practice a form of prayer that promotes healing of all your chakras, including the root. It is based on the immense, creative power of gratitude (it generates trust) and is entitled "My Gratitude Prayer."

This is not a structured prayer, but requires spontaneity, attention and a few moments every day. It can be prayed at any time (the moments just after awakening and just before sleeping are suggested) and in any place. You can incorporate the prayer into your rituals or use it alone. It simply involves saying "thank you" inwardly and outwardly for all the real blessings in your life. At first, if too much red and fire energy has overwhelmed you, it will be difficult but not impossible to summon up the feelings of gratitude. Stay with it and the healing will happen. And while it does, take in these words of wisdom:[257]

> "Gratitude is where freedom and destiny meet, because gratitude is a divine doorway to the fulfillment of destiny. When you [. . .] choose to express thanksgiving, this sets causation into motion to manifest your destiny of Wholeness in every experience of your life."

---

[257] Michael Bernard Beckwith, *40 Day Mind Fast Soul Feast*, Day 24, "The Alchemy of Gratitude."

Self-Healing Therapies: After Too Little Red and Fire Energies

When you have extreme physical fatigue, produced by physical and/or emotional malfunctioning and when there are psychological problems that manifest as a loss of the desire to live, a damaged root chakra is implicated. It cannot function because it lacks the red and fire (masculine) energies to stimulate its generative power. There is much healing work for you to do, including extensive spiritual counseling.

Body Work

Because you have somehow lost your connection to Earth's energies, **grounding** breath work is vital. Practice this extensively, especially if you are confined to bed. By combining the **grounding** breath work with visualization in this "Reinforcing and Balancing Exercise," you will hasten the healing process. It will stimulate the soul structures of the lymphatic system and, thereby, enhance the work of the circulation system that carries the red (blood) energies of life. You proceed as follows:

Take several **grounding** breaths.

With your roots firmly in place, see and pull up colorless energy.

With your mouth puckered, blow out black toxicities.

After several of these breaths, see clear red color.

Pull up this color on each inhalation and blow out the black.

After several of these breaths, see clear green color. This will reinforce and balance the new red energies. Pull up the green color with each inhalation.

If you have difficulty with this, you require more detoxification.

Go back and repeat the exercise, starting with the colorless energy.

Continue this breath work until you sense cleaner energies. Confirm with the assistance of the Observer.

Repeat this work several times daily, as long as you need it.

In addition to the breath work, you can "recharge" your root chakra, by toning the sound of its healthy vibrational frequency. In the Ayurvedic tradition, the sound of the root chakra is "LAM." Listen to the F below Middle C note on the piano and "tone" that sound by taking a deep **grounding** breath and releasing it slowly as your vocal cords generate LLLLLL . . . AAAHHHH . . . MMMMMMM. Focus your intent and attention on your root chakra. Create a strong, deep vibration that you feel in the chakra and in your mouth. Repeat this toning nine times for one "round." This, too, can be a daily exercise.

As your red energy builds, add physical body exercises for stimulation. (Always begin with **grounding** breath work and scraping.) These activities can include the **yogic poses** of "The Elephant" and "Pushing the Feet,"[258] **drumming** with the drum held between your legs

---

[258] Anodea Judith, *Wheels of Life*, pp. 94-97.

and sitting on and "bouncing" with your root chakra firmly placed on an imaginary or real exercise ball.

Finally there is "Undulating." In this body work, you are stimulating your kundalini with serpentine movement. One method of doing this is with "belly-dancing." Another very effective method is described as follows:

Get down on all fours in a "box" configuration, with your hands and knees at shoulder width apart and your tail bone up against a source of loud rhythmic sound, for example native drumming.

Focus on the sound and allow it to hit against and stimulate your root chakra.

The urge to move your hips will start and when it does, gently move with your thighs and hips in a figure-8 motion.

As the stimulation increases, the urge will come to start moving the figure-8 with your waist, as well.

As the urge increases, move your upper body and arms.

Finally, at the height of the stimulation, move your head. At that point, your entire body will be undulating vigorously.

With this exercise, start slowly and gradually increase the time that you are undulating. Practice this exercise (either alone or with friends) as long as you require those healing energies.

Earth Energies

The **crystals** that you can use to stimulate red energies are

Red Jasper helps you to move forward with courage and remain committed to your purpose of recovery.

Red Garnet balances and stimulates the development and movement of the kundalini energies and engenders deep healing in the root chakra.

Ruby energies that are intense and vivid will change your outlook on your life and help you to be creative while expanding your awareness.

Serpentine energy helps to open the way for the rise of the kundalini.

The **herbs** that will enhance the red energies of your root chakra are *borage*, *lemon balm*, *marjoram*, *red rose petals*, *thyme* and *violet*.

The **aromas** that will stimulate those energies are

Musk which is a sensuous aroma enlivening a depressed root chakra red energy.

Hyacinth which can be combined with musk or used alone to enhance pleasurable sensations in the root chakra.

Spirit Energies

The "Seeker's Lamp" meditation and prayer that have been given for too much red and fire energies are also immensely beneficial for too little, when they are incorporated into the "Body Work" and "Earth Energies" modalities. The energies of Spirit **know** what has to be healed. Since you are functioning within a **holistic** system, there will be benefits throughout your energy field.

In this lesson, you will begin a guided mediation that will also bring benefit when there is too little of the root chakra's color. Please prepare this time by doing the "Reinforcing and Balancing" breath work in which you "pull up" red energies and then green energies. This new guided meditation is a cumulative one that you will be able to do for the healing of too little of any color of energy. It takes you to a rich source of energy and starts, in this lesson, with the red of the root chakra. The title is the "Ring of Color." You proceed as follows:

Prepare a space of calm and peace. Wear loose clothing. Have a large glass of pure water on hand. Keep your journaling equipment on hand, as well. This can be either a sitting or a standing meditation. If you choose to stand, keep your feet shoulder-width apart and your back straight. Because you will be in a state of altered awareness with your eyes closed, stand behind something solid, for example, a tall-backed chair, for safety.

After stating your **intent** to connect with a rich source of red energy, start with several deep **grounding** breaths. Be sure that you are firmly anchored in Earth.

As you breathe deeply, turn your attention inward and see the elevator shaft that you have already used in the "Seeker's Lamp" meditation. See that shaft going downwards into your own depths of "unknowing." With each breath, move downwards in the shaft. It will be dark and you will descend into the darkness.

Keep your intent in mind as you breathe your way into the depths.

Let yourself continue to go down until you stop. At that point, the "doors" of the elevator open and you step out.

You find yourself in a place of green light. It is diffused in all directions and envelops you. As your eyes adjust to this unusual environment, you see that you are standing on a solid green "turf." And encircling your feet at a closeness of about twelve inches, there is a transparent, rope-like "ring." As you look at it, the ring starts to glow with shimmering intensity. The light gets gradually brighter until the color is clear crimson.

You **know** now that this is your source of red. While you continue to breathe deeply and evenly, you sense the red energies rising. With each inhalation, the red rises higher and higher. As it does this, you feel a warmth in your energy field. You feel a tingling and an increasingly warm sensation. As the red energy rises, the tingling and warmth increase. The red energy rises up over your head.

While you continue to breathe, the red increases in intensity and "substance." At a certain point, you will know that this is enough for the time being. With a sense of completion, you silently say "thank you" and continue to breathe deeply. Gradually the red energy and warmth will fade, but you will retain those energies.

When all the color has left the ring, you turn back toward the "doors." Re-enter the "shaft" and proceed upward. Continue to breathe deeply and "hold" the red and fire energies you have received. Gradually return to this dimension. Find yourself back where you started and slowly adjust to this "reality." Drink the glass of pure water. While you journal this experience, re-experience it. Rest.

Do this meditation as often as you need it.

(Please note that the self-healing therapies presented in this and any succeeding lessons are disciplines given to assist you to heal into wholeness. Because they are designed primarily to bring balance into your chakras and the structures they generate, all the therapies are also ?balancing" discipline/practices. Such is the path of "Coming into Being."

This has been an immense lesson. Before you leave this sacred space, please pause and experience the timelessness that you now know is here. With every trip you have made to this stone circle that same sense of "now" has been impacting on your soul field. Perhaps you are slowly realizing that you, too, are timeless. Allow that awareness to happen. It will simply be part of the journey.

You may leave the stone circle . . .

* * *

Soul Searcher, while on the path of "Coming into Being," you have continued "letting go" of some entrenched patterns, "letting be" what still have to be transmuted and at the same time you have been struggling (but succeeding in wonderful ways) to bring about balance not only into the "dancing" energies of your root center of consciousness but also those of your physicality. By now, you are likely realizing that struggle is a perfectly natural happening on this path! Before going to the next lesson, remind yourself regularly about who you are and your origins with and in the Spirit. You are a soul searcher engaged in a grand adventure of self-exploration and discovery. Please take your time!

Also be aware that your experiences of opening the way and of coming into being will continue into the next two lessons, along with your "work" of "letting go/letting be" and "balancing." The paradoxes will also continue! And, here is the final paradox of this lesson: did you notice that your path of "Coming into Being" has carried a **double** meaning; the first underlies your unfolding **past** process of physical soul structure development, while the second underlies your **present** process of spiritual questing? In the next two lessons, you will build on that paradox and experience yet more. In the meantime, really get to **know** your root chakra. It is an immense center of consciousness, a great archetypal power indicative of your origins and of your connection with Earth.

Peace and blessings

Lesson Four

YOUR SACRAL CHAKRA AND SOUL STRUCTURES OF EMOTIONALITY

In the warm and deep darkness of this midsummer night . . . hello and welcome: thank you for returning to the stone circle at such an unusual hour. Don't be afraid; here's my hand. Let's stand for a moment beside Long Meg's bulk and tune into the darkness. On these moors, the warm night energies are palpable. Let us allow them to embrace us. While our feet connect with supportive, sustaining Earth, our uplifted eyes absorb the cool, white light of the stars and moon. They are the only night lights on the moors. Can you imagine how many thousands of midsummer nights have come to this place? Long Meg has seen them all. And her Children, like stone sentinels, have created a sanctuary into which soul searchers like you could enter and find refuge. Here, in the dark night, with the sounds of moaning winds to stir them, long-buried emotions could arise. While you and I, in this time, look up at the stars and the moon, can you sense the energies of those long-ago others? Their emotions and ours, even after hundreds of generations, are not essentially different. Night promotes the emergence of emotions. Darkness and deep feelings are allied. Now, let me lead you to the center of the circle. Here are your ground sheet and a shawl. Be seated please . . . . Take several deep **grounding** breaths. For a few moments, I will leave you to sit and tune into the enveloping night and into those ancient energies.

Soul Searcher, on your path of "Coming into Being," it is often necessary to sit in the darkness of your "unknowing" and await, with trust, the new realizations that are opening the way. While you do this, you will remember from your last lesson that you carry an inner **knowing**. You will not (again!) forget your Divine origins.

Now take in these words by a visionary poet of the early twentieth century:[259]

---

[259] Kahlil Gibran, *Thoughts and Meditations*, Excerpted from pp. 91-96.

"O Night"

"O Night of lovers, inspirer of poets and singers,
O Night of phantoms, of spirits and fancies,
O Night of longing, of hopes and memories,
You are like a giant dwarfing the evening clouds
and towering over the dawn.
With the sword of fire you are armed, and with
the shining moon you are crowned, and with calm
and silence you are veiled.
[. . . .]
There I see you Night, awful and beautiful,
poised between heaven and earth, veiled in
mist, cloaked in cloud, laughing at
the sun, ridiculing the day, taunting the slaves
who sleeplessly worship before the idols.
[. . . .]
I have accompanied you, O Night, and followed you
until we became kin.
[. . . .]
In my dark self are glittering stars strewn
by my emotions.
And in my heart shines a moon lighting the procession
of my dreams.
In my sleepless soul a silence reveals
the lover's secrets and echoes the
worshipper's prayers,
And my face wears a magic mask. Torn by
the agony of death, it is mended by the songs of youth.
We are both alike in every way, Night.
[. . . .]
I am like you, Night, and we are both accused of
being what we are not.
I am like you even though twilight does not crown me
with its golden clouds.
I am like you although morn does not adorn the
hem of my garment with its rosy rays.
I am like you although I am not encircled by the milky
way.
I am night boundless and calm; there is no beginning
to my obscurity and no end to my depth."

Take some time to ponder these words. Do they stir any deep responsive images and feelings within you? If so, do not try to analyze them. Just sit with them for a while. You are being made ready.

Like the night, your paths of "Opening the Way" and "Coming into Being" are the paths of paradox, of both/and with which you are becoming acquainted. Now, you will leave behind the familiarity of your "gross" body energies; your soul structures of physicality and their archetypal root center of consciousness. You will continue, of course, to explore and experience them as your rebirthing journey unfolds. (While coming into being, you will also be opening the way, over and over again as you continue the discipline/practices of "letting go" of old **beliefs**, values, attitudes and habits, while "letting be" what requires further "work" and the "balancing" that started with your root chakra's energies.) Now your quest for wholeness draws you forward into new realizations. There is more adventure awaiting you!

You start by noting yet another paradox: your path of "Coming into Being" is not only parallel to and contiguous with your path of "Opening the Way" so that you can find yourself on both at the same time, but this path also contains three "lanes." Until now, while on the path of "Coming into Being," you have been on the first lane; that of exploring your root chakra and your soul structures of physicality. Now your simultaneity is becoming more complicated and you are required to proceed along the second lane. And as you are doing this, you will be experiencing yet more of your own multidimensionality. Just continue to let it happen — in yet more complex fashion — and enjoy!

On the second lane you will turn your attention to your first "subtle" body of consciousness. It constitutes a deep, deep dimension of you as an energy being, a soul field. There, as your first subtle body, your soul substance has been shaped by your sacral chakra into the soul structures of emotionality. Because those structures can be your "darkest obscurities," there is a strong similarity between you and the night.

Please pay heed to these words from an insightful woman who said:[260]

> "Now let us understand what causes human beings to particularly neglect, repress and cripple the growth of their emotional nature. This neglect is universal. Most human beings look mainly after the physical self. They do more or less what is necessary to make it grow and remain healthy. A good portion of humanity cultivates the mental side. In order to do so you learn . . . ; you absorb, you train your memory and your logical reasoning. All this furthers mental growth.
>
> But why is the emotional nature generally neglected? There are good reasons for that, my friends. To gain more clarity, let us first understand the function of the emotional nature in human beings. It includes, first of all, *the capacity to feel.* The capacity to experience feeling is synonymous with the capacity to give and receive happiness. To the degree [that] you shy away

---

[260] Eva Pierrakos, *The Pathwork of Self-Transformation*, p. 105.

from any emotional experience, to that extent you also close the door to the experience of happiness."

It is both sad and true that most people are unhappy energy beings. In the last lesson, you were given several reasons for this condition. In this lesson, you will be given more. To remind you of the initial "problem," please recall, again, the shaman's story about your incarnation. You, Little Soul, while carrying your nucleus of divinity (your inner guidance system), descended into this dimension from your origins in and with the Spirit. But the animal soul paradox was your starting position. In other words, **you who are an energy being, a soul field incarnated as an animal soul.** Having probed into, revealed and initiated the healing of your root center of consciousness, and thence, your soul structures of physicality, (remember: **form follows consciousness**) you are invited to undertake the same exciting healing quest involving your sacral chakra and your soul structures of emotionality.

There is much to be learned!

* * *

Enriched by Celtic mythology, by references to modern metaphysics and psychology, and by a "model" of the Buddhist Wheel of Samsara that incorporates Grimms' fairy tales, this lesson will deal in several ways with your sacral chakra; the center of consciousness that has generated, out of your soul substance, your soul structures of emotionality. In the context of that chakra's prime directive (its archetypal imperative) and "i-am" statement of consciousness, you will learn how and why these soul structures were formed. The impact produced by the inner and outer environments of childhood will be included. Then, you will learn about the sacral chakra's qualities and function, intrinsic to its enormous generative power. You will later become aware of the complexities of this power, while you delve into your own soul structures of emotionality. Deeper within that dimension and context, you will be shown how your "dancing," archetypal masculine and feminine energies have related to each other and how their interaction was heavily involved in the ongoing development of your egoic structures. Throughout this lesson, you will call upon the Observer to help you probe into the depths of your own emotionality. In this "work" you will be involved in yet more "letting go/letting be" You will also continue and add to the discipline/practice of "balancing." Finally, you will be instructed about a malfunctioning sacral chakra and, thereafter, given some self-healing therapies (disciplines), plus additional homework. This is a very full lesson!

Now, with an awareness of your divine origins as the light steadily guiding you, step forth on the second lane of your path of "Coming into Being."

Your Sacral Chakra

In your **holistic** human energy system, the microcosm of a macrocosmic generative power, your sacral chakra carries physical (root chakra), along with mental and spiritual components, as you would expect. But the prime directive of your sacral chakra since your conception is, and always will be, the generation and the maintenance of your emotionality. In other words, the archetypal imperative of your sacral chakra is your emotionality. Reinforced by that chakra's "i-am" statement of consciousness; "I feel (that is, I have emotions), therefore, I am," the prime directive wields an enormous power. This is revealed by an ego/self that says: "I am my feelings." Those feelings energies have been called the energies of relationship: they are crucial to your connections; with yourself, with all the others in your life and with your world.

Let us begin by tuning into those energies. While standing or sitting comfortably, take several deep **grounding** breaths and "scrape" your auric field. Then gently place your cupped hand on the area directly below your navel. In this third dimension, that is the seeming front "location" of your sacral chakra.[261] Turning your **intent** and **attention** inward, sense that wheel of light spinning beneath your hand. Call in the Observer to help you to tune into the energies that you are experiencing

With detachment and discernment, focus closely and steadily on the sacral chakra beneath your hand. Are you feeling excited? Scared? Guilty? Anxious? Abandoned? Rejected? Lonely? Are you feeling happy? Loving? Contented? Joyful? Carefree? Connected? Loved? Are you feeling numb? Alienated? Separated? Lost? What a repertoire of emotions and relationships can be conjured up, as you place your intent and attention on your sacral chakra! Stay with those feelings for a while. If images arise, allow whatever forms the feelings seem to take. Then leave your cupped hand in place, while you return briefly to the imaginal realm.

Please recall the purpose of mythology: that it reveals how people have evolved physically, emotionally, mentally and spiritually and that it has helped them to connect with their own being and with the natural world. Then, take in the ongoing myth about the Celtic warrior/ hero, Cuchulain; an archetypal motif of a physical-survival oriented root chakra consciousness. As recounted in the last lesson, Cuchulain, a fearsome fighter of great renown, had created immense havoc amongst the forces of a greedy woman who had threatened his safety and security. Great was the destruction inflicted by this mighty warrior, when he was possessed by his battle frenzy. The story concludes . . . .

Finally, when the battle was over and the enemy was fleeing, the servants of Cuchulain set out three huge cauldrons of cold water and awaited their master. He approached with whirling magical weapon and with red body enormously swollen and ghastly to behold. Nimbly trying to duck out of the way and often sustaining deep wounds, the servants sought to seize hold of the frenzied warrior. When they caught him, they threw him into the first cauldron. Such was Cuchulain's fiery heat that the water boiled. The second cauldron of cold water was in readiness and he was speedily put into it. Again the water steamed and hissed. Finally, after immersion in the third cauldron of cold water, Cuchulain's body resumed its normal

---

[261] Please note that your chakras might not be located, entirely or at all, in this third dimension. But you can sense them by scanning because you are tuning into them.

size, shape and color. The warrior/hero's fury and blood-lust were over, for the time being. He had returned to himself.

In this unexpected ending, you are given two important insights about your deep and dark emotional dimensions. First; the myth of Cuchulain reveals how the root and sacral chakras interact with each other in the holistic archetypal human energy system. Here, as metaphor, are both the survival-oriented physicality (the archetypal imperative) of the root chakra and the emotionality (the archetypal imperative) of the sacral chakra. Second; the myth reveals a further paradox on your path of "Coming into Being." It is this: the sacral chakra, with its focus on generating and maintaining emotionality, also carries the qualities (intrinsic to its generative power) that can provide, when they are healthy, the balancing required for coping with a highly excitable root chakra. The balancing (which you will later realize is enhanced by your discipline/practices) was illustrated by the myth, as you shall soon be made aware. Now, let us proceed to examine your sacral chakra's qualities, while relating them to the mythic Cuchulain.

Your Sacral Chakra's Qualities

In describing the "workings" of sacral chakra, Rosalyn Bruyere has noted that in the human energy system there must be a means of "quenching," when necessary, the root chakra's masculine red and fire energies.[262] This balancing is accomplished, in a healthy human energy system, by the sacral chakra's color orange and the element of water.

In the wheel of light that is your sacral center of consciousness, the predominant color "band" and sound energy is orange. The orange vibratory frequency, which **holistically** combines the root chakra's predominant red energies with the solar plexus chakra's predominant yellow energies (there is more in the next lesson), generates a vitality that can remain more within bounds than is often the case with the root chakra's red and fire energies (recall Cuchulain). In a healthy human energy system, that vitality is less primitive than simple red energies, because those energies are being balanced, somewhat, by the gradually emerging "will-power" of the solar plexus chakra.

Essentially, it is the orange frequency that sets the "feeling/tone" in your life.[263] The orange quality, the quality of your emotions, the quality of your relationships, the quality of your flexibility and flow, the quality of your pleasure and "pain" all reside in the sacral chakra. Clearly, these were not present in the basic red energies so vividly presented by the Celtic warrior, and quite clearly, they were needed.

Conjoined with the color orange is the element of water. In the world's cosmologies (including the Judeo-Christian) "water symbolizes the primal substance from which all

---

[262] Rosalyn Bruyere, *Wheels of Light*, p. 55.

[263] As already indicated in the "Prologue," I am indebted to Rev. Michael Bernard Beckwith for the phrase "feeling/tone," which he has frequently used in his sermons. I have interpreted the phrase to mean a profound, ongoing, **felt** sense of the **presence** of something intangible and alive. Although the orange frequency "sets" the feeling/tone, it can be influenced and enhanced as your quest for wholeness continues.

forms come and to which they will return."[264] The sacred water of wells, ponds, rivers and lakes has figured in many of the world's spiritual traditions. These waters have signified the deep mystery that underlies all of life: you were gestated in water. Throughout humankind's existence, water has been spiritually significant. Rituals of baptism and spiritual cleansings of various kinds, including exorcism, have involved the use of water. Water is also indispensable for your physical survival. Not only does water sustain your physical cells but it also assists fundamentally in their healing. Water energies are regenerative. Clearly, water is an element in which the "material" and the "spiritual" are one. In the myth about the frenzied Cuchulain, the quenching in water had to be done for the sake of everyone's survival and because he had to be brought back "to himself." In other words, he was regenerated, only after being immersed in water. Thus, the myth teaches that, paradoxically, the primitive, instinctual energies of your root chakra require the presence of water energies in order to preserve and maintain them. It is not surprising, then, that your root and sacral chakras are closely involved with each other.

In yet another paradox, the red and fire energies present in your creative passions are also in need of the water energies. Creative intensities can sometimes burn too furiously. In the water energies of the sacral chakra, there is present a persistent "flow," like a river relentlessly rolling within its banks toward its destination. In this movement there is both excitement and containment. Therein lie the necessary curbs and the balancing.

Yet, like fire, the power of water can be dangerous. Water, under control, can be used to generate the electrical power to light peoples' homes. Water raging out of control can drown those people and sweep away their homes. In your archetypal human energy system, the water energies of your sacral chakra can do the same to you. (With your cupped hand in place over your sacral chakra, breathe into and, with the help of the Observer, sense the power and mystery in those orange watery depths. Ponder on them and on the paradoxical ways that they can express in you.)

Contained within that paradox are the energies inherent in the soul substance that became your soul structures of emotionality. Those energies are your feminine force. (Please recall the attributes of the feminine yin energies from Lesson Two and continue to focus on your sacral chakra.)

Your Sacral Chakra's Feminine Force

Traditionally, the sacral chakras orange and water energies have been expressions of the archetypal feminine principle. Symbolically, the orange fruit tree was connected with wedding fertility rituals simultaneously representing a woman's virginity (the blossoms) and her fertility (the fruit). The element of water, conjoined with orange, has added more feminine power, for water has traditionally represented the feminine force. It has symbolized a surrendering unto, an accepting and an enfolding of whatever enters into it.

---

[264] Anthony Stevens, *Ariadne's Clue*, p.130.

In both sexes of human beings, the primordial feminine energies are required to focus the generative power of the emotion and relationship-oriented *sacral chakra*.

Those energies were vitally necessary from the moment of your conception. During your gestation, while your physicality and your physical survival needs were dominant, your sacral chakra's feminine energies formed the emotional component of your root chakra consciousness. (Age regression studies have indicated that a human fetus can experience deep emotions.)[265] After your advent, in the Dance of Shiva (and Shakti) that is your life, your root chakra's prime directive, expressed by the masculine energies, have been constantly partnering with your sacral chakra's prime directive, expressed by the feminine energies. Sometimes the partnership has been dysfunctional. Always it has been a paradox!

Immediately after your advent and for the first four years of your life, while animal soul physical survival needs remained paramount, the sacral chakra component of your root chakra was at work. Until age four, your sacral chakra was not functioning on its own, but its huge potential power was already evident in your root chakra's archetypal imperative. It was there as feminine force in your **holistic** energy system to provide some balance to the dominant masculine force of your root chakra. Sometimes, (as revealed by the Cuchulain myth), the feminine energies could be overwhelmed by the instinctual masculine energies. When that occurred, the emotions could express only as rage and/or fear. Then, they would have to be restored (sometimes dramatically!) by the sacral chakra's water energies. In your **holistic** energy system, during those crucial beginning years, the archetypal "dance" was well underway. How interestingly we human animal souls get shaped! (Are you beginning to appreciate the complexity of that process?)

While you are considering the feminine force of the sacral chakra, please note the intriguing psychological theory relating to people with "orange personalities."[266] Herein is expressed the self-identification arising out of the chakra's "i-am" consciousness and the dancing archetypal feminine energies. Although there are few, if any, "pure types," "oranges" are revealed by the following characteristics: they are loving, solicitous and sensitive and concerned about "basic human emotional needs;" they are instinctual caretakers and worry about those they care about; they are devoted, considerate and helpful team players; they love to bring people together; they are good listeners with whom others will willingly share their feelings; they are very cautious and hesitant to change anything in their environment; they are courteous people unless they are crossed, when they become "rigid, stubborn and hostile;" they have strong need for personal praise and signs of appreciation; they are careful to promote good feelings between themselves and their important "others;" they dislike conflict and will avoid it as much as possible; they "manage their resources well and plan for the future;" their self esteem and emotional stability are directly tied to and influenced by the quality of their relationships; they struggle deeply with having to cope with problems that are emotional in nature and sometimes the coping involves addictive behavior; extroverted "oranges" are hard

---

[265] For many examples, please consult the web site of the Institute of Clinical Hypnotherapy - Psychotherapy.
[266] Carol Ritberger, *Your Personality, Your Health*, pp. 129-136.

workers, who make the work interesting and fun; introverted "oranges" are "intensely private people," who are probably hard at work behind the scenes. (Ponder on those who might fit this description, including you. Do so with the help of the Observer by making assessments, rather than "moral" judgments.)

Now you are ready to examine the function and generative power of your sacral chakra.[267] With the Observer helping you to develop the necessary detachment and discernment, please tune into the front and then the back of that center of consciousness.

Your Sacral Chakra's Function and Generative Power

As a **holistic** component of your root chakra, while at the same time exercising its own unique power, your sacral chakra has functioned in an amazing (and paradoxical) fashion, while it generated your soul structures of emotionality.

Examining the physical component, you learn that through your sacral chakra front you have physically experienced your emotions, quite likely during your gestation and you have expressed them from the time of your advent. Screaming, crying, laughing, gagging, shaking and dancing are but a few of the physical ways that emotions can be manifested. Many people have discovered that their entire physicality could be taken over by the intensity of their feelings. Your physicality can even be re-shaped by instinct-driven emotions (as indicated by Cuchulain). The soul substance is extremely vulnerable. (After some deep **grounding** breaths, take some time to repeat what you did during the last lesson: with the help of the Observer, connect with the soul structures of physicality in which you sense strong emotions. If there are images, what "forms" do they assume? Are those structures physically healthy? Breathe into them for a while. Connect with the feelings but stay detached. Discern what you can about the energies. Then move on.)

In the front, your sacral chakra's predominant emotional component has carried your archetypal Pleasure Principle. Far more than sexual and survival-oriented, (although it is all of that in your root chakra), the Pleasure Principle, **when nothing interferes with it**, allows your sacral chakra to be involved with your soul substance in the spiritual intimacies required by a fullness of creativity and of love. Thus, it can shape your "material" creations and your relationships. But mainly, as already noted, that is not what happens in the lives of most people. Often there is lovelessness, an emotional energy that suppresses the Pleasure Principle; a lovelessness that can originate, as you have already learned, in both the inner and outer environments. Instead of love, there is fear rooted in mistaken **beliefs** that generate feelings of deprivation. Those feelings can create the need for overindulgence; thus addictions are formed. (If you are ready, observe without judgment the soul structures of your addictions. If you are ready, relate them to the activities of your perceptual filtering system. Accompanied by the Observer, go deeper, and discern the soul structures of lovelessness. Observe . . . observe . . . then move on.)

---

[267] See Cyndi Dale, *New Chakra Healing*, pp. 34-36, 97-98, 118-119, 140-143 and 243-244.

By the age of four, your root and sacral chakras were being influenced by a gradually developing mental component, present since your conception. (You shall learn more in the next lesson.) As noted in the last lesson, this development was in-formed by the working of your root chakra's DNA connection and the perceptual filtering system, both impacted upon by your internal and external environments. At an early age, in a nurturing, loving environment, although you were pre-cognitive and pre-verbal, your sacral chakra would generate out of soul substance a type of "understanding," as empathy, for the plight of others. This could continue as you moved through life. (Ponder on your early empathic experiences, if any. Ponder on those you gave and those you received. Ponder and remain detached. How did their presence or absence influence your life?)

The spiritual component in your sacral chakra front has been there from your conception. After your advent, if there were nurturing conditions in your early environment, your empathic feelings could have undergone deepening into the beginnings of gentle compassion. Thus, your root chakra's primordial instincts could have been greatly modified. If the nurturing love was sparse or completely lacking, your root chakra's primordial instincts might have taken you over. (Continue to ponder the previous question. Then ponder on this: if you have given/not given and received/not received empathy, perhaps from an early age, what degree of compassion do you have for yourself and others? While remaining detached, with the help of the Observer, answer this question: what soul structures of compassion do you carry?)

After observing and pondering on the amazing power of your sacral chakra front, go to the back and, with the Observer continue to experience this center of consciousness with detachment and discernment. The back of your sacral chakra is located in your lower lumbar region on your sacrum and opens to other dimensions.

The physical component in the sacral chakra back is a consciousness that changes. It can transform emotions, which are one form of energy, into colors and sounds, a sensory form of energy. It is, thereby, involved with your perceptual filtering system. If, for example, you are part of a group of people, all of whom are focused on one thing in which all of you believe, and all of you are highly charged emotionally, you can collectively experience a "vision." It has happened many times in the world's history to groups of both children and adults. It has certainly happened to individual children and adults caught up in intense religious, or quasi-religious, beliefs and their accompanying emotions. Because this chakra back opens to other dimensions, an emotional input from another dimension can be experienced. It could be suggested that those dimensions could be, in part, the imaginal realm; the source of myths and fairy tales whose symbolism, on occasion, can be quite incomprehensible.[268] That dimension exists. Human beings would, otherwise, have no means of "imagining" those experiences. (Perhaps you have had this happen to you. If so, please summon up the memory, call in the Observer and ponder on the suggestion that your "vision" or "imagined" experience was "real" but its interpretation by you or someone else could have been faulty.)

---

[268] It could also be the Akashic Field.

The sacral chakra back carries an emotional component that has heavily influenced all your emotional development. Again, from the time of your birth, your outer environment, especially the archetypal parenting figures, has played a crucial role. If you had been lovingly taught that **all** your emotions were acceptable and how **best** to experience and express them, then your early emotional development would have proceeded in a healthy fashion. Perhaps yours did and you were able to receive the nurturing energies available from other dimensions. But if you are like the majority of people, your sacral chakra back has required some healing. (Ponder on your situation. How did the parental figures in your childhood deal with their feelings and with yours? How did that affect your soul substance? What soul structures of emotionality do you discern? Remain detached. Then move on.)

The mental component in your sacral chakra back was heavily influenced by both your inner and outer environments. Even as a pre-cognitive and pre-verbal child, you were learning to adapt to life's changes. In many life situations you were required to cope. If you began to make judgments about the acceptability of certain feelings, or to deny them, you would early have been creating resistance to that necessary adaptability. As life went on, you would have become less and less flexible. That is, the crystallization of your soul structures of emotionality (and even your soul structures of mentality) would have been well underway. (Ponder your situation. Although it is very difficult to examine one's own disowned feelings, it can be done. With the Observer to help you, you will not get buried in guilt or judgment. Please remember that you are becoming "real" by focusing on the truth and learning to love yourself. This will be an excellent preparation for all the work you will do later with these feelings.)

The spiritual component in the back of your sacral chakra has been profoundly affected by your **beliefs** about yourself and about others. Please recall that your root chakra generates your biology of belief, including the molecules of emotion. As such, these are intangible soul structures of physicality. Yet, in a **holistic** archetypal energy system, these very structures have also been shaped, implacably, by the generative power of your sacral chakra. This is your emotional biology! Once more, there is the environmental impact of love or lovelessness to consider. From early childhood, you as an archetypal energy being, could have been held back or carried healthily forward in the "flow" of life. If you had been encouraged to open freely and happily to Spirit, to trust in the "divine right order," that all was well and all was truly well, you would have thrived, despite many (sometimes serious) problems and hardships that you might have been experiencing. (At this point you might want to ponder on your childhood spiritual training and relate it to your known beliefs. While remaining detached, consider the environmental impact of love or lovelessness. Allow the feelings to be there. If images arise, what "forms" do you discern?)

Clearly, your sacral chakra, both as energy in your root chakra and as itself, has been an enormous presence in your **holistic** archetypal energy system. As the generative power that in-formed your soul structures of emotionality that chakra has shaped your soul substance and, thus, your relationships, in ways that you will come to realize were virtually beyond your control. As has already been noted, since so much of that shaping has been the result of your interactions with your inner and outer environments, it is necessary to turn, again, to those formative energies.

The Environmental Impact

In preparation for what follows, please recall the instruction given in the previous lesson about the ways in which your inner and outer environments had sent sensory energies into your soul substance, by way of your root chakra's perceptual filtering system. Recall the creative, generative process by which those energies had formed your soul structures of physicality, your beliefs, attitudes and values and your initial egoic structures. Above all, please keep in mind your root chakra's "i-am" consciousness relative to the almost unbelievable intensity with which your outer environment impacted upon your soul substance and, thence, on your developing soul structures of physicality.

In your beginning years, while the sensory input had entered relentlessly, there were other environmental influences at work. They were mentioned briefly in the last lesson. But they required the context of awareness about your sacral chakra before they could be described in detail. We shall now focus on that description . . . .

From the moment of your conception, you, as soul field/substance have been malleable, impressionable, receptive and, above all, vulnerable. No matter how many years you have lived, those qualities still prevail, although your soul structures have likely undergone considerable crystallization. And in those first years after your advent into this dimension, the likelihood of trauma was virtually guaranteed. (This third dimension is a "hard" one to birth into!) If there was not actual physical abuse and sensory forms of trauma, there was emotional wounding that could occur.[269] (Please remember that your Sacred Contract with your parents included receiving Sacred Wounds. Your other Sacred Contracts could also have involved wounds of various kinds. If so, you probably received them!)

At this point, please recall the dramatic presentation entitled "The Turning Point" or "The Hand That Rocks the Cradle (Probably) Rules the World."

A Dramatic Presentation: Reprised

Recall from the first dramatic "turning point" when the mother exhibited great fear and explosive fear energies towards the beetle, that the infant was affected drastically. There was, despite her parental "love," an emotional trauma. From that day forward, the child was terrified of any crawling creature. After a few years of ingesting the energies of this fear-based mother and of the others who shared her perspective, the child was afraid of almost everything and felt very insecure. The child grew into an adult disgusted by a lot of natural phenomena, including physical body secretions. The **attitude** was one of aversion. The child also developed, as part of its **values**, a hate-oriented tendency to kill any bugs and other "lower life forms" that it encountered. The lovelessness had been established. The powerful **belief**, fostered by this and many similar incidents, was that these creatures were "bad", that is, dangerous to survival and must be exterminated without delay. Fostered over years, by

---

[269] For studies about emotional wounding, see Daniel Goleman, *Emotional Intelligence* Chapter 15; "The Family Crucible," Roger Wolinsky, *Trances People Live* and Peter A. Levine, *Waking the Tiger: Healing Trauma*.

these attitudes, values and beliefs there developed a lack of concern about life, feelings of fear about the world of nature and feelings of cruel superiority toward many living things. In-formed by these emotions, the human relationships of this person would inevitably carry this feeling/tone. The relationships would be a reflection of that long-ago trauma, repeatedly reinforced. (Ponder on the implications when hundreds of millions of people are shaped in a traumatic fashion. What would be the effect on the web of life and on world peace? Can you relate it to the present world political situation?)

Now, recall from the second dramatic "turning point" that the mother contained her love energies and remained calm, regardless of her feelings about the beetle. There was no trauma inflicted on the child. From that day forward, the child was unafraid of crawling creatures but respected their tendencies. After a few years of ingesting the energies of this love-based mother and of the others who shared the same perspective, the child was ready to meet the small challenges of the world. The child grew into an adult who could cope with the big challenges and feel at home in the world. The **attitude** was one of confidence and trust in the natural order. The child developed as part of its **values**, a sense of loving connection to the web of life that included all living things. The powerful **belief** that was fostered by this and many similar incidents was that all living things were here for a purpose and required safeguarding. In-formed by these attitudes, values and beliefs, the child developed a deep love for life in all its forms, feelings of connection with Earth and feelings of gratitude that such beauty and bounty existed. The human relationships formed by this person with this feeling/tone would be vastly different from those of the first child. (Ponder on the implications in the context of the web of life and world peace.)

The emotional environment within which you have spent your life has shaped you. The archetypal parenting energies present in your early infancy plus all the other emotional energies you ingested in your formative years and afterward were crucial to the generative activity of your sacral chakra. Although the dramatic presentation given in these lessons was overly simplified, there was an important truth to be learned. (Ponder on this: it has been said that there are really only two basic emotions that drive the choices that people can make; there is love or there is fear. Although the choices and how they are perceived seem to be infinitely varied, there are only those two fundamental emotions — love and fear. Out of these, the beliefs, attitudes and values that in-form humanity are generated.)

Now are you are ready to explore the depths of your soul structures of emotionality?

Your Soul Structures of Emotionality: The Astral Energies

The first of your "subtle" bodies of consciousness, your soul structures of emotionality, are the "forms" generated by your sacral chakra out of the **astral** consciousness energy of your soul substance. In order to understand what astral energy is, please recall (yet again!) the shaman's story about your incarnation and, this time, focus on your departure out of the Spirit. While you, Little Soul, descended along the ribbon of light, you passed through an enormous and extremely powerful "realm" of energy consisting of a series of dimensions. It was the astral plane. As your vibratory frequency decreased and you traveled "downward" through the astral dimensions, you "picked-up" and absorbed a quantity of its energy. It became part of your soul substance and it was present at your conception.

To help you understand further . . . the ancient Egyptians and the Greek philosopher, Plato (among others), knew about the astral plane and its energy. It was named after the word for starlight, because many of the ancients believed that their "souls" originated in the stars. For these people astral energy formed the duplicate body of every human being. (The Egyptians called it the "ka." It was the astral body that went somewhere in dreams, and it was the astral body that detached permanently from the physical body at death.) For many people, in later centuries, the astral plane was the Seven Heavens to which their "souls" returned. Lore about the astral energy and the astral body was included in the *Kabbalah* and became part of the formulations of the medieval European alchemists. The lore was also taken into the Rosicrucian and Theosophical teachings and it was part of the theories about human energies developed in the twentieth century by Wilhelm Reich and Rupert Sheldrake. Thus, while thousands of years have gone by and the content of the teachings about the astral plane and its energy has changed, a portion of the ancient lore has remained.

In this century, the idea of astral energy as a duplicate body that can astral project has a wide acceptance. Often conjoined with this idea is one about the astral plane; that angels and other spirit beings originate there and are invisible helpful presences in this Earth plane. In this modern day, there is also the idea that the astral body is the "body of emotions."[270] It is with the latter meaning that this lesson is concerned. **Astral consciousness energy is the energy of emotions.** These are the "feelings" energies that range from the "lowest," that is, rage, fear, shame, lust, hatred and greed, etc., to the "highest," that is, unconditional love, compassion, ecstasy, bliss, etc. It is an immense range of emotional energies. Thus, there is an enormous and multidimensional range of vibratory frequencies that indicate a person's astral energy. From the moment of conception, it is the sacral chakra of the human energy system that generates out of the astral energy (the energy of emotions), inherent in the soul substance, the first soul structures of emotionality. Since yours is a **holistic** energy system, the emotional component is present in all the chakras. But there is a crucial complexity to be noted (and here we must look ahead briefly to later lessons): the emotional structures are generated not only by the sacral chakra, present in all the chakras, but also by the heart chakra and by the third eye chakra, also present in all of them. These "higher" chakras generating the "higher" ranges of emotional frequencies are functioning in dimensions other than this one. Thus, the emotional "range" available to humans in this third dimension, begins with the "lowest;" the soul structures generated by the sacral chakra. The "range" can get progressively "higher" with the soul structures generated by the heart chakra and by the third eye chakra. But always there is present the sacral chakra component. Moreover, the development of the

---

[270] Keith Sherwood, *Chakra Therapy for Personal Growth & Healing*, p. 121. This author states that the astral body is not the duplicate body, but does have a symbiotic relationship with it. He is likely correct. This is an indication of the many conflicting views that currently prevail.

"higher" "ranges" is **not** automatic. Please note that in a loving, Spirit-filled environment starting in the uterus, the child would experience the wonderful emotional spirituality of the heart and the third eye, present as **possibilities** in the root and sacral chakras. These energies would ameliorate considerably the instinctual energies of those often out-of–balance centers of consciousness. But the prevalent "story" of people is that the soul structures of emotionality are initially those of the "lowest" vibration. And with enough lovelessness in the environment, they can remain that way throughout life. Perhaps the energy of emotions is not from the stars, but it is present in your soul substance. In the creative, generative process, that energy of emotions becomes the very troublesome and often neglected human "capacity to feel;" the emotional structures of animal soul.

Your Soul Structures of Emotionality: The Darkest Obscurities

To understand better the development of your soul structures of emotionality, imagine the following: you, Little Soul, have merged with the sperm and egg in the red cave of your mother's uterus and conception has resulted. You are enclosed in the blue light of the etheric womb and slowly undertaking your gestation. In-formed by your indwelling Spirit (your nucleus of divinity), the etheric matrix, and the kundalini, the creative, generative process by which you are formed is underway. The protoplasmic possibilities carried by your parental sperm and egg now merged with the consciousness energy in your soul substance are being shaped by your root chakra. Your tiny soul structures of physicality are forming. **At the same time**, the astral energy you brought with you in your soul substance is being shaped by the generative power of your sacral chakra and your soul structures of emotionality are forming. If your uterine environment is nourishing and nurturing, physically and emotionally, your malleable, impressionable, receptive and vulnerable soul substance can undergo the initial gestation process without trauma. You can incarnate peacefully. Your soul structures of physicality and emotionality will be readied for your advent. (Please note that you are being shaped by **both** your spiritual consciousness directing your energy system **and** by your mother's consciousness energies.) But if your uterine environment is marked by the energies of malnourishment and/or malnurturing, either accidental or deliberate, you will experience physical and/or emotional trauma. For example, if your mother is unable and/or unwilling to eat, exercise or sleep healthily, there will likely be physical trauma. If you are unwanted or your mother is carrying heavy feelings of fear, anger, shame, guilt, and/or hatred, you will likely be affected adversely, both physically and emotionally. Then, there comes your birthing, often marked by more trauma. (From this exercise in imagination, you are likely assuming that there are very few people who make their advent without already having undergone some physical and emotional trauma. The darkest obscurities can be there very early.)

As you have already been made aware, the newborn infant **requires** a loving, nurturing environment. And as you also know, what can often happen instead is more trauma. If you are beginning to suspect that the emotional life of most people is one of suffering, that the emotional structures of animal soul are those predominantly of pain, your suspicions are by and large correct. And your "capacity to feel" is further molded by the fact that your astral energy has carried into this lifetime the karmic content of, perhaps, hundreds of past lifetimes and their accompanying emotions. (Please recall from the shaman's story about your incarnation that you **chose** this as part of your Life Plan, and these energies are now part of the emotional "mix.")

There is a further complexity to consider when dealing with the darkest obscurities of your soul structures of emotionality. As already noted, the astral realm through which you traveled into this dimension was immense and multidimensional. Your soul structures of emotionality carry that immensity and multidimensionality. Not only are they huge in the "higher" dimensions (you will learn more about that in later lessons); they are also huge in the "lower" ones. Indeed, the emotional structures of animal soul generated by your sacral chakra can be compared to a massive iceberg, with only a very small portion above the "surface." That is, the emotions **that you are aware of** are a minute portion of those that lie in the darkest obscurities of your "unconscious." That is why you and the night are alike.

Needless to say . . .

Given their multidimensionality, size and content, not only from this lifetime but also from past lives, your beginning animal soul structures of emotionality constitute a tremendous power. And it is a power primarily not available to your awareness in this Earth dimension. In short, those energies mainly exist out of this time and space.[271] Generated by the sacral chakra out of your soul substance that carries the astral energy of both past lives and present possibilities, impacted upon by the inner and outer environments of this life time, your soul structures of emotionality begin to form their own patterns. These, in turn, can start to dominate your perceptual filtering system. Slowly the patterns are "set." As these patterns become crystallized, something else is happening. The beliefs, attitudes, values and habits of your biology, the patterns you encountered in the last lesson, become firmly embedded in the "subtle" structures of your emotions.

The patterns laid down in your early years (by the age of five) can already constitute such powerful structures of animal soul emotionality that they can take over control of your experience. Within your darkest obscurities, your deep dimensions of unknowing, the emotional structures of animal soul can eventually proceed to work as though they were "entities" separate from the rest of "you."[272] Those "entities" are not just emotions; they are also the biology of your beliefs and (as you shall soon be made aware) they constitute a portion of your egoic structures.

---

[271] Chris Griscom, *Ecstasy is a New Frequency*, p. 11.

[272] *Ibid*, p.11. The idea of hidden inner "entities" that bedevil human beings is part of an ancient tradition often revealed in mythology. In the modern Hermetic tradition the energies are described in this way: "The life of all beings, without exception, is ruled by a primordial Force deep inside them. The nature of this force is *craving*: an appetite that is never satisfied, an endless restlessness, an irresistible need and a blind, wild yearning." See Julius Evola and the UR Group, *Introduction to Magic: Rituals and Practical Techniques for the Magus*, p. 15. In another context, some people have identified the "entity" as the "ego" and called for its destruction. Please note that this idea does not adequately address the reality of those energies.

As the years go by, **if there are no mitigating conditions** in your inner and outer environments, this structure is reinforced. The mitigating conditions are those of the "higher" energies of love, joy and connection. In a **holistic** energy system, these can be present. But there seems to predominate in this world the emotional energies, the soul structures of lovelessness, which in-form the "entities." At an early age, that soul structure of emotionality will start to resist ceaselessly any of your efforts to change it. At this level of emotion, it is the "lowest" energy that prevails. This is the energy of fear, rage, guilt, shame, greed, lust and hatred. As these feelings slowly permeate your soul structures, they become addicted. You will seek out people and experiences that "feed" them. Although you might want to escape this situation and seek out "higher" levels of emotional consciousness, your animal soul structures of emotionality cannot allow this to happen.

At this point, you might be struggling to comprehend this description. Perhaps you might want to reject it, as being "extreme." You might even be asking: how could soul structures of emotionality like this be possible? The answer lies in the connection between your sacral chakra's prime directive and the "i-am" consciousness; already briefly mentioned and now requiring further examination.

First; as an aside and as review . . . in the last lesson, you learned that the root chakra has, from its beginnings, expressed its "i-am" as "I sense (that is, I have sensations); therefore, I am." With its prime directive of physicality; "embodiment," survival, safety and security, sensation is all that it can "know." Out of that root chakra's archetypal imperative there emerged your beginning egoic structures linked mainly with your physicality, especially your "maleness" or "femaleness." In this development, your ego/self started to take shape within your social and family environment and was defined by the cultural meaning assigned to "masculinity" and "femininity." In the meantime, the archetypal masculine and feminine forces, inherent in your soul substance, were becoming part of your animal soul structures, including the egoic.

Now, while maintaining your awareness of that development, please note the connection between the sacral chakra's prime directive, that of emotionality, and its reinforcing "i-am" statement: "I feel (that is I have emotions); therefore I am." With that prime directive, feeling is all it can "know." The implications arising out of that archetypal imperative, the implications of an ego/self that says: "I am my feelings," are enormous, especially around relationships. Because you are likely ready for a deeper awareness of your consciousness energies that are emotionality, those implications, including those arising out of lovelessness, will now be addressed. You will examine closely the "workings" of your sacral chakra and those animal soul structures and delve into their often perplexing and even tormented obscurities. For your greater understanding, that exploration will take place within the framework of a psychological "model," the reasons for which will soon be revealed.

A Buddhist "Model:" The Wheel of Samsara

In many Buddhist traditions,[273] there are teachings about the Wheel of Samsara, also known as the "Wheel of Life, Existence, Suffering." According to the teaching, people in this third dimension are caught up in rounds of birthing and dying.[274] The imagery could be that of entrapment in a circular cage from which there is no escape. Driven by the three poisons of greed, anger and ignorance, each person must go through the six "realms" of Samsara until the "human realm" is attained. It is only in that realm that a person, although still driven by the poisons, can undertake the spiritual practices that could lead to "enlightenment." With that state of consciousness achieved, the person obtains release from the Wheel, because the rounds of birth and death have ended.

In the "model"[275] to be presented in this lesson, each "realm" of the Wheel of Samsara is analogous to the unhealthy condition of most animal soul structures of emotionality most, if not all, of the time. (That condition could be described in a psychological context as "neurotic suffering" that exists, with varying degrees of intensity in most people after, but sometimes before, the age of five.) In other words, they are wounded energy beings whose energy system, soul substance and soul structures of emotionality have been damaged. Each realm in the model will be presented as an archetypal image — a living disposition common to all humanity — embedded in a fairy tale from the Brothers Grimm. Within that framework, you will deal with the vital "dancing" archetypal masculine and feminine forces within the **holistic** human energy system and, in particular, how this "dance" takes place in the sacral chakra, the center of consciousness generating the soul structures of emotionality.[276] You will learn how lack, or even absence, of the feminine energies in the sacral chakra can happen and how the imbalance in the "dance" results in various types of malfunction in that chakra. You will also learn how the malfunction results in the shaping of soul substance into predominantly dysfunctional animal soul structures of emotionality (the realms of Samsara) and how this situation, in turn, in-forms the ego/self. Finally, you will learn how that ego/self expresses, in various ways, as emotional "identity." In the meantime, you will also find out, through inner exploration and discovery, how each realm of the Buddhist model can be applied to you, an energy being, a soul field. Be ready for a challenging experience!

---

[273] It is interesting to note that a "wheel" of suffering was also to be found in both the Orphic and the Pythagorean mysteries of "classical" Greece. See Joscelyn Godwin, *The Golden Thread: the Ageless Wisdom of the Western Mystery Traditions*, p. 35 and footnote #10 on p. 160.

[274] This "wheel/circle" can be imaged as a cage in which the being is forced to run from section to section.

[275] A psychological model has been defined as a "deliberately simplified, idealized and imaginary representation of a phenomenon with properties explicitly defined as physically built from which the properties are to be deduced by logical reasoning or by empirical observation of the model as a physical object. Inferences from the model apply only to the model and not necessarily to the reality that it purports to represent, but if the model captures the important features of the phenomenon, then such inferences may apply to the phenomenon itself." *The Oxford Dictionary of Psychology*, p. 471. Please note that the Wheel of Samsara is **already** a model, from which the one for this lesson has been derived. For the latter I am deeply indebted to Mark Epstein's *Thoughts Without a Thinker: Psychotherapy From a Buddhist Perspective* and to my Buddhist friends.

[276] In preparation, please recall the descriptions of these archetypal energies given in the "Prologue" and in Lesson Two.

But first . . . let's look briefly into the marvels of fairy tales. They have been part of the human scene for thousands of years.[277] Their great longevity is due to the simple fact that "fairy tales are [. . .] more than mere entertainment."[278] They are actually a means by which you can probe "into [. . .] powerful feelings that might otherwise remain hidden."[279] This delving is possible because fairy tales are engrossing portrayals of archetypal patterns found in the "collective unconscious,"[280] that is, the Akashic Field. The tales "represent the archetypes [as "motifs"] in their simplest, barest and most concise form"[281] within the animal soul structures of emotionality of most people.

Dealing with such subjects as cannibalism, child abuse, executions, immolations, murder, lust, rape, marital infidelity and incest, (to mention a few), fairy tales were never intended for children, in the first place. "Originally conceived of as adult entertainment, fairy tales were told at social gatherings, in spinning rooms, in the fields and in other settings where adults congregated – not in the nursery."[282] It has only been within the last century or so that fairy tales, after being carefully sanitized, became "stories" for children.

In the model to be presented in this lesson, the fairy tales will be restored to their original intent. As they are recounted, you will experience their dream-like quality, for they take you into the imaginal realm, from which they originated, and into your deep dimensions of emotionality. In that context, you will discover that fairy tales exhibit a remarkable awareness on the part of both their tellers and listeners: on the surface, the stories indicate a **knowing** about the multidimensions of animal soul emotionality and how this affects the relationships people have with each other; at a deeper level, the stories indicate an "unconscious" **knowing** about the "workings" of the human energy system. In particular, the stories indicate that **form follows consciousness** and how the archetypal masculine and feminine forces carried by the chakras (and inherent in soul substance) interact with each other during the shaping of soul substance into the soul structures of emotionality, including the egoic structures. Finally, because fairy tales tell mainly (but not always) about "journeys of triumph and transformation,"[283] they will provide welcome encouragement as you progress along the second "lane" of your path of "Coming into Being."

At the onset, there are two important instructions for you to follow: first, please **experience** these stories and enjoy them before you enter into the subsequent discussion, during which you will probe deeply into them and into your own reactions and responses; second, during the discussion, there will be necessary references made to other primary chakras besides the root and the sacral, because these "higher" chakras often impact upon the sacral chakra within its components and, thence, on the soul structures of emotionality. When this happens, please

---

[277] Marie-Louise Von Franz, *The Interpretation of Fairy Tales*, p. 3. Fairy tales have even been found in Egyptian papyri.
[278] Sheldon Cashdan *The Witch Must Die: The Hidden Meaning of Fairy Tales*, p.10.
[279] *Ibid*, p.17.
[280] Marie-Louise Von Franz, *Archetypal Patterns in Fairy Tales*, p. 17.
[281] Marie-Louise Von Franz, *The Interpretation of Fairy Tales*, p. 1.
[282] Sheldon Cashdan, *The Witch Must Die*, p. 6.
[283] *Ibid*, p. 38.

keep in mind that all of these chakras will be dealt with thoroughly in later lessons and that you are not required to know the details at this point. Now, let us proceed.

The Realm of Hell

In some Buddhist teachings,[284] the realm of hell corresponds to the fiery place of eternal torment found in other religious traditions. In that realm, the person suffers the horrible tortures of anger and extreme anxiety, "burning with rage and tormented by fear."[285] Thus, in addition to these afflictions, the person is carrying the burden of lovelessness. Indicating crystallized and crippled animal soul structures of emotionality, the suffering can start in early childhood and continue throughout life, unless there is a healing intervention.

In fairy tales, the archetypal motifs symbolizing the anxiety, aggression, rage and fear energies of the realm of hell are usually female. (In this there is an immediate indication of the sacral chakra's feminine force.) The images can be the evil mother, mother-in-law, stepmother or any female character labeled as a "witch." The feelings of this character are often depicted in the tale as envy, jealousy, hatred and malice. But the "hellish" emotions of anxiety, aggression, rage and fear are what really drive her actions.[286]

The Grimm Brothers' fairy tale entitled "The Juniper Tree,"[287] tells the story of a stepmother, a woman burning with rage and tormented by fear, whose evil actions, triggered by these emotions, thrust her into hell. Now, take in the story . . .

An uncountable number of years ago, there lived a rich man, whose wife was childless. Often she went into the garden to stand under a large juniper tree and wish for a child. One day in winter, as she stood under the tree and peeled an apple, she cut her finger. Three drops of blood fell on the white snow beneath the tree. "Oh," she sighed, "how I want a child who is as red as blood and as white as snow." In that instant, she quickened. As the months went by, both she and the juniper tree became heavy with fruit. When she delivered a child, a boy who was as red as blood and as white as snow, she was so overcome with joy that she died. Her grieving husband buried her under the juniper tree. He wept daily for several months. Then, he married again.

Soon there was another child, a daughter. The new wife dearly loved her girl-child and was "cut to the quick" by the thought that the boy would inherit all his father's riches. Then "the devil took hold of her" and her aggression and rage were focused on the boy. "She pushed him from one

---

[284] As is the case with many spiritual teachings changed over time, there are inconsistencies in the "order" of the realms. The order in this model reflects the process of development of the soul structures of emotionality.
[285] For more detail, see Mark Epstein, *Thoughts Without a Thinker*, pp. 21-25.
[286] To test this theory, read "Snow White and the Seven Dwarfs," "Cinderella," "The Sleeping Beauty," and "Rapunzel." Read the oldest version you can find.
[287] Excerpted from Joseph Grimm and Wilhelm Grimm, *Grimm's Fairy Tales*, pp. 355-364.

place to the next; she slapped him here and cuffed him there, so that the poor child lived in ceaseless fear."

One day in autumn, the daughter asked her mother for an apple that was stored in a chest covered by a large heavy lid with a big sharp iron lock. Gladly, her mother obliged. When the girl asked for an apple for her "brother," the woman obeyed the devil again. She sent her daughter away on an errand and awaited the boy's arrival. Smiling, she invited him to take an apple out of the chest. When the child bent over to do so, the woman slammed down the heavy lid. *Crash!* The boy's head flew off into the apples.

Then the woman panicked and ran to get a large white kerchief. Sitting the boy on a chair in the kitchen, she replaced his head, tied it on with the kerchief and put an apple into his hand. When the little girl came into the kitchen, she remarked to her mother that he was pale and did not speak. The woman instructed her to "box his ears." She did so. Horrified, the girl watched his head fly off. She began weeping bitterly. Her mother wickedly let her believe that she had killed him and told her that they would have to conceal the crime. The girl and her mother set to work, cut the boy's body into pieces and put them into a pot of boiling water. When the father came home for supper, the "stew" was ready.

Calmly the woman served the meal while the little girl wept. When the man asked after the boy, the woman replied that he had gone to visit relatives. After that, the man ate heartily and tossed the bones under the table. The girl continued to weep. When the pot was empty, she gathered the bones in a large silk kerchief and went out into the garden. Gently she placed the boy's bones beneath the juniper tree. As she did, the tree raised its branches as if rejoicing. At its center there appeared smoke and a flame out of which there came a bird, which flew over to the garden wall and sang:

> My mother, she killed me.
> My father, he ate me.
> My sister, she made sure to see
> my bones were all gathered together,
> bound nicely in silk, as neat as can be,
> and laid beneath the juniper tree.
> *Tweet! Tweet!* What a lovely bird I am!

Then the bird flew high into the air. The juniper tree was restored to its former shape. The silk kerchief was gone. The girl suddenly felt happy. "It was as if her brother was still alive."

Meanwhile, the bird had flown to the goldsmith's house and began to sing:

> My mother, she killed me.
> My father, he ate me.
> My sister, she made sure to see
> my bones were all gathered together,
> bound nicely in silk, as neat as can be,
> and laid beneath the juniper tree.
> *Tweet! Tweet!* What a lovely bird I am!

The goldsmith had been busily crafting a fine gold chain and when he heard the bird, he ran out into the street, with the chain in his hand. He asked the bird to repeat the song and the bird refused unless he was paid with the gold chain. Gladly, the goldsmith handed over the chain. The bird repeated the song and then flew off with the chain clutched in his claws.

He flew to the shoemaker's house and again sang his song:

> My mother, she killed me.
> My father, he ate me.
> My sister, she made sure to see
> my bones were all gathered together,
> bound nicely in silk, as neat as can be,
> and laid beneath the juniper tree.
> *Tweet! Tweet!* What a lovely bird I am!

The shoemaker was entranced with the bird's fine voice and quickly called to his wife and family to see this wonderful creature. They exclaimed over his red and green feathers, his neck that glistened like pure gold and his eyes, "that sparkled in his head like stars." But when they asked him to sing his song again, he refused unless he received a gift. Quickly the shoemaker's wife went into the shop and came out with a lovely little pair of red shoes. The bird then repeated his song and flew away carrying the shoes in his claws.

He flew far away to a mill, where there were twenty men hewing a mill stone. The bird perched in a nearby linden tree and sang his song:

> My mother, she killed me.
> My father, he ate me.

At that point, two of the men stopped working and listened.

> My sister, she made sure to see
> my bones were all gathered together,
> bound nicely in silk, as neat as can be,

Now only eight of the men were working.

> And laid beneath the juniper tree.

Now only one of the men was working.

> *Tweet! Tweet*! What lovely bird I am!

Then the last man stopped working to listen to the bird. When they asked that he sing again, he refused, unless he was given the millstone. When they all agreed, he repeated his song. It took all twenty men to lift the stone. Then the bird stuck his head through the hole in the stone and put it on like a collar. He flew away, with the gold chain in his right claw, the red shoes in his left and the millstone around his neck. He went back to the garden and the juniper tree.

Meanwhile, the stepmother, father and little girl were still in the kitchen. The little girl wept piteously. The father continued to exclaim over the wonderful meal he had enjoyed. And the mother fell deeper and deeper into fear. Soon, she was feeling as though there was fire running through her veins and her teeth were chattering. Then the bird flew into the juniper tree and began to sing:

> My mother, she killed me.

The little girl's tears gushed forth. "The mother stopped her ears, shut her eyes and tried not to see or hear anything, but there was a roaring in her ears like a turbulent storm, and her eyes burned and flashed like lightning."

> My father, he ate me.

At that moment, the girls weeping intensified. But the father decided to go outside, the better to see and hear the bird. Although the woman tried to stop him, he went out.

> My sister, she made sure to see
> my bones were all gathered together,
> bound nicely in silk, as neat as can be,
> and laid beneath the juniper tree.
> *Tweet! Tweet*! What a lovely bird I am!

After ending the song, the bird dropped the gold chain. It fell around the man's neck, where it fitted him perfectly. He was delighted and returned inside, where he showed the woman his gift. She was petrified and fell to the floor. The bird again began his song:

> **My mother, she killed me.**

The woman howled and wished herself "a thousand feet beneath the earth" so that she would not have to hear the song.

> **My father, he ate me.**

Then the woman fell down "as if she were dead."

> **My sister, she made sure to see**

At that moment the girl got up and went outside to see if the bird would give her something.

> **My bones were all gathered together,**
> **bound nicely in silk, as neat as can be.**

Then the bird threw down the red shoes and the girl put them on. She started to dance happily and to praise the bird's generosity. But nothing could comfort the woman. She felt as though "the world was coming to an end." She decided to go outside.

***Crash!* The bird threw the millstone down on her head. She was crushed to death. While the little girl and her father ran to the scene, smoke and flames were already rising from the spot. There was no trace of the woman. And when the smoke and flames cleared, the little brother was standing there. He took his sister and father by the hand and all three went back into the house. That is the end of the story.**

Please experience this fairy tale several times, while you immerse yourself in its multiple layers of meaning. Then return to this dimension to participate in the discussion. In this tale, there are several archetypal motifs that indicate the Buddhist realm of hell and, by analogy, the damaged consciousness energies of animal soul emotionality expressing as rage and fear.

The "juniper tree" has had a long tradition of being an entrance to the underworld. Thus, all that happens in the story involving the tree indicates those lower regions. The images are very complex: they can express both the place of fiery torment and the hidden places of the spirit. In the story, the little "girl," a motif of innocent spirituality, gently collects her "brother's" bones, the motif of badly damaged innocent spirituality, and places them under the juniper tree. The "spirit bird," the symbol of a messenger from the Spirit, can then appear. The "smoke and flames" out of which the bird appears are images of an underworld place of torment. The analogy is that out of the deep darkness of the animal soul structures of emotionality, the "higher" energies of spirituality can emerge, if they are invoked by an act of compassion. And the destructive forces, symbolized by the murderous "stepmother," could also disappear into and remain in that darkness. The hellish place is duplicated in the kitchen, usually a symbol of nourishment, but in this tale a hideous place of malice, deceit, grief and terror. In the animal soul emotionality, those feelings can all be present, generated by a sacral chakra whose feminine force (the "stepmother") has been completely perverted. Finally, the "devil" motif is an indicator of the woman's hellish feelings and actions. Her aggressive behavior, rage and fear, triggered first by what she anxiously believes to be her daughter's future deprivation are the "ground" out of which a "tempter" can emerge. Although the woman "loves," she is essentially loveless and this she expresses. When she allows the devil to guide her actions, she gives it the power to take over her choices. They become evil. She is possessed by the devil and descends figuratively and then literally into the realm of hell. For this she has to pay the ultimate price. She disappears into the underworld. This can happen with soul structures of emotionality that have collapsed into the ruin of psychotic behavior.

Having connected the fairy tale to the Buddhist realm of hell and, by analogy to the animal soul structures of emotionality, let us go into the deeper awareness revealed by the story. Because **form follows consciousness**, a more detailed discussion about the sacral chakra is required for your better understanding.

We begin with the spiritual component of the sacral chakra. In the tale, the boy's "mother," the motif of loving spirituality, has died and lies buried under the juniper tree, in an underworld where she has no apparent power, until there is the addition of the bones of her murdered "son." Meanwhile, the story has centered on the actions of the "stepmother," whose hellish feelings and deeds are all the motifs of immense evil. In the context of the sacral chakra, what has happened is that the instinctual, survival-driven masculine energies of the root chakra have overwhelmed the sacral chakra's feminine force. With that imbalance, (and implied woundedness not only in the chakra but also in the soul substance) all that appears to remain is the chakra's physical component expressing as rage and fear.

In the context of the sacral chakra's generative power, the stepmother is indicating damage to that chakra so immense that the feminine force can be destroyed. Since "devil" energies have traditionally been depicted as masculine, it could be assumed that the instinctual masculine energies in the chakra (the physical component) have become malignant and totally dominant. There is no "dance." The chakra is malfunctioning and its generative power has been badly compromised.

Within the darkest obscurities of animal soul emotionality (as this fairy tale brilliantly illustrates), the burning and tormenting realm of hell can be quite "real." And this tale further indicates how the feminine force and the mental component of the sacral chakra could fare in such circumstances. The mental component, which is the "higher" masculine force indicated by the "father" motif, could be reduced to unwitting subservience to a destructive feminine force dominated by a malignant physical component. That feminine energy would become increasingly capable of destroying the sacral chakra's spiritual component, indicated by the "children" motif in the story. The destruction could happen if there is no nurturing, or too little, in an inner environment, likely reflecting an abusive outer environment. Thus, the malleable, impressionable, receptive and vulnerable soul substance could be mis-shaped, or even fragmented.

In such a situation, the damaged soul structures of emotionality can be expressed by a crippled ego/self that says: "I am so afraid in this unsafe world that I am prepared to destroy whatever I perceive as a threat." As for the person's relationships with others; when there are predominant rage and fear energies, perhaps kept hidden most of the time, there are likely to be huge issues around a lack of trust. They link to the basic masculine physical survival instincts. If these trust issues are not healed, the relationships are not likely to survive.

(Please ponder on these observations and those that you have developed throughout this discussion. Bring them into your own soul structures of emotionality by enlisting the help of the Observer in making a detached discernment rather than a judgment. Take the time that is necessary to do this.)

Then, please recall the instructions that preceded the first tale. Let us go to the second "realm" in our Buddhist model of the soul structures of emotionality.

The Animal Realm

The animal realm, as described in the Buddhist teaching, is an advance over the realm of hell in that the torments are not so unspeakable. Yet the animal realm is also very unhealthy; one in which the person is misled by ignorance and driven by instinctual, biological needs, primarily those of hunger and sexuality; needs that require instant gratification. Because the pleasures of gratification are always fleeting, and the person always returns to a state of unrest and desire, a chronic state of imbalance, there is constant suffering. By analogy, the crystallized soul structures of emotionality are addicted and crippled; a condition that can be lifelong, unless there is a healing intervention.

In fairy tales, the instinctual biological drives are usually indicated by predatory animals and by men. In modern versions, the latter are often presented as "princes" or other unmarried males looking for "wives." By contrast, the older, unrevised versions presented the instinctual ingredient more explicitly.[288] The biological drives of hunger and sexuality in the following fairy tale are equally shared by a derelict soldier and a conniving witch.

The Grimms' tale is entitled "The Blue Light."[289] It is tempting to imagine that this story was told around small fires in long-ago army encampments . . .

---

[288] For example, "Sleeping Beauty" was raped by her prince charming and later gave birth, while still asleep. See Sheldon Cashdan, *The Witch Must Die*, p.6.

[289] Excerpted from Joseph Grimm and Wilhelm Grimm, *Grimm's Fairy Tales*, pp 210-214.

There was once a soldier, who had fought valiantly for the king in many battles. Yet, when the wars were over, the soldier had been turned out of the army without pay. As he headed homeward, starved and penniless, with only his pipe for comfort, he wandered into a deep wood. Walking wearily onward, he found himself at the house of a witch. He begged her for food and a place to sleep. He could have this, she said, if he dug up her garden. The next day he set to work, and after digging all day, finished the task. Again, he begged for food and shelter. Again, she gave it to him, but only if he would chop all her wood. Again, the soldier set to work, and after an entire day, completed the task. For the third time, he begged for food and shelter.

This time the witch complied, but only if he would go down into a nearby well and retrieve a blue light that was burning at the bottom. He agreed. The next morning, she tied a rope around his waist and lowered him into the well. There he found the burning blue light. He signaled to the witch, who pulled him up to the edge of the well and sweetly suggested that he give her the light. He saw through her trick and refused. In a rage, she pushed him into the well and let go of the rope. He found himself back at the bottom with the blue light. There in the mud he lay in despair. Then he remembered that his half-filled pipe was in his pocket and he decided to have a last smoke before he died. Then, he lit the pipe with the blue light.

In the first puff of smoke, there suddenly appeared a little black dwarf, who said: "Master, what do you command?" The astounded soldier was unable to reply, until the dwarf assured him that he was the master of the blue light and could have whatever he wanted. At this, the soldier asked to be rescued from the well. Immediately, he found himself safely on the grass. Still holding the blue light, the soldier then requested that the witch be put into the well. This was done. Afterwards, he and the dwarf ransacked the witch's house and collected all her gold. When this was accomplished, the dwarf took his leave after assuring the soldier that any time he lit his pipe with the blue light that he would respond. Much pleased with this turn of events, the soldier filled his knapsack and pockets with the gold and hurried off to town. He bought new, splendid clothes, moved into the best lodgings and ate sumptuously. With all this accomplished, he lit his pipe with the blue flame. Immediately, the black dwarf was there. "Master, what do you command?"

"When I fought for the king, I served him faithfully," said the soldier. "He rewarded me by turning me out without pay so that I could starve. Now I shall have my revenge. In the night, fetch me the king's daughter, so that she may wait upon me and do what I bid her." It was done exactly as the soldier requested. The dwarf took the sleeping princess out of her bed and carried her to the soldier, who had his way with her. The next morning, the dwarf carried her back to her bed.

At breakfast, the princess told her father, the king, about a strange "dream" she had had. Her worried father asked her to cut a hole in one of her pockets, and fill it with peas before she went to bed. If, indeed, she had been carried away, she could leave a trail. This might have succeeded except that the dwarf had been listening. After carrying the princess to the soldier on the second night, the dwarf spread peas throughout the streets and the trail was lost. Again, the princess did the soldier's bidding and was carried home in the morning. After she had again recounted her "dream" to her father, he told her to wear one of her shoes to bed and to leave it behind when she was carried away in the morning. Again the dwarf overheard the king and warned the soldier. But the soldier "would have his own way." Once again the princess was carried to the soldier. In the morning, she left her shoe behind. Then the king ordered that the town be searched. The shoe was found in the soldier's lodgings. But, forewarned by the dwarf to leave the city, the soldier had already run away. He had, however, waited too long. What was even more unlucky for him was that he had left behind his pipe, most of the gold, except one coin, and the blue light. He was soon apprehended and thrown into prison.

As he stood looking sorrowfully out through the grating, the soldier spotted one of his old army companions. "If you will go to the inn and pick up a bundle that I have there, I will give you a gold coin," the soldier promised his comrade. This was a task willingly undertaken and soon the gold and the blue light were in the soldier's hands. The trial soon was held. "The matter was sifted to the bottom; the prisoner was found guilty and his doom passed: he was ordered to be hung forthwith on the gallows-tree." As he walked to his execution, the soldier asked that he be allowed to smoke his pipe. The king granted his request. When the black dwarf appeared, the soldier ordered him to scatter the crowd and to cut the king into pieces. While the dwarf carried out the soldier's wishes, the king begged for mercy. To save his life, he agreed to let the soldier have the princess for his wife and to leave the kingdom to him when he died. That is the end of the story.

Again, please experience this fairy tale as often as is required to fathom its layers of meaning. Then return to this dimension for the discussion.

Although it is beyond the scope of this lesson to provide a complete interpretation of this very complex story, the archetypal motifs indicating the instinctual biological drives (hunger and sexuality) of the animal realm of Samsara are many and interesting. Driven by starvation, and comforted by his "pipe," a phallic symbol, a penniless, unemployed "soldier," a motif for a derelict man, enters a deep "wood," a common image for the instinctual "physiological processes of the body."[290] There, the soldier gets involved with a resident "witch," the motif of a wicked woman, often skilled in the arts of black magic. He begs for "food," a symbol of biological hunger. In exchange, he agrees to "dig up her garden and chop her wood." In some parts of the world, even today, those phrases indicate that the soldier is agreeing to have sexual intercourse with the witch. After each day's work, he begs for more food and shelter, which she gives to him for her own reasons. In all these images there are indications of the animal soul structures of emotionality expressing as biological hungers. There are more that will be presented later in the discussion. Because **form follows consciousness**, but we shall now deal with the first segment of the tale in relation to the sacral chakra.

That chakra's feminine force, imaged by the "witch" is embedded within "physiological processes," expressed as instinctual biological needs. How this came about is not indicated by the story. When the story begins, the feminine force of the chakra is already corrupt. In other words, the sacral chakra's feminine force is malfunctioning in its "dance" with the masculine energies symbolized by the hungry soldier and expressing the chakra's physical component. That corruption can be generated in animal soul structures of emotionality and express as lust and, by analogy, the animal realm of Samsara. This the story reveals. The tale might have ended there, with the soldier joining forces with the witch to waylay unwary travelers in the deep wood and to service each other.

But, let us return to the tale and its revelations about the sacral chakra. Somehow, the witch has become aware of a blue light at the bottom of a well. It is this light, the symbol of great spiritual power that she really wants.[291] In a sacral chakra there is a spiritual component that might be deeply buried and the feminine energies might be desirous of connection with it. (In the story there is no indication of **why** the witch wanted the blue light. But the implications are that she would use the spiritual power to augment her evil. In a sacral chakra, is that possible? Yes, it is. It is a mis-use of spirituality and happens frequently.) In the soul structures of emotionality that are generated there is somehow an awareness in their darkest obscurities (the "well") that there is a spiritual power (the "blue light") to be sought after. In the tale, the witch reveals her true purpose; that the soldier go down into a well to retrieve the blue light for her sole use. Why does she not go herself? In the context of the **holistic** human energy system, the "lower" feminine energies alone (even when they are healthy) are not strong enough to go into the depths. Those feminine energies must be interactive with both the "lower" masculine energies (the root chakra) and the "higher" masculine energies of the solar plexus chakra, in order that the light of spiritual awareness can be gained. (In this imagery, there is revealed the crucial need for balance in the "dance" of energies. There is also revealed the paradox of the physicality/spirituality of people.) In the absence of that healthy, balanced interaction, there is little likelihood that the spiritual treasure can be obtained. In the tale, this is what happens.

---

[290] Marie-Louise Von Franz, *Archetypal Patterns in Fairy Tales*, p. 64.
[291] It is the power of the throat chakra, which can create, through the vibrations of sound. Although this ns not the "highest" spiritual power, it is a very important one, as the tale soon reveals.

The soldier, connected to the witch by a "rope," (another phallic symbol), goes into the well and retrieves the blue light. But she, being wicked, wants to kill him and keep the blue light for herself. And he, being instinctual and unaware of the power of the blue light he is carrying, tries to protect himself. Apparently, the evil overcomes the instinct and the witch pushes him back into the well. And by doing this, she loses the blue light. This condition can be present in soul structures of emotionality because a malfunctioning sacral chakra, whose crucially important feminine energies are in-formed by a predatory lovelessness, will not "dance" with the masculine and actually rejects the means to achieve the "higher" spiritual power. In other words, the spiritual component of the sacral chakra is disallowed and the resultant soul structures of emotionality can express only hatefulness. In other words, the soul structures of emotionality, totally focused on the instant gratification of biological needs and drives, are functioning in the animal realm of Samsara.

Meanwhile, the soldier at the bottom of the well comforts himself before death by lighting his pipe with the blue light. In the context of the sacral chakra, when there is profound emotional trauma, the instinctual masculine energies of the physical component in the chakra, ignorant of the spiritual power readily at hand in the kundalini life force, can accidentally trigger it. In the story, a "black dwarf" appears. This is a complex archetypal motif: the "dwarf" symbolizes the power of a servant of the spirit and the "black" reveals the paradox that this power actually is: the creative energy of the Spirit (the One Consciousness, Creative Energy) will allow what is both "good" and "bad;" whatever a person desires and uses spiritual power to create.[292] In this tale, the black dwarf displays evident enjoyment in doing "bad" things; both those ordered by the soldier and those the dwarf conceives on his own. Regarding the latter activities: it is interesting to note that the dwarf is analogous to the energies of emotionality that are an "entity;" those dark feelings apparently beyond a person's control. So, the power of the blue light is used by the soldier to get out of the well and to put the witch into it. Then, with the help of the dwarf, the soldier steals her gold, the symbol of hidden treasure, and with it, ensures his comfort in the town.

Keeping in mind that **form follows consciousness**, please note that this part of the tale suggests that an instinctual (root chakra) masculine energy has completely negated the corrupted feminine force of the sacral chakra. Such is the state of imbalance that there seems to be nothing left of the crucially important feminine energy of the sacral chakra, with resultant incalculable damage in the soul structures of emotionality. Yet, the symbol of the gold, which hints at the possibility of a "higher" purpose and the motif of the "town" which indicates a more civilized environment, both suggest the potential for a more evolved emotionality.

But at first things get worse. The soldier, helped by the black dwarf, misuses the power of the blue light to wreak his revenge on the "king" by kidnapping and abusing his daughter, the "princess." This sexual and other abuse indicates soul structures of emotionality expressing the animal realm of the Wheel of Samsara. In the context of an out-of-balance sacral chakra, the instinctual masculine energies (the soldier) are mis-using spiritual power (the blue light)

---

[292] Carl Jung, *Four Archetypes*, p.117, discusses the "essentially antithetical nature of the spirit archetype."

and dark creative energy (the dwarf) to war against the "higher" masculine spiritual power (the "king/father") by abusing the "higher" feminine spiritual energy (the "princess") that could comprise the sacral chakra's spiritual component. The king has to intervene and does so by alerting his daughter, who tries to obey but is thwarted by the black dwarf. This is the sort of struggle that can go on in animal soul structures of emotionality between an intervening "higher" spiritual power and the resistant energies (the "entity") of a crippled emotionality. In other words, there is the archetypal conflict between the powers of "light" and of "darkness." In the end the struggle is won by the "higher" spiritual power; but not without some dramatic moments. In the story, there is a last attempt by the condemned soldier to continue his activity by using the dark energy of the dwarf, to overwhelm everybody, including the king. Because **form follows consciousness**, when the sacral chakra has become completely unbalanced by the absence of its feminine energies, the resultant soul structures of emotionality, lost in the animal realm of Samsara, can run amuck. But the king, by appealing for his life and giving the soldier the princess and the "kingdom" (the motif of great spiritual attainment), offers an alternative. Although the soldier could have gone on and, by mis-using the power of the blue light, perhaps destroyed the king and everything else, he chooses not to do so. Why is this? Possibly, two things have happened with the soldier. First, he realizes that he really is not in control of the dwarf and could be its next victim. Second, the soldier, who has had his revenge, chooses to accept the bounty that he is being offered, as being a safer alternative. By analogy, there are crucial moments when a person recognizes great spiritual danger and pulls away from it. This is the beginning of a change in consciousness. In this context, the indwelling Spirit can "call" and be heeded. Thus, the instinctual masculine energies of the sacral chakra can undergo change by connecting to the "higher" feminine spiritual energies and by doing so, both allow and evolve into a "higher" level of masculinity. This generative "work" is made possible by a sacral chakra that has slowly undergone a healing process and is starting to achieve a balancing of its masculine and feminine energies. Thus, there can come about the transformation of the soul structures of emotionality. By analogy, the person is ready to leave the animal realm of Samsara.

In the context of the "dancing" relationship between those masculine and feminine energies and the implications for the development of the ego/self, the soul structures of emotionality can carry and express bestial impulses. In this situation, both the masculine and the feminine energies can be depraved: instead of "dancing," they seek to destroy each other. In terms of the ongoing development of the soul structures generated by the **holistic** human energy system, there is a dysfunctional orientation towards instinctual physicality. This can happen in early childhood, in circumstances of extreme impoverishment, sexual abuse and the constant threat of death (either real or imagined). In those conditions, there is a shaping of the malleable, impressionable, receptive and vulnerable soul substance into soul structures of emotionality that are crippled. In them the instinctual root chakra masculine energies will predominate and the feminine "feelings" energies of the sacral chakra will be those of a threatened animal. The child that survives could have functioning soul structures of physicality, but the emotional, mental and spiritual soul structures would be badly damaged. The "i-am" consciousness of such a person could be expressed as: "I am so hungry for what I need to survive that I will kill you, if necessary, to get it." It is not much different, in this respect, from the realm of hell, but there is a possibility of redemption, as indicated by the story.

In the context of relationships to others, this person might be very charming and attractive to other people, and make full use of those attributes. But the inherent lovelessness and isolation of a true predator will eventually repel those who might, initially, have been attracted. The person living in the animal realm of Samsara is, primarily, a lone wolf "red in tooth and claw" who will remain so, unless the crippled soul structures of emotionality, whose generative sacral chakra has lost its feminine force, are in-formed by healing mental and spiritual energies.

(Please take the time to ponder on these observations and be aware of your emotional responses. Consider the "world" around and within you in terms of the animal realm of Samsara.)

Then, after reviewing the instructions that preceded your venture into the first realm, please proceed to the third "realm" of Samsara, as indicated in this Buddhist model.

The Realm of Hungry Ghosts

After struggling free of the animal realm with its instinctual biological torments, the person moves into a realm that is somewhat more advanced in that there are more than simply biological "hungers." This realm of the hungry ghosts is one in which the person is "empty" and longs for whatever can fill that void. In the teachings, the realm is occupied by "phantomlike creatures with withered limbs, grossly bloated bellies and long, thin necks,"[293] beings who "starve" because they are "hungry ghosts" who cannot ingest what they have craved and acquired. Thus, the person caught in this realm continually demands impossible satisfactions and fleeting gratifications. The deprivation results in constant suffering. Unless there is a healing intervention, those animal soul structures of emotionality and, by analogy, the "hungry ghosts," could continue throughout life.

In fairy tales, the archetypal motif of endless unsatisfied "hunger" is often an animal, for example, a wolf (or, in African tales, a crocodile). But, the archetypal motif of a hungry human being can be a person of either sex, adult or child. The greed is usually indicated by gluttony, but can also be revealed by a rapacious desire for power, possessions and wealth.

In the Grimm Brothers' tale that portrays the realm of hungry ghosts, a woman's insatiable hunger for the power and the authority usually carried by men brings about her downfall. The story is "The Fisherman and His Wife."[294]

Please take in this tale . . .

---

[293] Mark Epstein, *Thoughts Without a Thinker*, p. 28.
[294] Excerpted from Jacob Grimm and Wilhelm Grimm, *Grimm's Fairy Tales*, pp. 37-44.

There was once a poor fisherman who lived with his wife in a ditch close by the sea. Every day he sat and fished with his line out into the waters. One day, his line plunged deeply towards the sea bottom and after much struggle he landed a huge fish. But this fish, who was really an "enchanted prince," asked to be set free. This the man willingly did and the fish swam away.

That evening, when the fisherman told his wife about the incident, she scolded him for not having asked the fish for a favor in return for his freedom. She wanted a cottage to replace the ditch they were living in. Unwillingly, the man went back to the water's edge and called to the fish:

> O man of the sea!
> Come listen to me,
> For Alice my wife,
> The plague of my life.
> Hath sent me to ask a boon of thee!

Immediately, the fish responded. When the fisherman presented his wife's request, the fish replied that she was already in their cottage. The fisherman hurried home, where his wife met him at the door. It was a splendid little house. She was thrilled with all its amenities. For a week or two, things went well.

Then she became increasingly dissatisfied over what she now perceived were the inadequacies of their dwelling. She insisted that her husband ask the fish for a castle. He was reluctant to do this and begged her to be satisfied with what they had. But she would not relent. He unwillingly went to the sea. It looked "blue and gloomy." With heavy heart he called to the fish:

> O man of the sea!
> Come listen to me,
> For Alice my wife.
> The plague of my life,
> Hath sent me to beg a boon of thee!

It promptly appeared. When the request for a castle was presented, it was immediately granted. The fisherman hurried back home. He met his wife at the door of their enormous castle. It was grandly furnished, filled with servants, and complete with an animal park. The fisherman was certain that this would keep them contented for the rest of their lives.

But the very next morning his wife jostled him awake and demanded that he tell the fish that she would be the "king of the land." After a futile discussion, the man went away sorrowfully. "The sea looked a dark gray color and was covered with foam." The fisherman cried out:

> O man of the sea!
> Come listen to me,
> For Alice my wife,
> The plague of my life,
> Hath sent me to beg a boon of thee!

There was again an immediate response from the fish, who wanted to know what she wanted this time. When the request was delivered, it was instantly granted. Then home the fisherman hurried, to find himself at a palace surrounded by troops and his wife sitting on a "high throne of gold." When he timidly suggested that being king should be enough, she was quick to reply that she was already getting tired of it and thought she would be emperor. She also reminded him that he was her "slave" and that he would do her bidding without complaint. This time, when he got to the sea, "the water was quite black and muddy and a mighty whirlwind blew over it." Again he called the fish:

> O man of the sea!
> Come listen to me,
> For Alice my wife,
> The plague of my life,
> Hath sent me to beg a boon of thee!

Again, the fish fulfilled her request. This time, when the fisherman arrived at home, he found his wife, the emperor, sitting on a "lofty throne made of solid gold" and wearing "a crown full two yards high." Yet, she was already voicing her next demand. This time she could see no reason why she could not be pope. When her husband returned to the sea, "the wind was raging and the sea was tossed up and down like boiling water." Although he was very frightened, he called out to the fish:

> O man of the sea!
> Come listen to me,
> For Alice my wife,
> The plague of my life,
> Hath sent me to beg a boon of thee!

"What does she want now?" said the fish. "Ah!" said the fisherman, "my wife wants to be pope." "Go home," said the fish, "she is pope already." And she was. There she sat with "three great crowns" on her head. Quite

overwhelmed, the fisherman suggested that she would now be satisfied, for she could be nothing greater. Her reply was that she would "consider" it. But she did not sleep all that night for "thinking what she should be next."

The next morning while she watched the rising sun, she knew. Brusquely, she wakened her husband and presented her request. She would be "lord of the sun and moon." Trembling with fear, he went to the sea. Such a storm arose that the trees and rocks shook, the lightning flashed, the thunder crashed and the sea rolled "with great black waves like mountains." Again the fisherman called the fish:

> **O man of the sea!**
> **Come listen to me,**
> **For Alice my wife,**
> **The plague of my life,**
> **Hath sent me to beg a boon of thee!**

"What does she want now," said the fish. "Ah!" said he, "she wants to be lord of the sun and moon." "Go home to your ditch:" replied the fish. That is the end of the tale.

Please experience this story as often as is necessary for you to appreciate its many levels of meaning. Then return to this dimension for the discussion.

Although not apparent at first, in this tale the archetypal motifs indicating the soul structures of emotionality analogous to the realm of hungry ghosts are plentiful. We start with the "ditch" motif in which dwell the "fisherman" and his "wife." It is a place where dirty "water" flows. In the context of the hungry ghost realm, the ditch is a dwelling place containing no nurturance and the people who live in it are symbols of a state of extreme deprivation. In the tale, the "fisherman," a masculine motif of productive work, can go out seeking food, but in this condition of deprivation he is not very successful and when he does land a "fish," it is not edible. Then, there is the complex imagery of "water:" first, there is the dirty ditch water and the "wife" who is forced to remain in it. Both are indicative of highly toxic feminine energies, in this case the feminine force of the sacral chakra; second, there are the deep waters; the "sea" into which the fisherman diligently casts his line. In this "water" imagery there is, first, the symbol of the watery depths out of which created things emerge at the behest of the Spirit; second, the deep waters represent the submerged, dark dimensions of the soul structures of emotionality, out of time and space. The "fisherman," analogous to the "higher" masculine energies of the sacral chakra's mental component is seeking to connect with something in the depths. Meanwhile, he has not interacted well with his wife, motif of toxic feminine energies, whom he describes as a "plague." In other words, the archetypal masculine and feminine energies are not "dancing." When the "fisherman" is fishing in the "sea," he pulls out a "fish." Although this fairy tale indicates that the fish is really an enchanted prince, there are other versions of the story that do not mention this. Indeed, fish have been traditionally associated with divine female sexuality and goddess feminine power.[295] Thus, the fairy tale reveals that at a level of consciousness "higher" than the instinctual root chakra, the masculine energies of the sacral chakra can seek profound connection with the divine feminine (the chakra's spiritual component) and that this can happen. But it cannot happen in an out-of-balance, toxic sacral chakra and, by extension, in soul structures of emotionality analogous to the realm of hungry ghosts. This the story graphically illustrates. In the tale, the wife who surely is a hungry ghost seeks to consume what she cannot possibly digest. This kind of "hunger" is indicative of damaged soul structures of emotionality. In the context of the sacral center of consciousness, toxic feminine energies created by deprivation, can seek to mis-use the "higher" spiritual feminine energies to take over the power of all the **masculine** energies. In the story, although this ambition is completely "unnatural," it is successful at first, i.e., the hungry ghost seems to assuage her hunger. But in reality she cannot and she is driven to seek more gratification. Meanwhile, there is trouble brewing, symbolized by the stormy skies and seas that indicate the unnatural state of affairs that cannot continue. There is too much imbalance. In the end, the fisherman's wife abruptly returns to her original state of deprivation. All this could happen in the confines of a sacral chakra. Without the healing power of a balanced relationship with the masculine and without a functioning spiritual component that provides a clear inner **knowing** of how to develop properly, the feminine energies could become toxic and destructive. Without the proper development required by a human energy system, (there is a "problem" with the archetypal imperative, involving an unhealthy outer environment and the perceptual filtering system). This could happen, with the resultant damage to the soul structures of emotionality.

In the context of the "dancing" relationship between the masculine and feminine energies of the **holistic** energy system and the development of the ego/self, masculine energies even of the sacral chakra's mental component, can be "enslaved" by a toxic feminine force. If this happens in early childhood, perhaps in a situation in which the predominant energies are those of people focused on getting and keeping the things that spell survival, safety and security, the malleable, impressionable, receptive and vulnerable soul substance of the child could be shaped into soul structures of emotionality that are basically greedy. Here, indeed, is the realm of hungry ghosts! In other words, in the sacral chakra the prime directive and "i-am" consciousness of the root chakra in the physical component would be dominant. Without the balance of archetypal masculine and feminine energies, the "i-am" consciousness being expressed by the emerging egoic structures could be: "I am so hungry to acquire the things that will alleviate my basic fears that I will insatiably strive to possess and consume as much of the world's goods as I can get."

In terms of relationships with others, the acquisitive ego/self that develops cannot partake of loving interactions, except as "lunch." Usually the relationships are intense and short. There

---

[295] Barbara Walker, *The Woman's Dictionary of Symbols & Sacred Objects*, p. 374.

could even appear to be promiscuity, as partners are acquired and quickly discarded. There is, in reality, an energy consumption going on until either the depleted partner or the "hungry" one leaves.[296] The pattern can be life long, unless a dramatic change occurs.

(Please ponder on these observations and on any you have made. Again, be especially alert to those that have had an emotional impact on you. Take your time and with the help of the Observer, make detached discernments about your own soul structures of emotionality . . .)

It is tempting to add a sequel to this fairy tale . . . . Let us imagine that after the fisherman's wife finds herself back in the ditch, she realizes that she has to make some different choices. (While in the hungry ghost realm, a lot of people have done that, after disaster has befallen them and they finally allow the indwelling Spirit to be heard.) In the imagined sequel, the first choice made by the repentant woman would be to seek spiritual nourishment. With help from the spirit world, perhaps a "godmother" motif, she could get out of the ditch and detoxify herself. Then she could establish a different relationship with her "husband" and, thereby, create a new partnering with him. In other words, with the power of "higher" feminine energies, she would be generating a new "dance," a new interaction of the feminine and masculine forces. Thus, the sacral chakra would be restored to balanced wholeness and the resultant soul structures of emotionality would be healthy. In the context of these lessons, the fisherman's wife would be taking her first steps on a new and more evolved path of "Coming into Being." (You might want to add further details, based on your awareness of how the root and sacral consciousness energies interact and of the crucial importance of the spiritual component in both chakras.)

Again, please review the instructions given before you experienced the first realm. Then, let us move on to the fourth "realm" indicated in this Buddhist model of animal soul structures of emotionality.

The Realm of the Jealous Gods

After being delivered from the realm of hungry ghosts, with its insatiable cravings, the person can enter into the first of the "heaven" realms. It is the realm of the jealous gods. The Buddhist teachings tell us that in this realm there is a "wishing tree" over whose "fruits" the gods are aggressively competing. Within people, this imagery is experienced as an intense inner conflict. It involves having to choose between what is mistakenly perceived as the "good" things of life, all of them seeming pleasures that are coveted. At the same time the person, through ignorance, is unable to discern the real "goodness."[297] Striving without inner peace and continually disappointed, the person is immersed in suffering. This condition, indicating crippled soul structures of emotionality can last throughout a lifetime, if there is no healing.

---

[296] In some "hungry ghost" marriages that have apparently lasted, the depleted partner has likely long departed in all but the physical body, while the hungry one stays out of dependency.

[297] For more detail, see Mark Epstein, *Thoughts Without a Thinker*, pp. 34-36.

In fairy tales the archetypal motif of a person who is relentlessly competitive and unable to make healthy choices is usually a young prince who wants to inherit his father's kingdom by outdoing his brother, the rightful heir. But an equivalent **female** motif is not available in the Grimms' tales.[298] There might be one exception and in it the motif is there only by inference.

Since the history of fairy tales is marked by additions, revisions and other changes, including the merging of one tale into another,[299] the tale to be presented next has been changed in keeping with that history, so that the implied female motif can be made explicit.

The story, from the Brothers Grimm, is entitled "King Thrushbeard."[300] It is a tale about a princess whose childhood deprivation caused her to lack an adult's discriminating awareness. This created in her a destructive misperception of the "good," until she received an uncomfortable, but necessary, lesson. Here is the story.

In a long ago time and place, there dwelt a king, whose beloved daughter and only child was lovely to behold. Since it was time for her to marry, he called for only the highest ranking suitors to appear. There came dukes, counts and other nobility. But the princess only pretended to be interested in them. She accepted the necessity of marriage, she said, but then used her quick wit and sharp tongue to cause her suitors exceeding embarrassment. Invariably, they withdrew their offers and left, with the rude and cutting comments of the princess ringing in their ears.

The king, her father, was much troubled by this behavior, but he had a great love for his daughter and did not reprimand her, at least not at first.

Next is an addition from the imaginal realm . . .

{The king also recognized that he was partly responsible for his daughter's unseemly actions. When his dear wife had died while birthing the princess, he had mourned long and bitterly. His wife had been the one true love who had filled his heart. After the grief had somewhat subsided, his advisors had urged him to take another wife, who would produce a male heir. With reluctance, the king agreed and the call went out summoning all the fair maidens of the land. One by one they appeared and one by one they were graciously dismissed. The years flowed by.

---

[298] Please note that the wicked stepmother who is jealous of her younger and more beautiful and innocent stepdaughter and who conspires against her is more suited to the realm of hell than the realm of the jealous gods, where there is open and fierce competition.

[299] For more detail, see Jack Zipes, *The Complete Fairy Tales of the Brothers Grimm*, pp.xxiii-xxxvi. In the tale presented in this lesson, the indicated change is the inclusion of an imagined "childhood history" of the princess.

[300] Excerpted from *Ibid*, pp. 177-180. In the earlier publication, the title is "King Grisly-Beard."

In the meantime, the motherless princess had been wet-nursed by a local peasant woman who loved her dearly. After the weaning, the wet nurse stayed as the princess's maid. She often brought her own two boys to the castle to play with the lonely little girl. Meanwhile, no one seemed concerned about the situation. The child was ignored by the people of the castle, who gave her anything she demanded and quickly disappeared. The princess and the peasant boys were happy children together; with the princess fully participating in the rough and tumble play in the castle garden. Her father, preoccupied with ruling his kingdom, saw his daughter only occasionally and always enjoyed her quickness of mind. Because she loved her father dearly, the princess actively cultivated her words and wit. Eventually the boys, her companions, were granted the opportunity to become knights' squires and she, not to be outdone but aware of her higher social rank, decided that she would be a knight. After that, the three children spent many happy hours prancing around on their hobby-horses and jousting with their stick lances. How the princess loved it, especially when she could compete in mock tournaments and knock the boys off their "horses"!

This state of affairs continued, until the king's mother paid a visit to inquire after her son and granddaughter. What the old woman discovered so shocked her that the whole court was thrown into turmoil. The princess's maid and her children were sent away. With the king's consent, his daughter was placed into the watchful care of a governess of impeccable social position and a lady-in-waiting, whose tasks were to teach the girl proper decorum and other matters suitable to her station. The hoyden princess was above all to be taught that she was the daughter of a king and destined to be the wife of nobility and the mother of noble sons. Well satisfied with her work, the king's mother returned home, but not until after she had admonished her son for his neglect of his daughter and after she had left detailed instructions about the training of the child. They were carried out to the letter. What emerged after a few years was an apparently pliant princess.}

Now, let us return to the tale as recounted by the Brothers Grimm. The princess has been rudely interacting with her would-be suitors.

After all the suitors had departed, there came more. This time the witty remarks of the princess increased. The sharp tongue became sharper. One suitor was too fat. She called him a "wine barrel." One was too thin. She called him a "pin." One was too pale. She compared him to "death." Her wit was irresistibly funny, except to her disgruntled suitors. Finally there was only one left. He was a king and he had a crooked chin that looked, she said, like a bird's beak. Labeling him "King Thrushbeard," the princess sent him on his way. But after these unseemly actions, especially an insult to a king, her father's patience was at an end.

"Daughter," he said, "you will marry the first beggar who comes through that door." Two days later, there appeared a wandering musician, penniless and dirty. Despite the princess's horrified objections, she was compelled to wed him. Having now become a "beggar woman," she had to leave her castle home and travel, on foot, with her husband.

As they walked along, they came to a large forest. 'Tell me," she said, "who might the owner of this forest be?" The reply from her husband was: "King Thrushbeard owns this forest." As they journeyed further, they came to a vast meadow. "Tell me," she said, "who owns this meadow?" The answer again was, "King Thrushbeard." They came to a large city and she asked once more: "who owns this city?" And again the answer was, "King Thrushbeard." Then the princess began to regret that she had rejected this suitor.

They eventually arrived at a tiny cottage, which her husband Informed her was their home. When she inquired after the whereabouts of the servant, this daughter of a king was told that there were none. She would have to do the housework, including the cooking. She did not know how. Finally the musician had to help her, if he wanted anything to eat. The princess felt utterly miserable and wept bitterly.

Within a few days, their provisions were gone. Then husband told the princess that they would both have to work to keep from starving. She would weave baskets. This she tried to do, but the rough willows bruised her tender hands. Then he tried to teach her how to spin. But the hard thread soon cut her soft fingers and the blood began to flow. After that, he decided that they would set up a business with pots and earthenware in the market. At this, the princess was terrified that someone would recognize and scorn her. But there was no recourse and into the market she went. People gladly bought her wares because she was so beautiful. She and her husband were able to live off the proceeds for a little while. Then he bought a new supply of earthenware and she set up a stall at the corner of the market. Suddenly, a drunken hussar rode his horse over all the pots and smashed them to pieces. Although she was terrified of what her husband's reaction would be, she had no choice but to run home to tell him. All he did was find her work as a kitchen maid in the king's castle. The princess had reached the depths of humiliation. Every day she took home the table scraps so that she and her husband could eat. Every time the elegant guests came to the castle, she would go up from the lower regions to the door of the large reception hall and look inside.

Then one day, while she stood outside the door, the king's son saw her. He took her hand and asked her to dance with him. She was horrified because she recognized him as the King Thrushbeard she had so rudely dismissed. She tried to run away, but he held her fast. Then he said: "Don't be afraid. I am the musician who married you. I disguised myself out of love for you. I am the hussar who rode over your pots. I did this to teach you a lesson." Then she shed bitter tears and asked his forgiveness for her unseemly actions. His reply was gentle: "The bad days are over and now we can celebrate our wedding." An invitation was sent to her father, (who had actually helped King Thrushbeard in this venture) and to all his court. Everyone came. And what a celebration it was! That is the end of the story.

Please take the time to experience and ponder on the many levels of meaning in this fairy tale. Then return to this dimension for the discussion.

Again, we will deal with the archetypal motifs that indicate the relentless competition and lack of discriminating awareness of the realm of the jealous gods, and by analogy, damaged animal soul structures of emotionality. Because this tale is so complex, the discussion about the generative (and malfunctioning) sacral chakra that, again, reveals that **form follows consciousness** is closely interwoven into the interpretation.

The motifs that could indicate the state of consciousness of the realm of jealous gods appear almost immediately. Here is a motherless "princess," a double-motif that indicates the absence of a strong female presence along with an innocent and usually docile maiden. This girl is not, however, indicating those qualities. Her outrageously competitive behavior toward her noble suitors, the motif of "civilized" prospective mates, is horrifying to her "king/father" the motif of an absolute ruler, who expects obedience and loyalty. In the context of the sacral chakra, the story reveals that the essential feminine force is absent. And the "higher" feminine spiritual component of the chakra (the "princess") expresses as an overwhelming and primitive masculinity. In other words, there is a malfunctioning sacral chakra, dominated by the root chakra's masculine energies and inappropriately using the "higher" masculine energies (the "wit" and the "words" motifs) of the solar plexus and throat chakras to flout the authority of the "highest" masculine spiritual power (the "king/father"). The sacral chakra's unbalanced condition is further complicated by the fact that the feminine energies (the "princess") are not only a spiritual component but are also a potential feminine force. All of this malfunction could result in soul structures of emotionality analogous to the realm of the jealous gods. To explain this bizarre situation; there is the story of a legacy of childhood deprivation; an absence of the nurturing proper to a princess. The loss of her "queen/mother," (the motif of proper nurturing) and the failure to provide an adequate substitute has left the princess deprived from birth. In the context of the sacral chakra, all the feminine energies are so damaged that they are unable to "dance" with the masculine. This can happen when there is an inner and outer environment that loses and/or neglects the archetypal feminine. But, as the tale reveals, the king/father requires that the princess be a mature woman ready to fulfill her function. In other words, the archetypal intent of the sacral chakra has to be realized. The situation is intolerable for everyone concerned. Meanwhile, the princess is probably unable to understand her own reactions. They are quite understandable, however, in the framework of an out-of-balance sacral chakra and damaged soul structures of emotionality analogous to the realm of the jealous gods.

Having been loved primarily by a "peasant woman," the motif of earthy female energies that are biologically nourishing to an infant, the princess had started off life well. Indeed, in the context of the **holistic** human energy system, the love that had been lavished on her and her childhood boy companions had been vital in shaping both the feminine sacral chakra energies and the masculine (root chakra) energies, indicated in the physical component of the sacral chakra. But the "peasant" motif is also one of ignorance, not of the energies of Earth but of the **information** necessary for functioning at a higher level. Instead of developing as she would have, had her mother lived, the princess had been untaught, neglected and allowed to compete vigorously in male activities with "boys," the motif of immature but powerful masculine energies. She had also developed a scathing wit and verbal abilities, both symbolizing highly developed intellectual skills that were also masculine energies. In short, the princess had taken on the attributes of a rustic "prince." These were reinforced by always having her demands obeyed by the servants. All this had taken place in a "garden," the symbol of childlike innocence and in a "castle," the symbol of a strong, masculine shelter. Meanwhile, the spiritual energies imaged by the "king/father" motif were predominantly distant. In the context of a sacral chakra, this is a situation of severe imbalance, with only the very primitive feminine energies in evidence. With no (or very few) loving feminine energies in her outer environment, the princess could become a relentless, aggressive competitor who perceived as a "good" thing, the exercise of dominance and control. They were very pleasurable. By analogy, the soul structures of emotionality lost in the realm of the jealous gods, could exhibit those behaviors. The visit from the "queen/grandmother," a motif of a more suitable nurturing, and in the context of the sacral chakra, an indication of the "highest" feminine spiritual energies, was a necessary intervention in the life of the princess. But the childhood damage was not rectified, because the old woman did not stay. There can be a very limited spiritual component in the sacral chakra and this is expressed by the soul structures of emotionality. This can happen when the sacral chakra feminine force, that is essentially receptive, is unable to receive. In the tale, despite (or probably because of) several years of loveless "re-programming," the princess was in a state of inner conflict about who she was and what choices she could make. Here is the realm of the jealous gods. But in her situation, she was expected to assume the role of a woman who would partner with her noble husband and produce new life that would ensure the continuation of the nobility; the "good" she really required. Apparently aware of her duty, the princess nevertheless had used her masculine skills to compete with her suitors and to avoid the situation that she could not accept for herself. In the context of a malfunctioning sacral chakra expressing overwhelming masculine energies, this center of consciousness can be torn so badly that the feminine energy sinks deeper and deeper into the darkest obscurities. In this situation, the sacral chakra is powerless to generate healthy soul structures of emotionality without help. That help can come only in the form of spiritual intervention. It is the only vibration strong enough to heal a badly out-of-balance sacral chakra and to promote the healing of animal soul structures of emotionality.[301] In the story, the "king/father" and "King Thrushbeard" both motifs of absolute authority over the "princess," provide a necessary lesson. In the context of a powerless sacral chakra, they constitute the archetypal energies of an intervening spiritual power.

In many fairy tales, divine help comes in strange guises: often apparently cruel tricks and great hardships.[302] This is what happened to the princess at the hands of both her king/father and her husband, who forced a discriminating awareness upon her. In the context of soul structures of emotionality, there are spiritual interventions that appear in the form of painful experiences by which adherence to the old crystallized archetypal patterns is ended. A life change is unavoidable. Slowly, the old structures are transformed into those that serve life. This process is an arduous and always courageous re-shaping of soul substance (**form follows consciousness**!) through a transformation of animal soul consciousness. But, as indicated by the happy ending to the fairy tale, the rewards are immense. Essentially, in the soul structures of emotionality, the feminine energies become empowered. In the case of the princess, they are an awakened awareness of what the "good" choices are for her.

In the context of the 'dancing" relationship between the masculine and the feminine energies and the ongoing development of the ego/self, deprived, neglected, abandoned and even lost feminine energies can be revealed in overly "masculinized" behavior, differently expressed in male and female people. The imbalance generated by the malfunctioning sacral chakra could be expressed in an "i-am" consciousness of: "I am so depleted and so ignorant of what I must **know** that I cannot truly **be** or express what I am in the present." When this statement is added to the other "i-am" statements already "modeled" in these lessons, you can see the complexity of the egoic structures expressed within the patterns of the soul structures of emotionality. They are multidimensional and by and large outside the bounds of self-awareness. In other words, they can be emotional body "entities." When they are expressing the energies of the realm of the jealous gods, they are often marked by an inability to recognize the real "goodness" in life.

In terms of loving relationships, deprived and damaged animal soul structures of emotionality cannot deal with the "reality" of the "other." This happens because the "other" cannot truly be perceived and because there is a compulsion to compete with and to control that other person. In this state of emotionality, there are deep, unacknowledged fears and often anger in-forming the person. The loving "feminine" heart center qualities that might be there are submerged and appear usually in a crisis situation when the person is threatened with abandonment or rejection. The pattern can be life long, unless it is changed by an experience

---

[301] For more detail, see Chris Griscom, *Ecstasy is a New Frequency*, pp. 44-45.
[302] For more detail, see Carl Jung, "The Phenomenology of the Spirit in Fairy Tales," in *Four Archetypes*, pp. 94, 95, 98 and 105.

of divine intervention, often at the hands of a loving, courageous and emotionally mature human being.

(Please take time to ponder on all these observations and on those you have formulated. Be alert to your emotional responses, for they indicate where your own deep woundedness resides. Ponder whatever "comes up" with the help of the Observer.)

When you are ready, please review the instructions that preceded this section of the lesson. Then proceed to the next part of this ongoing Buddhist model of the animal soul structures of emotionality.

The God Realm

After struggling out of the realm of the jealous gods, the person can enter into a realm that is very similar. In this second realm of "heaven," the god realm, there are intense "pleasures" to be enjoyed at all times. The Buddhist teachings about this realm indicate that the person dissolves into an endless profusion of sensuous delights; sights, sounds, odors, tastes and touches, all of which are transitory. As such, they create a craving for more.[303] The craving generates endless suffering. A person can start in early childhood and be controlled by sensuous cravings throughout life. Exhibiting damaged soul structures of emotionality, there are many people who have done this and have, thereby, been emotionally crippled unless they have received a healing intervention.

In fairy tales, the sensuous archetype is usually depicted as a seductive but "innocent" young woman (or women), who entices one or several young men into her embrace. The sexual appetites of the young men bring about their misfortune. It is usually an older man, whose sexual urges have, presumably been brought under control, who eventually gets the woman.

The Grimms' fairy tale to be presented for exploring the god realm of the Wheel of Samsara is "The Worn-Out Dancing Shoes."[304] In this tale, there are twelve dancing princesses and princes, who enjoy varied and splendid sensuous delights until all their uninhibited pleasuring is brought to an abrupt end. Now, take in the story . . . .

There was once a king who had twelve daughters, each one more lovely than the last. They shared a large bedroom, with twelve little beds. Each night the king himself locked them, for safe-keeping, into their bedroom. But each morning he discovered worn-out dancing shoes discarded beside the beds. Unable to elicit the truth from the princesses, the king finally issued a proclamation stating that any man who could discover the reason for the worn-out dancing shoes would have his choice of princess for a wife and succeed to the throne. But if he failed after three attempts, his life would be forfeited. Many would-be suitors tried and failed. Their heads

---

[303] For more detail, see Mark Epstein, *Thoughts Without a Thinker*, pp. 31-33.
[304] Excerpted from Jack Zipes, *The Complete Fairy Tales of the Brothers Grimm*, pp. 432-439. This tale has also been entitled "The Twelve Dancing Princesses."

were removed without mercy, while the princesses looked on, smiling. And every morning there continued to be worn-out dancing shoes beside the little beds.

One day, an old soldier, no longer able to fight in the king's wars, bethought himself to try his luck at capturing a princess and the throne. As he walked toward the castle through the woods, he met an old woman, who asked him the reason for his journey. He gently informed her about his hopes and they had a pleasant chat. During the conversation, she told him that he could succeed in the venture, if he remembered to do two things: he must refrain from drinking any wine offered to him by a princess and he must wear a cloak of invisibility that the old woman would give to him. Enthusiastically, the old soldier agreed.

He was well-received by the king, who fed him sumptuously and even gave him new clothes. That night, the old soldier was taken to a room adjoining the princesses' bedroom. The door was left unlocked. The eldest princess graciously offered him a glass of wine, but the old soldier, mindful of the warning, only pretended to drink it. He then proceeded to feign sleep and to snore loudly. Laughing, the twelve princesses set about their evening's work

They dressed splendidly and donned new dancing shoes. Only the youngest princess had some trepidation about the situation. When she spoke about her worries, her sisters all united to calm her fears. Finally, the princesses were ready. The eldest rapped sharply on her bed. Immediately, the bed moved to the side and beneath it was revealed a set of stairs going down into darkness. Led by the eldest, one by one the princesses descended. Leaping up and donning the cloak of invisibility, the old soldier speedily followed them. Such was his haste that he stepped on the gown of the youngest princess, who cried out in alarm. She was, again, silenced by her sisters.

At the bottom of the stairs, there was a beautiful forest filled with the trees bearing silver and gold leaves. As he followed, the old soldier broke off a branch. The loud *crack!* startled the youngest princess, who cried out, but the others pressed forward. The group came to a lake and there, awaiting them were twelve handsome princes, who promptly claimed their sweethearts. Over the lake they rowed with the old soldier occupying the boat of the youngest princess and her lover. He remarked on the heaviness of the boat but she calmed his concerns. On the other side of the lake stood a dazzling palace filled with lights, music and other sensuous delights. Eagerly, the couples began their frolicking. They ate, drank, danced and enjoyed themselves with abandon. The old soldier joined into the fun. Finally, when the clock struck three, the eldest

princess called for an end to the festivities. The weary group, including the old soldier, returned to the lake. This time he rode in the boat of the eldest and ran to the stairs in order to be back in his bed before the princesses got home. When they arrived and slipped off their finery, he was busily snoring. They laughed merrily. The next night and the third night, he and the princesses danced the night away. On the last night, the old soldier took away one of their golden wine goblets for further evidence.

Then, there came the moment to inform the king. The princesses lined up behind the throne and happily awaited the old soldier's execution. Instead, he presented his evidence and accompanying story. The stairs under the bed were revealed. The princesses were forced to confess. When the old soldier was asked to select his wife, he chose the eldest. The marriage was celebrated the next day. The other princesses were punished only by being closely watched, especially at night. "The princes, however, were compelled to remain under a curse for as many nights as they had danced with the princesses." That is the end of the story.

Please experience this fairy tale as many times as are required to understand its many layers of meaning. Then return to this dimension before you participate in the discussion.

In this story, the archetypal motifs symbolizing the constant pleasure-seeking and cravings of the god realm, and by analogy, those of the damaged condition of animal soul structures of emotionality clearly indicate that the "pleasure principle" is potentially very addictive. Indeed, the "sins of the flesh," enjoyed by these soul structures have been the subject of countless sermons for many centuries. The symbol of the "stairs" under the bed is an indication of a descent into the underworld; the immense and dark obscurities of the soul structures of emotionality.[305] In the story, these are a dazzling world of forbidden and hidden sexual pleasures, indicated by the "bed." The "lake" over which the women are conveyed is another symbol indicating the murky depths carried by these multidimensional soul structures. The "palace" represents the allurement of all the instinctual pleasures of the root chakra's masculine energies that in the **holistic** human energy system are present as the physical component of the sacral chakra and in the resultant structures of emotionality. And the "worn-out dancing shoes" are the symbol of a sensuous craving that is always temporary, no matter how often those pleasures are enjoyed. In people, the physical appetites carried by the root chakra's masculine force can overwhelm the feminine of the sacral chakra, especially when that force has been corrupted and when the spiritual component of the sacral chakra is undeveloped or even lacking. Without those curbs, the physical appetites become obsessions. In this fairy tale, the "princes," the motif of untutored sons of "kings," display the appetites of the masculine root chakra as the physical component of the sacral. Yet, to complete the picture, as the sons of absolute rulers ("king/fathers"), they actually are part of a "higher" spiritual masculine

---

[305] Please recall that your "unconscious" is replete with its own forms of consciousness.

160

vibration. Thus you see demonstrated again the paradox of microcosmic "material/spiritual" energies. In the tale there are no reasons given for their undisciplined actions, but the princes could have been younger sons who would not have inherited any kingdom and were ignorant of any other traits of nobility. Hence, they have lapsed into roistering and pleasure-seeking behaviors that are insatiable. In this manner, soul structures of emotionality can inhabit the god realm of the Wheel of Samsara. Because **form follows consciousness**, this can happen to those structures that are generated by a malfunctioning sacral chakra, especially if the feminine force is corrupted and the "higher" feminine spiritual component is not functioning. That damage is what is indicated in this tale by the "princesses," the motif of the untaught and undisciplined daughters of the "king/father." Please note the absence of the motif of "queen/mother." (You might want to compare these princesses to the one in the story of "King Thrushbeard.") In the present tale, all the dancing princesses display a marked heartlessness, an indication of the absence of "higher" feminine spiritual energies and they all present the motif of corrupted feminine energy (especially the eldest). Thus, the crucial feminine energies of the sacral chakra can become totally instinctual and addicted to the sexual and other physical pleasures, exemplified by the "princes." This could be regarded as a very unhealthy "dance" of energies. In the tale, the merrymaking ends and all the participants are spared by the "king/father," for various reasons. In the context of animal soul structures of emotionality analogous to the realm of gods, the pleasure-seeking, addictive behavior must end and the sacral chakra undergo a period of healing. This is especially necessary for the eldest princess, the motif of a truly corrupted feminine energy, who becomes the "wife," the motif of a future "queen/mother," selected by the old "soldier" the motif of evolving masculine energies, which can help in the transmutation.

More probing into the archetypal masculine and feminine motifs found in this tale reveals how these could relate to each other in a sacral chakra and be expressed by the ego/self. Then, further probing could reveal how these egoic structures could relate to others.

There is the "king/father," the motif of an absolute ruler, and in the context of the sacral chakra, the "highest" spiritual masculine energies. Since there has been no balancing "queen/ mother," the motif of a "higher" spiritual power, the king/father has been disempowered and has failed to deal adequately with his "daughters;" feminine energies that were left untaught and, thereby, did not realize their spiritual potential. In the sacral chakra undisciplined feminine energies can negate the power carried by the spiritual component and, thereby, cripple the resultant soul structures (including the ego/self). Then there is the "old soldier;" mature archetypal masculine energies that are indicative of the sacral chakra's mental component. (He has come through the wars and has learned better.) In a **holistic** system, these energies are generated by the solar plexus chakra and reveal the constraints imposed by self-discipline. But the old soldier is also a motif of evolving masculine energies, as indicated by his gentle treatment of the "old woman," the motif of powerful, spiritual feminine energies. By accepting her help, the soldier is interacting with the feminine at a much higher level than did the soldier with the witch in the tale of "The Blue Light." In the context of a **holistic** human energy system, the masculine solar plexus energies can be enriched by those of the "higher" spiritual feminine centers. This higher vibration can help to balance the feminine force carried by the sacral chakra and promote healthy soul structures of emotionality. To add one more idea to this discussion: in the **holistic** energy system, the "old woman," like the "king/father" images a spiritual power that is sorely needed as the spiritual component of the sacral chakra. In their absence, the soul structures of emotionality generated by that chakra can be analogous to the realm of gods.

This fairy tale reveals that out of a malfunctioning sacral chakra in which the "dancing" (in reality, conflictual) masculine and feminine energies express the "i-am" consciousness of both the root and the sacral, (please recall that those "i-am" statements are: "I sense, therefore I am" and "I feel, therefore I am"), the resultant soul structures of emotionality can express overwhelming addictions; to sensuous pleasures and to whatever else becomes an obsession. Thus, there can be "entities" that take form in those soul structures. Linked to the biology of the beliefs, values, attitudes and habits that has slowly developed, and shaped by the microcosmic creative energies that constitute your archetypal human energy system, the egoic structures gradually emerge. If there is no equivalent of a good "queen/mother" or "old woman" in the outer or inner environment, (the soul substance could sustain injury), the egoic structures, in-formed by a malfunctioning sacral chakra, could be licentious. In the context of the god realm, the "i-am" consciousness could be: "I am so delighted with my sensory pleasures, that I shall persist in enjoying them, no matter what attempts are made to stop me." That could continue throughout a lifetime, unless there is a healing event (often unpleasant) that triggers different choices.

In terms of relationships to others; those crippled egoic structures could express as little more than appetites. If, for example, the person had been overly indulged or badly deprived in early childhood, the "self" could express in animalistic behavior covered by only a thin veneer of civility. There could be no intimate, caring relationships within that context. If, however, that early environment had carried the "higher level" (spiritual and mental) energies of consciousness; equivalents of an empowered "king/father," and/or "queen/mother," "old woman" and/or "old soldier," the ego/self could start to glimpse the higher levels of the path of "Coming into Being."

(Please ponder on these observations and on those you have developed both out of your experience of the fairy tale and out of your probing into your own soul structures of emotionality. With the assistance of the Observer, take time to focus with detachment and discernment on your own inner realm of the gods.)

Finally there is the realm that can be the means of obtaining release from the Wheel of Samsara. Prior to entering into this part of the Buddhist model, please review the instructions that preceded the first one. Then continue into the realm.

The Human Realm

After exiting the god realm with its frustrated cravings, the person can come into the human realm, where the search for "self" must be made.[306] Because "we do not really know who we are,"[307] the suffering arises out of feelings of emptiness, inauthenticity and alienation. Those feelings often occur as the result of a crippling lack of childhood nurturing by those who failed to provide recognition, attention and acknowledgement. In an attempt to feel "real," the person creates a "false self" that eventually buries the potential "real" one. This condition, expressed by unredeemed soul structures of emotionality, can prevail throughout life, unless there is a "transcendent insight" (usually achieved after much questing) into the "real" self.

In fairy tales, the archetypal motif of the search for "self" is a youthful human being either male or female. He/she embarks on a heroic quest seeking that which is precious. While dealing with many challenges along the way, the hero/heroine undergoes transformation and attains the goal. Then, he/she returns home to make known to others what he/she knows.[308]

The tale from the Brothers Grimm that illustrates the human realm of the Wheel of Samsara and the heroic quest is "The Maiden Without Hands."[309] This wonderful story unfolds like this: . . .

There was once a miller whose livelihood had dwindled, until all that he had left were his mill and, behind it, a large apple tree. One day, while he was out cutting wood, there appeared before him a little old man, who said to him: "Why are you cutting wood? I will make you rich, if you will promise to give me what is standing behind the mill." Believing that he was getting rich in exchange for only an apple tree, the miller readily gave his promise. With a mocking laugh, the little old man told the miller that he would return in three years to claim what now belonged to him. The miller went home and met his wife, who wondered why they suddenly had acquired new household furnishings, fine clothes and pantries full of food. When the miller told her about his encounter with the little old man and the promise that he had made, his wife cried out in horror: "You have made a pact with the devil! It is not the apple tree he wants, but our innocent daughter, who was sweeping the ground under the tree." Then the miller regretted what he had done, but there was nothing that could be undone.

---

[306] For more detail, see Mark Epstein, *Thoughts Without a Thinker*, pp. 36-38. In some teachings, the being can drop into the hell realm, if there has been no spiritual development. If there has been spiritual development, the being can carry the power to make choices into the human realm. See *Ibid*, p. 31.

[307] *Ibid*, p. 37.

[308] For more detail, see Joseph Campbell, *The Hero With a Thousand Faces*.

[309] Excerpted from Jack Zipes, *The Complete Fairy Tales of the Brothers Grimm*, pp. 109-113, Jacob Grimm and Wilhelm Grimm, *Grimms' Fairy Tales*, pp. 296-303 and Clarissa Pinkola-Estes, "The Handless Maiden," in *Women Who Run With the Wolves*, pp. 387-394. This tale, which has ancient origins, is also entitled:"Silver Hands" and "The Handless Bride."

The three years passed quickly and the daughter grew into lovely womanhood. At the exact time, the devil came to claim her. The maiden had prepared by carefully washing her clothes and body. Then she had drawn a circle around herself and waited. When the devil tried to touch her, he was hurled away by unseen forces. Angrily, he ordered the miller and his wife to prevent any further washing by the girl. She was kept away from water for one month. The devil reappeared and again tried to claim her. But she had wept into her hands so copiously that they were clean and again he was thwarted. In a rage, the devil ordered the miller to chop off both of the maiden's hands. When the miller weakly protested, he was told that he, his wife and all his neighbors would be punished horribly if there was any further refusal. The miller then sharpened his axe and asked his daughter for forgiveness for the act he was about to perform. She gently forgave and told him that she was obedient to all his requests. Then she held out her hands and he cut them off. The devil came back. But the maiden had wept so much over the stumps that they were again clean. Then the devil had to go away, for he had no more power over any of them.

The miller offered to keep his maimed daughter in the luxury that was his. But she chose to leave and depend on the kindness of others to supply her wants. Then, after wrapping her stumps in white bandages, she departed.

She walked for an entire day and finally arrived at an orchard that was full of pear trees laden with fruit. The hungry maiden sought to enter the orchard but it was surrounded by a moat filled with water. As she stood there, there suddenly appeared a white spirit who gently held back the water and left a clear, dry path for her. Accompanied by the white spirit, the maiden without hands went into the orchard and ate one of the pears. Then she hid in the bushes. Unknown to her, the gardener had watched her enter the orchard with the white spirit and eat. But, out of fear, he had done nothing. In the morning, the king, who owned the orchard, arrived to inspect the fruit. Finding one missing, he asked the gardener for an explanation. When the gardener finished his account, the king offered to stay with him and keep watch in the night. That night, the king, accompanied by a magician and the gardener sat under the tree and waited. At midnight, the maiden came out of hiding. With the white spirit beside her, she went to the tree under which the king sat and ate one pear. Then, the magician stepped forward and asked her if she was a spirit. Her reply was that she was no spirit, but a "poor creature forsaken by all the world." Then the king gently assured her that he would never forsake her. He took her to his royal palace and loved her greatly. He "took her for his wife" and had silver hands made for her.

One year later, the king had to go to war. He spoke to his mother, the dowager queen and asked that she take care of his wife and their expected child. The old queen, who loved her daughter-in-law greatly, promised to do so and to send him a message when the child was born. A little while later, the young queen gave birth to a beautiful boy. Delighted, the old queen mother sent off a message. But the devil was at work. When the messenger came to a stream, he was overcome by sleepiness. The devil exchanged the message for one that said that the queen had given birth to a changeling. When the king read this message he was much distressed but wrote back saying that his mother was to protect his wife until his return. Once again the devil was at work. The messenger fell asleep at the stream. The message he brought to the old queen was that she must have the young queen and her child killed and, as proof, to keep her tongue and eyes. Horrified, the old queen decided to disobey. She ordered that a doe be killed and the tongue and eyes kept. But she had to send away the young queen and her child. Gently, the old queen helped to affix the silver hands and tie the baby to the young queen's breast. Sadly, she departed.

All day she walked. She came into a great wild forest, where once again the white spirit was there to guide her. She arrived at a little cottage with a sign that said: "Free Lodgings for Everyone." Inside, there was another white spirit, who welcomed her as a queen and made her comfortable. The queen stayed there seven years and raised her son. During that time, her hands gradually grew back; first as little baby hands, "then as little girl hands and then finally as woman's hands."

Meanwhile, the king had returned from the wars. His mother, the old queen, reproached him bitterly for having ordered her to kill the innocent queen and showed him the tongue and eyes she had kept. Much distressed, the king denied having issued such an order and wept bitterly over his lost wife. Then his mother told him the truth about having sent the queen away with her child. Vowing to go without food or drink until he had found them, the king set out. For seven years he wandered and was kept alive by a "force greater than he." Finally he entered into the great wild forest and came upon the cottage wherein dwelt his wife and son.

He was met at the door by the white spirit, who welcomed him as royalty. Refusing food and drink, he lay down to sleep and the white spirit covered his face with a handkerchief. Then the spirit summoned the queen and told her that her husband was there. Taking her young son with her, the queen approached her sleeping husband. The handkerchief fell from his face. He awoke, to see them gazing down upon him. Startled, he asked her who she was. "I am your wife," she said, "and this is your son." The king did not believe her because his wife had been without hands. "Through my travails and yet my good care," she replied, "my hands have grown back."

The white spirit showed him the silver hands, which had been carefully stored away. Then the king rose and embraced his wife and child. After sharing a meal with the white spirit, the royal family went home to the old queen mother. "There was rejoicing everywhere. The king and queen had a second wedding and lived happily ever after." That is the end of the story.

Please enjoy this tale as often as you require to probe into its many-layered meaning. Then return to this dimension for the discussion.

There is a complex interweaving that must take place in this discussion. Because the tale contains an amazing "cast of characters," they can be part of an intricate tapestry that along with the many other symbols also found therein, can richly reveal not only the human realm of Samsara but also the potential of animal soul structures of emotionality; those generated by a balanced and healthy sacral chakra that can finally express the "dancing" masculine and feminine energies. We begin by collecting the tale's many motifs and symbols (the threads of the tapestry).

In the cast of characters (the motifs) indicating the masculine energies that are part of the sacral chakra, there are the miller, the gardener, the king, the magician, the messenger and the king's son. The cast also includes the feminine energies of the chakra: the maiden, the miller's wife, and the old queen. Then there are the motifs; the little old man (devil) and the white spirit guides and the symbols; the mill and the apple tree, of the otherworld. The symbols that enrich both the fairy tale and the analogy are the axe, the circle, the tears, the "real" hands, the white bandages, the moat, the orchard, the silver hands, the great wild forest, the cottage, the messages, the stream, the handkerchief and the second wedding.

Now, let us proceed.

With the imagery of the mill and the apple tree, both symbols indicating deeply hidden spiritual power,[310] the tale plunges us into the otherworld. There on the scene are the miller, whose fortunes have fallen so low that he is cutting his own wood, and a "little old man" (the devil in disguise), who has lusted after the innocent maiden (the miller's daughter), sweeping under the apple tree. The devil tricks the miller into giving him the maiden in exchange for worldly comforts and food. The miller's wife immediately sees through the trick, but she becomes aware too late to save the maiden. In terms of damaged soul structures of emotionality, the consciousness energies of "people" and "devil" exist in the hidden depths. They dialog and strike their bargains within those obscurities. In the context of an out-of-balance sacral chakra, the masculine energies (the "miller") have been reduced to root chakra physicality, intent upon survival. They have thereby become fair game for the "tempter." Meanwhile, the sacral chakra's feminine force, imaged by the miller's "wife," is also indicative of a survival orientation, the prime directive of a root chakra. (Although she cannot prevent the pact between the miller and the devil, the wife does nothing to stop what eventually happens

---

[310] Barbara G. Walker, *The Woman's Dictionary of Symbols and Sacred Objects*, pp. 57 and 479.

and shares in the bounty.) This is what can occur in the sacral chakra and in the resultant soul structures of emotionality, if there is a prolonged struggle for survival. The chakra's immature and unprotected feminine energies (the "maiden") are disempowered. Thus, what prevail are the soul structures found in the dark darkest obscurities (under the "apple tree" behind the "mill") where the spiritual antitheses can lurk. When the bargain is struck, the maiden has no recourse, except to fall back on spiritual energies. By washing with water, the balancing quality of the sacral chakra, and by encircling herself, she is summoning "higher" feminine spiritual forces.[311] She is able to defeat the devil but only temporarily. Her father and mother (the energies of a survival-oriented root chakra) do not nourish or protect her, but by their choices align themselves with the devil. This can happen in the sacral chakra in situations involving a destructive inner and outer environment, by which soul substance suffers trauma, the sacral chakra gets severely out-of-balance and the resultant soul structures of emotionality are reduced to primitive, instinctual survival mode. In the story, although both the chakra and the structures have been somewhat developed (the devil has waited for the maiden to grow older), they are not healthy enough to withstand the forces that can overwhelm. The maiden can save herself again only by weeping into her hands and in doing so cleansing a portion of her body by the "holy water" of tears. But again the feminine energies she symbolizes do not have the power needed to overcome the energies of "darkness." They attempt once more to capture her by forcing her father (the corrupted masculine energies) to cripple her. Her "hands," the motif of the human capability to bless and to divine,[312] are cut off. The instrument used is the father's "axe," the symbol of authority empowered to punish the disobedient.[313] But the holy water of her tears shed over the stumps is enough, finally to defeat the devil. Unwilling to remain with her parents, the maiden leaves. Thus, in the generative sacral chakra, the feminine energies can be disempowered but not destroyed by corrupt energies present in the chakra. As often happens, trauma can trigger the mental component ("higher" masculine energies) of the sacral chakra to rouse the feminine energies and they can start, hesitatingly at first, to seek empowerment. In the human realm of the Wheel of Samsara, the person starts the quest for "self," just as in the fairy tale the maiden with bandaged stumps leaves behind her innocence and naivety, as well as her loveless and dysfunctional "parents."

Like the wandering maiden, the feminine energies of the sacral chakra can be seeking nourishment and yet be unable to get it because the chakra's water element has become a barricade (the "moat") rather than a means. In the chakra, these are deep feminine energies, but because of trauma, (the maiden is newly crippled), they are not beneficial (the maiden is unable to swim or wade through them.) It is then that the "higher" spiritual energies can intervene. This can happen in situations of hopelessness, when no human action seems possible. In the tale, this occurs and the maiden is assisted into the "orchard," a symbol of natural nourishment from Earth, the archetypal energies of the Mother. In the context of the sacral chakra and the

---

[311] The symbolic meaning of the "water" is clear. The reference to the circle is to an ancient feminine symbol of consecrated or protected space. See *Ibid*, p. 4.

[312] *Ibid*, pp. 21 and 23.

[313] *Ibid*. p. 23.

resultant soul structures of emotionality, the feminine energies require this "fruit" and are duly nourished. Then, there appear the masculine energies needed by the feminine energies. In the story, there are three: the "gardener" the motif of uncorrupted instinctual energies, the "king," the motif of the "higher" spiritual energies and the "magician," the motif of the "higher" masculine mental energies. The fragile feminine energies are rescued and sheltered by the "higher" spiritual power. In the "marriage" to the king, the maiden can be "pregnant" with new life and, in that gestation, experience movement toward empowerment. In the human realm of the Wheel of Samsara, here is an indication of further progress in the quest for "self." In this part of her "journey," the maiden has the help of an immense feminine spiritual energy, the "old queen mother." All this can happen within a sacral chakra.

But the tribulations have not ended. Although no longer the innocent maiden, the new queen (the motif of more empowered feminine energies) remains crippled. Then comes the next great stage of her quest, when the king departs and leaves her in the care and keeping of the queen mother. The birthing of the "son" signals a new turn in events, just as the onset of new masculine energies can help shift the consciousness of the sacral chakra and, thereby, slowly change the soul structures of emotionality. But, in that turn of events, the "positive" spiritual power (the "queen mother") can be challenged by the "negative" spiritual power (the "devil"), already once thwarted by the immature feminine energies (the "maiden"). This can happen in soul journeying. At first, it would appear that the negative spiritual power has been able to overcome the positive: the "messenger" (the mental energies) between the two positive spiritual energies (the "king" and the "queen mother") is waylaid by the forces of darkness and the "messages" changed. This can occur in an out-of-balance sacral chakra and as a result, in the depths of the soul structures of emotionality. There is a doe (a motif of feminine scapegoat energies) killed in place of the "queen" and the "eyes" and "tongue" (the symbols of seeing and communicating) are kept. Finally, the queen mother believing that she has disobeyed the king is forced to send the queen and her newborn child away. In the context of the sacral chakra, however, this is exactly what is needed for the further empowerment of the feminine energies. Although much help has been provided by the queen-mother and the king, the queen requires further journeying. Thus it is with the sacral chakra. When those feminine energies of consciousness have been disempowered, they can be healed only by coming into their full "i-am." Feeding her "son" (a gift of the Spirit and a motif of new masculine energies) at her breast and wearing her "silver hands" (a symbol of inauthenticity that requires replacing), the queen, the former maiden, leaves.

Again there is a departure. And again there is divine intervention. The queen wanders into a "great wild forest," the symbol of the deep places of "unknowing" and finds the healing energies that she needs. In a place of refuge (the "cottage") in which the queen can undergo transformation, there is the nourishment needed to heal her "hands." Thus it is that in an inner environment of deep spiritual cocooning the feminine energies of the sacral chakra can be healed, while at the same time nurturing the emergent masculine energies. Then the soul structures of emotionality can also obtain healing. Meanwhile, the queen mother has reconnected with the king and the truth about the queen has been revealed. In the sacral chakra healing happens, when the light of truth is allowed. Finally, the "positive" spiritual energies appear to be winning. But the tale has not yet ended. In despair, the "king" sets out on his own quest. In a sacral chakra where healing is happening, there is the opportunity for a strong connection to occur between the mature feminine energies of emotionality and the "higher" masculine spiritual energies. And it is necessary that "he" finds "her." (The "Dance of Shiva and Shakti" requires this.) There is a quest undertaken by the king, a reflection of the quest undertaken by the evolving feminine energies (the queen). They meet after a long interlude (a necessary period of growth) in the "cottage" in the "great wild forest." It is an intensely sacred moment, indicated by the "handkerchief" (the symbol of a veil of illusion being removed). After obtaining nourishment once more in the spirit "cottage" the family returns to the king's residence and reunites with the queen mother. This part of the tale would suggest that the sacral chakra must become a powerful and healthy center of consciousness (**form follows consciousness**) in order that the soul structures of emotionality can function properly. With great rejoicing, the masculine and feminine energies can "dance" with each other. The feminine energies of the sacral chakra are no longer malfunctioning, but are expressing its immense generative power. Therein lies the **possibility** in a human energy system of an equal, androgynous partnership involving the feminine and the masculine energies.

In the context of the "dancing" masculine and feminine energies, there is a wonderful lesson in this fairy tale about the necessity of that dance in the **holistic** human energy system. When the masculine and feminine forces get separated by traumatic life events, there can be a descent into the darkness of unredeemed animal soul. When that occurs, the "i-am" consciousness being expressed is: "I am so empty and so disconnected from life that I can feel nothing." But there is another lesson to be learned: sooner or later, those archetypal forces must reconnect and the "dance" must take place in the dimensions of **human** awareness. Although this is a difficult undertaking, there is fairy tale of "The Maiden Without Hands" to indicate that it is possible. And the "i-am" consciousness that can slowly be expressed is "I am aware, more so than I have ever been, of what I am and I can experience a deepening sense of well-being and completion." This is the **possibility**.

In the context of relationships to others, the person who has progressed on the path of "Coming into Being" in the human realm of the Wheel of Samsara has started to understand his/her ego/self with a deepening appreciation of its authenticity and intrinsic value. The relationships entered into will reflect that attitude in that the connections with others will indicate an appreciation and a valuing of that other being.

The tapestry is complete.

We are at the end of the Buddhist "model." Please ponder on the insights you have gained as you traveled around the Wheel. Quite clearly, your soul structures of emotionality and the egoic structures that they express are multidimensional energies that are extremely complex and have required your profound understanding. This you will achieve by your awareness that you are an energy being, a soul field, whose sacral chakra, a center of consciousness of incalculable generative power, can be the means of both lifting you to the heights and of hurling you into the depths, even demolishing you, physically and mentally. Such is the power generated by your archetypal sacral chakra and carried by the resultant soul structures of emotionality, your first "subtle" body of consciousness. With the discernments you have gained, you already have a greater awareness of your darkest obscurities and how they were created. Continue to ponder and welcome new insights. Your sacral chakra constitutes a paradox of immense proportions with its prime directive, "i-am" consciousness, qualities and function, all indicative of its generative power. It is a power that you must **know.**

A parting thought . . .

The Wheel of Samsara can be very familiar, even in childhood. Ponder on this: within an inner and outer environment that is neither nurturing nor nourishing, that is, in-formed by lovelessness, a child can be caught up in rage and fear (the realm of hell), a condition worsened by having its biological needs not satisfied (the animal realm), experience a deep unsatisfied emotional hunger (the realm of hungry ghosts), become terribly confused and frustrated over what it really wants (the realm of the jealous gods) experience sensuous pleasures that are quickly snatched away (the realm of the gods), and get to be five years old and already feel empty, inauthentic and alienated (the human realm). Thus, when the sacral chakra is ready to function on its own, it is already malfunctioning and, what could be described as the "embryonic" soul structures of emotionality are already badly damaged. As the Buddhist "model" and the fairy tales have indicated, an out-of-balance and malfunctioning sacral chakra can be the reason why people can "neglect and cripple" their "emotional nature."

Your Sacral Chakra's Malfunction

Let us turn now to a discussion about the malfunctioning sacral chakra and add a few more items to your awareness. Please recall from the last lesson that while your soul structures of physicality had been developing since conception, so also were your soul structures of emotionality and mentality. While they manifested your archetypal endowment and imperative, there would have been a prescribed sequence in this unfolding. During the process, the inner and outer environments would be playing a crucial part. In this third dimension, at this time in mankind's evolution, the environmental impact would likely be damaging, Thus, in addition to the damage to your root chakra, please keep in mind that damage could be inflicted on your sacral chakra. Essentially, the energies of emotionally dysfunctional environments can be too powerful for a child to handle. With too much pain, there can be created an "armor plating" as self-protection and as a means of enduring an appalling childhood.

The physical problems of childhood that can be carried throughout a lifetime stem from a malfunctioning root chakra. But now you can add to that awareness the emotional aspect of a damaged sacral chakra. Colitis, diverticulitis and appendicitis are linked to emotional damage. So also are kidney and bladder problems associated with a child's flight or fight feelings of helplessness. And the "armor plating" can be expressed as fibromyalgia.

The psychological disorders you have already encountered in the Wheel of Samsara model. Others to note are co-dependency and obsessive-compulsive disorders and, of course, the addictions that can take over your life.

Although the combination of physical and emotional afflictions might appear to be overwhelming, healing is both possible and necessary on your path of "Coming into Being."[314]

Self-Healing Therapies for Your Sacral Chakra

Recall yet again that **form follows consciousness**. Your soul structures of emotionality can be changed, when healing consciousness energies are directed into your sacral chakra. (Although the structures are "subtle" bodies, they are forms, nevertheless.) Included in any therapy are the maintenance guidelines for your energy system given in Lesson One. Please also recall from the last lesson that the self-healing therapies you will learn are not a substitute for competent, caring professional help; they are given as disciplines and as a means for you to go inward and to prepare yourself for that help. Because your soul structures of emotionality are unique, your work of inner preparation is vital. Herein lies your increasing awareness of the "resistance" that can be generated by your soul structures of emotionality and your "doing" that is the undoing of that resistance. And, of course, the "doing" now involves the disciplines/ practices of "letting go/ letting be" that you will realize are ready to be done. There is no way of telling you when this will happen. You will simply **know** that the old beliefs, values and attitudes are no longer yours. And in that "work," your increasing capacity for detachment and discernment will be manifesting. This, in turn will enhance your capacity for balancing. That discipline/practice will also be expanded by the healing disciplines you will undertake now.

In other words, your **discipline** is essential. (Again, you are reminded that your daily discipline of meditation is very necessary.)

Remembering that each one of your chakras vibrates within a particular range of frequencies, you will introduce energies that vibrate synchronistically with a healthy sacral chakra. You are already aware, to a certain extent, of its state of health. When you are practicing the healing modalities that you will receive shortly, continue to tune in with the help of the Observer and to "track" the healing process, just as you are doing with your root chakra. Because the two chakras interact so closely, you will experience physical as well as emotional changes, when the transforming kundalini "shifts" occur and the sacral chakra consciousness energies are transmuted. This will take time and your patience is necessary.

First, be aware of your own sacred space and your immersion in it. Then, begin the self-healing therapies for the sacral chakra by ascertaining if the damage has resulted from an excess or from a loss of your orange and water energies.

---

[314] You might want to listen to a piece of music that expresses the deep wounding and wounds of many peoples' soul structures of emotionality. The music is the First Violin Concerto by Dimitri Shostakovich.

Self-Healing Therapies: After Too Much Orange and Water Energies

When there is an excess of those (feminine) energies, you are emotionally volatile and unstable. You experience drastic mood swings. The vitality of your orange energies has been changed into hysteria and hyperactivity. You fluctuate between "cold rages" and torrential weeping. If you are a woman (or a man dealing with a woman like this), you blame it all on PMS. Your relationships are damaged by your emotional states. With this excess, your energy field is totally out of balance and your orange and water energies are "drowning" you.

If too much orange and water energies has been a long-standing condition, you will benefit from the "breath work" indicated for the root chakra (review the last lesson) and additional body work.

Body Work

Begin by "scraping" your aura in preparation for breath work.

Please recall and practice the **balancing** breath work from the last lesson. Your important "relaxation" breath work will be enhanced if you consistently practice **grounding**. Continuing with this essential practice, you can go into the next exercise.

For sacral chakra healing breath work, there is the "Ida/Pingala" exercise that will help to "clear" your entire energy system and, thereby, help reduce the red and yellow energies of too much orange. You proceed as follows

Take several deep, grounding breaths.

Focus on your "roots" and "see" colorless energy.

Inhale deeply and "pull" the energies up through the "roots" and up your legs.

"See" the colorless energies converge at your root chakra.

Focus intently on the "ida" channel. (Recall Lesson One and Figure Two.)

Inhale deeply and pull the energies up through the ida channel to the top of your head.

Exhale while puckering your mouth and "blowing out" the "black" energies of physical and emotional toxicity.

Repeat several times.

Focus your attention again on your root chakra and pull the colorless energies on your breath up through the "pingala" channel.

Exhale again while puckering your mouth and "blowing out" the toxicities.

Repeat this several times.

Now, focusing your intent and attention, pull the colorless energies up both of the channels and "see" them going around each one of your chakras.

Exhale the "black" energies.

Continue until you sense a "shift" in your energies. This might be accompanied by a feeling of inner warmth rising. It is the kundalini.

Confirm with the assistance of your Observer.

Drink a large glass of pure water.

Continue daily until you no longer require this breath work.

Earth Energies

The healing crystals that you will use carry the energies of calming and balance.

Amethyst balances the energies of the physical and soul structures of emotionality and brings in the healing energies of serenity and compassion.

Butlerite facilitates emotional stability and adaptability.

Hematite can be used to facilitate the attainment of peace, self-control and inner happiness.

The **herbs** that bring calm to a root chakra are also very effective in the sacral.

The aromas derived from the plants of Earth that can calm the damaged sacral chakra are musk, patchouli and cedar wood.

Musk rose, which is usually an oil, produces a feeling of well-being.

Patchouli and *cedar wood* are aromas that help in the healing and calming of both the root and sacral chakras.

Spirit Energies

Remembering that, in reality, all the healing work is "spiritual," make "sitting" meditation and gratitude an everyday practice. Because your **beliefs** always carry an emotional "charge," your practice of the "Seeker's Lamp" meditation you learned in the last lesson will help greatly in healing both your dysfunctional root and sacral chakras. So, continue to practice this powerful meditation and to welcome the times when you "do" nothing except to stay in the inner stillness.

Self-Healing Therapies: After Too Little Orange and Water Energies

When there are too few orange and water (feminine) energies, you feel arid, empty, despondent, and depressed. Your lassitude prevents you from doing anything except the bare minimum. Your physical and mental health can also be affected adversely. Your energy field will be the color of burnt orange. If this condition has lasted for any length of time, you will certainly need extensive "clearing" of your root, sacral, and solar plexus chakras, by an energy healer.

When your feelings of tiredness and depression are accompanied by physical illness, practice the body work given in the previous lesson for the loss of red energy in your root chakra. Then add this . . .

Body Work

Because your orange and water energies are depleted, the **grounding** breath work is essential. Ensure that your "roots" are firmly attached to your Earth source. Take several **grounding** breaths. Then do the "relaxation" breath work. After that, add the following variation on the "reinforcing and balancing" breath work you learned in the last lesson. The exercise is entitled "Up the Sushumma" breath work:

"Scrape" your electromagnetic energy field.

After several **grounding** breaths, "see" a colorless energy.

Inhale that energy by "pulling" it up from Earth through your "roots," up your legs and up your sushumma channel into your sacral chakra.

With each exhale, pucker your mouth and "blow out" the "black" energies. These are the physical and emotional toxicity you are releasing.

After several of these breaths, "see" a clear "red' energy.

Inhale that color by pulling it up your "roots," up your legs, up your sushumma channel and into your sacral chakra.

Exhale the "black" toxicities.

After several of these breaths, "see" clear "yellow" energy.

Inhale that color by pulling it up, as you did the red energy, into your sacral chakra and exhale the "black" energies.

After several of these breaths, "see" clear "orange" energy.

Repeat the inhalation and exhalation process.

If you have difficulty with any step in this exercise, go back to the "colorless" energy and repeat from the beginning.

When you have successfully inhaled several orange breaths, "see" clear cobalt blue energy. Carefully focus your intent and attention on your "roots."

Inhale deeply while "seeing" this "balancing" and "reinforcing" energy flowing in with the orange energy. Pull both the cobalt blue and the orange energies up your "roots," up your legs, up your sushumma channel and into your sacral chakra.

Exhale while "blowing out any remaining "black" toxicities.

Continue until you sense a kundalini "shift" in your energy field. Check it out after summoning the assistance of the Observer.

Practice this breath work as a daily routine until you no longer need it.

To enhance this breath work, you can then "recharge" your sacral chakra by "toning" the sound of its healthy vibrational frequency. In the Ayurvedic tradition, the sound of the sacral chakra is "VAM". Listen to the G note below middle C on the piano and tone that sound by taking a deep **grounding** breath and releasing it slowly as your vocal chords generate WWWWW . . . AAAHHHH . . . MMMMMMM. Focus on your sacral chakra. Create a strong, deep vibration that you feel in the chakra and in your mouth. Repeat this "toning" nine times for one "round". When you are finished, rest and continue your **grounding** breaths.

Then, add the toning for your root chakra for one round plus an additional round for your sacral chakra.

You will also require physical body exercises for stimulating both your root and sacral chakras. Those for the sacral include the yogic poses of "The Goddess," "Pelvic Rock," "Hip Circles," "Scissors Kicks," and "Walking From the Pelvis."[315] You will also enjoy belly dancing and a "swinging" exercise that has been taught by Barbara Brennan. This is described as follows:

Standing with your back straight, your legs shoulder-width apart, and your knees deeply bent, place your hands at your hips and start to "swing" forward and back with your pelvis. Move gently at first. But as you continue to practice, increase the speed and the arc of the "swing."

While you are doing this "work," please have fun!

Earth Energies

The **crystals** that you can use to stimulate orange energies are as follows:

Polka dot agate helps you to release painful experiences and to bring on cheerfulness.

Amber emits a sunny and soothing energy which enlivens the disposition.

Malachite is the "stone of transformation" assisting in changing situations and clarifying the emotions.

Citrine is a variety of quartz that never needs clearing or cleansing. It enhances the energy of the root chakra, while it provides supplemental initiative coupled with emotional balance for the sacral.

The **herbs** that will stimulate the root chakra energies will work as well for the sacral chakra.

The **aromas** that will stimulate orange energies are as follows:

Rosemary as an oil is used to relieve debility and nervous exhaustion.

Ylang-ylang, as an essential oil, is effective in dispelling depression and nervous tension.

Spirit Energies

After successfully doing the "Up the Sushumma" breath work, you might want to work again with the "Ring of Color" you received in the last lesson. Please recall your preparation. When you are ready, proceed with that guided meditation, but this time "see" that the ring of color is orange and that it is gradually accompanied by a sense of "dampness."

After this experience, "journal" and re-experience those sensations of color and damp. When working with this color of orange, remember those energies.

---

[315] Anodea Judith, *Wheels of Life*, pp. 137-141.

There is yet another guided meditation that will enhance the power of the water energies of your sacral chakra. This can be done while you are using the crystals and/or the aromas. The meditation is entitled the "Pool of Rejuvenation."

Prepare your quiet space. Wear loose clothing. Have on hand a large glass of pure water and a pad and pencil for journaling. Sit or lie down comfortably. Proceed as you have already learned with the "Seeker's Lamp" and the "Ring of Color" meditations. After several deep **grounding** breaths, "see" the elevator shaft and descend into the depths of your "unconscious." Continue until you stop moving and the "doors" open.

"See" that you are in a quiet garden. Before you there appears a narrow, winding, white path. Slowly, you follow it. As you walk, you inhale the fragrance of flowers and clear fresh air. Now you hear the sound of splashing water and you feel a jolt of anticipation. You hasten your steps and, rounding a curve, you see before you a large, round garden pool. There are water jets splashing around the circumference. Without hesitation, you strip away your clothing and step into the water. Then you notice that there is a low bench in the center of the pool, just below the surface of the water. You walk over to the bench and you sit on it. The water reaches to your hips. Suddenly, the jets start to pour water towards you. It arches over your head and splashes on all sides. You sit inside this dome of water and feel it rising around your body. Higher and higher it rises, until it comes to your waist. Then the jets stop. You are sitting in still, soothing, warm water. You start to breathe very deeply, and as you do, you feel the energies of the water penetrating your field. They are comforting and invigorating at the same time. Gradually, you feel all your sensations of tiredness, emptiness, depression, and lassitude slowly seeping away. You continue to breathe very deeply. If you sense gentle hands washing you, while you are sitting there, allow this and allow the feelings. If you sense gentle hands lifting you, submerging you in the water and washing you, like an infant, allow this and allow the feelings. Slowly, you feel within your deepest, darkest places, a sense of lightness and vitality. As this happens, you experience an immense thankfulness. [Stay in this place of tranquility for as long as you desire.] You rise to your feet, the water recedes, and you walk out of the pool. With arms and legs stretched wide, you allow the gentle breezes to dry your body. Then you don your clothes and follow the white path out of the garden.

You turn and re-enter the elevator shaft. You ascend to this dimension. Slowly return to this "reality." Drink the pure water. Journal and review your experience.

Repeat this meditation as often as you require. Vary it by "walking" into other bodies of water (rivers, lakes, oceans) and by experiencing waterfalls and high waves pouring over you.

There is much pondering you can do with these experiences. Call in the Observer to help you to probe into the emotions that have arisen. If they are unfamiliar, stay with them and gently allow them. Your soul structures of emotionality that are tied to the Wheel of Samsara will create conflicts within you, at first. Trust your process and those conflicts will eventually recede.

And trust also that during this process there have been more changes generated in your soul structures of ego/self. (Please keep in mind the real purpose of the ego.)

We have arrived at the end of the lesson. Outside the stone circle, the darkness of night is giving way to the new dawn. Shall we stand here and watch the rosy hues as they advance across the moors? It has been a wonderful night. You are likely feeling both fatigued and exhilarated after such a vast amount of instruction and experience. There is much to ponder. Please do so by taking as much time as you require. Recall and review your responses while you worked with the Observer on your sacral chakra. Focus on the realms of the Wheel of Samsara that most apply to you. Practice the disciplines of the self-healing therapies you have received.

At this point on your path of "Coming into Being," you are into yet more paradox. Still within the paradigm of animal soul, you are dealing not only with both the past and the present; you are now also dealing with both your root and sacral chakras in parallel "lanes" and with whatever has been happening on the ongoing path of Opening the Way." Your **knowing** has been expanded hugely. This night has not been wasted!

You have been deeply involved with and tightly connected to the energies of this place. They are immense and so are you. Before you leave this stone circle, look around you and once more realize the timelessness that is in you and around you. This you are starting to **know.**

You may leave the stone circle . . .

*   *   *

When you are ready, add the following homework to the healing therapies. It is, again, necessary discipline.

Homework: Your "Emotional Clearing" [316] and "Worm Hole Work"

Eventually you will feel compelled to release the deep emotions that reside in the darkest obscurities of your soul structures of emotionality. During your times of deep pondering and probing you are allowing more of those feelings into your awareness. Then, when you are ready, you can begin the intense emotional clearing work that changes them. As you are already aware from the "Seeker's Lamp" guided meditation and your other probing work that you carry deep structures of "memories" of past trauma linked mainly with **beliefs.** In the process of your self-healing, you will become acquainted with them and experience the emotions attached to them. By doing this, you will increase your capacity to explore your anatomy of **beliefs.**

Truly experiencing your emotions requires that you **allow** them, **acknowledge** them and **accept** them. It is an intensification of the discipline/practices of "letting go/letting be" By

---

[316] Ann Wilson Schaef, *Beyond Therapy, Beyond Science: A New Model for Healing the Whole Person.* Consult the Index under "Deep Process." A word of caution … this work is very intense and should not be done without sufficient preparation and/or professional help.

doing this "emotional clearing," you will be healing your dysfunctional sacral chakra and, in doing so, you will be healing your soul structures of emotionality. You will also be giving yourself additional means to change the beliefs that are attached to these emotions and are antithetical to your life.

Now, let us begin.

Instead of just "feeling" your reactions to people, situations and circumstances, realize that they are messages from your deeply buried soul structures of emotionality and "catch" them before they can disappear. If you are in a quiet place where you feel safe, you may start your emotional clearing right away. If you are not, wait until you are and in the meantime remember your **intent** to explore those feelings.

In your quiet, safe place, lie down on the floor, start your **grounding** breaths. Then call in the Observer to help you remain detached and discerning and summon up the emotion. It will begin rather hesitantly.

Maintain your focus and patiently **allow**. Do not think about it; just allow it. As it increases in intensity, gently start trying to name it. Inwardly say: "I am feeling" [and name it]. You might have to try several times before the correct naming word comes. You will know this because you will get a sense of recognition.

By naming the emotion, you are **acknowledging** it. This will increase the intensity. Continue to allow and acknowledge it.

By this allowing and acknowledging, you are **accepting** it. As the emotion pours up your sushumma, the naming will cease and you will undergo physical reactions such as weeping, screaming, gagging, and even nausea. Continue to allow and accept. You might even start to thrash about. Continue to allow and accept.

Eventually, the emotional "storm" will cease.

You will experience tiredness and relief. Do nothing for a few minutes. Sometimes after one emotional clearing, the next one comes hard on its heels. Then start the process all over.

If nothing comes, you are finished, for the time being. Drink a tall glass of pure water and sleep.

This process will be required for all your deeply buried emotions. As you release them, they are transformed into the energies of self-awareness and calm. This will not happen immediately, but over time the change will come. In the meantime, you will be able to recognize them and to stop being their victim. When you become somewhat adept at recognizing an emotion, you may start your "worm hole" work.

Since the emotion does not exist in a vacuum, you can be certain that it is connected to a **belief**. You must eventually find it and correct it. You do this by "catching" the emotion. You allow, acknowledge and accept it. Then you focus inward and go down, down into what seems to be a "trail" that the emotion has left. That is the "worm hole."

Go down as far as you must and as you do allow the images and even words to come up. Finally, you will reach the bottom. The "worm" will be there. It is the **belief** that you must identify. Recall all the images and other clues you have already obtained. Then, with the help of the Observer start a gentle, non-accusatory "dialog" with the "worm." Listen to the answers. When the **belief** is totally revealed, stop the inner work and return to this dimension.

With detachment, start to ponder the vital question: "Is this belief **true** about life and/or about me?" Usually the answer is "no." Then ask the next vital question: "What is the true belief?" The answer might take you a little while to discern fully. Be patient. If more "worm hole" work is required, continue to do it. The path of "Coming into Being" requires all the letting go/letting be, all the balancing, all the faith and the fortitude that a soul searcher can muster. Since this is a Spirit-guided undertaking, they are available and you will use them.

Stay with this lesson, until you feel ready to move to the next.

Peace and blessings

Lesson Five

YOUR SOLAR PLEXUS CHAKRA AND
SOUL STRUCTURES OF MENTALITY

Hello: welcome to the stone circle . . . . What a delightful day it is! Like carefree children, the breezes are chasing the white clouds across the blue sky, playing "tag" around Long Meg and her Children and ruffling the lush grass. In this late summertime, after many weeks of rains and growth, the pastures are heavy with nourishment for the farm animals that live on these moors. You are surrounded by a truly bucolic environment. It is gently inviting you to participate; to merge into this beauty and to vibrate harmoniously with it. Stand very still for a moment and connect with all of this life and especially with Earth. While you take a few deep **grounding** breaths of warm, clean air take in, as well, the brilliant sunlight that permeates this place. Do you sense it; your oneness with this entire scene? Savor . . . slowly . . . Relax Enjoy. When you are ready, here is your ground sheet and a bottle of pure water. Come . . . Sit here in the center on this cushion of fragrant hay. This is a perfect occasion. And you are invited to a picnic . . . a somewhat unusual one. In this place, while you are immersed in the translucent energies of late summer and of "now," you will receive and "digest" some "food for thought."

It is necessary that you know about "thought," for it is thought that has brought you to this place. "Thought" is consciousness energy experiencing and expressing all the fleeting content: the inner statements, observations, decisions, images, impulses, "personas" and whatever else that constitutes your "ephemeral" soul structures of mentality. Yet, although there is the fleeting content, the mental consciousness energy that is your thought can also be a disciplined process: one of abstracting, conceptualizing and integrating so focused that you can solve immensely complex problems. Thought is also the mental energy that can take you, in a twinkling, into the past and into the future. Thought can be filled with memories both pleasant and painful and with anticipations both enchanting and terrifying. Thought can raise you to the heights and hurl you to the depths. You can both create and destroy with thought. Clearly, you the "thinker" and your "thought" are inextricably connected. Indeed, they are the two sides of the same coin.

As both thought and thinker you are like those pilgrims who journeyed here before you. Their thought **content** reflected what they **knew**, in all their dimensions. So does yours. Their thought **function** expressed who they "were," at whatever level of soul development they had attained. So does yours. Although it is almost impossible for modern soul searchers to comprehend the thought content and thought function of those bye-gone people, there is a linkage between you and them, between now and the past. That linkage is to be found in the Akashic Field (the "collective unconscious"). As archetypal pilgrims on a soul journey that was taking them as far as they could go, they were then what you are now. And in this circle of stones you might "hear" their energies of thought; in the "voices" of the breezes playing around the stones, in the presence of Earth into which you are **grounding**, and even in the stones themselves. (Who knows what they have absorbed!) All of it is an infinite and ever-expanding consciousness energy of which you are part.

Soul Searcher, while on your (often simultaneous) paths of "Opening the Way" and of "Coming into Being" you have been plunged into some confounding paradoxes. You have been required to open your awareness to deep parts of you that had been buried in obscurity. You have also been required to comprehend the reasons for both the burial and the opening. You have pondered and probed into your dimensions that have only slowly yielded up their secrets. You have discovered and uncovered some crippled soul structures, both "gross" and "subtle." You have given much "thought," both contemplative and analytical, to what you found. Throughout this endeavor, you have been encouraged to make detached discernments and to forego moral judgments. You have been called upon to use both your rationality and your imagination. You have made decisions and started reshaping your soul structures, including your egoic structures.

What a grand adventure it has already been! And, of course, the physical and emotional soul "work" continues, as you embark on the next stage of your quest. You have arrived at the point where you, still as an animal soul, are ready to learn about your archetypal solar plexus chakra, its generative power, and your amazing soul structures of mentality. Now you are poised to move into the third, and final, "lane" of your path of "Coming into Being." Again, be prepared for and allow simultaneity. You will continue opening the way, while letting go/letting be, and coming into being, while balancing. Push on and be of good cheer! It is while traveling along this "lane" that you can glimpse the possibility of becoming androgynous.

Now, enjoy these playful words from the poet Rumi as he describes animal soul "thought:"[317]

---

[317] Daniel Ladinsky, *Love Poems from God*, pp 70-71.

"The Chance of Humming"

"A man standing on two logs in a river
might do all right floating with the current
while humming in the
now.

Though
if one log is tied to a camel
who is also heading south along the bank—at the same pace —
all could still be well with the
world

unless the camel
thinks he forgot something and
abruptly turns upstream,
then

uh-oh.

Most minds
do not live in the present
and stick to a reasonable plan; most minds abruptly turn
and undermine the
chance
of
humming."

Most minds are like that! Yet, while you chuckle, perhaps ruefully, over this tendency of animal soul consciousness, please note the sense of humor that you are sharing with Rumi. That capability is precious. It is a treasure probably available only to the people in this dimension. So, too, are the other capabilities that are carried by your soul structures of mentality, your second "subtle" body of consciousness. Herein is yet more paradox: your soul structures of mentality can be both a treasure house and a junk yard. As such, those soul structures reveal that they are the manifestation of an immense generative power, that of your solar plexus chakra. They are soul structures that, along with those of your physicality and your emotionality, can enormously influence the course of your life and, collectively, the fate of this world. That is a large piece of information to "digest"!

While doing so, you might want to pay heed to these words from an insightful woman whose studies of the human "mind-field" spanned several decades in the late 20ᵗʰ century:[318]

> "I believe the focused mind-field has the power to tap into everything going on in the world. Many of us intellectually accept this as true, but our experience does not confirm it [. . .] Besides, most of us identify the mind with the cellular brain; we don't recognize it as a wireless transmitter and receptor. We acknowledge as commonplace that we can send and receive radio waves, bounce them off satellites, unscramble them and materialize information transmitted over a distance. How strange that we cannot accept that all the marvelous things we invent or discover "out there" are really prototypes of the body and the mind-field. The power of the human mind is such that we could monitor and decode all the major "goings-on" in the world. Without the news media, we could sense starvation and catastrophe when they occur. [. . .] The mind-field has the capability of sending instantaneous thought messages. Most of us try and are surprised when this works. We shouldn't be. [. . .] We can go beyond the stars by harnessing the non-physical power of the mind. The open mind-field concept says that all important thought is ours for the taking."

But it is a "taking" that can be entrusted only a **fully evolved human being**. In other words, animal soul consciousness is not sufficient to take people "beyond the stars," (except, perhaps, to "monkey" around and create disaster.) On the path of "Coming into Being," you have already learned that the protoplasmic physical consciousness energies of "I sense, therefore, I am" and the astral emotional consciousness energies of "I feel, therefore, I am" could be involved in the generating of an ego/self that was both primitive and crippled. On that same path, the enormous generative power of the solar plexus chakra, with its statement of consciousness and prime directive has been required both to shape and to civilize you as an energy being. That archetypal imperative has been an essential sprecursor of the mind-field. Here, in this circle of stones, you will explore the generative power of your solar plexus chakra and complete your discoveries about animal soul. There is much "food for thought" to be shared. Come, let us enjoy our picnic!

*   *   *

Once more utilizing the riches of Celtic lore, of fairy tales and of modern literature, metaphysics and psychology, this lesson will focus immediately on your human energy system's solar plexus chakra; the center of consciousness that has shaped, out of your soul substance, your soul structures of mentality. Again, the impact of your inner and outer environments will be considered, this time within the context of your multidimensional learning process and the ongoing **holistic** interaction involving both your root and sacral chakra consciousness energies with those of the solar plexus chakra. Within that framework you will learn about your solar

---

[318] Valerie V. Hunt, *Infinite Mind: Science of the Human Vibrations of Consciousness*, pp. 101-102.

plexus chakra's qualities and functions, intrinsic to the generative process that produced your soul structures of mentality. In that context, you will deal with the chakra's prime directive (its purpose, the archetypal imperative) and "i-am" statement of consciousness. You will also make further acquaintance with your "dancing" microcosmic masculine and feminine energies, their ongoing need for balancing and the continuing relationship of those energies to your developing ego/self. Then, while investigating your soul structures of mentality, you will learn about your intellectual development and explore your personality with its many personified archetypes expressing as your "selves." In this undertaking, you will get your first glimmerings of androgyny; major intimations of the full extent and purpose of your ego/self. (Please recall what you have already learned about those structures.) As this lesson proceeds, you will have the help of your Observer in probing into and discerning the truth of what you, an energy being are as "mentality." At the end, there is instruction about a malfunctioning solar plexus chakra and the self-healing therapies (disciplines) that again constitute "homework."

Here is a reminder: as you progress along this third "lane" of your path of "Coming into Being" and your quest for wholeness continues, always hold your light; your awareness of your divine origins and who you truly are. Because there are moments of discouragement on your journey, it is wise to remember (even if, at this point, for you it is still only "theory") this truth about yourself.

Your Solar Plexus Chakra

It is no accident that your solar plexus chakra is located (at least for the purposes of scanning) in the area over your kidneys and adrenals in the back and in the area over your stomach, pancreas, liver, gallbladder and spleen in the front. In that complex of organs you have a processing center, where in-taking and out-putting "operations" are constantly going on during the production of the nutritive power that drives your physicality.[319] In the same "locations" but in another dimension, there is another processing center where "operations" are constantly generating an enormous power. That "processing center" in your human energy system is your solar plexus chakra. It has been generating the soul structures that (metaphorically speaking) have been in-taking and out-putting while producing what many people regard as the power that "feeds" them, i.e., their cognitive abilities. And the "raw materials" for these "operations" have been the varied and constantly recurring sensory and feelings stimuli within your outer and inner environments. While impacting upon your malleable, impressionable, receptive and vulnerable soul substance, these energies have become your mental "body" in an amazing process that had its beginnings at your conception.

As part of your archetypal endowment, your solar plexus chakra has been diligently doing its "work." Its prime directive was and always will be the generation and maintenance of your mentality: the mental "body" that is your thoughts, perspectives, assessments and many other

---

[319] It is the part that that provides both the nutrition and the "getaway" response.

soul structures, including your "personality." Your solar plexus chakra's "i-am" statement of consciousness that, along with the archetypal imperative, is intrinsic to that center's generative power is: "I think, (that is, I have thoughts); therefore, I am." It is the declaration of an increasingly **self-aware** energy being.

In dealing with the "workings" of your solar plexus chakra, there is further reference to the root and sacral chakras that must be made. (Keep in mind the **three** "lanes" of your path of "Coming into Being"!) Here, let us pause briefly for one more look into the Celtic myth about Cuchulain and his adversarial relationship with Queen Maev.

The myth has already given you some insights into your deep and often dark dimensions of unknowing (the "unconscious"). You will recall that Cuchulain, an archetypal motif of an instinctual root chakra focused on survival, had been completely possessed by his red and fire (masculine) energies. He was brought back to himself by being immersed in water, the motif of the balancing sacral chakra (feminine) energies. You will also recall that this dangerous and well-nigh impossible task had been accomplished by Cuchulain's loyal "servants," who had anticipated the event (likely with a measure of dread), prepared for it and accomplished it. Let us further explore that mythological motif.

The "servants" in the Cuchulain myth are analogous to the solar plexus chakra's power, i.e., the servants are: indicating the chakra's "thinking" capacity; the ability of thought to anticipate, to plan and to problem solve. In this power, they are metaphorically expressing the "higher," i.e., the non-instinctual, masculine energies of the solar plexus chakra. But those servants are also willing to sustain wounds in their efforts to minister unto the frenzied warrior. (In the myth, their actions are vital in bringing Cuchulain back to himself.) In this activity, the servants are also metaphorically expressing the feminine "feelings" energies (both "lower" and "higher") that can also be present in the solar plexus chakra. (Why and how that occurs will be dealt with in a moment.) It is sufficient to note here that inherent in your solar plexus center of consciousness, there is the **possibility** of androgyny. With the ongoing healing of root and sacral centers of consciousness, your animal soul masculine and feminine consciousness energies can begin a fine balancing and, thereby, learn to "dance" the Dance of Shiva (and Shakti). Thus, the story of Cuchulain's relationship with Queen Maev has provided some amazing insights into the animal soul developmental process.

Let us now further explore those ideas.

Your solar plexus chakra, like your sacral chakra, is already functioning but not at full power, from the moment of your conception. The "dance" of energies gets underway with the root chakra predominating, because the protoplasmic biological structures have to be in place first. But very quickly the gestating fetus can be experiencing emotional impacts, as you have already learned. While all of this is happening, learning can be going on. (There have been some reports about mothers-to-be who taught their unborn children mathematics and music. After birth, the infants were able to master those subjects at an unusually early age.)[320] Experiments involving age regression into the uterus have revealed both emotional

---

[320] For information about prenatal learning, see the web site: "Baby Plus Prenatal Education System."

and mental awareness, usually traumatic, in the unborn child.[321] Thus, you did not make your advent ***tabula rasa***. Your "subtle" structures of soul, although not as obvious as the "gross" structures, were already being generated.

In past lessons, you have learned about the importance of environmental influences on you as animal soul, i.e., the ways in which your postnatal inner and outer environments could impact upon your root and sacral chakras. Now you can add to the mix the environmental impact on the solar plexus consciousness energies of an infant. (Hearken back again to your infancy and your early environments.) Although primitive, preverbal and precognitive, you have experienced thought "forms" that were your earliest soul structures of mentality. They were generated by your infant solar plexus chakra. Those forms interacted with the soul structures that were your physicality and your emotionality in your very earliest "dance" of energies. It is no wonder that childhood "memories" (especially those that are not remembered) have such a tenacious hold on a person. This will become more apparent after you learn about the qualities, force and function of your solar plexus chakra and later delve into the splendid experimental work of a major psychologist. Let us start with the qualities.

Your Solar Plexus Chakra's Qualities

In describing the energies of your solar plexus chakra, Rosalyn Bruyere has noted that in a healthy human energy system, there is an unfolding "concept" that is sparked in the root chakra, controlled, if necessary, by the dampening energies of the sacral chakra and flared into greater intensity by the energies of the solar plexus chakra.[322]

Those energies carry the quality of the color yellow; both the third "band" in the "wheel of light" and the sound of the chakra. Yellow energies are masculine. When healthy, they can stimulate mental prowess and activate memory by charging the soul structures that are the central nervous system. Like the sunlight on a clear day, yellow energy can "shine" with optimism, gladness, happiness and hope. Paradoxically, yellow color energies can also be indicative of cowardice, deceit, avarice and dishonesty. The yellow quality; the quality of your reasoning, logic, and problem-solving capability, the quality of your thoughts and of your developing self-identification, all reside in your solar plexus chakra.

With reference to that self-identification, there is a "personality" type that has been described as "yellow."[323] Although there are no "pure types," this personality has some interesting characteristics. They can be summarized as follows: "yellows" carry a lot of "self" power; self-made, self-motivated, self-fulfilled, etc: "yellows" are ambitious and capable of grasping opportunities; "yellows" confidently assume leadership roles and usually have no opposition except from "reds;" "yellows" are critical and opinionated; they think "out of the box;" they see the "big picture" and expect to be allowed to realize that vision; "yellows" also

---

[321] See Stephen Wolinsky, *Trances People Live*, in the Index under "Age Regression." After that publication (1991) much more research has been done.
[322] For more detail, see Rosalyn Bruyere, *Wheels of Light*, pp. 54-55.
[323] Excerpted from Carol Ritberger, *Your Personality, Your Health*, pp. 137-144.

live "out of the box" and struggle all their lives to conform to social rules; they are courageous in their thinking and will not surrender when they think they are "right;" "yellows" think deeply and enjoy the opportunity to change the thinking of others; "yellows" are competitive but, unlike "reds," they enjoy competing only against those they respect and can learn from; "yellows" require the freedom to expand their capabilities; they are "idea people" who utilize a "sixth sense" to solve problems; "yellows" can be arrogant perfectionists with both themselves and others; they are planners and organizers and like to anticipate everything; at their best, "yellows" are people who can cut through the "smokescreens of tradition" and focus on the crux of a situation; at their worst, "yellows" are "impractical, condescending, overly conceptual, uncompromising, verbose and nit-picky;" extroverted "yellows" are "hearty, frank, highly energetic, dynamic, charismatic people;" introverted "yellows" are creative, intuitive, independent, individualistic and cool under stress. (Perhaps you are acquainted with, or even closely involved with people of this personality type. Perhaps you fit this description fairly well. Ponder on the implications of both.)

Conjoined with the color yellow in the solar plexus chakra is the masculine element of air. In many of the world's cosmologies, there are stories about a "primordial air god," who separated Father Heaven and Mother Earth so that human beings and other animals "could have room to breathe." An ancient philosopher, Diogenes of Apollonia, theorized: "that which has intelligence is what men call air . . . it has power over all things."[324] In short, in the element air, just as in the elements of fire and water, the "material" and the "spiritual" are inseparable. With every inhalation, you take in the energies of life. Air is absolutely indispensable for physical survival and is the only element that is found in the others. Air is also the least stable of the elements. The gentle breezes blow wherever they please. Your "airy" thoughts can do that! They can be very pleasant and take you into all sorts of nooks and crannies. The gentle breezes can cool you on a hot summer day and send your sailboat dancing over the waves. Your pleasant and refreshing thoughts can (metaphorically speaking) do the same. Like the elements of fire and water, air can serve life. Yet, like those other elements, air can also destroy. When the wind of tornadoes and hurricanes descends on people, there can be immense loss of life and property. The results can linger for years. When the solar plexus chakra is dysfunctional, thoughts can be wild and ferocious. That is, they can express the primitive, crippled energies of unhealed consciousness centers of physicality and of emotionality with their accompanying "i-am" statements. When that happens, human devastation, individual and collective, usually follows. In other words, the microcosmic creative energies that are expressions of the macrocosm, and the possibilities connected with them can become "stuck" as animal soul. Yet, as the myth of Cuchulain has already shown, there are other possibilities available to a soul searcher. They are the promise inherent in your solar plexus chakra and are, indeed, an indication of its archetypal imperative. Let us explore those possibilities.

---

[324] For more detail, see Barbara G. Walker, *The Woman's Dictionary of Symbols and Sacred Objects*, pp. 334-335.

Your Solar Plexus Chakra's Masculine Force and the Possibilities

Conjoined with the color yellow and the element of air, the **masculine** force is vitally necessary to the generative power of your solar plexus chakra. That is true for both sexes of human beings in their evolutionary process. But the solar plexus chakra's masculine force is **qualitatively** different, in its potential, from that of the root chakra. Please recall that on "lanes" one and two of your path of "Coming into Being" you learned about and experienced the incredible interaction of masculine root and feminine sacral chakra energies. What you found is that there was a predominance of the primitive and the instinctual in animal soul interaction. Yet, in your own **knowing** and in the fairy tales illustrating the Wheel of Samsara soul structures of emotionality, there were indicators that animal soul consciousness could ascend to a "higher" level. In other words you, as an energy being, a soul field, could evolve. Already present in the imaginal realm, these are the immense **possibilities** inherent in human soul substance and the human energy system.

Present as archetypes in the soul substance and in the human energy system, the instinctual masculine root and feminine sacral energies have "danced" with each other, since your conception. In this **holistic** system, not only have these energies interacted and expressed the "i-am" consciousness of those chakras in your egoic soul structures but those same energies have also been interacting with those of the solar plexus chakra. This "dance" was very simple and unsophisticated, at first. But there existed the possibility that qualitative change could occur, that the primitive energies could evolve.[325]

This evolution can occur when two related conditions are present: when nourishing and nurturing energies are somehow there in your environments after your advent, and when the spiritual energies inherent in the root, sacral and solar plexus chakras are activated. Then, in the solar plexus chakra, the masculine and feminine "dancing" energies are raised to a higher frequency and the soul structures of mentality, including the egoic structures, can function as a prelude to your rebirth into androgyny. To help clarify this idea and reinforce your understanding of the "workings" of an animal soul solar plexus chakra, here is another tale from the Brothers Grimm. At this time, please remember the function of fairy tales: they teach adult lessons about the energies of soul, at their simplest, barest and most concise level.

This tale is entitled "Roland and May-Bird."[326] It goes like this . . .

There was once a wood-cutter, who lived with his wife and his little son, Roland, in a cottage beside a great forest. One day, while the wood-cutter was working in the forest, he heard a strange sound from overhead. There, caught in the branches of a tree was an infant girl, dropped by a vulture, who had taken her away from her sleeping mother. Gently, the wood-

---

[325] This is analogous to biological evolution in which adaptation to particular environmental conditions gradually occurs. The evolution referred to here involves the masculine and feminine archetypal forces in a **qualitative** change, a transmutation, which, at the same time, does not change the prime directive of the chakra. Later in the lesson, the work of Jean Piaget provides further indication of how the evolution occurs.

[326] Excerpted and quoted from *Grimm's Fairy Tales*, pp. 344-352.

cutter retrieved the infant and brought her home. She was named "May-Bird," because she had been found in a tree in the month of May. The years went by. The two children, Roland and May-Bird, became inseparable. "They were never happy but when they were together."

During those years, the wood-cutter became increasingly poor. Finally, there came the day when there was not enough food for the man, his wife and the two children. It was then that the woman decided that she and her husband would take the children into the forest and leave them. After much argument, the man agreed. Meanwhile, Roland and May-Bird, whose empty stomachs had kept them from sleeping, had overheard the plan. Calmly, Roland slipped outside and filled his pockets with the white stones that glistened in the moonlit cottage court yard. Early the next morning, the children were roused from their beds and led deeply into the forest. As they walked along, Roland carefully dropped the white stones behind him. After a long walk, the parents stopped and instructed the children to go to sleep. Pretending that they would cut wood nearby and return later for them, the wood-cutter and his wife abandoned them. When night came, a frightened May-Bird sobbed piteously. But Roland assured her that with God's help they would be able to find their way back home. After the moon had arisen, they could follow the glistening white stone trail. This they were able to do. They were sincerely welcomed by the wood-cutter, but the woman was not glad to see them.

In a few months, there was again no food for the family. Once again, the children overheard their mother persuading their father to take them into the forest where they would be left. Although the man wanted to share his last morsel with the children he eventually obeyed, because "he had done as she said once [and] he did not dare to say no." This time, when Roland sought to pick up the white stones in the courtyard, he discovered that his mother had locked the door. Still, he comforted May-Bird and assured her that God would take care of them. The next morning, the woman gave each child a crust of bread and the family departed for the forest. As he walked along, Roland crumbled the bread and left the crumbs for a trail. They went into a part of the forest "where they had never been before in all their life." Again, the parents instructed the children to sleep while they cut wood. Again, the parents abandoned them. When the night darkness came and May-Bird was frightened, Roland assured her that in the moonlight they would follow the trail of bread crumbs. But there was none; during the day it had been eaten by hundreds of little birds. Still, Roland was certain that he could find the way back. Taking May-Bird by the hand, he set out. Unknowingly, he led them deeper into the forest. By the next morning, he realized that they were lost. Still he tried to find his way out. For two days, they wandered. By the third day, they were starving and still had not left the forest.

On the afternoon of that third day, Roland and May-Bird came upon a "strange little hut made of bread, with a roof of cake and windows of sparkling sugar." The hungry children began to devour whatever they could reach. Within moments, the door of the hut opened and a little old fairy came gliding out. Sweetly she asked them why they were eating her house, when they could come in and have whatever they wanted. Then they went inside. She fed them a splendid supper and offered them soft, clean beds for their rest. Happily, Roland and May-Bird went to sleep. But the fairy was a "spiteful" one, who had made her hut in order to "entrap little children." While these children slept, she removed Roland to a cage where she would fatten him for eating. In the morning, she forced May-Bird to fetch water and cook. Then the old fairy went off to another place, while accidentally leaving behind her magic wand.

When May-Bird saw her go, she quickly freed Roland from the cage and urged him to flee. He agreed, but first they had to steal the fairy's magic wand. This they did and off they went. When the old fairy returned home, she angrily used her magic powers to "see" them and used more magic to overtake them. But May-Bird saw her coming and used the magic wand to turn Roland into a lake and herself into a swan swimming in the middle of it. Although the old fairy used many arts to lure the swan to shore, it did not come. The fairy was forced to return home. Quickly, May-Bird turned herself and Roland back into their usual forms. They walked the rest of the night until the dawn. Then May-Bird turned herself into a rose in the midst of a thorny hedge. Roland sat down beside it and played his flute. The old fairy came striding along and asked if she could pick the rose. As she tried to do so, Roland continued to play his flute. The music was so magical that the old fairy could not stop dancing. On and on she cavorted and deeper and deeper into the hedge she went. Finally, she had torn off all her clothes and was stuck fast. By this time, May-Bird had become very tired. So Roland told her to wait there, while he went for help. After that, he assured her, they could get married. In order to be safe, May-Bird turned herself into a rock in the corner of a nearby field. Then Roland departed.

But, on his journey, Roland met with another maiden who pleased him so much that he forgot all about May-Bird. She waited a very long time for him to return. Then poor May-Bird felt such sorrow that she decided to turn herself into a daisy so that someone would tread on her. Instead, she was found by a shepherd, who thought the flower was so pretty that he took it home and placed it in a box. After that, wonderful things began to happen. Every day the shepherd's house was cleaned, the water was fetched and good meals were put on the table. Although he liked this well enough, the shepherd was puzzled. He went to a "cunning woman" who told him that there was "witchcraft" in it. She instructed him to watch to

see and throw a white cloth over whatever it was. When he saw the daisy come out of the box, he threw the cloth over it. Instantly, May-Bird stood before him. She was so beautiful that the shepherd asked her to marry him. She refused because she wished to be faithful to her "dear Roland." But she stayed and kept house for the shepherd.

More time went by. Then Roland decided to marry the maiden he had found. Since it was the custom in that land for all the maidens to go to a wedding and sing the praises of the bride and groom, May-Bird was asked to go. She was so heartbroken that she refused for a long time. Finally she went, but remained behind all the others. Then she could not help coming forward. The moment Roland heard her sing, he remembered her. "His heart was opened." He rushed to her side and declared that she was his "true bride." So, May-Bird was married to her dear Roland. And that is the end of the story.

Please experience this fairy tale several times before you enter into the discussion. Identify and ponder on the archetypal motifs and symbols with which you are already familiar. In addition, this tale carries deep symbolic meaning about the solar plexus chakra: about its masculine and feminine energies, about their androgynous potential and about the soul structures of mentality that this chakra can generate. Finally, the story provides an illuminating description about an evolving animal soul consciousness.

Let us begin the discussion with a reminder about your **holistic** energy system: the "wood-cutter" is a motif for the solar plexus chakra's masculine survival-oriented root chakra energies. But, mitigating these energies, there are the more evolved feminine love energies (of the heart chakra) that will rescue an infant and have tender feelings toward offspring. There are also small hints of spiritual energies that realize that all life is sacred. Yet, when altruistic choices are to be made, the feminine spiritual energies the wood-cutter carries are overwhelmed by the energies of his "wife." In this pattern, there is the symbolism of a solar plexus chakra in-formed by an unbalanced root chakra possessed by fear-driven emotionality. In the "wife" motif there is an echo of the woman you have already encountered in the tale of "The Juniper Tree." In this story of "Roland and May-Bird" the wife is so totally survival-oriented and her instinctual survival energies have possessed her so completely that she is even willing to forsake her natural child in order to "feed" herself and her "mate." In this pattern there is the Wheel of Samsara "realm of hell" symbolism of a seriously dysfunctional sacral chakra, now vibrating holistically in a solar plexus chakra. This imbalance can generate seriously damaged soul structures of mentality. Those structures would be expressed by contradictory actions: there would be occasions when the person could be "humane" and others, if security was really threatened, when only the instinctual masculine and feminine energies would prevail. The actions would reveal a descent into the lowest vibrations of animal soul.

The "children" are also archetypal motifs, symbolizing not only the masculine ("Roland") and the feminine ("May-Bird") energies of the solar plexus chakra but also its spiritual potential. There are, however, fundamental differences between those "children" and between them and their "parents." Those differences, which are important to an understanding of the power of the solar plexus chakra, will now be addressed.

In the symbolism of "Roland," the offspring of the wood-cutter and his wife, there is an indication that the "higher" masculine energies of the solar plexus center of consciousness can be influenced holistically by the instinctual energies of the root chakra. But, as the narrative about "Roland" also reveals, the solar plexus chakra's masculine energies can evolve, despite a tendency to regress to old patterns of survival and, thereby, vibrate at a higher frequency than the primordial, instinctual root chakra survival energies (the "wood-cutter"). The evolutionary process (and the fundamental difference between "Roland" and his "father") is indicated by "Roland's" gradually increasing capacity to plan and problem-solve. But, as the story unfolds, there are still a lot of instinctual masculine energies that can in-form "Roland" and, by analogy, a solar plexus chakra. He reveals his beginning planning and problem-solving skills by finding the way back home after he and "May-Bird" are abandoned in the "forest." When they are again abandoned, he seeks to repeat the pattern but fails because his planning skills (and by inference, his "thinking" skills) are not sufficiently developed. (He fails also because seeking safety by going "back" is not the direction to be taken by evolution.) And because his next venture has no direction whatsoever, he becomes completely lost and is captured by the "old fairy," the motif of instinctual and predatory feminine energies. (All of this can take place in a solar plexus chakra and impact upon its generative power. Then, all of this can be expressed by the soul structures of mentality.)

As the story unfolds, "Roland," after being rescued, begins a brief experience of evolutionary change: he is turned into a "lake," which symbolizes the "water" of deep, clear feminine energies. But he quickly reverts to the lower frequency of root chakra masculine energies (indicated by his involvement with his "flute," a phallic symbol.) Yet the masculine energies "Roland" symbolizes have acquired and fostered the necessary foundations for a healthy solar plexus chakra and soul structures of mentality. How has this come about? He has connected with his feminine "opposite within;" his adopted "sister," "May-Bird." It is she who has rescued him.

It is the "May-Bird" motif of feminine energies that makes this a truly remarkable fairy tale. The unusual manner of her arrival, introduction to "Roland" and her name would all indicate that she is a special gift from the Spirit. The two "children" become inseparable. In the context of a generative solar plexus chakra, the "Roland" masculine energies and the "May-Bird" feminine energies develop a deep connection: Roland becomes the protector of his vulnerable little "sister."

To sum up the discussion thus far: in an animal soul solar plexus chakra, carrying unbalanced root chakra energies (the "father" motif) and "realm of hell" dysfunctional sacral chakra energies (the heartless "mother" motif) , the solar plexus masculine energies can still be functioning at a "higher" level, because of its spiritual component. But the masculine energies, as the "Roland" motif indicates, can be very unpredictable. In this they are expressing the air and yellow qualities of that chakra. There must be healing changes that take the form of "learning" before there is stability. By analogy, the animal soul structures of mentality are being generated by a solar plexus chakra whose masculine energies are evolving

In the beginning, however, "May-Bird," the motif of a "higher" feminine spiritual energy (she has come from "above") that can inform the solar plexus chakra, has no means of dealing with either the heartless "mother's" toxic energies or a rather unstable "Roland." She is the victim of the one, while being a fellow-traveler with the other who shares in his lost-ness. (This can happen in a solar plexus chakra and be revealed in soul structures of mentality.)

Then comes the turning-point in the tale. Both children appear to have become starving instinctual energies. When they arrive at the "old fairy's" hut, they simply start to eat it. She is the motif of a dark feminine energy from the deep places of the soul structures of emotionality. In this, she reflects the wife of the wood-cutter, but she is even more heartless; her "hut," placed there as a lure and a snare, is the motif of the addictions that can damage a solar plexus chakra and cripple soul structures of mentality. She "feeds" the "children," entraps them and plans to "eat" them. (Like the dwarf in the story of "The Blue Light" and the devil in the story of "The Maiden Without Hands," she is revealing the hatred that can lurk in the emotional "darkness" and seek to destroy the "higher" energies of light.) But she fails to take into account the love (the "higher" level feminine and spiritual energies) that "May-Bird" has for her "dear Roland." It is "May-Bird" who assumes the leading role and rescues him. Then he briefly takes charge and instructs her to take the old fairy's magic "wand;" a symbol for the transformative power of the divine feminine.[327] With this power, "May-Bird" can perform some fundamental changes. She first transforms "Roland" into **feminine** energies, that of water, symbolized by the "lake," while she is the "swan," the **masculine** motif of a knight protector.[328] By these actions "May-Bird" is indicating that "higher" feminine love energy can impact upon the solar plexus chakra and start to produce the changes that can lead to the androgynous "dance." But she encounters some further challenges. When the root chakra masculine energies impel "Roland" to lapse into primitive sexuality, "May-Bird" transforms herself into a "rose," which is another motif of the divine feminine[329] and provides the means of trapping the "old fairy." Then an exhausted "May-Bird" stays behind while "Roland" embarks on yet another venture. (Have you noticed the similarities between "Roland's" journeys and those of the maiden/young queen and her king/husband in the tale of "The Maiden Without Hands"? As the motif of solar plexus masculine energies, both the king and Roland have more learning to do.) By analogy, this process can often happen in an evolving solar plexus chakra and, by extension, the animal soul structures of mentality. But instinct takes over and "Roland" gets lost again. (At this point, pause and ponder on these observations and how you are responding to them.)

---

[327] Barbara G. Walker, *The Woman's Dictionary of Symbols and Sacred Objects*, p. 32.
[328] *Ibid*, p. 411.
[329] *Ibid,* p. 433.

Then more can happen within a solar plexus chakra, as this fairy tale relates. There follows a period of change for "May-Bird," the motif of the feminine spiritual energies that can be at "work" in a solar plexus chakra and, thereby, be expressed by the soul structures of mentality. As a "rock" (a mineral consciousness) and as a "daisy" (a vegetable consciousness), she evolves. Empowered in this manner, she deals with the instinctual masculine energies symbolized by the "shepherd" and establishes a balanced relationship with him.

In an animal soul solar plexus chakra, there can be a period of change when unbalanced and instinctual root chakra energies and dysfunctional sacral chakra energies are modified by the "higher" feminine spiritual energies of love. Those energies are of the heart center of consciousness (there is much more in the next lesson). Changes can also occur by means of the spiritual component of the root, sacral and solar plexus chakras. In a **holistic** system, all can be in the solar plexus chakra and expressed in the animal soul structures of mentality. Partly, the qualitative changes are also explainable by referring to "divine intervention," which can also be referred to as "upward" and "downward" causation.[330] In other words, the indwelling Spirit has been calling out.

Then the story enters into its final phase and, in its motifs, the account of the ongoing development of a solar plexus chakra. A seemingly helpless "May-Bird" must undergo a period of much distress and growth. This can happen to the spiritual energies in the human energy system. When a betrayed and grieving "May-Bird" reluctantly attends "Roland's" "wedding" (a coupling of instinctual masculine and feminine energies), she "sings" (sound is an immense creative energy) and with the great spiritual power that she embodies (the downward causation), she re-awakens the "higher" masculine energies that he symbolizes. Then, "Roland" finally remembers her and his "heart" opens. He recognizes his "true bride." In the context of a solar plexus chakra, there is the recognition of the "higher" feminine spiritual energies that can "dance" with the masculine. Because **form follows consciousness**, the soul structures of mentality that are generated will exhibit the wholeness and balance of that center of consciousness.

The ongoing development of animal soul can involve all the lapses and changes indicated in this fairy tale. Yet, when the necessary conditions prevail, the work of the solar plexus chakra can be the precursor of an androgynous transition in your quest for wholeness. (There is more to learn in a moment.)

To continue in the spirit of the fairy tale . . . . the **function** of thought is androgynous: the process of *abstracting* is essentially feminine; a taking in, while *conceptualizing* is essentially masculine; a working upon. The process of *integrating* involves both forces in the "dance." But as the fairy tale reveals, there are many challenges to be lived through before that androgyny

---

[330] Ken Wilber, *The Eye of Spirit*, p. 37. Please recall the story of "King Thrushbeard" in Lesson Four. In the **holistic** human energy system, there is always "more" as development proceeds. The "lower" levels can influence the "higher" ones through upward causation. And the higher centers can exert a powerful influence on the lower centers through downward causation. See also *The Essential Ken Wilber: An Introductory Reader*, p. 58.

can be realized. The mere **possibility**, however, can be an encouragement on your path of "Coming into Being."

Take the time to ponder these observations and any that you have developed. Then, let us continue exploring the ways in which the possibility can be expressed by your sacral chakra.

Your Solar Plexus Chakra's Function and Generative Power [331]

In preparation, please scrape your auric field. Then take several **grounding** breaths and call in the Observer. With your cupped hand over your solar plexus chakra, tune into that wheel of light; into its color, rotation and vibration. As you have already done with the root and sacral chakras, you will explore all the components, front and back, of this chakra and deeply ponder on your past and present experiences. Because you will be exploring a paradoxical and **holistic** center of your energy system, you will experience physical and emotional reactions. (Please remember to **acknowledge**, **accept** and **allow** them. Take whatever time you need to practice that important healing discipline.) Then do the exploring while keeping what you have learned from "Roland" and "May-Bird" in mind.

In the front, begin by focusing inwardly into the energies of your solar plexus chakra's physical component. You generate your "gut" level ideas, thoughts and understanding by means of this component. Your "mind" can literally be in your "gut." Sometimes your best awareness can be a "gut feeling." (Recall a few instances.) At other times, you can also feel pain, especially in your stomach, when your solar plexus chakra is generating "sickening" thoughts. And you can experience sexual arousal when your chakra is generating exciting thoughts. In both cases, there are unexamined emotions that are a powerful accompaniment to, or even a precursor of, those thoughts. (Recall a few instances.) Because your soul structures of emotionality are mainly hidden in your deep dimensions of unknowing (until you focus on healing them), their energies can and do shape your thoughts by forcibly impacting on your solar plexus chakra.[332] In many instances, there will be a physical/emotional response. When you "remember" a pleasant or unpleasant flavor, for example, you can literally "taste" it and re-experience the emotions that are part of the "memory." (You might want to re-call those memories and with the Observer close by, sense the "forms" they are taking. Observe your responses. Ponder on this: since there is protoplasmic storage of belief and of emotion, there is likely protoplasmic storage of thought.)

In addition to the emotional experiences already noted, there is an emotional component that is crucial to your solar plexus chakra. In this chakra front, your self-identification, involving your ego/self, now comes to the fore. If there has been a nurturing environment and the chakra is healthy, the emotion informing the chakra is **self-esteem**. If that is the case, the masculine yellow and air qualities of the chakra are expressing as positive generative power. You have a sense of personal empowerment. If that is not the case, there is a preponderance

---

[331] See Cyndi Dale, *New Chakra Healing*, pp. 36-39, 98-99, 119-129, 144-147 and 244-247.
[332] Please recall again that the "unconscious" has its own forms of consciousness.

of unhealed emotional soul structure energies that are adversely influencing the generative power of the chakra. This can manifest as "conflicts" that rage in your "mind." These will be accompanied by feelings of personal inadequacy. (With the help of the Observer, probe into the sense of self-esteem you carry. If, at this point, you believe that having an ego/self and having esteem for that self is not "good," please accept and allow those feelings and thoughts while you learn more about the soul structures of mentality.)

The mental component of your solar plexus chakra front clearly indicates this chakra's prime directive. The mental component is an intelligent power, your rationality, that in-forms your understanding by shaping your awareness of this third dimension "reality" and of your place in it. That intelligent power also carries your "will" as a means of focusing that understanding, that awareness and where you are in all of it. Thus, this soul structure is an immensely important part of your mentality. But it must be understood very clearly that this intelligent power does not confer superiority, if you have developed it or inferiority if you have not. This is a power that, like all the others carried by animal soul, must be balanced. In other words, intelligent power of whatever size is not the "be all and end all" of you as an energy being, a soul field. (Can you relate to that idea? With the Observer along, your **intent** and focused **attention** will help you to identify your beliefs, attitudes and values around this very important subject. Take your time to explore while realizing the "social conditioning" that in-forms you. If necessary, do the intense "letting go/letting be" disciplines/practices of "emotional clearing" and "worm-hole" work).

Through the solar plexus chakra front, the spiritual component allows for a mental "empathy," which is a way of **knowing** that a particular idea is absolutely vital for your spiritual growth. It is an illumined awareness that is different from the rationality that is the mental component. (If you go deeply within, you can tune into those different energies. Again, balance is required. But, ponder on the occasions when you absolutely **knew** that a particular idea was nourishing your entire being, i.e., you as a soul field. It might have been an idea totally new and different from any you had ever encountered. It might not have even seemed rational, but your immediate, Spirit-guided response was "yes!" This, too, is what your solar plexus chakra can generate.

Clearly, your solar plexus chakra carries an incredible generative power that is manifesting its prime directive and "i-am" consciousness. While enjoying your "picnic," you have already received much "food for thought" There is more to take in, while you learn about the back of your solar plexus chakra. It opens to other dimensions and allows for an even greater generative capability.

A boon to healers, the physical component of the solar plexus chakra back connects into the metabolic centers of your physicality. As such, the chakra's generative energies that shape soul substance determine your protoplasmic stamina and strength. It is through the solar plexus chakra back that healing energies can be directed to help a faltering root chakra. In a **holistic** energy system, this assistance will benefit all the others. This is certainly the case if the perceptual filtering system has been malfunctioning, with the resultant physical and/or emotional dis-ease.

Through the back of the solar plexus chakra the emotional component opens to the energies of self-acceptance. These, in turn, assist in the all-important formation of self-esteem. (Do you note the loving energies that are implied in this? If your early training has not encouraged self-acceptance, stay with and ponder this insight for a while, while you remember that you are learning to love yourself. Then move on.)

Through the back, the mental component of the solar plexus chakra allows in the energies that can **alter** your thought patterns, especially. With the assistance of the Observer and your "will" power, those energies which are essentially those of loving, positive thoughts can be focused on the task. (If your beliefs do not encompass those of self-acceptance and love, what beliefs and resulting thought patterns have to be changed? What new ones are required? What are the emotions that are heavily involved? Are more intensive letting go/letting be emotional clearing and "worm-hole" work necessary?)

Through the back, the spiritual component of the solar plexus chakra can take in knowledge of the seen and the unseen. This requires an immense openness that you can **cultivate** while the chakra's emotional and mental components are receiving the attention they require. The spiritual awareness that you are fostering can help you to generate the **knowing** of what your Life Plan really is. (Please recall the shaman's story about you as Little Soul!)

If you are realizing that your solar plexus chakra back is almost shut down, do not be surprised. Your perceptual filtering system is probably implicated. Moreover, among stress-filled North Americans, it is often the case that the solar plexus chakra has suffered trauma. In many parts of this culture, there is such an emphasis on "rational thought" from such an early age that the chakra is being forced into a premature operation, that is, the inner guidance system is being circumvented, and the chakra cannot receive through the back in a normal fashion. At the same time, there is often a situation of "chakra displacement" in the front.[333] In an environment in which people are often "neurotic," (please recall the Wheel of Samsara!) this condition is related to a lack of **grounding**, which prevents the flow of energy up the sushumma and other channels. As a result, all the chakras are displaced upward: the root sits where the sacral should be; the sacral sits where the solar plexus should be; the solar plexus sits where the heart chakra should be, and so on. If you suspect that this is the case with you,[334] there might be chakra displacement. In addition to the self-healing therapies (disciplines) that you will receive later in the lesson, you might require professional healing help in order to re-align your chakras.

Yet, despite the hazards that you, as animal can encounter, it is clear from what you have already learned that you carry great power in your solar plexus center. Indeed, your possibilities are immense! Let us further ingests them.

---

[333] For more detail, see Rosalyn Bruyere, *Wheels of Light*. pp. 85-88.

[334] For example, in your probing and pondering you have encountered too many anomalies. Or you have experienced much difficulty in doing the self-healing therapies for the root and sacral chakras.

Your Soul Structures of Mentality

Please recall the information you have already received about your soul substance. Just as there was a protoplasmic energy consciousness that was shaped into your soul structures of physicality and an astral energy consciousness that was shaped into your soul structures of emotionality, there was a unique energy consciousness that was required for the shaping of your soul structures of mentality. Like the others, this consciousness energy was inherent in your soul substance. Unlike the others, this consciousness energy came with you, as Little Soul, from the Spirit.

An explanation is necessary.

As you recall the shaman's story about your incarnation, go back to the beginning, when you as Little Soul, decided to become a human being. There followed an immense amount of preparation. In that work, you were assisted by an all-wise Soul Keeper, by your all-knowing Celestial Guides and by the Council of Ascended Earth Masters. You were required to prepare a Life Plan that anticipated your human experience and even included a relevant portion of your Akashic Records. Implied in all of this, there is the presence of a purposeful, creative **intelligence**.[335] As a microcosmic energy being, you, as Little Soul, carried that intelligence with you into this dimension. Paradoxically, that intelligence was both a *quality* of your indwelling Spirit and, therefore, a vital part of the Spirit-directed creative, generative process that brought about the formation of your soul structures, and it was a *catalyst* for the intellect carried by your protoplasmic DNA. Expanding on the story of Little Soul; during your gestation, while your root chakra's DNA connection was involved in generating your protoplasmic soul structures (biological) and your accompanying emotional and mental infrastructures (also biological), and your sacral chakra was generating your first "subtle" structures of emotionality out of the lower frequency astral energies you had "picked up" on your descent into this third dimension, your solar plexus chakra was at work generating your first "subtle" soul structures of mentality. They were being shaped out of your soul substance carrying the purposeful, microcosmic, creative **intelligence** that you had brought in with you.

After your advent and for the next eight years of this lifetime, your solar plexus chakra was constantly at work, **but not on its own**, as you slowly learned how to function in your outer environment. In those years of physical and emotional as well as mental development, your solar plexus chakra was intricately involved with your root and sacral chakras in an incredibly complex interpenetration of energies. (This you have already discovered from the fairy tales and other commentary.) Keeping this in mind, you will explore the development of your soul structures of mentality.

But first please note a necessary qualification.

---

[335] Please note that "intelligence" in this context is **not** the same as "intellect" and therefore available only to those with a "normal" to "high" I.Q. In these lessons, intelligence is to be regarded as a property of the **knowing** that is the gnostic awareness of the Divine.

It is beyond the scope of this lesson to provide the details of the learning process required by people. For in-depth study, please consult the wealth of information available in the various disciplines of psychology.[336] As an energy being experiencing the root, sacral and solar plexus chakras of your archetypal energy system, you have already begun to discover the "why" of this process: an animal soul's process of "Opening the Way" and "Coming into Being." And you have already begun to explore the "how," as you have slowly realized your own creative power, probed into your own multidimensionality and become aware of the development of your ego/self. Thus, the account of the learning process to be given in this lesson will be enough only to whet your appetite for your own explorations. Meanwhile, you will continue the journey by receiving more "food for thought."

Having been adequately prepared by the previous lessons, you are ready to take in an essential new idea. It is this: your multidimensionality and the "how" of your "bodies" that are constituted of soul structures, including your egoic structures, can be better understood in the context of the ideas about "evolutionary holarchy" you have already briefly encountered[337] Ken Wilber, a great modern philosopher, has described this "developmental sequence" as follows:

> "In any developmental or growth sequence. as a more encompassing stage or holon [an increasing order of wholeness] emerges, it *includes* the capacities and patterns and functions of the previous stage (i.e., of the previous holons) and then adds its own unique (and more encompassing) capacities. In that sense and in that sense only, can the new and more encompassing holon be said to be "higher" or "wider." Whatever the important value of the previous stage, the new stage has *all* of that plus something extra (more integrative capacity, for example) and that "something extra" means "extra value" *relative* to the previous (and less encompassing) stage." "[. . .]."[338]

In undertaking the shaping of your mental "body," the soul structures of mentality, your archetypal human energy system has provided some compelling evidence to support the concept of evolutionary holarchy.[339] When dealing with those soul structures and their relationship with those of your physicality and emotionality, you will now turn to the insights provided by the child psychologist, Jean Piaget[340] and others. Since these important ideas must

---

[336] This vast body of scientific research grows daily and includes the Internet web sites of journals dealing with child developmental and behavioral psychology.

[337] Please recall that the idea of holarchy was first presented in Lesson Two re: the ZPF and the macrocosmic Unity.

[338] Ken Wilber, *The Eye of the Spirit*, p. 37. For more detail see pages 36-45. Please note that a "holon" can be a "whole" in one context and, in the holarchy, become part of the wider whole.

[339] Intuitively, it could be stated that the other animal soul "bodies" are also holarchic and that this provides another compelling reason for healing them. (This complex idea will not be addressed in these lessons Herein is an opportunity for future investigation.)

[340] Jean Piaget and Barbel Inhelder, *The Psychology of the Child*. With permission, this lesson presents the major insights contained in the complete text including the "Forward" by Jerome Kagan.

be balanced with the insights provided by additional theorists, the Piagetian findings will be given in two parts.

The Insights of Jean Piaget: Part One

Piaget refers to the "three great periods" in the child's mental development and how this development seems to be guided by an "internal mechanism," which is observable in each transition from one stage to the next. Although Piaget denies the existence of a "pre-established plan," and regards all of this process as "a gradual evolution," he can describe it only in relation to cybernetics: "self-regulation; that is, a series of active compensations on the part of the subject in response to external disturbances and an adjustment that is both retroactive (loop systems or feedback) and anticipatory, constituting a permanent system of compensations."[341] What triggers the "compensations" is not addressed. (From your studies thus far, you might want to suggest what that trigger is.) Despite that omission, there is much you can learn from Piaget.

In Piagetian teachings, the "First Great Period" of mental development is described as "sensori-motor intelligence."[342] (This period corresponds to the generative functioning of your root chakra and the development of your soul structures of physicality, in your first three years.) In this great period, there are **six stages** which proceed in a "remarkably smooth succession." Stage One is characterized by the "spontaneous and total activities of the organism" that provides the "groundwork" for the more differentiated "reflexive" activities, for example arm, hand and mouth coordination. In Stage Two, there is the formation of the first habits, attained by a "necessary succession of movements." Stage Three introduces "the next transitions after the beginning of coordination between vision and prehension – around four and a half months on the average." In Stages Four and Five, there are "more complete acts of practical intelligence," in which the child first coordinates "means and ends," for example, retrieving an object that has "disappeared" behind something, and then progressing (Stage Five) at around eleven or twelve months, to use the previous learning to understand spatial relationships, for example, retrieving an object by pulling on the string to which it is attached. In Stage Six, the child finds "new means not only by external or physical grouping but also by internalized combinations that culminate in sudden comprehension or *insight*." In this final sensori-motor stage, there is the inclusion and completion of all the others. (In the context of these lessons, it can be noted that this is a process of development undertaken by the root chakra and involving the nucleus of divinity, the etheric matrix, the kundalini and an increasingly sophisticated perceptual filtering system.)

Within that development, which begins with a symbiotic relationship with the nurturing "parent," there unfolds the slow "differentiation" described by Margaret Mahler [343] and by

---

[341] *Ibid*, p. 153 and 157.

[342] For more detail, see *Ibid*, pp.4-27.

[343] The work of this great pioneering psychologist has been frequently cited by A. H. Almaas in *The Pearl Beyond Price*, various paging. Please also note the critical commentary on some of Almaas's conclusions in

Piaget as a "kind of Copernican revolution, or, more simply, a kind of general decentering process in which the child eventually comes to regard himself as an object among others in a universe that is made up of permanent objects (i.e., structured in a spatial-temporal manner) and in which there is at work a causality that is both localized in space and objectified in things."[344] (In other words, there are the first intimations of an ego/self. Up to that point, the child is pre-egoic. Please recall the dramatic presentation and the discussion in Lessons Three and Four.)

This development of the soul structures of mentality occurs in the first eighteen months of your life, unless there are environmental conditions, external and/or internal, that interfere with healthy root chakra functioning. Then, its "i-am" consciousness could be seriously impaired. In your **holistic** human energy system, your solar plexus chakra would also be impaired and the unfolding evolutionary holarchy would be curtailed accordingly.

But, if things go reasonably well, then, according to Piaget the "universe" in which the child is functioning starts to consist of permanent objects; he learns that "an object does not cease to exist when it disappears and he learns where it does go." Within the sensori-motor learning process, all of which is related to "perception," i.e., the evolving sensori-motor awareness of objects, there is a gradual awareness of space and time. In that development, the child gradually relates the permanence of an object (for example a baby bottle), to constancy of form. In the same period, there develops the perception of constancy of size. Then comes the first primitive awareness of causality; "a tactile-kinesthetic perceptual causality," which is totally dependent on body movement. (Thus, there is a huge involvement with the root chakra.) Then there appears the beginnings of concepts (still mainly linked to sensori-motor intelligence and perception) and of "operations," which are the internalization of actions "grouped into coherent, reversible systems,"[345] in short, the ability to formulate "thoughts." The latter does not appear, however, until about the age of eight years, i.e., the age of onset of the solar plexus chakra. (We shall deal with this in greater detail in Part Two.)

Still prior to age eight, we deal now with Piaget's next major insights; with the sensori-motor intelligence, there is also a "marked parallelism" with the emotional development of the child. At first there is the same lack of differentiation. But there gradually develops the "emotional investments which attach the differentiated self to other persons." (Herein lies the prime directive of your sacral chakra and evidence of the workings of a **holistic** energy system. **The child's emotional development is concurrent with the Stages Two to Six of the sensori-motor process**. There is, according to Piaget and others, a "single integrated process" that is occurring. That structuring "constitutes the source of the later operations of thought." We shall return to that emotional development later. Meanwhile, let us continue with the discussion of sensori-motor intelligence, as the complexities of soul structures of mentality are further revealed.[346]

Ken Wilber's *The Eye of Spirit*, pp. 365-375.

[344] Jean Piaget and Barbel Inhelder, *The Psychology of the Child*, p. 13.

[345] *Ibid*, p. 91.

[346] For more detail, see Jean Piaget and Barbel Inhelder, *The Psychology of the Child*, pp. 28-49.

In the meantime, the period of sensori-motor intelligence has developed into the "Second Great Period" described by Piaget as "the semiotic or symbolic function."[347] This period, which indicates a **holarchic** development, that is, **it includes and continues** the preceding period, is marked by the increasing ability of the child to "represent something: object, event, conceptual scheme, etc. by means of a 'signifier,'" which is language, mental image (very primitive before the age of eight years), symbolic gesture (expressed in play and in drawings) and so on. Within that "semiotic function" there gradually appears the crucially important role of **imitation,** which leads into "representation." (This idea relates to the impressionability and receptivity of soul substance.) Conjoined with the development of imitation is that of **memory** and within that complexity, language evolves. All of this semiotic or symbolic function "makes thought possible." At the same time, the function "evolves under the guidance of thought, or representative intelligence."

In discussing these findings, it could be stated that the solar plexus chakra has been doing its generative work, as well as it can, while not being fully functioning. At the same time, as we shall now discover, the root and sacral chakras' masculine and feminine energies have been "dancing" with each other and with the gradually strengthening power of the solar plexus center of consciousness. Meanwhile, the child's emotional development has been underway. As you have already learned, the root and sacral chakras can be heavily involved with each other. In this interaction, the importance of the child's early environment, including the parenting function cannot be over-emphasized. In the worst case, the child can be caught on the Wheel of Samsara and in the best case there can be difficult (and wounding) emotional situations that arise. No human life is completely free of them. The result in the evolutionary **holarchy** of your mental development is the effect of "upward causation." As indicated by the fairy tales, your soul structures of mentality, including your "moral" concepts, can be dramatically influenced by what your root and sacral chakras have been doing. **Indeed, your ego/self that is manifesting within your soul structures of mentality can be regarded as the holon resulting from the generative "work" of the first two chakras.** (This awareness is crucial when you start to explore the "selves" of your "personality." They emerged in a process of evolutionary holarchy.)

In the Piagetian theory, the emotional and relational development "follows the same general process" as that required for "operations" because the emotional, social and cognitive aspects of behavior are "in fact inseparable."[348] (That will come as no surprise to someone aware of the **holistic** nature of the human energy system.) The emphasis, however, is on the child's interpersonal relations with adults and with other children. The focus is on the child's growing awareness of self, which "constitutes a valorization much more than an introspective discovery . . . [but] also brings the child to try to win other people's affection and esteem." Indeed, before the age of eight years, the child's "self" is not characterized by autonomy but is a self that "wants to be at the same time free of and esteemed by the other." (Implied in this

---

[347] See also *Ibid*, pp. 51-91.
[348] Jean Piaget and Barbel Inhelder, *The Psychology of the Child*, p. 114.

observation is the socialization of the child. In the beginning years, the child is centered on itself and gradually learns social skills. In this area, it is interesting to note how gender figures into the training of children in relationships and morality in those early years.)[349] In Piaget's research, the turning-point for the emergence of "self" and the other lines of early development is age eight. As already noted, this can also mark a turning-point in the generative functioning of the solar plexus chakra. This turning-point heralds the explicit manifestation of what in these lessons is described as the "soul structures of mentality." It is at this age that a healthy solar plexus chakra can undertake its most advanced work of soul structuring. In the ensuing pre-adolescent period, immense changes and growth can occur. (Take time to ponder Piaget's findings and relate them to your own mental development. If yours was different from the process observed by Piaget, how was it different and why?)

Here, we must interrupt our exploration of Piaget's insights to pick up other important ones also dealing with the solar plexus chakra and the soul structures of mentality. We shall return to Piaget.

It is at this point that you are ready to probe deeply into the soul structures of mentality that express your physical patterns of "behavior," along with your emotions, the mental consciousness energy that is your thought, your masculine and feminine energies and your ego/self. In short, you are ready to explore what has been called your "personality." It has been described as being "the ways in which people differ from one another but remain true to themselves."[350]

Your Personality

In yet another paradox, you as an energy being, both **are** a personality, that is, you relate to other people in a particular way, and **have** a personality, that is, you relate to yourself in a particular way. (Sometimes, those "particular ways" do not match each other. Hence, we have these immortal words of the poet Robbie Burns: "Oh wad some power the giftie gie us, to see oursels as ithers see us!") Thus, your personality is a remarkable soul structure. It is also, despite years of "personality" theory and research, somewhat of a mystery.[351]

In the word "personality" there are three inter-related words that provide a descriptive distillation of those soul structures. The words are "person," "persona," and "personal." In the word "person," you immediately envisage a uniquely individual human being; a personality whose "i-am" ego/self consciousness energies are differentiated from everyone else's (even an identical twin). In the word "persona," there is a reference to the theatre, where actors wear masks and play roles; an indication that there are many different individuals differently relating to others and to "self" in one personality. In the word "personal" there is both the idea that the ability to be related to oneself and to others marks the culmination of ego/self

---

[349] For more information, see Carol Gilligan, *In a Different Voice.* See in particular the chapters "Images of Relationship" and "Concepts of Self and Morality" pp. 24-105.

[350] Judith Rice Harris, *No Two Alike: Human Nature and Human Individuality*, p. 21.

[351] *Ibid.* See the prefatory material and various paging.

development,[352] and the idea that this ability and culmination really mark the beginning of a greater human development.[353] In the latter, there is the hint of the real purpose of your ego/ self. (You shall deal fully with this in the next lesson.) Thus, you approach the final steps along the paradoxical path of "Coming into Being."

Let us explore your personality.

It began long before the emergence of your "autonomous" ego/self at age eight. Indeed, as a new-born you were already exhibiting some distinct personality traits that the people around you soon began to associate with "you." Since this came, presumably, **before** any cognitive development, you may assume that your personality started in the uterus. Because there is strong evidence of genetic inheritance, it is safe to say that you received a portion of your personality through your protoplasmic DNA. You can connect certain traits (physical, emotional and intellectual) with those of your biological parents and grandparents. But there is more . . . .

Since your heritability apparently accounts for only 45 per cent of your personality,[354] you might assume that the effects of your outer environments account for the remainder. But that is not entirely the case.[355] There must be other linkages to investigate. Indeed, your personality likely started **before** your incarnation into this lifetime.

First, there are metaphysics to consider. They involve those past lives you chose to make an impact upon this one. You recall that these energies became part of your soul substance while you descended, as Little Soul, through the astral dimension. There is scientific evidence to substantiate this part of the shaman's story. Modern psychological research has strongly indicated that some personality traits and the corresponding "selves" that people exhibit are the energies of past "personalities."[356] In reincarnation, there is a continuity of personality;[357] related to the Law of the Conservation of Energy. To clarify: the soul substance that carried those energies of personality into this lifetime was shaped by your root, sacral and solar plexus chakras. And as your **holarchic** development progressed, the emerging personality manifested in physical mannerisms, in emotional patterns and in 'ideas" **that you had not learned in this lifetime**. (Take some time to ponder on how you might have been the carrier of past life energies. Please recall what you already know about the Akashic Field.)

---

[352] This is implied in the Piagetian teachings and stated clearly in the object relations theory of Margaret Mahler and others.

[353] This theory is developed by A. H. Almaas in *The Pearl Beyond Price*. In this work, "personal" is the "personal element," that links ego with the "Personal Essence," an aspect of the indwelling Spirit.

[354] Judith Rich Harris, *No Two Alike: Human Nature and Human Individuality*, p. 99. This is the conclusion reached by the author after an intensive study of psychological research.

[355] *Ibid*, p. 40. Harris indicates that the home environment accounts for a very small percentage of "personality." Then she develops a theory of "mental systems" that involves a person's social environments in a very complex interaction with the inherited predispositions. She explains the puzzling parts that do not quite fit the "nature/ nurture" combination by referring to "evolution" and to "developmental noise." The latter is not defined.

[356] See, for example, Roger J. Woolger, *Other Lives, Other Selves*.

[357] C. G. Jung, *Four Archetypes*, p. 47. Edgar Cayce, who explored the Akashic Records many thousands of times, gave detailed "readings" about the ongoing energies of "personalities." See Kevin Todeschi, *Edgar Cayce on the Akashic Records*.

Still within the metaphysical framework, you brought into this incarnation your nucleus of divinity; (the indwelling Spirit) the essential Source of power in the creative, generative process that shaped your soul substance into your soul structures. As you have already learned, your ego was the first intimation of your Self. In the consciousness energy that is personality, the "personal" was, from its beginnings, your connection with the personal aspect of your indwelling Spirit. That personal aspect, from your conception, had made your ego/self possible. It was a possibility carried by your soul substance. (Some studies have indicated that even a fetus can have a sense of "ego/self.")[358] After your advent into your particular home environment, that possibility underwent further actualization under the impetus of the prime directive and the "i-am" consciousness of each one of your creative, generative animal soul centers of consciousness.

Finally, within the context of metaphysics and psychology, you brought into this incarnation the microcosmic masculine and feminine forces, essential to the functioning of your animal soul chakras. How those centers of consciousness shaped you was an archetypal "journey" uniquely yours. You have already explored much of that journey, with more to come. The Cuchulain myth and all the fairy tales you have been given thus far have been the means to illustrate the ways in which those forces could express in the generative "workings" of your root, sacral and solar plexus chakras. Those forces have been instrumental in shaping your ego/self, and thus, shaping your "personality," right from the beginning.

Clearly then, that unique "person" that you are was already taking shape at your advent, and your path of "Coming into Being" was already underway.

In your first home environment, you connected, through imitation, with your early role models and tried on their "masks." Many times, you kept them. They were a vital piece involved in soul shaping and, thence, in the development of your ego/self. The effects of childhood's early outer environment have already received much attention in these lessons. The shaping of malleable, impressionable, receptive and vulnerable soul substance often resulted in damaged soul structures that later required healing attention. The earliest wounds were the most difficult to find and to change. But the child was already expressing them. You were expressing yours.

During your early school years, in a complex socialization process, you refined your first roles and developed more. In your interactions with peers, you began to establish how you, as ego/self, "fitted" into the social scene and related to the separate "others" in your wider environment. During this period, you had to deal with your "gender identity," (or as much of it as you could and/or would allow, after soul wounding, or with past life energies and/or genetic inheritance influencing you). As those "formative" years went by, your ego/self roles and masks changed along with your developing cognitive power. By the time you reached age eight, you had laid the foundations for the "person" that was emerging. (There was, of course, more to come. We shall deal with that later.)

---

[358] Age regression research has clearly demonstrated this. In age regression spirit journeys, many of my students have encountered themselves as fetuses.

Those ego/self roles and masks were tightly connected to the masculine and feminine forces both inherent in your soul substance and essential in the creative, generative power of your root, sacral and solar plexus chakras. All were related to the "i-am" statement of those centers of consciousness. These energies were, in turn, tightly connected to the archetypes-as-such present in the Akashic Field; the "collective unconscious." (Please note that the archetypes-as-such are likely the accumulated energies of millions of years of human ego/selves.) In your activities of playing roles and donning masks, you were **invoking**[359] particular archetypal images. They were gradually being personified **through** you, **in** you and **as** you. Within your ongoing development, they were assuming their unique guises. Eventually, there was produced in you "a general sense of being a person, an individual with a sense of self or identity."[360] But in reality, that mental soul structure called "personality" contained a plurality of "selves," your archetypal "personas." Let us turn to these now.

The Personified Archetypes

In preparation, here is more Celtic lore. It is a portion of the legend of Taliesin, a British sage of great fame . . . this portion being an account of how he first acquired his prodigious intellectual skills. It provides insights into the "personas" of "personality." The legend is told like this . . .

There once lived, at the time of King Arthur of the Round Table, a man whose wife's name was Ceridwen. They had a most ugly and slow-witted son, a child whose chances of marriage or gainful employment were slim. To compensate for these failings, Ceridwen, who had recourse to books containing magic formulas, resolved to turn him into a sage. After much study, she borrowed from her neighbor a great copper cauldron and set to work. Into the cauldron she placed the ingredients of the brew that would make of her unfortunate child a man who would have supernatural skills.

How very hard she labored! The cauldron had to be kept boiling for a year and a day. As the brew developed greater and greater potency, only three drops were required for the magic to work. While Ceridwen provided the herbs and uttered the incantations, she had blind Morda on hand to feed the fire and a boy, named Gwion Bach, to stir the mixture.

One day, near the end of the year, while Ceridwen was away gathering more herbs, three drops of the brew flew out of the cauldron and lighted on Gwion Bach's finger. Spontaneously, the boy put the burned digit into his mouth. Immediately, he became gifted with the supernatural skills intended for Ceridwen's son. Gwion Bach realized that she would kill him if she could and he ran away.

---

[359] Jacquelyn Small, *Embodying Spirit: Coming Alive With Meaning and Purpose*, p. 33.
[360] A. H. Almaas, *The Pearl Beyond Price*, p. 53.

When Ceridwen came back to the cauldron, she sensed what had happened. So great was her fury that she smote blind Morda and struck out his good eye. Then she set out in pursuit of Gwion Bach. Her screams of rage had alerted him. When he saw her, he changed his form into that of a hare. She quickly became a greyhound. He leaped into a river and became a fish. She became an otter and continued to chase him. He became a bird and she a hawk. Then he shape-shifted into a grain of wheat and dropped among the other grains in the grain bin. She changed into a black hen and ate him. The chase had ended.

Then along came the woman who owned the farm. She killed the hen and ate her for supper. Nine months later, the farm woman, who had no husband, bore a male child. So great was her shame at having done this that she would have killed him, except for his great beauty. Instead, she placed him into a bag and threw him into the sea.

There, a fisherman found the floating bag and took it home to his wife. Inside, the boy child was safe. So beautiful was he that the fisherman and his wife named him "Taliesin," which meant "radiant brow," and raised him as their own. Great good fortune followed them all their days. After Taliesin grew to manhood, he went to King Arthur's court and fulfilled his destiny as a great sage.

That ends the portion of the legend of Taliesin.[361] Whereas, on the surface, it seems to be a credulous tale of magic and witchcraft, at a deeper level, it conveys important insights about the creation of the personas exhibited by the soul structures of mentality known as "personality." We will deal briefly with them now.

Let us begin with the symbolism of the cauldron; often mentioned in Celtic lore. You have already encountered it in the myth about Cuchulain. You will recall that in that story the servants set out three cauldrons of water and plunged the frenzied warrior into them. Thereby, he was restored to himself. In the Celtic spiritual tradition, cauldrons were sacred containers filled with holy water into which people (usually dead warriors) were placed for regeneration.

In the legend of Taliesin, the contents of the cauldron were intended for that very purpose; the physical and mental re-formation of someone ugly and slow-witted into a larger-than-life human being. The creation of the cauldron's contents, a "substance," was a lengthy process requiring constant tending and nurturing. The substance itself was a sacred and transformative mixture, which could, when even a tiny portion was ingested, generate a shape-shifting power. In all this symbolism, there is an analogy to a human energy field (a "container"), which carries the inherent power (the human energy system) to shape out of soul substance

---

[361] Distilled from T. W. Rolleston, *Celtic Myths and Legends*, pp. 412-416.

(microcosmic consciousness energies) whatever archetypal "selves" (personas) are necessarily invoked for survival.

If, indeed, Ceridwen's "brew" would have worked on its intended recipient, we shall never know. You will note that Gwion Bach, who did receive it and who had been a "normal" person, had to "die" and be "reborn" before the power he had ingested was truly his. (We shall return to this theme in the next lesson.) In the shape-shifting part of the story, you are made aware of some of this power. Each one of the living "forms" he became in order to escape Ceridwen, carried great symbolic mental power that is still available to people.[362] When the male Gwion Bach finally turned himself into a "wheat seed," it carried immense accumulated mental power, while the female Ceridwen, the "hen," carried the opposite. In the uterus of the "farm woman," a motif of Earth energies, the power of the brew (intelligence energies) was symbolically joined with the masculine (seed) and feminine (egg) energies analogous to the root, sacral and solar plexus chakras. Since Taliesin was no ordinary human, he had to be birthed into this third dimension, but brought forth from another. Hence, "Radiant Brow," a supremely intelligent human energy was not only conceived immaculately but also retrieved from out of the "sea." (Please ponder on the complex symbolism of those images.)

And how does this legend "speak" to you about your "personality" and its personas? It is a soul story that tells you that, right from conception, your soul substance can be shaped uniquely by the consciousness energies of your human energy system, and especially by your solar plexus center of consciousness. It also tells you that after your advent, while your soul structures of mentality were being formed in the three great **holarchic** stages indicated by Piaget, you were developing, in an interaction with your (sometimes "unsafe") outer environment, the multiplicity of "selves," the personas, that would express as the ego/selves of the soul structures of mentality referred to as your "personality."

The personas were defined by Jung as a means "to designate the characteristic roles we individually adopt in relating to others."[363] Jung also stated that "the persona is that which in reality one is not, but which oneself as well as others think one is."[364] Moreover, this inner "group" can be very complex. Carol Pearson, who has done extensive work in identifying the personas, has described our personified archetypes in this manner:[365]

> "[. . .], each one of us lives with inner plurality – plurality that is usually not even integrated. Indeed, we generally are capable of living with such inner plurality because we repress knowledge of the parts of us that do not fit our image of ourselves. Or we engage in self-improvement projects to try to get them to fit. Yet it is part of the human condition that we will experience some radical plurality in our lives; different parts of ourselves, for instance, will want different things."

---

[362] For more detail, see Ted Andrews, *Animal Speak,* various paging.
[363] Anthony Stevens, *Archetypes: A Natural History of the Self,* p. 299.
[364] C. G. Jung, *Four Archetypes,* p. 57.
[365] Carol S. Pearson, *Awakening the Heroes Within: Twelve Archetypes to Help Us Find Ourselves and Transform Our World,* p. 67.

Having noted all of this, you may safely conclude that your inner plurality could consist of many archetypal images. There are literally dozens of them that you can invoke as your "cast of characters." Some would be expressive of your gender identity; for example, King/ Queen, Prince/Princess, Seducer/Seductress, Warrior/Amazon and Knight/Lady. Others would be included in both sexes but expressed differently; for example, Perfectionist, Doubter, Workaholic, Critic, Judge, Protector, Whiner, Controller and Busybody. Many could be totally different from those of your friends and lovers. Thus, getting to "know" each other would be an interesting undertaking! And if you removed yourself from one culture and went to another, there would be further complications, as you connected with people whose inner pluralities reflected only their own development and culture. That is one reason why relations, international and personal, can be very challenging. (Has this happened to you? Ponder for a little while on the "selves" that you have encountered in your neighbors, family members, friends and lovers. Focus on those that you have found confusing and/or annoying. They are the ones that you could not "relate" to and which might have created serious difficulties in your relationships. With the aid of the Observer, start to probe into your own personas. Put a name, "face" and "form" to them. You might begin with those that you have been told are your basic personality traits.)

While there are numerous personas that reveal human differences, there is one that is common to all people.[366] And that one common personified archetype is correlative with three others. You will now deal with this persona and its "relatives." While doing so, you will be dealing again with paradox. That is, you will explore both the persona and its "shadow." In the process, you will connect these consciousness energies to the ego/self (or selves) of your "personality." How very complex are the soul structures of mentality generated by your solar plexus chakra!

The personified archetype common to all of us is the ***Child.***

Your Child Archetype and Its "Relatives"

With animal soul energy beings, it is both annoying and delightful to know that they can "grow up" and still remain children. Not only can that happen, but there can be several "children" contained in the same "adult" personality. (Before we proceed, please tune into the child(ren) that you carry.) You have already been made somewhat aware of them in these lessons on the path of "Coming into Being.")

To continue . . .

There are many of the world's fairy tales that deal specifically with the linkage between mother and child.[367] In these stories, it is clear that the child is something so precious that there should not be, on any account, any damage inflicted. Yet, most of the tales convey the opposite: the mother, "knowingly" or not, "kills" the child. Given what you now know can

---

[366] I am indebted to Carolyn Myss and Carol Pearson for providing the insights in this part of the lesson.
[367] For example, see Marie-Louise von Franz, *Archetypal Patterns in Fairy Tales*, Chapter Five, "The Tale of Mrile," pp 146-166.

happen to an incarnating soul, from the moment of conception and thereafter, this likely comes as no surprise.

What the tales indicate is that the incarnating human being is always a Divine Child. (At this juncture, please recall the shaman's story about your incarnation.) Here is Little Soul, who enters into this dimension carrying the wondrous nucleus of divinity. Sometimes, until the age of eighteen months, "[children] still have one foot in eternity; they are not yet completely incarnated into an ordinary, earthly human being and their eternal personalities continue to hover around them.[368] Rare indeed is the parent who recognizes this Divine Child and rarer still is the environment, before and after birth, wherein this Child is given the nourishment it requires. That is essentially the case with animal souls and that is the message of the fairy tales. The "mother," especially, gets blamed. Yet, given the malleability, impressionability, receptivity and vulnerability of soul substance, plus the developmental path required by human beings in the first years, the complexities of the inner and outer environments and Little Soul's own Life Plan, could it be otherwise? So, the Divine Child aka the Innocent, Magical or Enchanted Child rarely stays. It does not do well in this third dimension "reality."

He/she has been depicted, as have all the other representations of the Child, in modern literature. The Divine Child (for example, Esmeralda in Hugo's *The Hunchback of Notre Dame*) does not usually survive childhood. The Innocent, Magical and/or Enchanted Child is the one who does not live in this world of ordinary "reality." He is a Peter Pan and she is a Tinker Bell. (See the movie "Benny and Joon, Over the Moon" with Johnny Depp, for a modern example.) There is also the Nature Child, (for example, the young Tarzan raised in a paradisiacal setting by non-human beings.) There is the Adult Child, (for example, Little Nell in Dickens' *The Old Curiosity Shop*), who is an "old soul" here to raise his/her parent(s). Often, that child enters into adulthood carrying the deep wounds of having been "invisible" during childhood and not realizing the real purpose of his/her early life. Thus, this child can also be the Wounded Child, of which there are two "types;" the Step Child (embodied by Rawling's Harry Potter) and the Orphan (embodied by Dicken's Oliver Twist).

It is with the Wounded Child that you are likely identifying, because that is essentially your story. (It is essentially the story of humanity.) Most people in Western cultures can readily "identify" with Harry Potter and/or Oliver Twist. There are depicted, in these stories, familiar patterns of painful interactions between a child and adult(s). People can carry into adulthood the crystallized soul structures created by those interactions. Therein lies another paradox on the path of "Coming into Being; the Wounded Child as an adult can often be both the "positive" persona and its opposite, that is, the "shadow."[369] For instance, that person can be very helpful, caring, engaging, socially responsible and productive. That same person can range from being "moody" to chronically depressed. In extreme cases, there are those who

---

[368] *Ibid*, p. 149.

[369] For greater detail, see C. G. Jung, *Aspects of the Feminine*, pp. 165-167; Jacquelyn Small, *Awakening in Time: The Journey From Codependence to Co-Creation*, various paging; Anthony Stevens, *Archetypes: A Natural History of the Self*, pp. 210-243 and Carol Pearson, *Awakening the Heroes Within: Twelve Archetypes to Help Us Find Ourselves and Transform Our World.*, various paging.

are "sunny" most of the time, while they are hiding their wounds (Pollyanna) and the shadows appear only rarely and unexpectedly. Or there are those who can be "mean-spirited" and driven by their wounds (Ebenezer Scrooge). The shadows are dominant. Thus, there is a wide range of consciousness energies at work. They are all the result of the generative power of the human energy system (the centers of "i-am" consciousness) within the context of a particular environment and a Life Plan.

Let us pause here and deal briefly (there will be more in the next lesson) with the consciousness energies known as your "shadows."

Your Shadows

Your shadows can be the energies of role models you ingested from dominant personalities in your early years. For example, although you might have detested your father's behavior patterns and you might have worked hard to develop a different "character," you can find yourself acting the same way. Often, these patterns will appear in dreams and require healing attention. There are also the shadows that indicate the underlying energies of past lives. You have unfinished karmic business to deal with in this lifetime. For example, you might be disturbed to note malicious tendencies in yourself and you know that they are not related to this life. Those consciousness energies also reveal themselves in dreams and require healing. (You shall receive more instruction about that in a moment.)

The shadow most often reveals itself in "projections," that is a tendency to "cast [the] shadow out onto the world, expunging these "evils" from [oneself] and seeing them only in others."[370] Those projections are often aspects of you that you have rejected and/or disowned. In many instances, they were your "hidden treasures;" expressions of your indwelling Spirit that were deemed to be "unacceptable" in your environment and/or culture. They might have been "inappropriately" linked to your gender. And/or in the religion in which you were raised, they were often labeled as "sins" or "failings." They have found their way into your adulthood and are the soul structures that now require healing.

(Ponder on these observations for a while. With the aid of the Observer, put a "face" and "form" to your shadows, which are essentially your Wounded Child(ren). As an exercise in identifying your projections, you might want to play a "parlor game" with a few friends in which you discourse freely on the subject of "The Kind of Person That I Cannot Stand." Note how quickly you reveal your own shadows. Your friends will help. You might receive a pleasant surprise!)

In the context of the shadow world of the Wounded Child, there are three universal "relatives" that require your attention. These personified archetypes are the Victim, the Prostitute and the Saboteur.[371] All three interrelate with each other, that is, when there is one present in the "personality," the others are there, too. They indicate a profound lack of self-

---

[370] Jacquelyn Small, *Awakening In Time*, p. 47.
[371] For details, please refer to the series entitled *The Language of Archetypes: Discovering the Forces That Shape Your Destiny*, CD #1, by Carolyn Myss.

esteem, the evidence of a damaged and malfunctioning solar plexus chakra. All three can blight your life and your relationships. Although there are innumerable ways in which these archetypal consciousness energies can express in thought, action, words and imagery, there are (metaphorically speaking) several basic physical, emotional and mental "i-am" statements of animal soul ego/self that they express:

The Victim: "I am broken and weary; I am helpless and ineffectual; I am angry; I am distrustful and afraid; I am defeated; I suffer. Of course, I want loving relationships! I just have to control them, because people will hurt me and I must avoid abuse; otherwise, I will not survive."

The Prostitute: "I am hungry and empty; I am seductive and insatiable; I am angry; I am distrustful and afraid; I am needy; I pretend. Of course, I want loving relationships! I just have to control them, because people will want the "real" me and I must avoid exposure; otherwise, I will not survive."

The Saboteur: "I am inflexible and alert; I am deceptive and charming; I am angry; I am distrustful and afraid; I am malicious; I destroy. Of course, I want loving relationships! I just have to control them, because people will expect me to be different and I must avoid change; otherwise, I will not survive."

Like the Wounded Child, the Victim, Prostitute and Saboteur archetypes are indicating a dysfunctional inner and outer environment. Like the Wounded Child, they can be invoked at a very early age and, through steady reinforcement, become crystallized egoic structures expressing in your "personality." All three participate in the Wheel of Samsara and all three have the power to control your "thoughts." Indeed, these ego/selves have (mistakenly) been made synonymous with "evil."[372] (Please recall the fairy tales you have been given and, after inwardly locating these personified archetypes, relate them to what you now **know** about your animal soul centers of consciousness and structures.)

Finally, the personified archetypes that are the Victim, Prostitute and Saboteur are **androgynous** soul structures of mentality, generated by your solar plexus chakra in its interactions with your root and sacral chakras. In this, they heavily express your biology of belief (with its emotional "charge") and the 'i-am' consciousness of those chakras. Then, the "i-am" consciousness of your solar plexus chakra expresses those shadows as "selves." These egoic structures are usually buried in your deep places of "unknowing" and remain well hidden behind your masks. Although you might have retained traces of your "positive" Divine Child, Innocent, Magical and/or Enchanted Child who were, of course, androgynous, your first androgynous soul structures of mentality were very likely your shadows; those that now require your deep healing attention.

---

[372] For example, see Eckhart Tolle, *A New Earth: Awakening to Your Life's Purpose*, p. 22.

Probing into the energies of the Wounded Child can often reveal the five "character structures" described by Barbara Brennan.[373] Her thousands of encounters with adult Wounded Children led to her awareness that children who have been physically and/or emotionally traumatized by parental figures, prior to or at puberty, revealed a particular physical, emotional and mental dynamic. In other words, their soul structures had been shaped and reinforced into crystallized "bodies" that expressed the shadows of a Wounded Child. Here is a summary of her findings. (As you encounter them, please note the power of **beliefs** in maintaining the woundedness of the Child and note the presence of the Victim and/or Prostitute and/or Saboteur. Then, connecting at a deeper level, allow yourself, with the help of the Observer, to recognize your own character structure(s)):

The Five Brennan Character Structures

The "**schizoid**" character has been traumatized before or at birth by an openly hostile mother. In defense, the person "goes away" into the spirit world and grows up believing that she/he does not have the right to exist. There is very little connection to this third dimension "reality." The soul structures of physicality in adulthood are elongated with right/left imbalances, indicating imbalances of the masculine and feminine energies. Relationships involve sex and fantasies in order to feel the life force. There are feelings of terror that cover rage that cover a terrible pain of needing a loving, warm and nourishing connection with another human being. That is extremely difficult because there is at the same time little or no sense of connection with an inner "self." Interactions are marked by intellectualized and depersonalized language. Healing requires an immense focus on all the animal soul chakras.

The "**oral**" character has been traumatized in early infancy by abandonment (physical and/or emotional) by the mother. The belief is that love will be withheld, no matter what the need. In defense, the person becomes "independent" at a very early age and as a result becomes unwilling and afraid to ask for what is truly needed. This can result in spiteful passivity. Because the feelings are those of emptiness and hollowness, relationships mainly involve sex for closeness and contact. But in these the person experiences disappointments and rejections, which result in feelings of bitterness and a greedy need for more that is never enough. There is a deep need to be nurtured. The soul structures of physicality in adulthood include a thin frame with a collapsed chest and flaccid smooth muscles. Interactions involve speaking in indirect questions that are meant to evoke mothering from the other person. Healing involves an intense focus on the animal soul chakras.

The "**psychopathic**" character has been traumatized in early childhood by a covertly seductive parent of the opposite sex. In defense, the person becomes controlling and manipulative, either by dominating or by seduction and reaches adulthood believing that he/she has to be "right" or die. As a result, the person is torn between dependency on people and the need to control them. Relationships are often hostile, fragile and frequently homosexual.

---

[373] I am indebted for these insights to Barbara Brennan, *Hands of Light*, pp.109-127.

There are feelings of defeat, humiliation and aggression. There is a deep need for creative self expression that has to be released. The soul structures of physicality are top heavy with an inflated chest and cold legs and pelvis. Interactions involve dictating and direct manipulation. Healing requires an intense focus on the animal soul chakras.

The "**masochistic**" character has been traumatized in childhood but before puberty by controlling, dominating parental figures. The person reaches adulthood believing that he/she has to strike first before someone else seeks either to humiliate or "kill" him/her. In defense, the person tries to hold everything inside and turns into a seething mass of spite, negativity, hostility, rage, superiority and fear. Relationships often involve sexual impotence and an interest in pornography. There are feelings of entrapment, defeat and humiliation and a deep need to release all the inner tension. Interactions involve indirect manipulation by means of "polite" expressions often accompanied by an "air" of disgust. The soul structures of physicality are heavy with a head that is thrust forward and cold buttocks. Healing requires an intense focus on the animal soul chakras.

The "**rigid**" character has been traumatized in early puberty by being rejected by the parent of the opposite sex. The person reaches adulthood believing that there really are no "right" choices. In defense, the person holds back all feelings and identifies strongly with physical reality. Relationships often involve demanding love and sexual responses from others but being competitive rather than committed to them. There are feelings of terror and vulnerability well protected by a wall of "unfeeling." There is a deep need to surrender to the unexpressed feelings. Interactions include habitual indecisiveness. The soul structures of physicality are well formed but the back is rigid and the pelvis is cold and tipped back. Healing requires an intense focus on the animal soul chakras.

The Wounded Child that has been expressed in these character structures can have many variations. What is clear is the dreadful damage that has been inflicted upon the animal soul chakras and, by implication, to the egoic structures. (Perhaps you have already experienced these energies in you and your acquaintances. They can also express in a collectivity. Please stay out of judgment and observe, with compassion, the deep wounding and probable soul fragmentation. If the latter is the case, shamanic healing involving soul retrieval will be necessary.)

Thus, by the age of eight years, you could be carrying the androgynous "shadow" soul structures of mentality that you would take into adulthood. In addition, many of the other "persons," "personas" and "personal" components of your "personality" could already be in place. But physically, emotionally and mentally you would still have a lot of "growing up" to do.

With all that awareness in place, let us return to the insights of the great Jean Piaget and to his findings relating to the workings of your solar plexus chakra after age eight, in your pre-adolescent years.

The Insights of Jean Piaget: Part Two

Piaget has designated the life span after age eight until age sixteen as the "Third Great Period." In it there are developed the capacities for "thought and interpersonal relations."[374]

In defining and explaining the pre-adolescent development, Piaget uses the words "concrete operations." These are "*actions* characterized by their very great generality." That is, thought processes are actions. They are also "reversible," "never isolated" but always "capable of being coordinated into overall systems." The actions of thought are "common to all individuals on the same mental level" and enter into both "private reasoning" and "cognitive exchanges." In concrete operations the child is dealing first with objects and not with the "verbally stated hypotheses" that come later. Yet in this early thought, the child progressively remembers and applies increasingly complex ideas of classification, arrangement, numbering, space, time and speed. As this learning continues, there evolves a more mature approach to causality and chance. And the "operations" also involve the development of "moral" beliefs. These, as you have already learned, have an early advent and are later expressed, according to Piaget, in certain "feelings" and in the setting down and acceptance of certain "rules" of behavior, in games and so forth. It is these that indicate the emergence of a truly "autonomous" self.

(Please remember that all of this amazing process had its beginnings in sensori-motor intelligence informed by emotions. The process culminates and provides a readiness for the next stage at age eight. Also note that the process reveals both **evolutionary holarchy** and the "workings" of a microcosmic creative power; an archetypal human energy system whose complexities cannot be understood solely in a scientific context but require the **knowing** present in mythology and fairy tales.)

Now, let us continue.

In the last great Piagetian stage of your mental **evolutionary holarchy**,[375] your solar plexus chakra has greater generative power than in the early years of your development. This has a relationship to your phylogeny, in which there was much more power residing in your root and sacral chakras than the solar plexus chakra. But there comes at age eight, after much development, a "new structure of thought," [. . .] which "constitutes a natural culmination of the sensori-motor structures [. . .] and of the groupings of concrete operations."[376] Briefly, what happens is described by Piaget as follows:

> "It would seem [. . .] as if the child first realized that signs were distinct from things and was then led by this discovery increasingly to regard thought as internal. This continuous and progressive differentiation of signs and things, together with the growing realization of the subjectivity of thought, appears gradually to lead him to the notion that thought is immaterial."[377]

---

[374] For more detail, see Jean Piaget and Barbel Inhelder, *The Psychology of the Child*, pp. 92-129.
[375] For more detail, see Jean Piaget and Barbel Inhelder, *The Psychology of the Child*, pp. 130-151.
[376] *Ibid*, p. 131.
[377] Jean Piaget, *The Child's Conception of the World*, p. 87.

In addition to these changes, there are emotional and social developments that must occur. In these the child has to be "autonomous" but at the same time be must become sensitively aware of the "others" in his environment. (In studies conducted by Carol Gilligan and others, there is evidence that the female people in Western culture are more advanced in this respect than are the males.[378] But on closer examination, the effects of socialization based on gender become clear. It would appear that the females' sensitive awareness is not a "moral" decision but an inculcated desire not to hurt another person's feelings.)[379] In the context of these lessons, sensitivity to others would indicate the beginning of an awakening out of the consciousness of animal soul. Nevertheless, the pre-adolescent human has evolved into the next **holarchic** stage. The child becomes capable of "reasoning correctly about propositions he does not believe in, or at least not yet."[380] Within the next four years, the child has become successful at dealing with the basic scientific propositions of negation, notions of proportion and certain forms of probability, among others. Then by age eleven to twelve, the child reveals the "spontaneous development of an experimental spirit"[381] in the undertaking of certain scientific procedures. In the meantime, "pre-adolescence is characterized by an acceleration of physiological and somatic growth and by the opening up of new possibilities for which the subject is preparing himself [. . .].[382] (The latter is an indication of the workings of the emotional, mental and spiritual components of the solar plexus chakra.)

In discussing these final findings of Piaget, in the context of the human energy system, there is the distinct possibility that with the ending of pre-adolescence the child would be ready to leave the animal soul consciousness behind. Although the root chakra has to continue the physiological unfolding, the sacral and the solar plexus chakras could be poised for an immense transition. This is the stage when the heart chakra consciousness energies can truly begin. In the developmental process up to that point, there could have appeared the first glimmerings of androgyny in soul structures of mentality and the emergence of a unique "person" and "personas." At that juncture, the Child could have been a "fully developed positive child," replete with trust and a sense of responsibility.[383] The child's ego/self would have been poised on the edge of immense new awareness.

Instead, there likely were malfunctions, especially in the sacral chakra and thence, the soul structures of emotionality. These, in turn, had impacted upon the workings of the solar plexus chakra and the generating of the soul structures of mentality. (If that was the case with you, stop here and ponder on your development until the age of twelve years. Instead of

---

[378] For more detail, see Carol Gilligan, *In a Different Voice*. See Chapter Three, pp. 64-105.

[379] *Ibid*, p 67. "The essence of moral decision is the exercise of choice and the willingness to accept responsibility for that choice. To the extent that women perceive themselves as having no choice, they correspondingly excuse themselves from the responsibility that decision entails. Childlike in the vulnerability of their dependence and consequent fear of abandonment, they claim to wish only to please, but in return for their goodness they expect to be loved and cared for."

[380] Jean Piaget and Barbel Inhelder, *The Psychology of the Child*, p. 132.

[381] *Ibid*, p. 145.

[382] *Ibid*, p. 150.

[383] Carolyn Myss, *The Language of Archetypes*, CD #1.

culminating your path of "Coming into Being," and moving into the next great stage of your evolution, where were you?)

Now recall the story of "Roland and May-Bird" with its deep insights into the "workings" of the human energy system; in particular the "dancing" masculine and feminine energies as they are expressed in the solar plexus chakra. It is at this point that there arises the possibility of androgyny. It is at this point that the next "path" of your journey into wholeness begins. Again, please note that these lessons on your path of "Coming into Being" have given you two "journeys" to keep in mind. The first is the one you have undertaken into the "past" of your childhood and into what brought you to this point and the second is the one you are undertaking now. The process of re-birthing into androgyny requires that you continue doing both, while you continue to heal. We turn next to your damaged solar plexus chakra and then to some self-healing therapies.

Your Solar Plexus Chakra's Malfunction

As you have progressed through this lesson, you have become increasingly aware of the ways in which your animal soul chakras are **holistic.** They are indicative of an incredibly complex energy system that operates with absolute precision; the prime directive, the "i-am" consciousness, the generative power of each of those centers of consciousness and the creative, generative process by which soul structures are formed are all splendidly organized and directed. It is an amazing microcosmic process of creation. Yet, in this third dimension, at this time in human evolution, there is probably no human being whose energy system functions perfectly. Why? Despite the beauty and the bounty of the Earth "home" that people occupy, they have used their creative power to set up and promote a "world" in which people can unknowingly cause their chakras to malfunction. As you have likely already realized, it is the lovelessness that so much prevails in the "human" situation that has been instrumental in promoting this malfunction. Thus, people can be crippled physically, emotionally and mentally. (Although there are geographic, cultural and economic factors that also make their impact, please ponder on the ways in which the lovelessness that people have for themselves and for each other has influenced those factors.)

In the preceding lessons, that malfunction has been described for your root and sacral animal soul chakras. You have been given many means to restore your damaged creative power. With your awareness that **form follows consciousness**, your soul structures of physicality and emotionality, including your egoic structures, can also be changed as your consciousness changes. Now, let us focus on the last of your animal soul centers of consciousness; your malfunctioning solar plexus chakra.

You will recall that there can be chakra displacement, mainly brought about by a lack of **grounding** linked to the unhealthy activities of the sacral chakra, whose generated soul structures have been compared to the Wheel of Samsara. To add more detail, the immense emotions generated by the sacral chakra are "pressures" that can bring about the chakra displacement. Those pressures also find expression in a cultural emphasis on intellectual achievement in the push to "get ahead in the world." This can start in grade school (sometimes earlier) and create in the child an over-identification with "doing." Although intelligence energies are essential in the shaping of soul structures of mentality, the findings of Piaget would indicate that they require a gradual development involving more than scholastic efforts. With an over-emphasis on the latter, the result can be "neurotic" problems, all connected with a lack of self-esteem, and unhealthy energies in the solar plexus chakra.

With this chakra, the physical and "psychological" problems are combined. Since the solar plexus chakra carries the power of "will," any malfunction will physically indicate power issues that are centered in the middle of the physical body. Those issues would express as emotionally charged thoughts. (You can see how personified archetypes, for example, the Perfectionist, would be involved with a malfunctioning solar plexus chakra.) Thus, liver problems in either a man or a woman indicate animosity against men or one's own masculine energies. Spleen problems in either a man or a woman indicate animosity against women or one's own feminine energies. Stomach problems indicate a tendency to "swallow" other peoples' opinions. Gallbladder problems in either a man or a woman indicate resentments or grief about men or about one's own masculine energies. Pancreatic problems indicate the lack of ability to hold "sweetness," the likely result of having been under-nurtured. Adrenal and kidney problems indicate survival issues carried over from childhood; for example, "I always have to have extra food in the house, because something terrible could happen and I would go hungry."

When these physical and psychological problems are added to those of the malfunctioning root and sacral chakras, the list of "ills" that can afflict people as the result of a malfunctioning energy system is appalling. But, as was the case with the root and sacral chakras, there is hope for healing.

Self-Healing Therapies for Your Solar Plexus Chakra

Once again you are reminded that the guidelines for maintaining your energy system, provided in Lesson One, still apply. You are also reminded that the self-healing therapies given herein, are **not** a substitute for the help provided by competent caring professionals. The work you will do in healing your own soul structures is a necessary adjunct to that done by others. When **form follows consciousness**, your structures are healed because the chakra has gradually been healed. A kundalini "shift" of energies has occurred and the energies of the structures have been transformed. Thus, your self-healing work is a discipline that you willingly maintain. (And sustaining that discipline is your daily practice of meditation; an essential discipline.). Please recall that discipline is the doing that is the undoing of your resistance to awareness!

Since this is a **holistic** system, you can deliver healing energies into other chakras, especially the sacral and the heart, in order to heal the solar plexus chakra. Much of the work you have already undertaken with the sacral chakra has benefited the others. As a result, there has already been a reduction in the resistance set up by your soul structures of emotionality. In other words, the "entities" have been disappearing. Remember to practice the disciplines and to be patient; the process unfolds gradually. You can "track" your healing process by tuning into your own energies with the help of the Observer. Just observe.

Self-Healing Therapies: After Too Much Yellow and Air Energies

Before you begin, be aware of your connection with your own sacred space. Then, focus on your damaged solar plexus chakra. Too much yellow (masculine) energies can trigger extremes of both "positive" (happy, exuberant, optimistic, focused. Deep-thinking, ambitious} and "negative" (deceptive, dishonest, cowardly, critical. Perfectionist, uncompromising, condescending) attributes in your soul structures of mentality. Too much air energies can trigger destructive extremes of both the "positive "and "negative" attributes. How these extremes are related to a malfunctioning sacral chakra cannot be determined exactly. But all of the chakra's components are probably involved and the out-of-balance "dance" is happening.

Your **grounding** breaths, connection to Earth, stress-reducing breath work, breathing (and balancing) up the "Ida" and "Pingala" channels and the "scraping" remain important aspects of the healing work. The spirit energies from meditation and prayer are likely now assuming a prominent place. (Your grounding and gratitude are always there to empower you.)

Body Work

Continue these therapies and add the following practice for your solar plexus chakra malfunctioning because of too much yellow and air energies.

To **control** yellow, you need purple. To control air energies, you require focus. (The focusing in the breath work for your malfunctioning root and sacral chakras has already been healing your solar plexus chakra.) Keep that in mind as you undertake this visualization: it is entitled "Pouring Purple Paint."

When there is conflict going on in your personality among various personified archetypes, each wishing to dominate, for example, a "quarrel" among your "Complainer, Pacifier and Perfectionist, you do **not** have to feel like the helpless Victim. What you do instead is "Pour Purple Paint" like this:

See those warring energies as being within your solar plexus chakra. Put a "face" and "form" to each one of them.

Step up into the area of your heart chakra. See it as a huge room behind you.

See in that space a large warehouse filled with gallons of purple paint.

Gently speak to the warring energies below and ask for silence.

If none is forthcoming, reach behind you and pick up a gallon of the paint.

Find a paint can opener in your pocket.

Crack open the gallon of the purple paint.

With gentle detachment, pour the paint over the combatants.

One can is usually enough. But if more is needed, pour it.

This is a very effective way to stop the conflicts that many people feel within.

Repeat this exercise as often as you need it, especially if there is a problem with the Saboteur. (Under no condition do you get into a battle or even a discussion with the Saboteur. If you pour enough purple paint on this immense energy, it will be changed, likely into that of alert and kindly detachment. This can happen, but only gradually.)

Earth Energies

When there is too much yellow and air energy, the **crystals** that are needed to balance and restore your solar plexus chakra and thence your soul structures of mentality are the following:

Amethyst (you are already using this to heal the sacral chakra) balances the root and sacral consciousness energies and brings into the solar plexus chakra the healing spiritual energies of serenity and compassion.

Antlerite, which enhances mental clarity, helps to promote an unbiased evaluation of your feelings and a loving evaluation of your thoughts.

The **herbs** that are helpful in dealing with too much yellow and air energies are **thyme** (in baths), **skullcap. Lady's Slipper and valerian** (all with sedative powers).

The **aromas** that will quieten too much yellow and air energies are

Rose, which helps you to develop an amiable tolerance.

Vetiver, which is deeply relaxing, helps you to deal with the insomnia that is often expressing too much yellow and air energies.

Please recall from Lesson Three the ways in which aromas can be used. Deep body massage using either the Rose or Vetiver aromas in oils is also very healing, when the excessive yellow and air energies are present.

Spirit Energies

Although at first it will appear to be an impossible task, your daily "sitting" meditation practice, done in conjunction with your "Body Work" and Earth Energies, will bring you into balance and into peace. As this happens, you are able to deal successfully with your difficult personified archetypes and to invoke new, more agreeable ones. (You will even be dealing successfully with karmic energies and making major strides with your Life Plan.) To assist you further in your meditation, add the "Ida/Pingala" breath work. Because there is so much unbalanced emotion involved with too much yellow and air solar plexus energies, the "Seeker's Lamp" meditation can also greatly assist you by helping you to "uncover" the **beliefs** that are likely contributing to the problem. Then, follow up with your intensive letting/go/letting be "worm-hole" work. And remember in the midst of all this busyness to welcome those times of being held in the inner stillness.

Self-Healing Therapies: After Too Little Yellow and Air Energies

In a damaged solar plexus chakra, when there are too little yellow and air (masculine) energies, there is not enough generative power to shape (or continue to shape) the soul structures of mentality to their maximum development. Your intellectual capacities are curtailed. Your personality expresses this curtailment. Your ego/self is diminished, along with the self-esteem and the will that are so essential for truly coming into being. When the damage has been prolonged over time, the soul structures of mentality will be heavily crystallized and require extensive ameliorative work. In the case where the damage has had a more recent origin, such as in a traumatic "shock" (which often involves soul fragmentation), the healing of the chakra can be less prolonged, but there is much work to be done. In either instance, you will likely require the help of an energy healer.

Body Work

Grounding breath work is essential. Your connection to Earth energies is vital for the healing of unhealthy energies in all three of your animal soul chakras. Thus, the "Ida/Pingala" breath work can be practiced extensively. The more toxicity that is released, the more the center of consciousness can be healed. In this work, commitment with intent and attention are vital.

An effective combination of breath work and visualization to increase the yellow and air energies is as follows. It is a variation of the "Up the Sushumma" breath work you have already learned:

"Scrape" your electromagnetic field thoroughly. Take several **grounding** breaths and firmly attach your "roots" to your energy source.

Take several deep **grounding** breaths.

See a colorless energy.

Inhale deeply while "pulling" that energy up your roots up your legs and up your sushumma into your solar plexus chakra.

Exhale while puckering your mouth and "blowing out" the "black" toxicities.

Take plenty of time to do this step.

Then, see a clear yellow energy.

Inhale deeply while you pull that energy up into your solar plexus chakra.

Exhale the "black."

If you have difficulty with this step, return to the beginning and work more with the colorless energy.

After considerable practice in pulling up the yellow energy into your chakra, continue until you sense that the black toxicity has been greatly reduced.

See a clear purple "reinforcing" color.

Inhale **while pulling up both the purple and the yellow energies** and placing them into your solar plexus chakra.

221

Exhale whatever remains of the black energies.

Continue until you sense cleaner energies, which you confirm with the assistance of your Observer.

Continue this exercise on a daily basis until you no longer need it.

You can enhance the breath work and help "recharge" your solar plexus chakra by "toning" the sound of its healthy vibrational frequency. In the Ayurvedic tradition, the sound of the solar plexus chakra is "RAM." Listen to the A note below Middle C on the piano. "Tone" that sound by taking a deep **grounding** breath and releasing it slowly as your vocal cords generate RRRRR . . . AAAHHHH . . . MMMMM. Focus on your solar plexus chakra. Create a strong, deep vibration that you feel in the chakra and in your mouth. Repeat this toning nine times for one "round." If you find it difficult, you are hitting your damage. Persist in the toning. After having successfully practiced this sound, add the toning for your root ("LAM") and sacral chakra ("VAM"). In your **holistic** energy system, they will help to heal each other.

As your yellow energy builds, add physical body exercises. These activities include jogging (to overcome inertia) and sit-ups (to increase the muscle tone over your solar plexus chakra). The yogic poses you might try are the "Bow Pose," the "Belly Push," the "Pike Pose" and "Making the Sun."[384] Stimulating the kundalini with "belly dancing" and "undulating" is necessary (and a lot of fun!) for healing your animal soul root, sacral and solar plexus chakras.

Earth Energies

The crystals that you can use to stimulate yellow energies are

Alexandrite, which carries power for centering your being and reinforcing your self-esteem.

Hematite, which is called "the stone for the mind" and which can be used for assisting in mental attunement, memory enhancement and original thinking.

Berlinite, which is used to stimulate independence and autonomy and opening to self assurance and self-sufficiency.

The herbs that will help in promoting more yellow energy are **speedwell** combined with **celery root**, and **St. John's Wort** tincture.

Spirit Energies

When the yellow energy is depleted through traumatic "shock," there is the likelihood of soul substance fragmentation. In addition to the necessary counseling there is a way of retrieving the "part" that has been "lost." This can be done only if professional healing help is not available. It is a shamanic practice that will take you into the "spirit world." Do not undertake this work unless you are certain that there has been a traumatic shock that has left you with

---

[384] Anodea Judith, *Wheels of Life*, pp, 177-181.

the strong sense that there is "something missing." Before making the attempt, prepare with considerable body work and **grounding** in Earth's energies. Make further preparation by doing the "Ring of Color" guided meditation, but this time "see" the color as clear yellow and sense air energies as you experience the power entering your field. Take your time with this work; by now you recognize its great power. If you experience any emotional hesitancy, you can also establish a great inner calm by repeating the "Pool of Rejuvenation" meditation. And, of course, you remain in the inner stillness until you **know** that you are prepared. With that readiness, you may undertake the intense shamanic experience entitled "Soul Retrieval."

Sit in your calm and peaceful space. Start with some deep **grounding** breaths combined with the "Ida/Pingala" breath work. Clearly state your **intent** to retrieve the fragment of your soul substance that you have "lost." Then focus within and start to go "downwards" very deeply. With each inhalation, go deeper and deeper into the "darkness" and clearly "know" your **intent**. At a certain point, you will "see" a veil or a curtain in front of you. With courage and intent, go through the veil. You will find yourself in the "place" where your missing soul fragment is located. (Do not be surprised at what this is.) You will likely meet a "spirit guide" to help you. But if there appears to be none, press onward with trust. Remember your intent. Your soul fragment will appear. (What it will look like cannot be stated. It will look like what it is.) Deal with it lovingly and gently. Ask it to come back with you. If it requires reassurances, give them. If it is injured and/or crippled, pick it up and carry it. Otherwise, take it gently into your hands. Turn around and go back through the veil. Very slowly, ascend and return to this dimension. When you are completely back, place the energies of that retrieved soul fragment into your heart chakra by "breathing" them into that center of consciousness and then into your crown. Then drink a large glass of pure water. Carefully and thoroughly journal this experience. Please do not lapse into amateur psychologizing. Ponder with deep compassionate awareness those parts that you recognize as damaged soul structures.

Those returned energies will require loving assimilation. If you experience emotional difficulties, work with the "Seeker's Lamp" meditation to uncover the **belief** that is likely triggering those emotions. Do your "worm-hole" work. Work also with the "Pool of Rejuvenation" meditation to help heal the emotions. Take all the time that you need to come through this stage of your quest for wholeness.

Be assured that on this path and in all this process of learning, experiencing, pondering and healing (form follows consciousness!) **your egoic structures of soul have also been undergoing regenerative change**.

We have arrived at the end of the lesson. It has been a grand picnic and you have received a lot of "food for thought." Later on, you will be given the opportunity to "digest" it and, thereby, make it part of the evolutionary holarchy that constitutes your mental "embodiment." We have also completed the lessons on your "lower" centers of consciousness and the soul structures they have generated. You have journeyed on all three "lanes" of your path of "Coming into Being," and you have become increasingly capable of balancing the "dancing" masculine and feminine energies that are so essential to the "workings" of your centers of consciousness and to the health of your soul structures, including the egoic structures. You have also journeyed on the simultaneous and parallel path of "Opening the Way" while letting go/ letting be old patterns of beliefs, habits and attitudes that have in-formed you. Soul Searcher, your learning has been intense and your **knowing** has grown immensely!

Before you leave, please look around and know that you are part of the timelessness of this sacred place. At this juncture, you are likely more comfortable than you used to be with just being in the "now." Good! That is a strong indication of the healthy "shifts" in your animal soul consciousness and of your androgynous possibility.

You may leave the circle of stones.

* * *

Soul Searcher, take whatever time you need to rest. On the next stage of your rebirthing into androgyny, you will be on a new path. While you gather up your energies for continuing your journey, please keep in mind that you are a multidimensional energy being, a soul field who embodies an immense creative power. And remember also that you are finding out, at last, all that you truly are. When you are ready, go to the "Second Interlude."

Peace and blessings

SECOND INTERLUDE

Let us pause together in the South for yet another interlude; again, a period of assimilation. This you will do so that the teachings contained in the last three lessons can become (as did the first two) part of you as a soul field. Into this second interlude, you will take all that you have already become; all the inner empowerment that you are already sensing. And you will undertake yet more "stretching;" more beginnings, both inward and outward.

In this interlude, you may choose as you did in the first, to return to the stone circle or to create your own sacred space. (For the latter, please recall the instructions you have already received for "casting the circle.") Also note that within your sacred space, there are now many more ways of inner exploring. You have learned these ways both in the lessons and in your experiences. In this period of assimilation, while you go even deeper into inner explorations, you will more and more come into the **knowing** that is becoming your new **being**. That **knowing** is heralding an approaching androgyny.

And there is more work to be done.

But, here is a note of encouragement: have you noticed that after internalizing your rich legacy of wisdom teachings that you felt more confident to continue on your journey? Have you noticed that after working closely with the Observer in the letting go/letting be of your old patterns of **beliefs**, values, attitudes and habits, that your inward (and outward) detachment and discernment have become easier for you? Have you noticed that the opposite is also true? And have you noticed that your practices of "balancing" (especially your breath work) have not only helped you to become increasingly aware of the out-of-balance "dance" of energies that have promoted those old patterns, but have also helped you to become more comfortably with paradox? Have you also noticed that your increasing capacity for detachment and discernment has enhanced your capacity for balancing? Finally, have you noticed something quite wonderful: while you have continued to experience your soul field/soul substance energies and to probe into soul structures, that your slowly developing inner empowerment has a feeling/tone of purity, simplicity and unity[385] that seems to "glow"? And although there are many parts of you as animal soul that are still "dark" and "heavy," you are not "in" them in quite the way you were. In other words, the insights that you have already acquired have been

---

[385] These words will not be defined because they are triggers" that are meant to invoke your own insights. They require that you tune in very deeply.

astonishing.[386] Soul Searcher, you have done well. You are waking up to the marvelous reality of life, not just life in general, but your own in particular. Be assured that you are already well advanced in your transformation, liberation and regeneration.

Now you go deeper.

In this second interlude, your necessary "work" is to assimilate and make part of you, as a soul field, the very **personal** directions for inner probing given in the lessons themselves. Go back into them. Probe more deeply than in a new exploration. Allow yourself to go into your murkiest, heaviest obscurities. They require your focused attention. Allow yourself to face your worst fears. They will present themselves, when you look for them. While you are doing this, always with the help of the Observer, you will become aware that your disciplines/ practices of letting go/letting be and of balancing, when combined with your healing disciplines and with probing and pondering are fostering an even greater sense of inner empowerment with its feeling/tone of purity, simplicity and unity. And with that awareness, you will also become aware that your "dancing" masculine and feminine energies are expressing as a more balanced interaction within your **holistic** energy system and as more mature egoic structures. Thus, this period of assimilation will result in even more **knowing** that becomes a greater **being**. And there are not words to describe it. You will find your own.

Please take whatever time you need. Work with courage and concentration. Allow a "settling" to take place after each experience of uncovering and discovering yet another dimension of you.

And while you ponder and probe ever further into the soul field that you are, you will become increasingly aware that the sustaining undercurrent of Life that was with you in the East and remains with you now has been augmented by the qualities of another aspect of your indwelling Spirit (your nucleus of divinity).

Here in the South, as shamans know it, the aspect is Light. In essence, it is "Ground" Luminosity; the Light that has also been permeating your soul field as the colors (and sounds) of your chakras.[387] In your ponderings, you will realize that the light that you have been carrying to illuminate your path of "Coming into Being" and the inner "glow" you have already noticed have all along been reflections of the Light whose qualities have gradually been expressing in you. And, those qualities have been combining with those of the Life aspect to enable you, with the help of the Observer, to "work" the healing therapies (disciplines) and

---

[386] If you are familiar with the work of Dr. Abraham Maslow, you have likely seen how his insights about the hierarchy of human needs closely connect with your explorations of your root, sacral and solar plexus chakras and the corresponding soul structures. If you are not familiar, see Abraham Maslow *Motivation and Personality*. For more development of the ideas, see his *Toward a Psychology of Being*. If you require further information, there are excellent audio downloads of Dr. Maslow's 1968 lectures available at abrahammaslow. com/audio.html.

[387] In *Genesis*, Chapter One the creation story tells that God spoke and abstracted the energy of Light out of the darkness of the void. Out of the Light (the spectrum of Consciousness) all things were made, including human beings, the microcosmic expression/manifestation of the One Consciousness, Creative Energy. But the Light itself remained in God. You are the microcosm (recall the nadis.) To put it another way, your **holistic** energy system manifests the sound and color spectrum of the One Consciousness.

the disciplines/practices. You are healing your animal soul centers of consciousness and you are becoming "real."

And as this interlude of assimilation continues, there will be a deepening trust in your "process." That trust has come about despite the inner resistance expressing unhealed animal soul structures. Here in the South, you **know** that trust is the feminine other side of "faith."[388] In this moment, you might want to pay heed to these words by a spiritual teacher of the twenty-first century:[389]

> "Follow the light. It will always help you. The light is God's gift of certain confidence in yourself when all the world seems to have deserted you. It is your friend in a time of need and your comforter in a time of sorrow. [. . .] Never believe that God could leave you. This is the only condition in all the universe that is impossible. [. . .] When you feel your world disintegrating, turn to God. [. . .] While you are following the Light that is God, God is following the light that is you."

During this interlude you will increasingly **know** that the indwelling Spirit is guiding you in amazing ways: in the "accidental" encounters you have with those who are actually your soul contracts; in the unexpected opportunities for greater awareness that "come" your way, and in the "flashes" of understanding that "pop" into your mind. With the undercurrents of Life and Light to sustain you, trust the journey and the process.

Please remain in this second interlude and do the "work" of assimilation until you have come into a new (and larger) sense of readiness for the continuing quest.

Farewell . . . until we meet again at the stone circle,

Peace and blessings

---

[388] Whereas the masculine "faith" looks outward for evidence, the feminine "trust" looks inward for **knowing.**

[389] Alan Cohen, *The Peace You Seek,* p. 69.

PART THREE

THE PATH OF THE WEST:

"ENTERING WITHIN"

THIRD INTRODUCTION

Knowing that all living things are part of a sacred web of life, shamans "journey" into the spirit world in order to acquire the spiritual knowledge necessary for serving life on Earth. Shamans fulfill this responsibility with love.[390] They serve life by story-telling, counseling, teaching and healing. On your quest for wholeness, you have already encountered those loving, giving shamanic energies. They will continue.

By now you have also experienced the many rigors and joys of a rebirthing journey; in the East on the path of "Opening the Way" and in the South, on the path of "Coming into Being." And you are already experiencing the immense powers arising out of the disciplines/practices of letting go/letting be and of balancing. While you continue on your quest, the energies of the East and South will be there to serve you in the ongoing expansion of your **knowing** and **being**. But now you are ready to enter upon the third, and preparatory, stage of your rebirthing and of your quest for wholeness:

You surrender to the power of the West. It is the cosmic realm of ripeness and fulfillment. The West contains the power that invariably expresses in this third dimension as the energies of the day's evening with its setting sun and as the seasonal energies of autumn, with its pungent and vibrant coolness. The West also contains the power that invariably expresses in Earth's living things, including people, as the energies of maturation and ripening into late adulthood. All those powers are freely bestowed by the cycles of "nature." The West also contains the power of "containing;" a possibility that, like the others on this journey, must be actualized. The "containing" power

---

[390] Of course, there are exceptions. But shamans who do not love and who, as animal souls, mis-use their power usually bring about their own physical, emotional, mental and (above all else) spiritual destruction.

of the West is essential, for your ripeness and fulfillment involve carefully holding and carrying — while at the same time you are allowing — the changes that are taking place in you. During this time of maturation you start to realize the **holarchy**[391] that is being generated: i.e., while the power arising out of letting go/letting be continues to be actualized, it becomes part of the power arising out of balancing. And, in turn, both together are generating an enhanced capacity for containing.

Embracing the power of the West, you set your feet on the path of **entering within**. On this path you explore and heal the consciousness energies of your heart center "bridge" and its multidimensional soul structures. While doing this "work," you are preparing to encounter your own higher "mysteries." Meanwhile, your androgynous **knowing** and **being** are completing their gestation in you.

Shamans know that in the West, the **macrocosmic** energy of **Love-as-Such** is paramount. Eternally unchanged and unchanging Love is an aspect of the Spirit. Shamans also know that at the same time the **microcosmic** love energy is constantly beginning and constantly renewing itself. Thus it is that love energy is vibrating as every particle/wave of all creation (the manifested cosmos), including you. An awareness of that energy is what you require now. Ripening and fulfilling mean accepting and allowing Love/love.

Let us go to the stone circle.

---

[391] Please recall the instruction about holarchy given in Lessons Two and Five. The holarchy that will emerge in the coming lessons is undoubtedly related to the evolutionary holarchy indicated by the Piagetian findings, but at this beginning stage of theoretical development will be dealt with separately.

Lesson Six

YOUR HEART CHAKRA AND "BRIDGING" STRUCTURES OF SOUL

Hello: on this foggy late-autumn evening, welcome again to the stone circle. The mists spread themselves over the moors with a silent, chilly presence. Beyond the circle, the yellow leaves hang limply from the trees and the brown grass lies awaiting the frosts. Here at the enclosure, the damp fog surrounds us and wraps wispy arms around Long Meg and her Children. In this deep stillness not even the curlews are calling. Yet the very murkiness itself seems to vibrate with the energy of expectancy. Please take this ground sheet along with this warm poncho covering and go to your accustomed place in the center of the circle. Sit there very quietly and tune into the energies of the fog . . . . Now, with deep, **grounding** breaths connect with Earth . . . . Focus your attention on the cool, damp stillness and listen . . . listen . . .

Do you hear them? . . . Listen . . . Behind and all around you there are the sounds of shuffling feet. It seems that other beings have entered the circle and taken up their positions in front of the stones. Remain very still and listen . . . . What you are sensing behind and around you are the energies of the ancient ones. They are holding hands and facing inward. Listen . . . listen. The sounds of shuffling feet intensify. The ghostly circle seems to be moving around you . . . . Very softly the singing begins. You strain to hear the words. Then, you realize that this is a language you do not understand with tonal cadences that are unfamiliar . . . . It occurs to you that you have slipped into another dimension, while remaining in this one.[392]

The ancient beings are giving you a ring dance; sacred movement that was often performed when the stone circle was the site of recurring pilgrimages. You sit here, enveloped in the damp, cool fog and you listen. With awe and wonderment, you sense your deep connection with the energies of adoration and joy that are being generated around you. As the dance continues, you feel your heart center expanding. And you feel, perhaps for the first time, a deep love for those long-ago pilgrims who had come to this circle. They and you, in this moment, have bridged the many centuries separating you. Then you realize that this enclosure is a sacred container in which past and present have merged. In the murkiness of this autumn

---

[392] There is ancient teaching that there were stone circle "choirs" whose purpose was to "enchant the landscape." See Joscelyn Godwin, *The Golden Thread: The Ageless Wisdom of the Western Mystery Tradition*, p. 20.

evening, you and the ancient pilgrims are a unity of consciousness. You strain to see them. There is a fleeting impression . . . and they are gone. But they have left you filled with reverence and peace.

At this moment, please be aware that while you are connecting with Earth energies, you are also being in-formed by other, cosmic, energies. As a multidimensional energy being in a multidimensional universe, you are fully capable of experiencing this. Trust the possibility. It, too, is heralding your approaching androgyny.

*   *   *

Soul Searcher, please also be aware that your journey has entered into a new stage. It is beckoning you into a vast new **knowing**. And, herein lies yet more paradox: your new "path" is both well-traveled and untrodden; you know it already, while you do not know it at all.

It is the path of "Entering Within."

On the well-traveled path, you have already experienced deep probing and inner exploration; an immense entering within. All the lessons here in the stone circle have required that you plumb those depths; your "lower" centers of consciousness and their structures of animal soul. Thus, all of your journeying was a necessary preparation for this new stage. And on the new untrodden path, you can expect an even more profound entering within; a connection with your "higher" centers of consciousness, the "spiritual" centers, and with their structures of soul.

On the well-traveled path, you have learned about the function and generative power of each of your animal soul chakras. And you have developed an awareness of the functional and generative possibilities contained within the spiritual component of each of those chakras. In your **holistic** energy system, while the "lower" chakras remained unhealed, the possibilities inherent in each spiritual component could barely be actualized, if at all. You have required the journey along the paths of "Opening the Way" and of "Coming into Being" to bring about the healing of your animal soul chakras and to open you to the great power of your "higher" spiritual centers; the power that had, by and large, remained unexpressed in the animal soul chakras.

While you venture now along the untrodden path of "Entering Within," you will be receiving **both** the spiritual gifts increasingly available from your "higher" spiritual centers of consciousness **and** the healing that is necessary for your ongoing quest. All of this is required for your rebirth into androgyny. Soul Searcher, you have accomplished amazing changes in your human energy system and in your structures of soul! Now, while you quest along your untrodden path of "Entering Within," there will be a further expansion of your **knowing** that will become new and greater **being**; an indication of imminent rebirthing.

For you to comprehend better the complexities of this next stage of your journey, you shall be given two images. The first is that of a "bridge." It is by means of your heart-center-generated "bridging" structures of soul that you can successfully travel your path. As you have likely already guessed, this untrodden path actually involves you with both ascending and descending consciousness energies. That upward and downward causation can be described this way: while you healed the "lower" centers of consciousness, you raised their vibratory frequency and opened to the higher frequencies of your "higher" centers. That was the well-traveled path that will continue. As a result, in your **holistic** energy system, while the lower energies are going upward, the higher spiritual energies now are free to go downward. That is the untrodden path. And all are going across your heart "bridge." (The image of a heart "bridge" requires further detail which you will soon receive.)

The second image to help you is that of a 'crucible;" a container in which immense changes can be wrought. It is actually by means of and through your heart "crucible" that the energies of your animal soul centers of consciousness have been transmuted and will continue to be, with the resultant transformation of their soul structures. (Although you have been given hints of this re-forming of animal soul energies in previous lessons, it was necessary that you come to this point in your journey before the details could be given to you. You will receive more later in this lesson and in the next.)

Now take in a shaman's story. It tells about how and why your heart connection with your "higher" centers of consciousness can result in your rebirthing into androgyny and, thence, into wholeness.

Before the beginning there is the Mystery;
The eternal "now"
Out of which all beginnings come.

In the beginning there flowed out of the Spirit;
The One Consciousness, Creative Energy,
An androgynous "Image and Likeness"
So huge that it filled the entire Cosmos.
It was Cosmic Man; it was the Anthropos.

For the Germanic people, the Anthropos was the giant Ymir.
For the Chinese people, the Anthropos was the divine man P'an Ku
For the people of India, the Anthropos was the ancestor, Yama.
For the Iranian people, the Anthropos was the giant, Gayomart.
For the ancient Jewish people, the Anthropos was the giant Adam Kadmon.

At first, the Anthropos was Everyman, the "all as one;"
It was not an individuated consciousness;
There was no ego/self.
Then the Anthropos began inching towards self-awareness;
A consciousness that was a "knowing."
And as the "knowing" slowly progressed,
It began to evolve into being.

After his first death, P'an Ku was reborn as a bringer of culture.
After Yama died, there arose the Purusha, who represented
The Self that indwells all things.
From the giant Gayomart, murdered by the evil Ahriman
There sprang humanity's great sages and cultural innovators.

From the Adam Kadmon, there came the first Adam.
And with the first Adam the androgyny was divided,
Thus, there came about "men" and "women,"
Who sought out each other for completion
And began to multiply on the face of Earth.

These people were given the blessing;
A love relationship with the Spirit/Creator.
A relationship expressed as a "covenant,"
Between mankind and the Spirit/Creator,
A relationship that has continued
Throughout all the succeeding centuries.

The covenant carried the promise of mankind's spiritual evolution
And a return to androgynous wholeness
Through obedience to the Spirit/Creator,
Through a gradual awakening out of Ignorance,
In a heart connection that was eternal.

When the first Adam's descendants lost their way,
The Spirit/Creator sent great prophets
Who called for repentance and a return to righteousness.
There followed a slow spiritual evolution,
But always a relapsing into Ignorance.

When mankind continued to lose its way,
The Spirit/Creator sent Siddhartha Gautama of the Sakyas,
As the Buddha, the "Awakened One,"
Whose teachings and example
Have brought enlightenment to many
And inspired the *bodhisattvas* to return
To help mankind evolve into humanness.

When mankind continued its waywardness,
The Spirit/Creator sent Lao Tzu,
Who came as the Sage, the Old Boy,
And gave mankind *The Way and Its Power*:
A teaching which has promoted grandeur in its adherents
And put that consciousness into the world.

When mankind continued to be lost and unenlightened,
The Spirit/Creator sent Yeshua ben Joseph,
Jesus of Nazareth,
Who incarnated the Anthropos as the second Adam,
The Son of God and Man,
Whose life and teachings of love, even unto death,
Have opened countless hearts and connected them
In a "new covenant" with the Spirit/Creator.

He has joined the ranks of those who had gone before
And of those who have come after,
Those, who like the Prophet Muhammad
Brought the message of God's love for man.
All those who have incarnated the "image and likeness,"
All those who have taught the "covenant;"
The covenant of love, of the heart,
The covenant of connection.

All those who have taught the path of "Entering Within."

For herein lies the path into rebirthing,
The only path; the inner path,
The path that you began as an expression *of* the Spirit/Creator,
As Little Soul, who chose to incarnate in this dimension.
And you have journeyed toward the Spirit/Creator,
Upward to the heart bridge,
And to the heart crucible,
Upward in a process of self-realization,
Upward to the "knowing" that you are also
An androgynous "image and likeness,"
That you are also an anthropos.

That ends the shaman's story.[393] It continues your rebirthing journey by bringing you into your heart center and providing the purpose of your heart "bridge" and "crucible." They are there to act as vehicles for the Love energies of your nucleus of divinity (the indwelling Spirit), while expressing the "covenant" that has always been there nurturing you.

*   *   *

---

[393] Excerpted from the account of the "Cosmic Man/Anthropos" in Marie-Louise Von Franz, *Archetypal Dimensions of the Psyche*, pp. 133-157. The remainder of the story is taken from the *Holy Bible*, both the Old and the New Testaments, from Huston Smith, *The World's Religions* and from Philip Novak, *The World's Wisdom*.

On the untrodden path of "Entering Within," you will return once more to your sacred legacy of wisdom teachings; focused this time on those dealing with the energies of the "heart." With that foundation in place, you will be ready to explore your own heart center of consciousness; the chakra that forms out of your soul substance your "bridging" structures of soul. In that context, you will learn about the qualities and function intrinsic to the heart chakra's generative power and about that power itself, which splendidly reveals the chakra's prime directive and "i-am" statement of consciousness. Probing deeper, you will experience, explore, and start to repair and regenerate your "bridging" structures of soul. To help you into deeper understanding, you will be given yet more Celtic mythology and other references from literature. And you will augment that awareness by discovering and utilizing the power of your dreams and the power of your heart archetypes. Still on the untrodden path of "Entering Within," you will continue your connection with your "dancing" masculine and feminine energies and yet again relate these to your ego/self. Meanwhile, you will be continuing the healing disciplines and practices – the letting go/letting be and balancing — that have served you so well. And you will begin a new discipline/practice; that of "containing." All of it is necessary, while you continue the process of transmuting your animal soul consciousness energies and, thereby, transforming their soul structures. Since these include your egoic structures, you will be changing them and coming yet closer to realizing your androgynous self. **At the same time,** you will be healing your heart chakra and the "bridging" structures it has generated. Finally, you will learn about a malfunctioning heart chakra and receive the self-healing therapies (disciplines) that will constitute your ongoing "homework." Soul Searcher, although this lesson will be very full, you are ready for it and for this stage on your quest for wholeness.

Come; let us eagerly venture along the untrodden path of "Entering Within."

Ancient Wisdom Teachings about the Heart

In most of mankind's cultures, the language about the human heart has indicated many centuries of reflection about this center of consciousness. And words about the heart qualities such as "warm," "cold," "soft," "hard," "open," "closed," "loving," "fearful," "full," "empty," "broken," "mended," "stormy," "peaceful," "good," and "evil" have been found in the world's myths, legends, literature and songs and depicted in the great works of art and drama. Passed down from generation to generation, the "heart wisdom teachings" constitute the huge legacy that is the foundation for this stage of your journey.

From the ancient Egyptian wisdom teachings you learn that of the seven "souls" a person possessed, the "heart soul" was the most important. It had come from the heart of one's mother, a part of her divine blood, which had descended into her womb and then formed into her child. In the Hall of Judgment, after death, that person's "heart soul" would be weighed in the balance scales against the feather of Truth. If, after an honest and honorable lifetime, the heart soul was found to balance with Truth, there was the reward of continuing life. If the heart soul was found wanting, it would be fed to a hungry crocodile, poised to receive it.[394] Later Egyptian wisdom teachings, even then concerned with the ignorance afflicting humanity, called for "guides" to help people go to the "House of Knowledge," where they would "see with the heart, the brilliant brightness."[395] In this teaching, the heart was a tool of perception, but it perceived only that which was sacred and connected with Light.

In the wisdom teachings of Judaism, the human heart was paired with the "soul" and "mind" in order both to feel and to know the essential connection of people with God. Throughout the entire Old Testament, the "heart" teachings reveal that the human/Divine connection had been established right from the beginning. Thereafter, it had evolved through many vicissitudes and many centuries and had covered the full spectrum of emotion and thought. That connection has continued, even unto the present day, because the soul and mind of God's people were linked in a covenant with God.[396] It is a teaching about how the Spirit has continually reached out to people while they, by and large, have steadfastly remained in a state of ignorance.

In the Hindu wisdom teachings, there are four paths ("ways,") that people can take in order to get to God. The way of the heart, the *bhakti* yoga of love, has been the most popular. In this teaching, the devotee was required "to love God deeply – not just claim such love, but love God in fact; love God only (with other things loved in relation to God); and love God for no ulterior reason (not even from the desire for liberation, or to be loved in return) but for love's sake alone."[397] In addition, the devotee was required to love God in one of His/Her many chosen forms. Most readily chosen was one of God's incarnations, for "God can be loved most readily in human form because our hearts are already attuned to loving people."[398] Thus, the "heart is made pure by that yoga"[399] and the devotee has received the covenant, for this Hindu teaching states:

> "I am equal-minded toward all beings.
> They neither enrapture me nor enrage me.
> But if they worship me lovingly,
> they are in Me and I in them."[400]

---

[394] Barbara G. Walker, *The Woman's Dictionary of Symbols and Sacred Objects*, pp. 175 and 317.

[395] Timothy Freke and Peter Gandy, *The Hermetica: The Lost Wisdom of the Pharaohs*, p. 129.

[396] The Old Testament Concordance lists several hundred references to "heart." The "love" was commanded by God and there are many stories of the Israelites turning away from that love. With their hardened hearts, the connection was lost. Yet God's love was seen to be everlasting and redemption was always possible. In the *Book of Jeremiah*, 31: 3, 18 and 20, the Spirit, i.e., Jehovah, speaking through the prophet, compares the Israelites to "an untrained calf" [i.e., the animal soul] while referring to them as the "darling child" and declaring that "I have loved you with an everlasting love; therefore, I have continued my faithfulness to you." This translation is given in Ninian Smart and Richard D. Hecht, *Sacred Texts of the World*, pp. 63 and 64.

[397] Huston Smith, *The World's Religions*, p. 34.

[398] *Ibid,* p. 36.

[399] Philip Novak, *The World's Wisdom*, p. 32.

[400] Quoted from the *Bhagavad Gita* in Ninian Smart and Richard D. Hecht, *Sacred Texts of the World: A Universal Anthology*, p. 219.

In the vast heritage of Buddhist wisdom teachings, there has been much emphasis on the "goodwill which is the heart's release." This goodwill was much more to be cultivated on the path of rebirthing, than "good works."[401] In the development of Loving-Kindness, one was enjoined to be of a "blissful heart" and . . .

> "Just as might a mother with her life
> Protect the son that was her only child,
> So let him then for every living thing
> Maintain unbounded consciousness in being.
> And let him too with love for all the world
> Maintain unbounded consciousness in being
> Above, below, and all round in between,
> Untroubled, with no enemy or foe."[402]

Just as there was a covenant between God and humankind taught in Judaism and Hinduism, there was a covenant teaching in Buddhism; expressed in "The Lotus Sutra." In this wonderful story, there is revealed the unending love of "the World-Honored One" for all people, while they continued to be "deluded and ignorant." Finally, some would realize that they were "Buddha-sons."[403]

In the wisdom teachings of Taoism, the great path was the way of the heart, the way of compassion. It was first of all the compassion one felt for oneself. Then, there could follow a harmonious relationship with the infinite, eternal, ever-flowing Tao. In that connection, one could "save the world from the degradation and destruction it seems destined for."[404] The key lay in turning inward and working first on one's own self-awareness. In this teaching

> "If you want to awaken all of humanity, then awaken all of yourself.
> Truly the greatest gift you have to give is that of your own self-transformation."[405]

Also from the Orient, in the wisdom teachings of Confucianism and Shintoism, the heartfelt compassion that was necessary for a peaceful co-existence with others received much emphasis.[406] Thus, loving connection with the Creative Power, with oneself and with others in-formed centuries of Eastern wisdom teachings about the heart.

In the wisdom teachings of Christianity, the sacred heart of Jesus the Christ has been the symbol and the exemplar of an awakened **knowing** of total connection with the inner Kingdom of God. It was the "I-Am" consciousness of the Christ that would be the "way and the Truth

---

[401] *Ibid.* p. 267.
[402] Philip Novak, *The World's Wisdom*, p. 74.
[403] For more detail, see Ninian Smart and Richard D. Hecht, *Sacred Texts of the World*, pp. 239-241.
[404] Philip Novak, *The World's Wisdom*, p. 170.
[405] *Ibid.*, p. 170.
[406] Gail Godwin, *Heart: A Personal Journey Through Its Myths and Meanings*, pp. 52 and 58.

and the life" necessary for that linkage.[407] The words and actions of Jesus, the Son of Man, provided the examples. Over and again he focused on the divine Love and the need for people to allow It to flow through them and out to others. The love was to be expressed in charitable acts, (the Parable of the Good Samaritan) and in forgiveness (the Parable of the Prodigal Son). The surrender into love was indicated in the Beatitudes, the trusting love was spoken in the Lord's Prayer, the love for oneself was defined in the Sermon on the Mount and the example of unconditional love was given by the Crucifixion and Resurrection.

While the Christian wisdom teachings evolved, there came those whose experience of the Divine bore proof of the truths that Jesus had taught. These were the teachers who stated: that "God became a person so that persons might become God;"[408] that "prayer has great power which a person makes with all his might [. . .] it draws down the great God into the little heart, it drives the hungry soul up into the fullness of God;"[409] that "Christ's birth is always happening and yet if it doesn't happen in me, how can it help me? [. . .] everything depends on that;"[410] that "I have been called an extremist [. . .] was not Jesus an extremist in love [. . .] and in some not too distant tomorrow the radiant stars of love and brotherhood will shine over our great nation with all of their scintillating beauty;"[411] finally, that "without heart we are not truly human [. . .] and the possibility of having an authentic and deeply satisfying human life is only a pipe dream when our love is not directed to what truly fulfills the heart."[412] Thus, the wonderful legacy of the Christ "heart" teachings has continued into the present.

In the wisdom teachings of Islam, there have been many calls for "heart" actions "to feed the hungry, to help the afflicted, to lighten the sorrow of the sorrowful, and to remove the wrongs of the injured, to assist any person oppressed, whether Muslim or non-Muslim, to honor an old person, to follow up an evil deed with a good one, to control one's tongue, to say what is true and to avoid the shedding of innocent blood."[413]

The heart has been central to the Sufi wisdom teachings. It is the organ of true **knowing**. In these teachings, the 'heart' consciousness has been attained when the enlightened "soul" has joined with the indwelling Spirit. That connection has been the result of a lengthy, dedicated process of learning and liberating, during which the animal soul has been transformed into humanness. The "heart" consciousness was described by a 9th century Sufi teacher in these words:[414]

> "God made this hollow piece of flesh into His treasure trove. He has given it eyes to see the invisible and ears to hear His words, and he has fixed in it a window in the chest, for the heart is a lamp whose rays of light shine in the

[407] The *Gospel of John*, 14: 6.
[408] Clement of Alexandria; quoted in Philip Novak, *The World's Wisdom*, p. 265.
[409] Mechthild of Magdeburg, quoted in *Ibid*, p. 268.
[410] Meister Eckhart, quoted in *Ibid*, p.270.
[411] Martin Luther King, Jr., quoted in *Ibid*, p. 278.
[412] A. H. Almaas, *The Unfolding Now*, p. 1.
[413] Distilled from Philip Novak, *The World's Wisdom*, pp. 315-318.
[414] Al-Hakim at Tirmidhi, quoted in Sara Sviri, *The Taste of Hidden Things: Images on the Sufi Path*, p. 4.

chest. Thus God has made this hollow piece of flesh into the source of true knowledge, which is supreme wisdom and mystical understanding. God placed within the heart the knowledge of Him and the heart became lit by God's light. Then God spoke in a parable and said: "*compared to a niche wherein is a lamp*" (Qur'an 24:35). The lamp of the Divine Light is in the hearts of those who believe in the Oneness of God."

In later Sufi wisdom teachings the inner heart light was augmented by the need to "polish the mirror of the heart" in order for the Divine Light to descend into humanness, "for that is where the mystical life is lived."[415] In this process, the "heart" would become individuated as the "True Ego,"[416] the inner *mysteria* ecstatically described by Abu Yazid al-Bistami who declared: "I shed my self as a snake sheds its skin, then I looked at myself and behold *I am He*! Glory be to me! How lofty I am!"[417] This awareness of the unity of the human heart with the Divine Love and Light was splendidly expressed by the 9th century Sufi "heretic," el-Hallaj, who prayed for his executioners, while he could still speak, by saying:[418]

> "Forgive and have mercy upon these Thy servants,
> assembled here for the purpose of killing me;
> for, had Thou revealed to them what Thou hast
> revealed to me, they would not act thus."

Quite clearly, during many centuries of wisdom teachings, the heart consciousness energies have been regarded as central to human spiritual development and to true humanness.

Modern Teachings about the Heart

In addition to the wisdom tradition, modern scientific discoveries in medicine and in psychotherapy have contributed to an awareness of the importance of "heart" connectedness in promoting physical, emotional and mental well-being. For example, recent research into the healing power of prayer has provided secular proof of the holy covenant given to human beings so many centuries ago.[419] In that work, the loving intentions of those praying for people who are total strangers have connected indwelling Spirit with indwelling Spirit and demonstrated the unbreakable heart linkages between people (the microcosm) and the Divine.

As the wisdom and scientific teachings would suggest, in the work of repairing and regenerating your "bridging" soul structures, you will eventually develop a greater sense of connectedness with the indwelling Spirit and leave behind, in your rebirthing process, the stage of journeying toward It. To encourage and sustain you in this "labor" and to give you

---

[415] *Ibid*, p.,16.
[416] A. H. Almaas, *The Inner Journey Home,* pp. 599, 602, 607, 616 and 631.
[417] Sara Sviri, *The Taste of Hidden Things*, p. 20.
[418] Idries Shah, *The Sufis*, p.425.
[419] See the work by Larry Dossey described in his book *Healing Words: The Power of Prayer and the Practice of Medicine.*

that sense of your covenant with the Divine, here are the very personal words of the *Lord's Prayer* translated from the Aramaic language spoken by Jesus:[420]

"Abwoon (Father-Mother of the Cosmos)"

O Birther! Father-Mother of the Cosmos,
Focus your light within [me] – make it useful:

Create your reign of unity now –

Your one desire now acts with [mine],
as in all light, so in all forms.

Grant what [I] need each day in bread and
Insight.

Loose the cords of mistakes binding [me],
as [I] release the strands [I] hold
of others' guilt.

Don't let surface things delude [me].

But free [me] from what holds [me] back.

From you is born all ruling will,
the power and the life to do,
the song that beautifies all,
from age to age it renews.

Truly—power to these statements –
may they be the ground from which all
my actions grow.

Pause here while you resonate with those words.

Then, let us examine the consciousness energies of your heart chakra.

---

[420] Neil Douglas-Klotz, *Prayers of the Cosmos: Meditations on the Aramaic Words of Jesus*, p. 41. Please read and experience the longer translation, interpretation and body prayers given in pp. 12-40.

Your Heart Chakra

Begin with several deep **grounding** breaths, When you are ready, focus your attention on your heart center of consciousness which is seemingly located between your breasts. Gently "scan" it and with the help of the Observer, note the shape, size and rotation. Tune into the feeling/tone of the energies you are sensing. They are astral energies. (Please recall that your sacral chakra's consciousness energies are also from the astral dimension, but at a much lower frequency.)

Your heart center astral energies were present at your conception. They were your first linkage with your parents. If they were "making love" instead of simply "making out" (or worse), you made a "heart connection" with them that is unbreakable. During your gestation, the emotions (astral energies) indicating your sacral chakra's interactions with your root chakra's survival orientation were affecting your heart center. And after your advent, all the events of animal soul development were also impacting on that center. Although your heart chakra would not start to function on its own until your puberty, its generative power was at work in a reduced fashion from before your birth. Your "bridging" structures of soul were being generated, with the likelihood that any prenatal or postnatal wounding (often the indicators of lovelessness) that would cause damage to your animal soul structures would also cause damage to the "bridge." Yet, with even minimal love nurturing, your **holistic** astral energies would have been expressing in your animal soul centers of consciousness and in the resultant structures. (**Form follows consciousness**!) As indicated by the story of "Roland and May-Bird," there was the possibility, from the moment of your conception, of androgynous humanness.

This possibility existed because the prime directive (archetypal imperative) of your heart chakra right from the beginning has been the generation and maintenance of your inward and outward connectedness (sometimes referred to as the "heart cords" or "heart strings"). Thus, the "bridging" structures of soul have been that of relationship; a heart connection that has expressed the energies of love in all its permutations, including the energies of reconciliation.[421] Reinforcing that prime directive, your heart chakra's "i-am" statement of consciousness has been from the beginning; "I am the sensations, feelings and thoughts of loving relatedness." Thus, the connective and regenerative power of your heart chakra have always been crucial in your quest for wholeness.

At this juncture, it is necessary to note an important development that previously could only be touched upon. It has required the lessons and the "Interludes" until this point. That development can be described in these words: in your ongoing quest, you and the truth-

---

[421] Although the word "relationship" has also been used in these lessons in describing the prime directive of the sacral chakra, there is a vast difference to be noted. The sacral chakra's relationships are based on the pleasure and pain principle and express animal soul consciousness. In the heart center, relationship expresses the Love energies of the indwelling Spirit. The word "reconciliation" carries its modern meaning but also carries its old meaning; a restoration of peace through the reconsecration of a sacred place sullied by violence and bloodshed.

oriented Observer have already had many hours of experiencing your soul substance/soul field and many more hours of letting go/ letting be the old patterns of **beliefs**, attitudes and values. Out of that "work," especially the discipline/practice, you have steadily been acquiring the powers of detachment and discernment. **Those powers of detachment/discernment are the actualization of the letting go/letting be**. Meanwhile, you and the Observer have also experienced many hours. of balancing. Out of that discipline/practice there have arisen the increasing powers of a dynamic equilibrium between the "dancing" masculine and feminine energies inherent in your soul substance and expressing in your animal soul chakras and structures. **Those powers of dynamic equilibrium are the actualization of the balancing**. Both disciplines/practices have augmented each other and will continue to do so. And at this point please note that the important development involves the coming together of their actualized powers in an emerging **holarchy**.[422] It is by means of that development, with the mutually enhancing powers of detachment/discernment and of dynamic equilibrium, that you have promoted your increasing sense of an inner empowerment with its glowing feeling/tone of purity, simplicity and unity. In all of your previous "work," you have splendidly prepared for the "heart work" of this lesson.

Now you are ready to adopt a new discipline/practice. It is a heart work that began during the ring dance in the stone circle, when you experienced your heart center expanding with deep love. It is also another step toward your coming into being an androgynous, human, energy being. The discipline/practice is that of "containing." It can be described as a focused "ingathering" of the **knowing** that you have steadily been acquiring about the "real" (the truth) of you. When "containing," you are deeply **grounding** and then inwardly "seeing" your expanded heart center as a love "container." Into that container you gently gather and hold the healed physical, emotional and mental consciousness energies that you already **know** are "you." These will be expressing various soul structures, but primarily expressing your transformed egoic structures. (You have been training to do this during your many moments of pondering, probing and "tuning into," during your hours of "work" with the healing therapies (disciplines), with your discipline/practices of letting go/letting be and balancing, and during the "Interludes." You are ready.) Begin the new discipline/practice of "containing" now. It is the necessary accompaniment to what follows in this lesson.

Your Heart Chakra's Qualities

Now, let us explore and experience the immensities of your heart center of consciousness.

You will first focus your inner attention on that chakra's color and element. Then, you learn about its force, function and generative power. While you do this, please maintain your discipline/ practice of containing.

In the "wheel of light" that is your heart center of consciousness, the predominant color "band" and sound energy is green. The green frequency, which holistically expresses the solar

---

[422] To recall the information about holarchy, see Lesson Five.

plexus chakra's yellow energies interacting with the throat chakra's blue energies, generates powerful and paradoxical energies. (Please recall that it has been through the solar plexus chakra's generative power that the soul structures of mentality carrying the "possibilities" of your androgynous rebirthing have been formed.) In the heart chakra, the power of the "warm and active" yellow solar plexus chakra energies, when interacting with the "cold and passive" blue energies of the throat chakra, produces a "transitional or intermediary color, neither active nor passive but potentially both."[423] And, paradoxically, the seeming "blend" of those masculine color energies produces the feminine green of the heart connection. As feminine energy, the color green can be associated with both life and death; the fresh green of new plants in springtime, and with the green of decay and putrefaction. That paradox can also be found within the heart chakra's consciousness energies. In a healthy human energy system, there is a wondrous interaction of life energies from both solar plexus and throat chakra that carries the loving, compassionate and tender qualities of the "second feeling." In these words, Rosalyn Bruyere has indicated that the instinctual, primitive animal soul feeling energies of the sacral chakra can be raised to a higher, more human vibration.[424] And the color is clear, vibrant green.

But the opposite can also be true. This was clearly indicated by Jesus, the Christ, who taught his disciples (and us) that "the things that come from the mouth come from the heart, and those things [can] defile a person. For out of the heart [can] emerge evil intentions, murders, adulteries, sexual immorality, thefts, false witness [and] blasphemies. These are the things that [can] defile a person."[425] Thus, there is often the need to heal the heart center of consciousness; to "repair" the heart bridge; to transmute and transform the old while generating the new.

And here is a final aside dealing with the chakra color "personality" types. We shall deal this time with those that have been described as "greens."[426] Although there is seldom a "pure" type, the "green personality" is essentially intuitive, idealistic, hopeful and optimistic. "Greens" seldom live in the present, but thrive in the past and future. They "think in metaphors and analogies" and see life in terms of the "complete picture." Greens" are deeply sensitive to the "emotions and feelings of others" and strive to create opportunities that will "meet the needs of everyone involved." Being intuitive, rather than logical, "greens" are masters at finding hidden meanings and in "reading" body language. "Greens" are open and receptive to new ideas, especially those that give them a clearer picture about themselves. They also love "the experiences that life offers" and thrive on change. But "greens" look more for the fun and spontaneity than the structure and repetition that planning requires and seldom stay with a skill or project long enough to master it. Yet "greens" are serious people. They seek to understand their life's purpose, and they see the events of life as "lessons." They follow their hearts and tune into their "inner feelings and belief systems." They are often involved in

---

[423] Anthony Stevens, *Ariadne's Clue*, p. 147.
[424] Rosalyn Bruyere, *Wheels of Light*, p. 55.
[425] *The Gospel of Matthew*, 15: 17-20.
[426] Carol Ritberger, *Your Personality, Your Health*, pp. 110-111 and 145-152.

"new movements of thinking." They will champion causes like the environment and human rights. Wanting to actualize their authentic selves, "greens" endlessly search and seldom find, basically because they are more imaginative than practical. In their search, however, they are often inspirational and motivational leaders that can persuade and motivate others. "Greens are attracted to and seek out others who think like they do and who allow them to get in touch with their deepest feelings without being judged." They are "warm, sensitive, gentle, emotional people," who develop deep and lasting friendships and seek to create a safe environment where "people can be themselves." But in many cases, their need for relationship causes "greens" to create relationships that are "co-dependent and not healthy for either party." And "greens" can be the "chameleons of the personality world:" they can become quite "red" when they feel that others have taken advantage of them. For extroverted "greens," life is full of "endless possibilities and alternatives and a host of interpersonal encounters just waiting to happen." And in these encounters, extroverted "greens" can be relied upon to encourage and maintain the enthusiasm, while they often change their minds and leave others wondering. For introverted "greens," the opposite is the case. Seldom are they out in the forefront. They are "calm, quiet, reserved and even shy." They stay with themselves, but they are "loving, warm people," whose friendship is worth cultivating. "Being reflective, contemplative, meditative and inwardly-focused people, they derive pleasure from interacting with their own active imaginations." It is this type of "green" who will find living in a strife-torn world so difficult that they will withdraw, "just to survive."

In these observations about the "green" personality, the expression of the varied qualities of the heart chakra color is vividly clear. Indeed, the heart consciousness energies, the life and death energies, are sometimes confounding. Of course, so are people! When you combine these observations with those you have already received about the "red," "orange" and "yellow" personality types, you can gain yet more insight into you and into the immense journey you have undertaken.[427]

Conjoined with the color green of the heart chakra is the element of earth. In most of the world's mythologies, earth is feminine: it is the power of birth, fertility, life and regeneration.[428] In this dimension, in your **grounding** connection with the nurturing and nourishing Earth energies, you have already been awakening and/or enhancing the life energies of your heart center. With every breath, you have been bringing in that life. It is a splendid attribute of your microcosmic creative process. Yet, as is true of the feminine green, earth can also symbolize death, with entombment and a descent into the Underworld. And, although the Earth can be richly fertile, it can, without water, become a barren desert. In terms of the heart center of consciousness, the absence of a regenerating "water" power can create a lifeless terrain. (Please recall your awareness about water. In a **holistic** energy system, the healthy energies of water are required both for the sacral center of consciousness and for the heart center.) While

---

[427] If you would like more information about those personality types as they express as "you," refer to Ritberger's book on pages 115-119 for a "personality inventory" you can take.
[428] Anthony Stevens, *Ariadne's Clue*, pp. 124-125.

describing the power of the earth element of the heart chakra, Bruyere has suggested that if the energy that started in the root chakra as the spark of fire is not quenched by the water energies of the sacral chakra and is further inflamed by the air energies of the solar plexus chakra, there is the possibility with the "second feeling" that the spark must be changed or extinguished. In that case, it can be "smothered" by the earth element and not allowed expression.[429] In that sense, "death" would be necessary so that a new spark could be generated.

Your Heart Chakra's Feminine Force

Having encountered your heart chakra's powerful and paradoxical feminine energies as color and element, you will not be surprised to learn that the force that in-forms your heart center is feminine. Closely relating to the feminine energies of your sacral chakra, these of the heart are from a much "higher" vibration of the astral plane and also relate to the mysteries of spiritual consciousness. In the heart center's "i-am" consciousness and in its prime directive, there is an indication of the incredible power of those feminine energies. Above all else they carry an immense **receptivity**, which explains why your heart center can be so easily and so badly damaged. When that feminine energy of receptivity has been "stuck" or damaged, your heart bridge and crucible have malfunctioned. Thus, a healthy heart center is essential. When you deal in a moment with the function of this chakra, you will better understand what that health would entail. Later, there are healing therapies (disciplines) to be undertaken.

Meanwhile, here is another myth about the Celtic warrior/hero Cuchulain.[430] It will illustrate how the feminine energies of the heart center of consciousness can affect animal soul centers of consciousness and, thereby change not only their vibratory frequencies but also the soul structures they generate.

In previous lessons, you will recall, Cuchulain has been presented as an archetypal motif of primitive, instinctual animal soul energies; a predominantly root chakra consciousness interacting with the sacral and solar plexus chakras. Also recall the purpose of myth, before you delve into this one and into the consciousness energies of the heart. It is especially important to remember that myths, which originate in the imaginal realm, provide amazing insights into the inner "workings" of people.

As the myth begins, the warrior/hero has been fighting battles for many years and has become a leading figure in the group of Ulster warriors who had raised him from infancy. In the meantime, he has married a woman who had chosen him and who "knew him well." Although Emer, his wife, has been faithful in the marriage, Cuchulain has taken a variety of paramours. His infidelity has grieved her greatly, but she has accepted the situation. The story continues . . .

While visiting the warriors' encampment, Emer and the other wives were walking at the edge of the lake. Suddenly there appeared a flock of

---

[429] Rosalyn Bruyere, *Wheels of Light*, p. 55.
[430] Excerpted from Peter Beresford-Ellis, *Celtic Myths and Legends*, pp. 79-96.

large white birds that settled tantalizingly close on the water. In great excitement, Emer sent a message to the camp requesting that Cuchulain set aside his favorite board game and capture the birds. Reluctantly, her husband left his game and, much annoyed, speedily cast his sling and captured the birds. He presented a bird to each woman, except Emer. But seeing her distress, he promised that he would capture the next one for her.

There immediately appeared two splendid birds, one red and one green, that flew majestically over the water towards them. Yet try as he might, the great warrior was unable to capture either one. They flew westward and cleverly eluded all his attempts. In a rage, Cuchulain leaped into his chariot, whipped up the horses and sped after the disappearing birds. He pursued them for hours and miles until they landed on a far distant lake. Then, realizing how exhausted he had become, the warrior sat on the ground beside his chariot, laid his head against an ancient pillar stone and fell deeply asleep. As he lay there, two women, one dressed in red and the other in green, came to him and began to beat him with rods of rowan. With each stroke, the "strength and vigor went out of his body."

The next day, his charioteer and the other warriors found him. They were unable to rouse him and carried him back to the camp. In the meantime, Emer had gone home to await him. Thus it was that another woman, a former lover, was enlisted to tend to Cuchulain. He lay in a "strange wasting sickness" for so long that he began to die. In desperation, his attendants decided to take him back to the ancient pillar stone where they had found him. This they did, while feeling remorse that no one had informed Emer about her husband's condition.

The instant that his head touched the stone, Cuchulain again met the woman in green. In a friendly fashion she informed him that he would not die, if he would return the love of her sister, Fand, whose husband, the sea god Mannanan, had deserted her. Cuchulain was most reluctant to accept this proposal for several reasons: it was frequently unsafe to get involved with the beings of the Otherworld; the husband of the woman in green wanted Cuchulain to fight three of the husband's deadly foes before even seeing Fand and, finally, the warrior himself was too sick "to get up let alone fight anyone."

But he finally agreed to send his trusted charioteer to meet with Fand and to assess the strength of the deadly foes. After a day, the charioteer returned with his report; that Fand was more beautiful than any mortal woman and that the foes' armies, including a group of demons, were as thick as ants on the plain. In response, Cuchulain asked that Emer be brought to him. When his wife arrived, she was horrified by the situation and enraged by the fact that her husband's former mistress had been attending to him. But she was a wise woman who knew that "her husband would only be truly released when the Otherworld folk had let him go." Seeing no other alternative, she berated Cuchulain and shamed him into getting up and recovering his strength. Then, accompanied only by his faithful charioteer, Cuchulain drove to the water's edge and disappeared into the Otherworld.

What a horrific battle ensued! Aided by a small Otherworld army commanded by the husband of the woman in green, Cuchulain went into his battle frenzy. The slaughter was immense. Even the demons were decimated. In short order, the outcome was clear and the warrior had to be brought back to himself in the usual three cauldrons of cold water. Afterwards, Cuchulain bathed, scented himself and entered into Fand's presence. She had been eagerly awaiting him.

At his first sight of her, all thoughts about Emer and any of the other mortal women he had ever loved left Cuchulain's mind. He became Fand's lover and for one month of Otherworld time he thought of nothing but being with her. Then he began to get restless and yearned to return to the mortal world and to Emer. Although the lovesick Fand tried to keep him, she finally had to let him go. But she had extracted from him a promise that at each quarter moon, he would meet her at the Strand of the Yew Tree's Head. Then Cuchulain and his charioteer went home.

Within a few months, it became clear to Emer that her husband was regularly making love with another woman. In a rage, Emer armed her handmaidens with knives and resolved to kill either one or both of them. But Fand heard them coming and was able to alert Cuchulain just before Emer and the other women arrived. Then there came about an amazing confrontation. Starting in mutual rage, it ended in a moment of great tenderness, when Fand and Emer briefly saw into each others' hearts and Fand realized that Emer loved Cuchulain enough to let him go, if that was his choice. But Cuchulain, who realized that he loved *both* Emer and Fand, for different reasons, could not make the choice. At that moment, Mannanan, Fand's estranged husband, arrived in his silver chariot to reclaim her. She had seen both the love Emer had for Cuchulain and the changeable indecisiveness that informed the warrior/hero. Then Fand realized that she had to go back with Manannan. As they rode away in the silver chariot, Cuchulain ran after them with dreadful cries of despair.

Then there came many months of grieving. The warrior/hero wandered in the mountains, "living among the wild animals, scarcely eating nor drinking nor even sleeping [. . .] and no one would go near him." Then Emer appealed to his dear friend, King Conchobhar, who sent singers to

remind Cuchulain about his heroic deeds, about his comrades in arms and about his wife, whom he had once loved. When Cuchulain fell asleep, he was carried home, where King Conchobhar's Druid called on Manannan to release him. The god waved his Cloak of Forgetfulness between Fand and Cuchulain and all thoughts of her were erased from his memory.

Thereafter, Cuchulain lived quite contentedly with Emer. But she was unable to forget that he had once rejected her. Her jealousy took over her thoughts. Finally, she confided in an old nurse living at King Conchobhar's palace. The old nurse told the king, who in turn informed his Druid. One evening, when Cuchulain and Emer were dining at the palace, the Druid placed three drops of a special potion into their beverage. After awaking from a deep sleep, Cuchulain "had no memory of his passions but there lingered in him a deep sorrow, the reason for which he could not recall." When Emer awoke, "her anger and jealousies were gone and once more she was her natural self, the sweetest and most loving of wives."

That ends the telling of the myth and leaves you, perhaps, with some perplexing thoughts about the paradoxical ways in which heart consciousness energies can impact upon animal soul, while the reverse can also happen. Here are the masculine energies of the root chakra interacting with the feminine energies of the sacral chakra, whose motifs are the archetypal Cuchulain and Emer. Here are also the solar plexus consciousness energies, symbolized by the archetypal "servants," this time including the charioteer. (You are already familiar with the symbolic purpose of the "servants" and the cauldrons of water. The charioteer is a special motif indicating the solar plexus chakra's power to generate the "thoughts" that can take you into the "higher" centers of consciousness and take you out, if you choose to leave.) The "higher" centers are symbolized in this myth by the personages of the Otherworld: the "lady in green," the "king" who is her husband and, most importantly, by Fand. They are the combined motif of a "calling" into a greater awareness and capacity for love that the primitive masculine energies of root chakra consciousness (Cuchulain) at first resist but later accept. Emer, the motif of the primitive sacral chakra feelings energies, expresses qualities of caring, but she also carries deep angers and jealousies. When her situation is reasonably stable, she can function in the sacral energies. In her later inner turmoil are revealed unhealed soul structures of emotionality, as in the Wheel of Samsara realm of hell. To reinforce that image, there are Emer's "handmaidens," who are quite willing to help her commit murder. **At the same time** there are depicted the energies of the heart center that temporarily "called" forth a "higher" love in Emer. Meanwhile, Cuchulain had been "called" into a "higher" love (Fand) in the Otherworld. Although the warrior had received the assistance of a "higher" masculine energy (the "king") and had successfully defeated "demons," he was still dominated by his own nature and was ultimately unable to choose that "higher" consciousness. He had to go back to a consciousness in which he is "at home." Cuchulain, the motif of the essentially instinctual root chakra masculine energies, is really capable only of relating to Emer, the motif of essentially primitive feminine energies. But having once tasted the ecstasies of "higher" love, he feels ever afterward, an inexplicable sense of loss. She, on the other hand, who has only slightly and temporarily connected with "heart" awareness, undergoes a healing of her worst damage in a temporary connection with "higher" consciousness energies symbolized by the "old nurse," "King Conchobhar" and the "Druid." Afterward, Emer remains "content" in a state of simply being who she is. That has often been the way of animal soul consciousness. What an immense paradox of heart center energies has been revealed by this wonderful myth![431]

Your Heart Chakra's Function and Generative Power

While you continue the discipline/practice of containing, summon the Observer and tune into the front of your heart chakra. Although it is not in this dimension, the heart center's feminine force causes it to be receptive to all the environmental influences (healthy and unhealthy) carried by this dimension. Having learned about them in previous lessons, you are aware of their impact on your soul substance and "lower" centers of consciousness. (This journey has been about healing those centers and their damaged soul structures.) Please note that in your **holistic** human energy system, the unhealthy environmental influences were equally damaging to your receptive heart chakra. They will be alluded to, as you examine the function and generative power of that center of conscious. Now let us turn to the connection of the heart center of consciousness with animal soul by considering the generative function of your heart chakra. While you explore your own heart consciousness energies please keep in mind the paradoxes revealed by the Cuchulain myth.

Dealing with the physical component of your heart chakra front, you are reminded that you can experience a variety of physical sensations that express deeply-rooted emotions. (Your biology of **beliefs** carries an emotional "charge.") On this journey you have been exploring and healing the strong interconnection between your soul structures of physicality and emotionality. Now, go further and fully realize that your feelings and thoughts have the capacity to trigger huge physical responses in your heart center of consciousness (as when your heart "leaps"). Your heart can physically feel "light" and very "large." It can "sing" and "laugh." Indicating its archetypal imperative, your heart center can experience a heart connection that seems tangible. These "heart strings" often accompany the freshness of being "in love" and the loving excitement of happy encounters, situations and events.[432] (Pause here and ponder on those sensations in your life. Recall the 'high" energies of those occasions and how the world seemed to be a new and wonderful place.) The physical sensations of the heart can also be "tight," "burning" and "cold." Your heart center can feel "stifled" and "shut down." Those sensations are triggered by something in your outer or inner environment that

---

[431] In the stories that continue the saga, Cuchulain remains unchanged and eventually is killed by a greater warrior.

[432] For an interesting discussion linking the physical heart with the "emotional intelligence" postulated by Daniel Goleman, see Ervin Laszlo and Jude Currivan, *CosMos: A Co-Creator's Guide to the Whole-World*, pp. 141-142.

is connecting with your **beliefs**. Instead of love, there are the "heavy" energies of lovelessness; fear, anger, guilt, shame and pain. (Here is a reminder of the Cuchulain myth.)

Pause now and explore: at the junction of your ribs and breast bone, there is a "grief spot" that can actually be sore to the touch. It can indicate the presence of the Wounded Child. If you are carrying those energies, you can tune into them, into their feeling/tone, by gently pressing on this spot. Your "crying" heart can be heard, felt and relieved. If you allow this to happen, you can actually experience the physical sensations of "letting go" and of the receptivity as "opening." (Take time to do this. Stay in the containing.)

Turning to the emotional component of your heart center front, summon the Observer and probe deeply into the feelings energies that you carry. You already know about the emotionality of fear, anger, hatred and pain. Because yours is a **holistic** energy system, those energies can be found in your heart. So, also, can the "higher" vibrations of love. When you love, the world is a wonderful place. Your feelings of joy, gladness, and happiness can permeate every cell of your physicality. They can also attract loving relationships to you. They come, it would appear, from the outer environment and you are happily receptive to them. But they also express your heart center's prime directive. (If the vibrations in your heart center are not those related to love energies, then probe yet more deeply and allow what are there to express in images and feelings. Do you resonate with the Cuchulain myth in this respect? If the images and feelings are those of darkness, use the "Seeker's Lamp" meditation to help you probe into them. If the "letting go" of emotional clearing and "worm-hole" work is needed, do so without judgment and remain in the containing.)

Focusing now on your heart chakra's mental component please be aware that there are ways of thinking and of understanding with love and compassion about yourself and others. They can be described as ways of heart connection. (At this point, please recall the wisdom teachings about that kind of thought and understanding. Also recall the thought-full and compassionate "servants" in the Cuchulain myth. Do you resonate with that kind of heart connection? It indicates **belief** structures that have been healed.) Yet, in the heart chakra's mental component, there can also be the unhealed energies comprising the "character structures" presented in the last lesson. They are "holes" in your heart bridge that require repairing. Reflecting an unhealthy and malnourishing outer environment, a lovelessness by which the "higher" heart energies have been unrecognized and/or ignored, these character structures of soul have been closely allied with both the Wheel of Samsara soul structures of emotionality and the "shadows" of the Wounded Child archetype. Thus, they have impacted hugely upon the heart center. (If this is the case with you, continue to "work" diligently with the balancing healing therapies (disciplines) for the sacral and solar plexus chakras, while you continue to probe into your soul structures of emotionality and mentality. The kundalini "shifts" that indicate the healing of your lower" soul structures will also signal successful repairs to your heart bridge. Stay with the "containing.")

Finally, your heart chakra front spiritual component has the capability of receiving messages and guidance from many sources.[433] Present since your conception, those messages have been generated both in the "higher" dimensions and in this third dimension. From the higher dimensions, the messages enter the heart center through downward causation. But the receptivity, the heart "openness," might not be there. Indeed, this will be the case, if there has been too little or no childhood (and later) nurturing. If that is so, there will appear to be little or no receptivity of the downward causation or the upward causation from this dimension. (Please remember that the heart chakra's prime directive of connectedness and the feminine force can become "stuck" if there has been more lovelessness than love and insufficient healing of the "lower" frequencies. This was indicated in the Cuchulain myth.) But the receptivity is there and, even if much healing is necessary, a loving input can lead to the transformation of the "bridging" structures of soul. In particular, the spiritual concerns of receiving and living your "heart's desire" are input, guided and healed through the heart chakra. (Take time to ponder on your heart's desire and how it has, or has not, been realized. If the latter is the case, meditate with the "Seeker's Lamp" to locate the **belief** that will provide insight. Then do some "worm-hole" work that will help with the "letting go.")

Opening to other dimensions, the back of your heart chakra can be a receptor of energies whose power is immense. They can also be overwhelming. (This can happen if your "lower" centers of consciousness still require healing, as indicated in the myth of Cuchulain.) Here is a reminder, then, that your ongoing quest involves all three of your paths and all their "lanes" and that the simultaneity of journeying on them will likely continue. Keep in mind also that your quest requires the letting go, letting be and balancing that are actualizing the powers of detachment/discernment and of dynamic equilibrium in your emerging holarchy which is enhancing your inner empowerment and its feeling/tone of purity, simplicity and unity. After this reminder, please maintain the new discipline/practice of "containing." And walk with the Observer on this untrodden path of "Entering Within" as you proceed to explore your heart chakra back.

The physical component of your heart chakra back serves as an entry point for the archetypal energies (sometimes referred to as the "spirit guides") that can spur you to take the physical actions necessary to actualize your true "calling." After having perhaps taken years trying out various careers, there comes a sudden awareness that you have a physical yearning to move forward in a particular direction. Thereafter, you are inspired and strengthened to expend immense physical energies to achieve your goal. (Perhaps this is still to come or it has already happened to you. Ponder on this while you focus on the back of the chakra. If you discern an "ache" or even a sense of "tightness," tune into it and allow it to reveal its source. In relation to the myth of Cuchulain, it seems that the warrior/hero had received a higher "calling," but he was not ready for it. Has that happened with you? Is it happening now?)

The emotional component of your heart chakra back can express an unconditional love for yourself and for others. As already indicated, this is not common in the history of humankind.

---

[433] For example, there are Schubert's "Unfinished" Symphony Number 8 and Rumi's poetry.

At this level of relationship into which you slowly evolve, your heart center is gradually opening and becoming clear of the encumbrances thrown up by unhealed sacral center energies and by your animal soul egoic structures. (In the Cuchulain myth, these obstacles prevented the hero/warrior from staying in the "higher" energies that he had entered. Ponder on this in your experience. You might discern the need for further healing. If so, "work" with the healing therapies (disciplines) for balancing the sacral chakra and with the "letting go" of emotional clearing. Make no judgments. With the Observer to assist you, stay on your path.)

The mental component of the heart chakra back is quite powerful. (This was clearly indicated in the Cuchulain myth by the "charioteer.") You have a capacity to think lovingly. That is, while you continue to transmute your sacral chakra energies and transform their soul structures, you can start to love without fear and judgment. This will enhance the quality of your thoughts, especially your ideas about relationships. The conditionality that has likely indicated your **beliefs** will be replaced by a decision to express love in authentic relationships. (Ponder on yours and again refer to the Cuchulain myth.) Although this energy shift will require a lot of courage and commitment, it will be well worth the effort. (There is more detail later in the lesson.)

Finally, the spiritual component of your heart chakra back can be an intake portal to messages from the Spirit. You allow in guidance from angels and other holy guides. This is yet another avenue of heart connectedness and yet another indicator of heart center receptivity. They happen while you are following your paths, maintaining the healing disciplines and the discipline/practices and "opening" to the Spirit. (With a final reference to the myth of Cuchulain, you can perceive the results of a choice to remain at the root chakra level of consciousness. Ponder on the choices that you have made.)

Having learned about your heart chakra's generative function, you are ready to explore what that chakra generates; your heart "bridge," aka the bridging structures of soul. You are on the threshold of rebirthing. Persevere on the untrodden path of "Entering Within."

Your Heart "Bridge"

So far in this lesson, you have been given many word images of a damaged heart center of consciousness and of wounded soul structures. When we move from the context of myth into this time and space to deal with the personal experience of many people, it could be described like this: the damage to your heart center of consciousness could have started at your conception in malfunctioning relationships between your parents and/or between you and your mother. After your advent, the damage and wounding could have been reinforced by further malfunctioning relationships and by your beliefs, values, attitudes and habits. Within an unloving environment, the "higher" astral energies of your heart center that would have been instrumental in raising the vibratory frequency of your animal soul centers of consciousness would not have been noticeably present. And why is that? Your heart center can be imaged as a "bridge" with those "higher" astral energies which carry the higher emotions – compassion, tenderness, sensitivity, kindness, gratitude, gentleness and caring – being part of the soul substance shaped by your heart center into your "bridging" structures of soul. As such, your heart "bridge" is the connector between your "lower" and "higher" centers of consciousness. And that connector would have been too damaged to allow for the generation of those structures; hence, there would not have been the vitally necessary downward flow of energies in your human energy system. Meanwhile, your animal soul egoic structures, developing since your conception, would have continued to be those of "I am my physicality; I am my emotionality; I am my mentality." Because **form follows consciousness,** the "identity" that had been generated and that was expressing the out-of-balance masculine and feminine forces of those animal soul centers, would certainly be implicated in your heart center damage. When that chakra actually came into its own functioning at your puberty, its creative power would have been horribly compromised. In the words of "bridge" imagery, your heart center would have been unstable, with missing parts. (The response that triggered your quest for wholeness was a "cry" from your heart center.)

In a brief aside: the physical and emotional stresses that have marked animal soul puberty have often been noted. In recent decades in Western societies especially, these stresses frequently have assumed major proportions and have been revealed in a "teen-age sub-culture" that has often rejected adult mores. Although some worried attention has been given to this situation, the underlying "causes" have been only partially addressed. With a better understanding of the human energy system and, in particular, of the animal soul structures of physicality, emotionality and mentality, some of the teen-age behavior could be comprehensible. But it would be only with an awareness of the function of the heart chakra and the "dance" of these consciousness energies with the others, that clarity could be achieved. The reason is likely this: it is at puberty, when the heart center can start to function on its own, that the possibilities of development into an androgynous human being can begin to be actualized. In a healthy human energy system, that development can really get underway at puberty because there is a readily accessible downward causation from the "higher" centers through the heart bridge. But the "reality" is usually vastly different. Carrying such widespread damage to soul structures including those of the heart bridge, the teen-age sub-culture has expressed very little except woundedness. One indicator of the power of the heart chakra and how different the situation could be lies in the "idealism" of youth. The stories of the Knights of the Round Table, for example, bear witness to those receptive energies. This idealism has been revealed in many ways. One modern example involves the response of youth to charismatic political figures who have promised "change." In law-abiding countries, idealistic youth have marched with slogans and banners. In less stable countries, they have joined "revolutionary" armies. In order to understand what has happened, you must be fully tuned into your heart chakra bridge.

Let us return to the lesson.

Soul Searcher, please note that from the moment your quest for wholeness got underway, you have been healing your consciousness energies of animal soul. Moreover, because this is a **holistic** energy system, you have slowly been making headway on repairs to your heart bridge.

Thus, you have greatly expanded your **knowing** and **being**. (Take some time to ponder this while you tune into your heart center of consciousness and allow it to "speak" to you. Tune in. Let your heart center reveal the progress made by the emerging holarchy (the powers of the detachment/ discernment and the power of the dynamic equilibrium) which is developing in you. Let it tell you about your deepening sense of glowing inner empowerment and its feeling/tone of purity, simplicity and unity.) Although you must continue with your quest for yet a little while, you have already done remarkably well.

After your pondering, please take in the next teaching. It is meant to promote in you an even greater awareness about your heart center. It is meant to remind you, yet again, about you as an energy being. And it is meant to prepare you for your next "heart" image:

Like your other centers of consciousness, your heart chakra's generating power arises out of your microcosmic, archetypal, **holistic** human energy system. Hence, your "bridging" structures of soul have been and will continue to be generated out of soul substance with the "higher" astral energies, in accordance with your heart center's prime directive (archetypal imperative), its "i-am" consciousness, its qualities and its function. Now, expand your awareness to encompass this:

In your human energy system, your heart center of consciousness has been involved, since your conception, in both the developing and the healing of animal soul's connection with the indwelling Spirit. It is an amazing "story" that reveals the presence and power of your inner guidance system. We pick up the "story" with your heart "bridge." If you were like most people, it would have sustained terrible damage in the same loveless environment that had brought about the damage to your animal soul structures, even before your birth. (You have already been given a great deal about that part of the story!) Before your healing journey began, the function and generative power of your heart center would have been curtailed in direct proportion to the amount of lovelessness impacting upon you. After the onset of your quest for wholeness, your healing disciplines and the practices have been crucial in helping to heal your heart "bridge." And why is that? They have slowly brought about the transformation of your animal soul structures through the healing of your "lower" centers. This transformation, in turn, has resulted in the further healing of your "lower" centers. Thus, you can be made aware of the incalculable power of the heart "bridge" in upward and downward causation; that it was the connector over which the ascending and descending consciousness energies could flow. In all of this unfolding, there has been revealed the "working" of your inner guidance system. But there has been more to the "story." You are now ready to deal with the second "heart" image you were given at the beginning of this lesson; namely, the heart "crucible."

Your Heart "Crucible"

The "crucible" image is an ancient symbol of essential change that makes clear the immense power of your heart center of consciousness. That center is the locus of an inner alchemy.[434]

---

[434] I am indebted to Reverend Michael Bernard Beckwith, whose sermons first gave me this phrase. Afterward, the idea has been enhanced by explorations into the hermetic wisdom tradition. The main sources were

Thus, your heart center can be given the same attributes as an alchemical crucible. And here is yet another insight that you are ready to receive. Throughout your journey, while your animal soul structures, in particular your egoic structures, have undergone transformation, there has been the alchemical change of animal soul consciousness energies taking place in your heart "crucible." And what has been the catalytic agent? In that amazing process, which has involved your heart center's prime directive and "i-am" consciousness the catalytic agent in the crucible has been love. Love has fostered both an ongoing restoration to wholeness of your "lower" centers and an ongoing expression of your covenant with the indwelling Spirit. It is love has fostered an incredible connectedness, reconciliation and **knowing**. This is the process in which you have been and continue to be involved.

And in that fostering, which has also involved your heart center's "higher" feminine energies, the "lower" masculine and feminine energies continue to be transmuted while your animal soul egoic structures are being transformed and your heart chakra's "i-am" is being actualized. In that fostering, your practice of containing is crucial. The reason is this: your heart crucible, with its catalytic love energies has also been involved in the repairing of the old bridging structures. The love energies have been there all along in the "workings" of your inner guidance system. Now they are being manifested through downward causation. They will continue and gradually become stronger, as you continue the upward causation of your healing quest. The alchemy will continue. But it requires your ongoing discipline/ practice of containing. And the reason is this: in the fostering of heart connectedness by the love energies, the powers carried by the emerging holarchy have been expanding. Now, the powers actualized by your containing are being added. And the developing and the healing of animal soul's connection with the indwelling Spirit, especially the "i-am" egoic structures, are part of the continuing "story."

Clearly, your heart chakra involvement in your rebirthing journey has already been a grand adventure. In that "work," your heart center and especially the crucible have been given direct assistance in two wonderful ways. Let us explore them now.

Your Dreams

The first of the "wonderful assistance" given to your heart center has been provided by the dreams you have likely been experiencing since childhood. (Indeed, your legacy of wisdom teachings includes the ancient awareness of the power of dreams.)[435] In a moment, you will realize why. The only difference between your childhood dreams and those that you can have during your quest is that you can now be aware that your dreams give you direct help from the indwelling Spirit.[436] They symbolically reveal in much the same fashion as fairy tales, the

---

Julius Evola, *The Hermetic Tradition: Symbols and Teachings of the Royal Art* and Joscelyn Godwin, *The Golden Thread, The Ageless Wisdom of the Western Mystery Traditions*, in particular Chapter 13; "The Inner Alchemy."

[435] For more detail, see Anthony Stevens, *Private Myths: Dreams and Dreaming*, pp. 8-34.

[436] Marie-Louise Von Franz, *Archetypal Patterns in Fairy Tales*, pp 28, 34, 36, 39 and 45.

contents of your buried and usually traumatized consciousness energies. Up out of the dark depths there emerge sensations, images and feelings, all to be lovingly transmuted in your heart crucible. In your dreaming you are also given symbolic representations of the discord between your masculine and feminine energies, with the possibility of healing them. You dream about people (male and female) you know and people you do not know. They are all your own masculine and feminine energies revealing themselves to you. And because you are there in your dreams as the "dreamer," you receive both direct and indirect messages related to you as an ego/self. Your egoic structures might even be revealed as animal forms. Thus, it is wise to take your dreams seriously. In doing this, you will be healing your heart chakra and you will be both repairing and generating your "bridging" structures of soul. Here are some words of encouragement:[437]

> "When we dream we enter a realm which may be legitimately described as magical in the sense that literally anything can happen without any reference to the normal constraints of nature: we can fly, travel to far-off places, hold conversations with animals and with the dead and witness extraordinary transformations. Moreover, dreams are not infrequently experienced as miraculous in their effects in that we are both animated and transformed by them. On waking from such dreams, it is not unusual to feel ourselves and our world to be different. Nothing will ever be quite the same."

The following account of a series of dreams that spanned almost twenty years in a quest for wholeness will illustrate how dream messages can ensure that "nothing will ever be quite the same."

*   *   *

In the first dream, the dreamer, a fifty-five-year-old woman, who had not started her quest for wholeness but who had been getting insistent "readiness messages," was given a sudden insight that forced her to begin to pay attention.

She is in a vast, semi-dark and windowless underground basement with a dirt floor. She is walking with someone who is a quiet, gentle presence. She and the presence are slowly moving past obviously sick people who are lying covered with sheets, except for their heads, on slabs of marble that look like raised, horizontal tomb stones. The dreamer feels very sad at the sight of such misery and she stops occasionally to look with pity at a sufferer before moving on. After some time, she notices a large hole in the wall of the basement. The wall has been broken through and she sees the rubble outside. There is sunlight streaming in through the hole. Eagerly she hastens toward it and steps through. There in front of her is a heap of debris with some large chunks of concrete balanced on it. Above and beyond the rubble, she

---

[437] Anthony Stevens, *Private Myths: Dreams and Dreaming*, p. 171.

sees clear, blue sky and brilliant sunlight. Without hesitation, she starts to crawl up the pile of rubble. Then the dream ends.

Unable to forget the dream, the dreamer carried a profound sadness for several months. She realized that the "basement" was her own inner depth and that the "sick" people lying there were parts of her. But she was disinclined to take note of much of the "message" because she was too busy trying to cope with disturbing events in her life.

Then there came the second dream.

She has been idly looking over and picking up lingerie in the women's clothing section of a large department store. Suddenly, she hears over the usual noise, the sounds of singing. It is a "thin" voice and the music is the "blues." Curious, she follows the sound and comes upon a potted fan palm tree that obscures her vision. When she walks around the tree, the singing becomes very clear and the words are distinguishable as: "I don't love you and you don't love me." She looks around for the singer and sees no one. Then she looks down. There at her feet on a baby blanket is an infant, naked except for its diaper and propping itself up on its stomach. With a start, the dreamer realizes that this infant has been singing the "blues." As the dreamer looks down on the baby, it stops singing and looks up at her with coal black eyes that are filled with hostility and pain. Then the dream ends.

The dreamer was left shaken and upset, but this time she paid greater attention to what was obviously a powerful message about her. She began pondering the words she had heard and allowed herself to feel the pain enclosing her heart area. She also became aware of a "spot" of coldness behind her left breast that she identified as lovelessness. After she began recalling incidents from her childhood, she gradually allowed her wounds to enter her awareness. Very slowly, she started to feel warmth towards that inner adult/infant she carried.

Several years after that dream, she received another dream message.

She is walking in a thick and murky forest. She suddenly emerges into a sunlit clearing surrounded by trees. As she walks forward, she realizes that there is a picnic table in the center of the clearing. Seated on either side of the table are four children ranging in age from about six to puberty. As the dreamer approaches the table, a boy seated at the far end of the left side of the table stands up and looks at her. He is a teenager and rather chubby and plain in appearance but he carries an air of maturity. In a tired voice, he says: "I'm so glad that you have finally come." The dreamer is astounded and cannot comprehend. She looks at all the other children in turn and sees that they are girls, who are returning her gaze with sullen hostility. Then she sees that there are stainless steel plates, bowls and eating utensils on the table. The dishes are shining clean. There is no food. The dreamer feels alarm and distress. She says to the boy, who is still standing and waiting: "Where are your parents?" He does not reply. At that moment, she feels a hard tug on her skirt. Looking down she stares into the angry face of a little girl, age about three, with red, corkscrew curls springing from her head. The little one tugs again and angrily demands: "Isn't anybody going to pay attention to me?" Utterly astounded, the dreamer gazes at the little girl and asks: "Who are you?" Then the dream ends.

By the time this dream took place, the woman had read extensively about the inner child and had explored her own woundedness. Quickly, she realized that the dream children were her own inner children who required much more nourishment than she had been providing. Her "warmth" towards the adult/child of the second dream had possibly brought her to a higher awareness, but there was a long journey ahead. This was indicated by the third dream. In ordinary "reality," she did not connect well with children. She was uncomfortable with the thought of this relatedness. In dealing with this dream, she struggled with her emotional "resistance." Then, one day she felt that she had found the truth: she could not love, except non-threatening people and things. She concluded that her wounds had shut her heart down. After more "inner child" work, she concluded that she was not able to love because she feared being rejected. This had been a large part of her childhood experience. When that realization surfaced, she felt an immense grief that continued for some time. Greatly distressed, she turned for help to her indwelling Spirit. The insight was rapidly forthcoming. Her heart had not shut down; she had simply equated love with the sadness and hurt of rejection and she was grieving the love she had given and not received. It had been her greatest treasure and it had been discounted. Instantly, she experienced an energy shift. She felt her heart center open and she began to feel joy. Here was a transmutation that resulted in wondrous repair to her bridging structures of soul! And her quest continued. Years later, after much discipline and commitment, there was a fourth dream.

She has recently moved into her new home and is seated on a lounge chair on her driveway. She is relaxing and reading. She is fully aware that she is experiencing her own physical body as it is in ordinary "reality." Suddenly, a huge red fire truck rolls onto the driveway and stops within a few feet of her. She is surprised but not frightened and stands up, while keeping her finger between the pages of her book. Bemused, she watches as eight firefighters, huge in size and clad entirely in yellow firemen's garb, line up facing her in front of the truck. As she continues to gaze at them, the firefighters raise their hands in one motion and remove their helmets. Their long auburn hair tumbles down over their shoulders. She is astounded to see that they are all beautiful women, identical in appearance. Then the one in the center steps forward, looks keenly at her and says: "Do you know where we can get something to eat?" The dreamer feels overwhelmed and stammers her reply: "No, I just moved here and I don't know where the restaurants are." Riveting her with a stern gaze, the firefighter replies: "Oh, yes you do!" The dream ends.

Having spent years nurturing herself, the woman was embarrassed when she remembered what she had done in her dream. While pondering, she realized that the "firefighters" were her own evolved selves, that she had developed hugely from the "sick" people in the "basement" and that all she had had to do in the dream was to invite the "women" into her new home. Her refrigerator was well stocked. Why had she not done that? Her insight was that she was still, in some respects, loveless and not able to trust enough. She was, in effect, still rejecting these parts of herself. It was a huge step in self-awareness. Then the work of self-acceptance came to the fore. It took more journeying and years before she realized that this had been a dream of her future; her egoic structures, in particular, would be nurtured enough that she would be an empowered androgyny and **know** her own **being**. Then, her quest began in earnest.

*   *   *

Even if you seldom remember your dreams, you can cultivate this capacity. It will greatly assist you on your quest. Paying attention to your dreams will involve you in two tasks: the first is **pondering**, while you rely increasingly on your intuition and imagination to provide insights. In doing this, you will already be linking to your "highest" vibration. (This will be explored thoroughly in the next lesson.) Since this is a gradual process which cannot be rushed, it is usually not wise to rely heavily on your own interpretations of your dreams. The second task, therefore, is to **connect** with an intuitive analyst, who will assist you in your discoveries. Dream analysts have undergone a great deal of transmutation and transformation themselves and are actually listening to their own spiritual input. As you work with them, they will teach you to do likewise. In this way, you will be following the untrodden path of "Entering Within," while both repairing and generating your heart bridge.

Meanwhile, you will also be receiving yet another wonderful assistance in the "workings" of your heart crucible. It is the help that has been available from your very earliest years from your androgynous heart archetypes.[438] Let us explore those amazing energies.

Your Heart Archetypes

In the manner of your conception, the importance of the love connection between your parents has already been noted. Of crucial importance was another love connection, already noted; the symbiotic relationship between you and your mother during your gestation and for several months after your birth. **In that symbiosis, you and she were one consciousness and the love connection between you was vital for your later human development.** Not only were your root, sacral and solar plexus chakras involved, but also present was your heart center.

The nurturing environments and experiences of childhood have already received much emphasis in these lessons. Now here is another reason for the necessity of childhood nurturing. It is this: in your symbiotic love connection (if it had been present), you would have been

---

[438] These wonderful universal energies have been described by Angeles Arrien in *The Four-Fold Way: Walking the Paths of the Warrior, Teacher, Healer and Visionary*, pp. 13-45, 47-76, 77-105 and 109-128.

made receptive to the immense energies of the heart archetypes. They would have been there, perhaps before your birth, but certainly afterward. In that vital connection with your mother, she would already have "called" them into her being from the "collective unconscious," the Akashic Field. During your developmental years of animal soul consciousness, your heart archetypes would have been expressing, but in a limited way. Meanwhile, your soul structures of emotionality, in particular, and your developing physical and mental egoic structures would have been in-formed by that mitigating influence. To be sure, you would have been animal soul, because that is the evolutionary way. But the woundedness and its primitive manifestations would have been much less than "normal." Your heart bridge would have required much fewer repairs to enable downward causation. And your heart crucible would already have started its alchemical "work." (Please take some time to ponder again on your first love connection with your mother. If this was not the case with you because you were an unwanted fetus and/or given up for adoption, you have important "inner child" work to do. Do not be discouraged! Your heart archetypes are awaiting you. Now, receive the teachings about them.)

Their immense power stems from the fact that each of your heart archetypes embodies a "principle" that expresses Love. Just as the Life and the Light of the first paths of your quest indicate guidance from the indwelling Spirit (the nucleus of divinity), so, too, does the Love of your third path, the path of "Entering Within." It is the Love aspect of the Spirit that not only in-forms your heart archetypes but is also, as you have already learned, the main catalytic "agent" in your heart crucible.

As an aside: in the Sufi teachings about the heart, there is a word, *himma,* which means a "concentration of heart that can produce a creative energy powerful enough to give objective body to the heart's intentions."[439] Your heart archetypes can become that "real" in your life. They can actually become "embodied" as you.[440]

Let us continue . . .

The first archetype of the heart is the Teacher. This creative energy embodies the principle of being aware of the outcome but not desiring to control it. In other words, the Teacher archetype is uninvolved with expectations. In-formed by Love, the healthy Teacher expresses in you as trust and going with the flow. The Teacher also expresses as the loving detachment that trust requires and, thereby, slowly fosters a growing commitment to Truth. In all this, the Teacher allows the developmental process to be what it is. By invoking your Teacher archetype, while you are arriving at your own healing insights, you will be able to deal successfully with the resistance set up by your unhealed soul structures of emotionality that can drag you into the depths. The heart message of the Teacher is for you to have loving trust in your Spirit-guided developmental process.

Without this awareness, the Teacher archetype can be expressing woundedness; deep wounds often inflicted within an environment of lovelessness. Then, the wounded Teacher "shadow" rises to the fore and tries to control outcomes in every possible way. There is a

---

[439] For more detail, see Gail Godwin, *Heart: The Story of Its Myths and Meanings,* p. 245-246.
[440] Please recall that archetypes express **in** you, **as** you and **through** you.

linkage here with a body of **beliefs** and attitudes that emphasize security and safety. As already indicated in previous lessons, many of those beliefs can be false. Thus, quite early in childhood, the shadow can be expressing as both a disregard of and a distrust of truth, including that of loving heart connections. (Recall the dreamer you have recently encountered.) All that time, there is a fear-based refusal to trust in (or allow) any process of inner development. Impacted upon by the Teacher "shadow," the energies of the Life Force are curbed and channeled in a particular direction. Meanwhile, the physical, emotional and mental egoic structures are crystallizing and the heart-generated "bridging" structures are experiencing trauma.

On your quest for wholeness, when you are struggling to let go of your old **beliefs** and to open the way to the new, the Observer has been a stalwart aid.[441] With the Observer to help, you can now start to "call" in your Teacher archetype. That archetypal energy will gradually enter and be involved in the loving work of transforming the soul structures of beliefs, fear and distrust. At first, the wounded Teacher shadow will seek to control the outcome and actually prevent the healing. But as your quest continues, the alchemical action of your heart crucible will gradually bring about a kundalini "shift," through the transmutation of the unhealed energies of your root, sacral and solar plexus chakras. Eventually, your healthy Teacher will be present to you as a loving inner guide, whom you will have learned to trust; a Teacher who is oriented only toward Truth. In your **holistic** energy system this can happen in the following manner: when your root and solar plexus chakras, along with your sacral chakra and its generated soul structures of emotionality undergo healing, this, in turn, has a healing effect on the damaged energies of your heart "bridge." As a result, the downward causation of the "higher" consciousness energies can get underway or, if there has already been some activity, be much improved. The receptive heart center opens or opens further. With that opening, your heart crucible can undertake or improve upon the alchemical "work" of transmuting the consciousness energies of your unhealthy "lower" centers. Thereby, the healing of the animal soul structures will be brought about. Throughout all of that splendid development, your healthy Teacher archetype of the heart can be coming to the fore and, indeed, can be assisting you as a guide.

The second archetype of the heart is the Warrior. The principle embodied by the Warrior is to show up and to stay present. In other words, the Warrior archetype is uninvolved with entitlement. In-formed by Love, the healthy Warrior expresses in you as three universal powers: the first is the power of presence; an unchanging commitment to being what is Truth: the second is the power of communication; an unflinching commitment to presenting what is Truth: the third is the power of position; an unwavering commitment to supporting what is Truth. The heart message of the Warrior is for you to have the loving courage to recognize and welcome all the truths that will be there on your journey.

Without this love and courageous awareness, the wounded Warrior "shadow" can dominate your feelings, thoughts and actions, from early in your life. If your **beliefs** are rooted in survival

---

[441] Please recall that the Observer helps you to **know** the truth about you and, thereby, helps you to love yourself. With this help, you become "real."

needs and you have, perhaps, experienced rejection and/or abandonment, the healthy Warrior archetype can be replaced by the "shadow" presenting the face of an angry rebel, who rejects all perceived forms of "authority." Or the shadow will present itself as a victim, who will either lash out or cower when the situation is perceived to be "threatening." In adulthood (and sometimes in late childhood), the shadow can be expressed as fraudulent leadership powers of presence, communication and position which can lead the unwary into disaster. Sometimes the shadow can become the "power behind the throne" and in this hiding place manipulate political and other life-changing events for thousands of unsuspecting people.

On your quest for wholeness, you summon the Observer and "call in" your Warrior archetype of the heart. While you gradually increase the strength of your commitments to the three Warrior "powers," the Observer will help you to remain focused and maintain the necessary inner balance. As you continue to let go, open the way and do the work of coming into being, your Warrior archetype will become increasingly present. This highly evolved spiritual energy will be there as a discipline in your dealing with the wounded Warrior shadow and with the resistance of your soul structures of emotionality. (Please recall that those energies can also be expressed physically, as in screaming excitement and enthusiasm and mentally as in sophisticated arguments for sidestepping the truth in an event, situation, even a relationship.) As already indicated for your Teacher archetype of the heart, the self-healing therapies (disciplines) you have been assiduously undergoing gradually bring about, in your heart crucible, the alchemical transmutation of the unhealthy energies of those "lower" centers. And in your **holistic** energy system, while your damaged heart bridge is being repaired, your "higher" energies of consciousness can move in downward causation. Thus, your Warrior archetype, like the Teacher, will eventually manifest as a trustworthy guide courageously expressing the truths of what you are as a multidimensional energy being, a soul field.

The third archetype of the heart is the Healer. This creative energy embodies the principle to know and practice all the ways that human love can be expressed. In other words, the Healer archetype is uninvolved with sentimentality. In-formed by Love, the healthy Healer expresses in you as the awareness of the many different types of love, yet at the same time the recognition of the unity of consciousness they manifest. All are an indication of a true covenant in relationship: between mates and lovers; between parents and children; between colleagues and friends; between therapists and clients; between your own inner "selves," and between you and the indwelling Spirit. The heart message of the Healer is for you to be so profoundly "in love" (in unity and in truth) that all duality and falsity disappears.

Without that awareness, the wounded Healer "shadow" can promote a deep rift between you and the "treasures" of your heart. If the energies of your early childhood environment were a combination of harshness and sentimentality, your **beliefs** and attitudes about love were likely in-formed by fear and by conditionality. Thus, your beliefs about how to express and how to receive love would be false and your "love" feelings would not be real. You would experience the frustration of desiring something that continually eluded you. (In this description, please recall the god realms of the Wheel of Samsara.) In adulthood, the shadow of the Healer often expresses as a martyr, who cries out against the apparent heartlessness of those he/she "loves." The martyr energies are implicated in the "guilt trips" that can be inflicted on lovers, family, colleagues and friends. Another form the shadow takes is addictions; not only, or necessarily, to substances but also to emotional intensity (the "drama queen/king") and to "perfection." The controlling and manipulating Healer shadow can be a travesty of true love and can promote a deep despair in the person whose love needs can never be satisfied.

On your quest for wholeness, you summon the Observer and "call in" your Healer archetype. As your journey unfolds, the Observer can assist you in your practice of containing, by helping you to maintain a commitment of love toward your as yet unhealed animal soul structures. As you persevere with healing their centers of consciousness and shift into healed soul structures, your Healer archetype will be manifested. The wounds that have been a huge constituent of the resistance put up by your soul structures of emotionality will be soothed and eventually cease to give you pain. During your heart crucible alchemy, the still-unreconciled masculine and feminine forces of your "lower" centers will enter into a more balanced "dance." Your egoic structures, in particular, will undergo yet more positive change. Now, your Healer heart archetype with its power of true love, along with your Teacher and Warrior can be present as inner guides and your heart bridge will carry the flow of downward causation.

The fourth archetype of the heart is the Visionary. This creative energy, that you likely did not know was there, carries the principle to "see" and express Truth without judgment or blame. In other words, the Visionary archetype is uninvolved with hypocrisy. In-formed by Love the healthy Visionary expresses in you as a highly evolved **knowing** that has always benefited humankind. The capacity for "seeing" and expressing Truth takes you beyond the literal level of "seeing" and beyond the symbolic level to the level of paradox. At that level, there is only the unity of a multidimensional "reality" and that is what you **know**. The truth is that there is neither separateness nor duality and you live accordingly. The heart message of the Visionary is for you to experience the connectedness of all things and to commit to being and practicing authenticity.

Without this awareness, the wounded Visionary "shadow" can express all the falsity that can distort a person's life. The distortions can start in early childhood, when the child copies the adult "games" he sees all around him and seeks praise and acceptance by doing the same thing. Or the child has been punished for speaking the truth and quickly becomes cynical and self-protective in his interactions with others. After years of pretending, posturing and play-acting, the child's ego/self is a falsity. In adulthood, he/she can be part of the group of people who lie to each other without any qualms for the sake of the social "correctness." They hide behind their "masks" and are deeply fearful of being "found out." Eventually, they even start to believe the lies they are telling and are being told. In their business dealings, politics and relationships, inauthenticity is the norm.

In your quest for wholeness, it is again the Observer who assists while you "call in" your Visionary archetype of the heart. During your search for the truth about you, while you courageously probe into and ponder your inner landscape, especially your **beliefs**, the

Observer is an unwavering presence. If you start to lie to yourself (or to others), the Observer vanishes. Meanwhile, in the alchemy of your heart crucible, the consciousness energies of your "lower centers" that generated your physical, emotional and mental egoic structures are being transmuted. The more you plunge into paradox and the more you acknowledge, accept and allow the truth about you to come up, the more authentic you become and the more will be your sense of freedom and realness. You will cease rejecting yourself. Thus it is that you will **know** Truth and you will love yourself. In all this undertaking, you are invoking more and more of your archetypal Visionary. Gradually it will join with your Teacher, Warrior and Healer to guide and sustain you. In this process, your heart bridge will continue to heal and to undergo regeneration. And you will have learned an invaluable lesson: that fear and falsity are inseparable partners. The new partnership you will gain by invoking your heart archetypes will be that of L/love and T/truth. And, eventually, your heart archetypes will express, not just **in** you, but **as** you and **through** you. They will become part of the containing. Thus, there are great blessings awaiting you! (Please ponder on this teaching while you do your deep inner probing. Although you might still be experiencing pain and resistance, be assured that the Observer will readily assist you and that the Love will see you through.)

It is clear by now that in your **holistic** human energy system, the healing of your heart center of consciousness can be assumed with the healing of your root, sacral and solar plexus centers. But that assumption is not entirely correct. The heart chakra itself also often requires direct healing, mainly because your malleable, receptive, impressionable and vulnerable soul substance has been badly wounded by an unhealthy outer (and inner) environment and then misshaped by a heart chakra crippled by the childhood (and later) trauma that has also produced the malfunctioning root, sacral and solar plexus chakras. As you have probed and pondered, throughout these lessons, you have become very familiar with those traumas, with the causes, the impact on your animal soul centers of consciousness and their resultant soul structures. When the trauma included lovelessness, the heart center — bridge and crucible — could sustain direct damage. Then its function and generative power would be horribly compromised.

Let us now turn to an examination of a malfunctioning heart chakra. Summon the Observer. Please remain detached and discerning. And continue the discipline/practice of containing.

Your Heart Chakra's Malfunction

Within an unhealthy inner and/or outer environment, the trauma inflicted on your sacral chakra can be repeated in your heart center. Although these consciousness energies (astral feelings energies) exhibit different ranges of frequencies, your **holistic** system will manifest the damage. Thus, the malfunction in your heart chakra will reflect early childhood physical and emotional trauma, especially sexual abuse and all that came later out of the original trauma. Your heart center will also be damaged by negative **belief** structures, including the belief in your own "badness" and by the thoughts that are triggered by those energies. And all of it can express as lovelessness.

The physical expression of a malfunctioning heart chakra can include heart and/or circulatory disease and blood pressure problems. All are related to an excess of red root chakra energies. Those energies can actually lodge behind your physical heart organ. Further physical expressions of a malfunctioning heart chakra are lung and breathing related problems, asthma, bronchitis and sleep apnea. The latter can indicate persistent wounds so serious that the person tries to escape by going out-of-body. The psychological expressions of heart chakra dysfunction include those of an unhealed sacral chakra, plus a worsening of relationship problems. Then, the inability to experience physical "intimacy" with another human being becomes a major problem on three levels; the physical, emotional and mental.

Since both your heart bridge and crucible are crucial in the "working" of your human energy system, it is essential that you undertake the self-healing therapies (disciplines) that are required for your heart center of consciousness.

Self-Healing Therapies for Your Heart Chakra

Please recall again the maintenance guidelines given in Lesson One and the caution that you must exercise in applying the suggested therapies. By now you are fully aware that **form follows consciousness**; that by healing the chakras, the kundalini "shifts" you experience will indicate the healing of soul structures. As you have already discovered, this is a gradual process and requires your continued patience, discipline (including daily meditation) and commitment. While you undertake this "work," and discern the results, please maintain your discipline/practice of containing.

As was true for the "lower" chakras, the healing must focus on the excess or the lack of the color and elemental energy of the heart chakra; the color green and the element earth. In the case of your heart chakra, there can also be an excess of red energies that must be addressed.

Self-Healing Therapies: After Too Much Green and Earth Energies

There are some spiritual practices, in which people are encouraged to "pull down" from the highest dimensions a "love" energy that seemingly fills the heart. At the same time they ignore (and sometimes even negate) their "lower" chakras. These practices are often characterized by an absence of **grounding**, which promotes an excess of green and earth (feminine) energies. The practices can also promote a rejection of animal soul consciousness. Included in these practices there can be a regular pattern of astral projection (also known as out-of-body experiences)[442] and a focus on an "otherworldly" spirituality. All of this is understandable, in light of the trauma that can be inflicted on the animal soul centers of consciousness in the

---

[442] The subject of astral projection is not addressed in these lessons. Since it connects with the sacral, heart and third eye chakras, and with the emotional body consciousness, it is a complex subject that requires further investigation.

uterus and in early childhood. But this type of spirituality leaves out an important detail.[443] Anyone truly committed to a quest for wholeness, will accept the existence of those "lower" chakras and set about healing them. The reason is this: without balance throughout the system, the potential **knowing** that can become true **being** will be lost. In the context of these lessons, that loss would be tragic.

The healing modalities for the heart chakra include those of all three animal soul chakras; the root, sacral and solar plexus. If there has been an excess of meditative and other practices, especially those focused on the crown and the third eye chakras, they must be set aside while the healing of animal soul structures is undertaken. There is a crucial need for balancing. Thus, the emphasis is placed on "Body Work" and on "Earth Energies."

Body Work

Your **grounding** work with roots deep into Earth will be foremost. This can be reinforced by the intense physical energies generated by vigorous dancing, undulating and drumming. All of the "body work" for your animal soul chakras can be undertaken, always assisted by the Observer. Since there is such an energy imbalance, it would be difficult to know to what extent the heart archetypes are present. But invoke their help and accept the help that comes.

Start with the "Ida/Pingala" breath work as follows:

After **grounding**, focus on your "roots" and "pull up" a clear (colorless) energy.

At the root chakra, send the energy up the ida and pingala channels to the termination point.

With each in-breath, continue to "see" the clear energy.

With each out-breath, breathe out green. It might be the "green" of putrefaction; let it be what it is. Put it into Earth for cleansing.

Practice this breath work daily, until there is a sense of balance when you tune into your lower chakras.

With an excess of earth energies, there is a visualization that involves transformation. It is entitled: "Planting My Heart Garden."[444]

After several **grounding** breaths, focus on your heart chakra.

Go deeply into that space and "see" the earth energies. (Put a "form" to them. They could be piled in heaps, covered with debris, corrupted, etc.) Also "see" a shovel, a wheelbarrow, a hoe, a rake and a large watering can.

With gentleness, use the shovel to fill the wheelbarrow as many times as are necessary to move out all the excess earth energies.

"See" each one dumped into uncorrupted Earth for cleansing.

You will experience a sense of balance when enough has been removed.

---

[443] Only advanced yogi masters can safely "pull down" energies, after having spent years of training in "pulling" them up.

[444] This visualization was provided by one of my students after a spirit journey.

With gentleness, use the hoe to break up any congealed remaining pieces.

And use the rake to smooth and spread the rich soil that remains.

Then, "see" around you many pots full of red, orange, yellow, green, blue, purple and white flowers.

"See" you on your knees, carefully planting each one.

When you are finished, gently use the watering can to "water" your heart garden.

This visualization might be required frequently while your root, sacral and solar plexus chakras are being healed. Eventually, the work will be finished.

Earth Energies

The herbs that are helpful in healing with too much green and earth energies are those that will **enhance** the color and elemental energies of the root, sacral and solar plexus chakras. Please recall those herbs and their power.

When there are too many green and earth energies, the healing crystal that is required is

Rose Quartz, which can attune each chakra by providing the healthy vibratory frequency.

The aroma that will assist in balancing too much green and earth energies is

Cabbage Rose, which promotes a sense of well-being. This aroma can be used in conjunction with the aromas that will **enhance** the color and element energies of the root, sacral and solar plexus chakras.

Please recall the ways in which aromas can be used. Deep body massage using the Cabbage Rose aroma in oil is also very healing.

Spirit Energies

Remember that in your **holistic** human energy system there has been a considerable healing of your heart center's excessive green and earth energies by the spiritual practices you have already undertaken with your "lower" animal soul chakras. More can be accomplished by uncovering and then "letting go" the **beliefs** that are contributing to the heart center's dysfunction. The "Seeker's Lamp" meditation, the emotional clearing and your "worm-hole" work are powerful means of doing this. And afterward, with a new discernment of balance, remain for a little while in your inner stillness.

When there are "heart strings," also referred to as "heart cords," connecting one person to another, there can sometimes be excessive green and earth energies. (You have already encountered these connectors earlier in the lesson.) Those cords can connect people through the heart center and through the "lower" centers as well. When the connection is healthy, as in the symbiotic joining of a loving mother and infant, or the joining of deeply committed adult lovers, the relationship is a profound loving intimacy. In those instances, the heart energies are large but not excessive and there is balance in the system. But often the relationship is that of an unhealthy co-dependency or even a love/hate connection. This would indicate the animal realm of the Wheel of Samsara soul structures of emotionality and an unhealthy sacral chakra. Then the green and earth heart energies can be both excessive and corrupt. When the healing of this relationship is undertaken, there is a "letting go" that can be done. The work, which is shamanic in its origins, is entitled "Recapitulation." It is carried out with loving intent and attention. If this is healing that you require, you must be completely aware and certain that you must let go of the relationship.

Before you begin, set up a quiet area as sacred space and ensure that there will be no interruptions. Set aside a tall glass of pure water.

Sitting on a straight-backed chair, prepare by stating your intent to let go of your unhealthy heart connection with the person, by name.

"See" an image of a "cutting" instrument, for example, a sword, scissors, a scalpel.

Keeping the intent in mind, take several deep **grounding** breaths.

Go into the "Ida/Pingala" breath work.

Continue, while you go deeply within and carry your cutting instrument with you. Maintain your intent.

"See" yourself sitting at the end of a long, straight road stretching before you to the horizon.

As you continue to look at the road, see a minute figure at the end of the road.

Watch intently, as the figure walks toward you and gradually becomes larger.

"See" that it is the person that you will be releasing.

Feel only love as you watch the approaching figure. If you feel anything else, discontinue the exercise.

See the person stop within a foot of you.

See the cords that are connecting you. (Sometimes they are as thick as ropes made of steel.)

Send a silent loving message of farewell.

Then, pick up the cutting instrument.

Without hesitation, cut the cords.

Watch them sever.

As each one falls, gently remove the end attached to you and place it on Earth.

When all the cords have been severed, continue to send loving messages to the person.

Watch as the person turns around and starts to walk back down the road.

Continue to watch until the figure vanishes.

Remain in that place and allow all the feelings that have arisen in you.

Then, slowly, return to the "now."

Drink the water. Ponder your experience and rest.

The work of recapitulation is usually required only once. If your soul structures of emotionality set up energies of resistance, calmly go back in memory to the moment of letting go. Focus on that, with love. Practice this discipline until the resistance is gone.

Self-Healing Therapies: After Too Little Green and Earth Energies

In a malfunctioning heart chakra, when there are too little green and earth (feminine) energies, the "holes" in the heart bridge indicate soul fragmentation. There is not enough generative power to repair the damage or to construct a new heart bridge. The archetypal imperative and the "i-am" consciousness cannot be realized and the whole connection with the "higher" spiritual centers is drastically curtailed. Thus, there is no downward causation and the potential of rebirthing cannot be fulfilled. Because the damage has started in the animal soul chakras, healing them will be vitally necessary for the healing of the heart center. Meanwhile, there are therapies for working **directly** on the depleted heart chakra. This healing requires patience, after such a prolonged time of malfunctioning.

Body Work

When there are too little green and earth energies the "Ida/Pingala" breath work can be undertaken. Also, an effective combination of breath work and visualization to augment the green and earth energies is a variation of the "Up the Sushumma" work you have already done. (There is one word of caution, however; if you have high blood pressure, do not undertake this therapy. In that case, there would be red energies behind your heart. These will have to be removed by a healer.)

To continue . . .

Scrape" your auric field thoroughly. Take several deep **grounding** breaths, while you are attaching your roots to your energy source in Earth.

"See" a colorless energy.

Inhale deeply while "pulling" that energy up your roots, up your legs and up your ida and pingala channels.

Exhale, while puckering your mouth and "blowing out" the "black" toxicities.

Repeat this step many times until you sense that you have fortified your energy system. Switch to the "Up the Sushumma" breath work.

Then, "see" a clear green energy.

Inhale deeply while you pull that energy up your roots, up your legs and up your sushumma into your heart chakra.

Exhale more "black."

Repeat this step many times until you sense change in the heart energies.

Continue, **unless you have high blood pressure**.

Then "see" a clear red "reinforcing" color.

Inhale while pulling the red up your sushumma into your heart chakra.

Exhale whatever remains of the "black" energies.

Do this exercise daily until you sense a kundalini "shift" in your energies.

As was the case with your animal soul chakras, you can enhance your breath work by "toning" the sound of a healthy heart chakra. In the Ayurvedic tradition, the sound of the heart chakra is "YAM." Listen to the Middle C note on the piano. "Tone" that sound by taking a deep "grounding" breath and releasing it slowly as your vocal cords generate Y Y Y Y Y . . . A A A H H H . . . MMMMM. Focus your attention and intent all this time on your heart chakra. Create a strong, deep vibration that you feel in the chakra and in your mouth. Repeat this "toning" nine times for one "round." Do not be surprised by sometimes strong emotions. After much practice, add the "toning" for the root chakra ("LAM"), the sacral ("VAM") and the solar plexus ("RAM"). Do one "round" for each sound. This is very powerful healing work.

As your green energy builds, add physical exercises such as "arm circles" and "windmilling." Some yoga poses to try are the "Cobra" and the "Fish."[445]

Earth Energies

The crystals you can use to stimulate green and earth energies are

Green Spinel, which can align and stimulate the heart chakra. Green spinel will also protect the kundalini and the soul structures of physicality during the kundalini rising.

Adularia, which can stimulate the opening of the heart chakra and an openness to love.

Mesolite, which helps to open the back of the heart chakra.

The herbs that will help in promoting green energies are **hawthorn**, **mistletoe**, **chamomile**, and a combination of **speedwell** and **celery root** (prepared as teas).

Spirit Energies

Your (by now) "standard" guided meditation; The "Ring of Color" can be used very successfully to enhance the green and earth energies of the heart. After your usual preparation, undertake the meditation using a clear green color and the element of earth. Please maintain your journal as you continue to experience the power of this meditation.

There are two new meditations that you can undertake to enhance directly the green and earth energies of your heart chakra. In both, you require the help of the Observer.

The first is extremely easy and at the same time very difficult. It is entitled "Mirror Work."

While standing or sitting in front of a mirror, take several deep **grounding** breaths.

Look deeply into your own eyes and gently say: "I love you."

You may add your name, if you wish.

Be prepared for upsurges of emotions. They will likely be a mixture of grief, pain and even angry resistance.

---

[445] Anodea Judith, *Wheels of Life*, pp. 220-222.

Continue to focus on your eyes and place either your right or your left thumb on the "grief spot" at the bottom of your sternum. Gently press on this spot. Slowly and softly repeat: "I love you."

Let the feelings happen. Your heart bridge will be healing.

Repeat this exercise daily until the grief, pain and resistance disappear and you truly experience what you are saying.

The second meditation also involves loving yourself. It, too, is very easy and very difficult. It is entitled: "Cradling."

You might want to prepare for this meditation by repeating the "Pool of Rejuvenation" meditation for your sacral chakra. Then proceed with the cradling.

In your quiet place where you will be undisturbed, clear an area and set down a soft mat and pillow.

Lie on your back on the mat and place the pillow under your head or knees.

Take several deep **grounding** breaths and gently wrap your arms around the front of your body.

As you continue to breathe deeply, start to say loving words to yourself.

They could be words like "precious," "sweetheart," "darling" etc.

Then add phrases like "precious child," "blessed little one," "wonderful person" etc.

Then add sentences that speak lovingly about you to you.

Again, you can expect emotional upsurges at first, while the soul structures of lovelessness are being transformed and your heart center is slowly opening.

Repeat this exercise often. You will feel your heart energies expanding and warming as you foster your relationship with you. While you continue in this loving interaction and with the disciplines of the other healing therapies, you will eventually experience the kundalini "shift." It is always an indicator of your enhanced inner growth and development. (Remember to add these to the "containing"!)

Yet, without the "lower" energies, nothing could have been accomplished. The reason is this: in your **holistic** human energy system, the healing brought about by the therapies (disciplines) and by the disciplines/practices of "letting go/letting be" and "balancing" has been slowly promoting a dynamic equilibrium; a splendid new "dance" of the masculine and feminine forces inherent in your soul substance and present in your "lower" centers of consciousness and soul structures.

And, all through the process, while your vibratory frequencies ascended and your animal soul structures, including the egoic structures, were being changed, your emerging holarchy was being created, your sense of a glowing inner empowerment with its feeling/tone of purity, simplicity and unity was being fostered and your new **knowing** was being generated. What has come about with the "workings" of your heart center of consciousness is both a transmutation and transformation of animal soul energies. It is little wonder, then, that for so long, so many of the world's wisdom teachings have been focused on the "heart"!

The lesson is ended. Before you leave this sacred enclosure, experience again its timelessness and your own, while you re-member your heart connection with the ancient ones and realize that in a multidimensional universe the "ancient" and the "now" are one and the same.

You may leave the stone circle.

*   *   *

Soul Searcher, your quest for wholeness has taken you along both the well-traveled and the untrodden path of "Entering Within." Your rebirthing journey has reached its culminating point. You have done very well! Please stay with this lesson until you have a sense of completion. Then move forward to the "Third Interlude." Stay with it for whatever time is necessary to prepare you for taking your place again at the stone circle.

Peace and blessings

THIRD INTERLUDE

Here in the West, let us pause, again, for an interlude of assimilation. Having already experienced those periods in the East and in the South, you are likely anticipating yet more development. You are correct: by internalizing the teachings from the lesson about your heart so completely that they become part of you as a soul field, you will be getting closer to your rebirthing. You are carrying into this interlude all that you have become since you first entered the stone circle. Although you can expect that you will undergo yet more "stretching," you have prepared well for that and you will receive it. In the meantime, your dedicated "work" with the healing therapies (disciplines) has produced transmutations that have raised your vibratory frequency (**form follows consciousness**). And the disciplines/practices (the letting go/letting be, the balancing and the containing) that you have undertaken, with the help of the Observer, have been splendidly actualizing the powers of the emerging holarchy. In all of this, you have continued to foster and strengthen your glowing inner sense of empowerment with its feeling/tone of purity, simplicity and unity. Already your journey has been a grand adventure. Already you are more "real" than you might have ever imagined. It is a strong indication of your ongoing transformation, liberation and regeneration.

In this interlude you may choose, as you have in the others, to return to the stone circle or to create your own sacred space by "casting the circle." Please do so when you are ready.

Herein, there awaits a "work" that is already familiar. Your first two interludes have prepared you. In this one, you will deal with a combination of the **impersonal** and the **personal.** Indeed, the distinction will become blurred, as you assimilate and internalize them. First, in the impersonal work you will absorb wisdom teachings, those dealing with "heart" consciousness. These you will obtain not only from the lesson but also from other sources. There are many ancient and modern wisdom teachings comprising many media. Be prepared to have them present themselves.[446] As you did in the first interlude, you will be strengthening your foundations and further enhancing your capabilities as a soul searcher. Second, in the personal work you will absorb and integrate into your soul field the ways of inner probing given in the heart lesson. Although you have already been exposed to them, you will now focus on and stay with them until you experience profound kundalini "shifts." And although

---

[446] For example, you might want to join with Deva Primal and Miten in the wonderful chanting of "Awakening" and "In the Light of Love" on their CD entitled "The Yoga of Sacred Song and Chant." (Please note that although chanting involves the throat chakra, the alchemy occurs in the heart crucible.) And/or you might want to plunge into the wonderful water colors by Doris Klein in *Journey of the Soul.*

you have already probed deeply during your second interlude, this probing might be your most difficult challenge thus far.

You are likely already aware of the reasons for this difficulty. On this journey, there can often be immense challenges facing a soul searcher dealing with heart center damage. The "bridge" can be full of "holes" and entered onto only with considerable pain and reluctance. In your experience of life, there might have been generated more soul structures of lovelessness than you realized. You might have become accustomed to heart feelings of coldness (your "armor-plating"), hardness, emptiness and/or brokenness. And while you pondered and probed during the second interlude, you might have uncovered some deeply buried **beliefs** about your own inadequacy and worthlessness. This journey has not been easy!

But it has been made much easier than it might otherwise have been because you have had the constant help of the Observer. That wonderful energy continues to assist you. You also have with you now your archetypes of the heart. In your personal work, while you continue to invoke them and heal their "shadows," you will increasingly "embody" their power. (Please recall that you will be in love and in the truth.) Thus, you will be able to deal with the challenge during this period of assimilation.

Here the West as shamans know it, the final heart "work" is awaiting you. With your capabilities as a soul searcher enhanced by your **impersonal** "work," you will be made ready. Take plenty of time for that. The wider, deeper and stronger your foundations are, the better!

Then embrace the **personal** "work" of fully entering within your own heart center. Allow yourself to become intensely immersed in your heart center consciousness; its woundedness, its great healing power and its involvement with your "lower" centers of consciousness. During this profound entering within, with all its permutations and hidden possibilities, you will continue the disciplines/practices of letting go/letting be and balancing and **know** that you can trust the detachment/discernment and dynamic equilibrium powers of your emerging holarchy. Meanwhile, you will be continuing to actualize the power of containing through that discipline/ practice and you will be experiencing with greater clarity your sense of inner empowerment with its feeling/tone of glowing purity, simplicity and unity.

All of it is important preparation for your next path and the experience of your "higher" centers of consciousness. For this heart "work" the rewards are huge: you will greatly advance the healing of your "lower" centers of consciousness and your heart "bridge" and, thereby, make wonderful headway in the process of upward causation. And you will greatly advance the emergence of your healthy heart archetypes and, thereby, make wonderful headway in the process of downward causation.

Be assured that during this interlude, you will continue to receive the "accidental" encounters with your soul contracts, who are there as part of your Life Plan. You will also continue to receive the unexpected opportunities for growth (possibly enhanced) that have likely become familiar. All this is possible because the indwelling Spirit (your nucleus of divinity) has been guiding and sustaining you. As there was during your quest in the East and in the South, there has been the sustaining power of an aspect of the Spirit. Here, in the West, as shamans know it, there has been the aspect of Love on your path of "Entering Within."

Throughout the lesson on the heart and especially in the instruction about the heart archetypes, you have already learned about the power of Love. Thus, it will come as no surprise that while you have been developing the "faith" that Life has given to you and the "trust" that Light has provided, there has been Love as your ever-present sustenance. You do not have to "feel" it or even "affirm" it, for Love requires none of that. It is the "covenant" (the heart connection) people have always had with the Spirit (Consciousness, Creative Energy).

In the sacred writings of Judaism, you read:

"Fear not, for I have redeemed you;
I have called you by name, you are mine.
When you pass through the waters I will be with you;
and through rivers, they shall not overwhelm you;
When you walk through fire you shall not be burned
and the flame shall not consume you.
[. . .]
Because you are precious in my eyes,
And [. . .] I love you . . ."[447]

And in later writings you read:

"Thus says the Lord
[. . .]
I have loved you with an everlasting love;
Therefore, I have continued my faithfulness to you."[448]

Describing love, a modern teacher of great spiritual awareness tells us:[449]

"Living from the level of awareness that says "I am love," means living from
a level where love can grow. In the early stages of personal evolution, most
people wonder about these essential states. They are confused about whether
they are lovable, trusting strong, valuable and so forth. You cannot find out
about these states by trying to prove them to yourself. Earning love by acting
good, being nice, learning the game of social attractiveness, etc., always ends
in failure, because once you stop behaving in those trained ways, the attitude
you are left with is doubt, which is where you began.

---

[447] *Book of Isaiah*, 43: 1, 2 and 4.
[448] *Book of Jeremiah*, 31: 1.
[449] Deepak Chopra, *Ageless Body; Timeless Mind*, pp. 184-185.

The end of the search for love is beyond behavior, because in time the mind decides to look inward, and when it does, the search changes into a search for the essential self, the me that knows "I am love."

There is truth about yourself at every level of your awareness, but [. . .] this is the most basic truth. You are love, you are compassion, you are beauty. You are existence and being. You are awareness and spirit."

Soul Searcher, you can be certain that Love has been another undercurrent present in your rebirthing journey. Macrocosmic Love has been (and is now) guiding and expressing in you, the microcosm. And in this interlude, as you enter more and more deeply within, as you "work" with the heart healing disciplines and experience your kundalini "shifts," there will increasingly arise the sense of a warm, gentle softening and opening. Yet there will be no sense of vulnerability. While you are letting go of soul structures of self-rejection and even self-hatred, while you are invoking your healthy heart archetype guides and while you are expressing your emerging holarchy of powers, you will become aware of an inner loving presence. Paradoxically, it is a presence that is both you and not-you. At this juncture, please acknowledge it and just let it be. Quite clearly, Love has involved you in an amazing connection with your nucleus of divinity. In all your personal work of assimilation, trust that you will surmount whatever challenge arises!

Now, deal with the challenge and allow yourself the time for becoming love rather than fear-based. In the "work" of the heart be assured that you will be actualizing the wonderful qualities of Love: empathy, compassion, tenderness, kindness and "relationship" to yourself and to others. Above all, be assured that this heart work is a great "work" of love, guided by Love. Stay with it until you sense your readiness to enter into the final stage of your rebirthing quest.

Peace and blessings

PART FOUR

THE PATH OF THE NORTH:

"FINDING WISDOM"

FOURTH INTRODUCTION

Shamans know that there is a cyclical pattern in which all living things abide; a Principle inherent in the Cosmos. It is an ongoing pattern expressing the One Consciousness, Creative Energy and indicating that all is in divine right order. Like the shamans, you can perceive that this is so, for you also abide in the cyclical pattern. On the final stage of your rebirthing journey, you accept with trust that in this quest, in this ongoing development, you can and you will become all that you truly are.

While rebirthing into androgyny, you have journeyed along the paths of the cosmic realms; in the East, on the path of "Opening the Way," in the South, on the path of "Coming into Being" and in the West, on the path of "Entering Within." And you have been generating a holarchy that has been emerging out of the disciplines/practices of letting go/letting be, of balancing and of containing. That concentration of powers will continue to actualize in you and, in this final stage of your rebirthing, express your wondrous possibilities.

As your quest nears its completion, you surrender to the power of the North. It is the cosmic realm of endings and transition. The North contains the power that invariably expresses in this third dimension as the energies of the day's midnight with its darkness and as the seasonal energies of winter with its death-like cold and stillness. The North also contains the power that invariably expresses in Earth's living things, including people, as the energies of "aging" and waning into "death." In addition to those powers, freely given in the cycles of "nature," the North contains the powers of "revealing/concealing;" a paradoxical possibility that like all the others must be actualized. Those powers will also become part of the emerging holarchy, while your journey continues. Then, when *all is in readiness, it is out of the North, the realm of cold darkness, dissolution and "death," that the androgyny can appear.*

*Embracing the power of the North, you set your feet on the path of **finding wisdom**. On this path, you are birthing your androgyny in the cosmic realm of endings. Yet at the same time, you are experiencing transition into a deeper and wider **knowing** and **being**; the necessary prelude to your next journey, after the "endings."*

*Shamans know that in the North, the **macrocosmic** energy of **Law-as-Such** is paramount. Eternally unchanged and unchanging Law is an aspect of the Spirit. Law is the constant ordering Power that both governs and sustains the Cosmos. Shamans also know that the **microcosmic law, i.e., the "natural law," is exactly the same**; implacable, impersonal and immutable, and that the **microcosmic** law vibrates as every particle/wave of all creation (the manifested cosmos), including you. An awareness of that energy is what you require now. It is Law/law, transcendent and immanent that makes your rebirthing and the "afterward" possible.*

Now let us return to the stone circle.

Lesson Seven

YOUR THROAT, THIRD EYE AND CROWN CHAKRAS AND SOUL STRUCTURES OF SPIRITUALITY

Hello: welcome to the stone circle. Thank you for braving the weather on this cold winter afternoon. The winds pile the snow along the pasture fence behind Long Meg and try to penetrate even the warmest clothing. Her Children stand like frosty sentinels. Inside the circle, the winds have swept the area clean and the frozen grass crunches underfoot. Watery sunlight illuminates but does not warm. Here again is your bottle of water along with your ground cover and poncho, with an extra scarf to shield your face and some hand warmers to hold. Please take your accustomed place in the center of the circle.

Now recall the "heart connection," when you encountered the ancient ones in the autumn fog. It was a timeless moment of loving interaction that wove together many centuries and many dimensions. Although you can no longer hear the shuffling feet and the ghostly voices, you can be certain that those long-ago pilgrims remain here with you. They are gifts from the Spirit; part of the wisdom legacy that has given you your foundations and strength. Please remember that timeless moment and note that all of it is "now." And there is something else . . . . Focus inwardly . . . . There it is: a deep vibration of expectancy. Tune into it . . . . Note the feeling/tone of warm aliveness. Focus and stay in the vibration . . . . Focus . . . And stay.

*　　*　　*

Soul Searcher, be assured that during your third interlude of assimilation, you accomplished a great "heart work." Here is a distillation of it: while you repeatedly journeyed on the untrodden path of "Entering Within," and at the same time along the others, the wondrous healing of your animal soul centers of consciousness and soul structures was taking place. That transmutation and transformation were unique to you and will continue to be, for you are a unique expression *of* the Divine. (Please recall the story of you as Little Soul!) With each kundalini "shift," your vibratory frequencies were raised. Throughout that intense experience, there was a healing interaction between animal soul energies and those of your

285

heart center (bridge and crucible). Meanwhile, as you "worked" with the healing therapies (disciplines), and continued the disciplines/practices of letting go/letting be and balancing, you were enriching a holarchy that was manifesting their actualized powers. Please recall that **the power of detachment/discernment had started (and continued) in your interaction with the Observer, that this power had resulted from the discipline/practice of letting go/letting be, that the power of dynamic equilibrium had resulted from the discipline/practice of balancing, and that these powers have augmented each other**. With the new discipline/practice of containing, you undertook a deep entering within. You focused on your healed soul structures, primarily your transformed egoic structures, and you began to ingather the **knowing** about the "real" you . . . the truth about you . . . which has been emerging throughout your journey. You have held that **knowing** in the heart "space" that was opened during the "heart connection" in the autumn fog. Thus, with the discipline/practice of containing you have been actualizing the **power which is the loving i-am/self**. It has now become a huge new part (a holon) of the emerging holarchy, whose other parts — the powers of detachment/discernment and of dynamic equilibrium – were a preparatory stage for this one and are now manifesting in a yet greater development. In all of this growth, your constant faith in the outcome and trust in the process have been crucial. (Your presence here in this stone circle would indicate that you have kept the faith/trust.) And have you noticed that your sense of inner empowerment with its glowing feeling/tone of purity, simplicity and unity has vastly increased?

The "shifts" taking place in you have signaled ongoing heart center openings that might have been frightening, at first. Old patterns of fear-based resistance had been waiting to be transformed. There were "shadow" heart archetypes waiting to be healed. It was a huge "work" involving hours of pondering and probing, many healing disciplines and the power of the emerging holarchy. And sustaining all of it was the Life, Light and Love that never failed.

But, as promised, the rewards have been great. What has resulted (and will continue to manifest) is *heart awareness*. Because your heart center is infinite in its scope, your heart awareness can seem to be huge. Let it be all of that. It will also seem to be both "empty" and "full." Let it be all of that. Your heart awareness is an empty/fullness; another paradox! From this moment, you will take your heart awareness with you on this journey . . . and into the "Afterward."

Within your heart awareness, you are bringing into this sacred space not only the memory of the "heart connection" but also the wonderful aftermath: your deep, rich and loving relationships with yourself and with others. These have been coming to the fore. They have flowed out of your many hours of intense "heart work," while you were immersing in your heart energies, healing your wounded archetypes of the heart and tending to your unhealed animal soul structures. Thus your deep vibration of expectancy is a natural outcome of your work on the path of "Entering Within:" you **know** that you are nearing the end of your quest for wholeness. Soul Searcher, you have journeyed splendidly.

All that you can be is increasingly ready to be expressed. It is all there in the empty/ fullness of your heart awareness. Then, because you have also actualized the powers of detachment/discernment, you likely realize that there is yet more to the journey. You are correct. Indeed, it will involve your greatest explorations and discoveries. And your heart awareness can provide the necessary "staging area." Awaiting your attention are your "higher" centers of consciousness. After having received this distillation and description of all that you have accomplished, you are ready to learn about and experience the "higher" centers.

Those wheels of light are essential not only in your **holistic** energy system but also for your approaching androgyny. The reason is two-fold:

First, all of what you have developed and become to this point is the result of the gradually increasing impact of the "higher" centers of consciousness on your animal soul centers. Through downward causation across your heart "bridge," those energies, almost negligible at first, have been doing their "work." Now you will have the opportunity to explore and understand them. This you could not have done without all your prior "work" with the "lower" centers and with the heart "bridge." Such is the evolutionary path. And, indeed, that "work" will be required still, for the healing of animal soul is not yet finished. Neither is the heart "work" fully complete. (You likely discern this.) Have you noticed, however, that the inner presence you have already experienced as being you and not-you seems to be stronger? It is quietly waiting.

Second; those "higher" centers offer the immense gifts of wisdom to any soul searcher questing for wholeness. In seeking wholeness and becoming "real," you are making yourself ready to accept your gifts. Thus, while you are in your staging area of heart awareness, you will be proceeding along the final path, the culminating path, of your journey; the path of "Finding Wisdom."

Now, take in a shaman's story about the "ancient one" who is you, and how you finally arrived at this moment.[450]

Before the beginning, there is the Mystery;
The eternal "now"
Out of which all beginnings come.

In the beginning, there flowed out of the Spirit;
The One Consciousness, Creative Energy . . .
An androgynous "Image and Likeness"
Known to the ancients as "Cosmic Man; the "Anthropos."
And from the Anthropos, there flowed out
Into this third dimension

---

[450] For this continuation of the shaman's story begun in Lesson Six and more insights into the macrocosmic and microcosmic anthropos, I am again, indebted to Marie-Louise von Franz See "The Cosmic Man" in *Archetypal Dimensions of the Psyche*, pp.133-157. Both this story and the "Story of Little Soul" carry many levels of meaning and must be understood symbolically.

All that mankind was to be;
All the possibilities
That were to be actualized.

It was an immense outflowing!

And in the beginning,
You were one of the possibilities;
A microcosmic "image and likeness,"
A holographic "particle/wave"
Of the outflowing Anthropos.

And after that,
You were birthed
Many hundreds of times
And you experienced death
Many hundreds of times,
On this Earth plane.

On this Earth plane, you were women and men,
Both beautiful and ugly.
You were stillborn, infant, youth, adult and old one.
You were murderer and mendicant,
Princess and pauper,
You were sinner and saint,
Warrior and wise one.

You were atheist and agnostic;
Muslim, Christian, Taoist and Sufi.
Hindu, Buddhist, Jew and Jainist,
Shintoist, Confucianist,
Pagan and Gnostic.
You were shaman, druid and priest,
Medicine woman, druidess and priestess.

You were "father" in many lifetimes
You were "mother" in many lifetimes.
And your progeny have covered the Earth.

On this Earth plane you, ancient one, lived in caves
And hunted woolly mammoths.
You lived in straw huts and tilled the soil.
You lived in igloos and fished through the ice.
You lived in both hovels and palaces.
You lived in all the countries of this Earth.

You were dark-skinned and light,
Red, white, yellow and black.

You fought in many battles in many wars
You procreated many children
And you butchered many others,
While you were raping and pillaging.

You were murdered and killed in combat.
You were hanged and burned at the stake.
You were dismembered and you were beheaded.
You died when very young
And you died in advanced old age.

You often lived a peaceful life
In which you toiled or idled,
Made your "mark,"
Or accomplished nothing,
Lived in a family,
Or lived alone,
And, repeatedly, you passed from the scene.

You lived and died here on Earth
While lifetime followed after lifetime
And you accumulated experiences and karma.
You established your Akashic Record, in the Akashic Field.

And you were evolving.
You, a microcosmic "image and likeness" were evolving,
You, a holographic particle/wave were evolving,
For the Spirit had always been with you
And after many lifetimes, (excruciating slowness!),
You were finally ready.

You had sensed, however dimly, your divine origins.
You *knew*, somehow, that you were
Out of and *part of* the Spirit.
Part of the great outflowing
Out of the Anthropos.

In this lifetime, in this space
You heard the "call" and obeyed.
You chose to be a soul searcher.

You began your rebirthing quest whose goal was

The androgynous wholeness you *knew* you were.
The journey has consumed your every moment.
It has brought you through much opening of the way
And "letting go/letting be,"
Much coming into being
And "balancing,"
Much entering within
And "containing."

On this journey, you have dis-membered with pain,
And re-membered with rejoicing.
You have struggled alone through raging inner storms
And you have been sustained in loving arms.
You have wept and laughed,
Crawled and soared.
You have sagged with emptiness and
You have swelled with fullness.

And now you, ancient one, are culminating
Into who you truly are;
The fully self-actualized
And completely self-aware
Holographic particle/wave,
Microcosmic "image and likeness;"
Of the androgynous Anthropos.

That is the end of the shaman's story. It was given to you so that you can cultivate an even deeper awareness of your "story" and of its magnitude. Please take a moment to reflect on your own meaning. Then prepare to experience yet more.

* * *

Because this lesson can best be presented in dreamlike imagery, mainly that of Celtic lore and myth, you will venture again into the imaginal realm. And you will complete your quest by being on your path of "Finding Wisdom," while you stay in your heart awareness "staging area." Within that empty/fullness, you will explore and understand all three of your spiritual (i.e., "higher") centers of consciousness: first, your throat and third eye chakras and later, when you are ready, your crown chakra. You will explore the generative function of those chakras and probe into the generative power itself. You will do this within the context of their prime directive and "i-am" consciousness. And you will realize how crucially important those "higher" centers of consciousness are in your human energy system. The "work" will include dealing with the archetypal "dancing" masculine and feminine energies of those "higher" centers; primarily their connection with your changing egoic structures, while you are also

290

focusing on your other soul structures of spirituality; the soul structures of transcendence. In doing this, you will be arriving at the threshold of your second birthing; this time as a self-realized androgynous human being; a microcosmic anthropos.

Meanwhile, you will be making more repairs to your heart "bridge" and healing your "lower" centers. (It is an incredible simultaneity! But you have prepared for this.) During the forthcoming "work" (always undertaken with intent), you will promote yet more inner empowerment with its glowing feeling/tone of purity, simplicity and unity. You will also have a greater sense of the presence that is you and not-you. This you will achieve by continuing your healing therapies (disciplines) and disciplines/practices. From the latter, there will come more of the emerging holarchy. And all this time, on the path of "Finding Wisdom," you will be in the empty/fullness of your heart awareness, in that deep vibration of expectancy. Now, set your intent, stay in your heart awareness and step forth onto your culminating path of "Finding Wisdom."

Your "Higher" Centers of Consciousness: An Overview

Your throat, third eye and crown chakras, apparently located in the small space between the bottom of your neck and the top of your head (but actually out of this third dimension) were present at your conception. Their power was available from that moment. Enclosed in a healthy etheric womb and in a human uterus completely filled with nurturing love, those "higher" centers of consciousness would/could have made an enormous impact on your gestating fetus.

As an aside . . .

It seems that the evolutionary path of a human energy being always starts with hominid. But this statement requires qualification. There are sometimes pronounced differences within hominid energies: there are, occasionally, newborns who are evolved "old souls." They quickly "go through" their animal soul phase. Throughout human history, the few who did this often realized that they had come to teach and inspire the rest.[451] They were the rare exceptions that provided wondrous examples (and lessons) of human greatness that eventually brought greater awareness to the rest of humankind.

Let us return to the lesson.

Throughout your early childhood and later development, those "higher" centers of consciousness would/could have mitigated, by downward causation, the ways that your soul structures were being formed. But that would have required a stronger connection with them. (Please recall from the fairy tales and myths about your root, sacral, solar plexus and heart centers of consciousness the motifs for the powers of the "higher" centers. They were there from the beginning, but they were mainly disempowered. In your interludes of assimilation

---

[451] For example, there are the great ones such as Jesus the Christ, Prince Gautama, Lao Tzu and the Prophet Muhammad. There are many others at this time who **know** that they have come into this third dimension to be a lesser "Messenger of the Light."

you have likely realized this.) Now, as you eagerly explore those spiritual centers and add to your understanding of them, please stay in the empty/fullness of your heart awareness.

Let us begin that exploration by turning to Celtic lore.

The ancient Celts believed that a person's immortal "soul" resided both in the physical head and in the Otherworld. As a "duplicate person," the "soul" could travel from this world, through a "veil," into the realm of spirit and return, sometimes after a long delay. In-formed by this belief, the warrior Celts, both men and women, revered not only their own valiant heroes but also their valiant foes. With the latter, the Celts believed that there was a special valor that indicated the high quality of their immortal "soul." Thus, when a Celtic warrior defeated and killed a valiant foe, the head would be taken as a sign of respect. After the flesh had fallen off and the skull was dry, it would be used as a drinking vessel at a sacred well believed to contain the waters and energies of life. There were many such wells in the Celtic world.

In Celtic legend, there is the account of Bran the Blessed, a valiant High King of the British Celts, who led his warriors to Ireland on a mission of revenge. While there, he was poisoned by a treacherous former brother-in-law. As he lay dying, Bran commanded his warriors to return home to Britain and to carry his head back with them. With great sorrow, they complied. On the journey, the head was placed on the dining table. While the warriors were at supper, the head of King Bran, thereafter referred to as Bran the Blessed, spoke wise counsel and emitted a radiant light. Thereafter, for many years, Bran continued to rule his kingdom wisely and well.

The myth reveals the importance of the human head as the locus of the "higher" centers of consciousness. This overview of those centers can be concluded here.

Your Throat Chakra's Qualities

The myth also provides a symbolic example of the power of the throat and third eye chakras. They are the centers of consciousness that give you "voice" and "vision." They are also centers for expressing Truth, a paradox that you will encounter in a moment.

Let us continue by dealing first with your throat chakra. Gently discern its size, shape, rotation and direction of "spin," front and back. Please note that although you can tune into it by scanning your neck and chin, your throat chakra is not in this dimension. Remaining within the Celtic framework, you will explore the qualities of your throat chakra. As you do this, please remain aware of its sacredness.

The color of your throat chakra is blue; regarded since ancient times as a sacred color. Blue is the color of clear, healing water and clear skies (often paired in the lore as the divine parents) and the color of the robes of the divine feminine.[452] According to the lore, before a major battle, the Celtic warriors (male and female) would daub sacred blue clay on their naked bodies. The clay, they believed, would protect them during the fighting by helping them to "voice" their courage and ferocity. In this manner, the color blue carried great power.

---

[452] Anthony Stevens, *Ariadne's Clue*, p.149.

Yet, the sacred color of the throat chakra can also carry paradox: the blue can be both clear and murky. Within this paradox there is a deeper one that you are invited now to consider: what is "voiced" through your throat can be both the clarity of the truth and the murk of untruth.

At this point, you are asked to become aware of the paradoxical nature of Truth. The paradox is this: in expressing the truth, it is Truth itself that is the paradox, i.e., Truth can both reveal and conceal what is there. Thus, there are those who can open to and receive Truth, while there are others who cannot. On your rebirthing journey, while you have deeply probed and pondered, continued the disciplines/practices, actualized your emerging holarchy, fostered your inner empowerment and become aware of a presence that was you and not-you, you have been encountering and (perhaps) recognizing the paradoxical nature of Truth. It is often confounding but, for this journey, totally necessary. Soul Searcher, on your path of "Finding Wisdom" you will focus only on being in Truth. The reason is this: by using your throat chakra for "voicing" the truth about you and your situation, you will be actualizing the fourth power of your emerging holarchy. It is this: **with the revealing and concealing discipline/practice of focusing only on Truth, you will be actualizing the power of translucent knowing**.

And, in truth, the actualizing started in your first contact with the Observer. The actualizing has continued with that connection during all the hours of letting go/letting be, balancing and containing, especially during the latest interlude of intense "heart work," when you explored your heart archetypes, healed their "shadows," and probed into your paradoxes. During that "work" of assimilation, you had been gradually embodying the power of your healthy Teacher, Warrior, Healer and Visionary heart archetypes, whose immense shadows had been slowly healing in your heart crucible. Thus, there came about (always with the help of the Observer) your ever-increasing capacity to **be** those archetypes. Now, recall their power of Love and Truth. By invoking the archetypes, you had reached the full expression of revealing/ concealing. And out of the intense "heart work" experience, the translucent knowing was already developing as the last great stage in your emerging holarchy. That power, which contains and expresses all the others, will expand as you "work" with your throat chakra (and later with the other "higher" centers).

While "voicing" the truth about you and your situation through your throat chakra, you realize the power of Truth and your loving capacity to accept and allow it. (Do you perceive how the actualized powers of detachment/discernment, dynamic equilibrium and loving i-am/self can enhance that capacity?) Thus it is that while expressing Truth (i.e., by using the discipline/practice of revealing/concealing and actualizing it in the power of translucent knowing), you are — in your **knowing** and **being** — both unfettered and "secure." In other words, you have both unlimited freedom and unlimited safety. (At this juncture, tune into your heart archetypes of the Teacher and the Warrior; they are connected with your throat center of consciousness. When they are without woundedness, they are in-formed by Love and express and live only Truth. Then, realize the immense power that you have been developing.)[453]

---

[453] In the Kabbalistic teachings, when something powerful is "concealed and clothed in a garment, it is revealed … by concealing and clothing itself, it reveals itself." Daniel C Matt, *The Essential Kabbalah*, p. 91.

The element of your throat chakra is ether. The "duplicate person" who could travel into and out of the Celtic Otherworld, was the "etheric double." Every living organism has its etheric double. Your etheric double is connected with your throat chakra (referred to as your "etheric matrix"), through the elemental power of ether.[454]

Ether, which was a familiar "fifth" element in ancient metaphysics, later became shrouded in superstition and was eventually discarded by science. Now it is being accepted again, as quantum physics explores "empty" space and provides an understanding of the real power of the ether. Meanwhile, there have been many accounts of the "etheric double" of a person presenting itself, after physical "death," to loved ones.[455] (Perhaps this has happened to you or to someone you know. It is a profound experience and must not be dismissed or discounted.)

Your etheric double (sometimes referred to as "phantom DNA"), is the non-physical duplicate of your physicality. Hence, the prime directive of your throat chakra, with the elemental power of ether, is the generation and maintenance of your spiritual, i.e., transcendent, physicality. That archetypal imperative is reinforced by the chakra's "i-am" statement of consciousness: "I am an expresser of Truth." (You will be given more details about that "i-am-ness" later in the lesson.) At this point, please recall that you gestated in a human uterus within an etheric womb. The transcendence was already there. Now, let us examine that transcendent physicality.

Your Throat Chakra's Function and Generative Power

Your throat chakra as part of your **holistic** energy system functions with a physical, emotional, mental and spiritual component, as do all the others. In these "workings," the chakra is expressing its archetypal imperative; that of generating and maintaining your soul structures of spiritual, i.e., transcendent, physicality, while its "i-am" consciousness makes it an expresser of Truth. Within those parameters, your throat chakra functions in the following manner:

In the front of your throat chakra, the physical component which is very strong, channels your physical means of communication; the energies of speech. These energies of sound and meaning are more than expression. They are a creative power and helped to bring into your

---

[454] There is an immense lore about the "ether." In ancient times, it was thought to be the "substance" filling all space. After modern science debunked this idea, there were many attempts to conduct experiments involving "empty" space with limited success. Now the idea of "ether" has returned as the "Zero Point Energy Field" in the "quantum vacuum," the "A-Field" and the "quantum sea." See Ervin Laszlo, *Science and the Akashic Field*, various paging. Some writers have suggested that it is the "ether" that constitutes the "substance" out of which everything is created. Laszlo has quoted Alice A. Bailey, whose channeled works have been very influential in modern metaphysics. She wrote that "this word 'ether,' is a generic term covering the ocean of energies which are all interrelated and which constitute that one synthetic energy body of our planet … the etheric or energy body, therefore of every human being is an integral part of the etheric body of the planet itself." These insights have been corroborated by the latest scientific findings. See Ervin Laszlo, *Science and the Akashic Field*, p. 161.

[455] The gospels of the New Testament tell that Jesus appeared unto many after his death. Although his corpse had not been removed from the tomb, it had disappeared. Only his etheric double had remained. In his autobiography, Paramahansa Yogananda told about his encounter with his deceased teacher, the beloved Sri Yukteshwar, whose physical remains had been cremated.

life those experiences that you have likely labeled as "good" and/or "bad." People are just beginning to realize that words, spoken and/or thought are a means of connecting with the Spirit, both immanent and transcendent. Hence there is now a large body of information on affirmative prayer, on "positive" affirmations, and other ways of communicating beneficially with the universal powers. When these words are combined with "positive" beliefs, (which you recall are soul structures of physicality) the results can sometimes be astounding.[456] That sound is a creative energy is borne out in the Biblical account of creation, when God said: "let there be Light."[457] It was the **sound, i.e., the vibration** and the **meaning** of the words that got things started. Through the throat, the words can be delivered in many ways, from whispering to screaming, from talking to singing and chanting. They can convey your feelings and thoughts, both peaceful and warlike and trigger many reactions/responses in the listener. As the great orators of humanity have repeatedly demonstrated, words can help to "bring forth" both wonderful and diabolical activities in human beings. (After summoning the Observer, take a few minutes to ponder on the uses you have made of speech. How have you "voiced" your beliefs, attitudes and values? What meaning have you expressed? How have you communicated with those you have encountered in various life situations? What did this reveal about your detachment/discernment and dynamic equilibrium? What did this reveal about your ego/self? What was revealed about you as animal soul? What healing has already been achieved? What discipline/practice "work" is still required?)

Interacting closely with your throat chakra front physical component is the emotional component. Through your throat are transmitted the energies of your feelings. At this level, your ability to communicate your emotions can make the difference between simply "sounding off" and truly expressing how you feel. And, you can literally close your throat with unexpressed emotions that can indicate a deep resistance to acknowledging, accepting and allowing Truth. This resistance, in turn, can adversely affect your physical well-being.

You can help yourself to heal physically and emotionally by telling your "sacred story," which is both a recognizing and a rendering of the underlying **meaning** that you realize has been unfolding along with your Life Plan. (After pondering on your ability to communicate your feelings, you might want to start the account of your "sacred story." It is much more than your autobiography and requires some deep insights into your "sacred contracts," into your emotions and above all, into your **beliefs** that trigger so many of those emotions. In this moment, recall the teaching about the Wheel of Samsara and how it was an indicator of your soul structures of emotionality. Probe into their present state of health and what healing is still required. The Observer will assist you greatly in this "voicing" about you and in the letting go. While you do, stay in your heart awareness.)

The mental component of your throat chakra front is closely involved with the "meanings" of your vocalizations. In your early childhood, before language, your throat chakra was your means of sending messages that helped to ensure the necessary attention to your survival.

---

[456] One example is the content in the Abraham/Hicks materials
[457] *Genesis* 1: 3-5.

As you matured, so did your linguistic ability. Within a nurturing, supportive environment, primarily your home and school, but also your surrounding culture, you would be developing the power of your throat chakra. It would be expressing your increasing depths of thought and understanding. (Recall all that you have realized already about your soul structures of mentality. Focus on their present and future requirements.) Your throat chakra would be helping to expand your multidimensionality. You would be invoking your empowering "personality" archetypes and revealing your remarkable personhood. (Ponder on the "reality" of your throat chakra's mental component; what it was and what it is now. With the help of the Observer and with your enhanced powers of detachment/discernment, ponder without judgment. What meanings of your vocalizations are you finding? Are they expressing the truth about you and your situation? Does your solar plexus chakra require more "work"? If so, return to the therapies (disciplines) and the discipline/practices that are required.)

The "spiritual" component of your throat chakra front is predominant. At its highest vibration that chakra can be the means of expressing psychic abilities, especially clairaudience. Although there is great benefit to be derived from this ability, it is not the most important capacity for you to develop. And, indeed, it might be a detriment, if you forget your real purposes and start trying to gain fame and fortune. Your most important throat chakra spiritual skill is to "voice" the truth about you and your situation. As you have already learned, your Teacher and Warrior archetypes of the heart are invoked and empowered through that capacity. It does not require that you become a great philosopher. But it does require that you focus both your inward and outward intent and attention on what is authentic, what is real. (Recall that becoming "real" is what you are seeking to achieve. Include the Observer in your pondering.)

Being "real" can be much enhanced through the back of your throat chakra. Therein are the portals to other dimensions. Again, there are the four components to consider.

The physical component, very closely tied to your "etheric double," opens to the divine guidance that a healthy physicality requires. Essentially, this "opening to" involves an "intuitive" awareness of the energies of nourishment and other physical "maintenance" you need. Without that awareness, you could leave that portal completely unguarded and subject to access by "entities." Those energies, that are by no means imaginary,[458] can cause you physical harm, and also financial and relationship distress. In ancient times, people knew about "possession" and safeguarded against it, with amulets and prayers. In "primitive" modern societies, people still do. (With the Observer, take some time to ponder on the health of your throat back portal. By placing your hand over it, you might even detect energy "leakage;" an indication of a lack of shielding.)

---

[458] There are still people who perform exorcisms. They are still required. People who have taken a walk as tourists through the Roman catacombs have occasionally traveled home with an attached entity. There are other places on Earth where they loiter. When well-meaning people open closed vortices, they can often unwittingly set those entities free. Essentially, they are the darkest, coldest, unhealthiest and most loveless energies of animal soul.

That energy leakage is also an indicator of the emotional component of your throat chakra. If fear and rage are still part of soul structures of emotionality, you will have leakage. This will inhibit the healthy input of intuitive feelings about people and situations. Those intuitive energies that connect with your inner and outer relatedness enter from the higher dimensions. (Be careful, however, when dealing with intuitive feelings. If there are unhealed animal soul structures of emotionality, the intuitions require verification before they can be accepted as Truth.) And shamans, who spirit journey, enter into and exit from the Otherworld through this same portal. Thereby, they acquire the greatly enhanced intuitive awareness that they refer to as "spiritual knowledge." This level of awareness has always been possible for you. (Continue pondering on the health of your throat chakra back portal. Tune into the feelings that arise as you focus with the Observer. What are they "telling" you about your present inner and outer relatedness and the need, if any, for more healing therapies (disciplines?))

In the mental component of your throat chakra back you will discern a major part of your anatomy of beliefs and the "ideas" they have expressed. These are the "tapes" that people will say "run through their heads," especially during highly-charged emotional and/or intellectual situations. As you are aware, they can be both healthy and unhealthy, true and untrue. You have already recognized this while you continued to heal your "lower" chakras. In addition to those "tapes," you have carried your Life Plan's "sacred contracts," both healthy and unhealthy. That linkage can be closely entwined with your "heart strings." During a healing kundalini "shift," there can be a sudden change in the "tapes," when a new message enters through your throat chakra back and flows downward into your heart "space." This is a profound experience of opening that signals a major healing in both your sacral chakra and heart "bridge." (Again, with the Observer ponder on your throat chakra back mental component. What have been the predominant messages of the "tapes"? What are the messages now? What are you discovering about the sacred contracts you have had with others? What are the contracts now? Where has truth or untruth come into the picture? Where is Truth now? It is a vast area for you to explore and, where necessary, heal. Do this while staying in your heart awareness and take your time.)

Here to help you is the spiritual component of the back of your throat chakra. It has been through this portal, when you focused with loving intent and attention, that you have received your healthy Teacher, Warrior, Healer and Visionary heart archetypes. (Continue to ponder, without judgment, and tune into that center of consciousness. What is happening here? Are you detecting the residue of the wounds that caused you to invoke their "shadows"? Make gentle note of the healing already achieved and what is still required.) Then turn to your second "higher" center of consciousness.

Your Third Eye Chakra's Qualities

Stay in the empty/fullness of your heart awareness and on your culminating path of "Finding Wisdom" while you explore your third eye; the chakra that you have already learned expresses "vision." With great gentleness, scan its energy field, front and back. Note its size, strength and rotation. Now, deal with its qualities and note its paradoxes.

The color of your third eye is purple; a color that along with blue has traditionally been regarded as sacred. A combination of the primordial creativity of red with the sanctity and clarity of blue, purple has been believed to be "the most mystical of the colors."[459] Like many of their modern descendents in England, the ancient Celts revered the purple of kingship. And their kings were required to be wise leaders and great warriors, (as the story of Bran the Blessed would indicate.) Yet with the color purple, there is also paradox, for red is the color of the root chakra's masculine energies, with their (sometimes) destructive creative power, combined with the masculine blue of the throat chakra, with its (sometimes) destructive power of expression, to produce the feminine purple. (Please remember the paradoxical nature of Truth.)

Thus, while the third eye is the "visioning" chakra whose feminine energies allow it to "take in" the raw energies of wise and life-serving insights, that immense power can also be used by people of obsessive ambition (and, usually, deep unacknowledged wounds), to subvert the truth. The results are invariably disastrous. There is the example of some charismatic people, such as Adolph Hitler, whose "vision" of a new world order and persuasive "voicing" of that vision, as Truth, changed the course of history. Although the Truth itself is paradoxical, there is no way of subverting it, at least, not for long. Throughout mankind's history, this has been attempted with distressing frequency.

You are being reminded, Soul Searcher, that your path of "Finding Wisdom" requires that you focus on Truth. While "seeing" the truth about you and your situation through your third eye chakra, you again realize the power of Truth and your loving capacity to receive and allow it. (Do you again perceive how the actualized powers of detachment/discernment, dynamic equilibrium and the loving i-am/self can enhance that capacity?) Please also note the enhancement of freedom and safety in your **knowing** and **being** because your discipline/ practice of revealing/concealing is actualizing in your emerging holarchy as the power of translucent knowing. At this juncture, recall your heart archetypes of the Healer and the Visionary. They are connected with your third eye chakra. They "see" into and beyond this third dimension of surface appearances and they both take in and "voice" the "higher" realities. When they are without woundedness, they are in-formed by Love and express and live only Truth. Recall its paradoxical nature and again realize the immense power you are carrying and continuing to develop.)

The element of the third eye chakra is radium. Since radium is a source of powerful radiation, the light of the Celtic King Bran's head could have symbolically originated in his third eye chakra. In the world's literature, references to light abound in relation to the third eye (pineal gland). In the Christian wisdom teachings, there is the statement that "when the eye is single, the body is filled with light."[460] In that sacred context, you will recall, the Light

---

[459] David Fontana, *The Secret Language of Symbols*, p. 67.
[460] The *Gospel of Matthew*, 6: 22.

is an aspect of the indwelling Spirit. Thus, the third eye (gland and chakra) that "visions" beyond the world of appearances can be guided internally and in-formed by light. The Celtic warrior, for example, would "see" into and fight to counter the skills of the opponent. As a result, there could be a deep emotional connection developed with the foe though the third eye. That same deep connection can also be developed in loving ways with those people you truly desire to "see into." This is the pinnacle of good relationship. The "seeing into" is also an indication of the prime directive of your third eye chakra: the generation and maintenance of your spiritual, i.e., transcendent, emotionality. This archetypal imperative is reinforced by the chakra's "i-am" statement of consciousness: "I am a seer of Truth." (There is more detail about that "i-am-ness" in a moment.)

To summarize briefly and add a new observation . . .

Your throat and third eye chakras vibrate at the high frequencies of spirituality, i.e., of transcendence. Their powers, as indicated by their colors (which, you recall, are also sounds) and by their elements, are immense. At your advent, you carried their wondrous possibilities. Yet, even at this level of vibration, there is paradox and the possibility of wounding. That possibility has always been present, because these centers of consciousness can be healthy only with "voicing" and "seeing" Truth. Meanwhile, the paradoxical nature of Truth can lead to wounding, when there is **ignorance** that prevents allowing and accepting (and thereby prevents the development of transcendent knowing). That real deficiency of awareness is often present as soul structures of false beliefs that appear to be "true." Many are in the lowest dimensions of "unknowing." In the **holistic** human energy system, the consciousness energies of the unhealed animal soul centers that generated those beliefs will be present in the throat and third eye chakras. Therein lies the generative source of the wounded heart archetype "shadows." (Please recall what these energies have been in you and how far along in the healing process you have come. Remember to stay in the empty/fullness of your heart awareness and on your path!)

Your Third Eye Chakra's Function and Generative Power

Exploring further into your "higher" centers of consciousness, focus on your third eye chakra. You will recall that its prime directive is the generation and maintenance of your spiritual, i.e., transcendent, emotionality, while its "i-am" statement of consciousness; ("I am a seer of Truth") reinforces that "visioning" archetypal imperative. While examining its function and generative power, please also recall that like the other chakras in your **holistic** energy system, your third eye carries four components, front and back.

Your third eye's physical component, front, uses its ability to "see" and visualize images that give you insight into what physical needs and/or addictions you might be indulging, overlooking, ignoring or even completely oblivious to. Thus, for example, you can get recurring images of food, water or sexual encounters. In this imaging, other physical sensations can be experienced, if the need and/or addiction is strong. In the case of addictions to chemical substances, the same type of images can be experienced. (Ponder on your experiences of this nature. Have they been prominent in your life? Have they diminished or even disappeared during your healing process?) Another way of experiencing the third eye capacity to "see" is by scanning an auric energy field. Please recall that by scanning, you are seeing with your hand and with practice, you will be seeing into multiple dimensions. In this context, the third eye chakra gives some people the capacity literally to see auras. They can do this by switching from ordinary sight into their "higher sensory perception" and seeing the dancing spectrum of light that encloses all living things. Although seemingly rare, the ability to see and to read auras is something that you can increasingly develop, while you are healing your animal soul centers of consciousness. (It is possible that you are already able to do this.)

The very strong emotional component of your third eye chakra front gives you yet another "seeing" capacity; that of probing into situations made murky by animal soul emotionality and suddenly seeing what is really there. In other words, you are seeing Truth. It is a way of "shedding light" on wounded, malfunctioning soul structures, of raising the vibratory frequency of damaged centers of consciousness and bringing about a kundalini "shift." Many of your healing visualizations, especially those involving the "Seeker's Lamp," have been utilizing this discerning capacity. (Ponder on your experiences, in particular those involving the realm(s) of the Wheel of Samsara. With an energy shift, there can often be a strong sensation of "light." Please realize that your sacral chakra has undergone considerable healing and that the energies of your soul structures of emotionality have been extensively transformed. Then with the help of the Observer and the powers of detachment/discernment of your emerging holarchy, ponder on what remains to be healed.)

A practical and intriguing "seeing" capacity of your third eye front has involved the mental component. When thoughts are enhanced by imaging power, you, as the image maker, can get the "whole picture" of an expanded thought. With this capacity, you can "see" the completed project and you can see each detail as you put your plan into place. It was said that Michelangelo "saw" his statue of the David in the flawed block of marble that had been brought into his workroom. Then, all that was needed was to chip away the extra marble; the flaw was unimportant! (Ponder on your own "practical" applications of enhanced imaging power. It is an immense "seeing" capacity that you have had all your life. Ponder also on your healing experiences involving both thought and imaging and how they have freed you from a purely cerebral sort of technique that could not take you into your depths. Ponder deeply on what is still required. Then set about doing the "work.")

Finally, with the predominant spiritual component, the radiant "seeing" capacity of your third eye center of consciousness attains its fullest function. This is its wonderful potential. When you are opening fully to see, you can envision what your life can be and eagerly continue your rebirthing journey. You never try to control it, but you have a better idea of what possibilities there are. You can also see what the rest of humanity could potentially become. In your close encounters, you can see what is behind the appearance of people and situations. By doing this, you are expanding your capacity to see Truth. This, in turn, results in even greater **knowing** and **being**. (Ponder on the distance you have already covered on your journey. Ask yourself: "In what ways do I see what was once hidden from me? In what ways do I still hide from the truth about me and my situation?" Although there is more detachment/discernment in the offing, you have come a long way!) In this you have had the power of the Observer to help you. You have also been helped by the energies entering through the back of your third eye chakra.

The physical component of your third eye chakra back functions by providing an enhanced sense of physical ability to turn your "vision" into a reality. Although this is difficult to explain, what seems to happen is this: there is a "message" sent to your soul structures of physicality to alert them to the physical necessities of your vision. To be sure, there will already be the skills and strength that you have cultivated, perhaps in another capacity, or those you will now start to develop. But here, through downward causation, there comes the feeling/tone of an ability to turn your vision into a third dimension "creation." It is amazing to realize that little Michelangelo (who was barely five feet tall) could have summoned the physical skills and strength to create the David. (Take time to ponder on your own visions, those you brought to fruition and those that you found to be "impossible." After clearly distinguishing between "vision" and "fantasy," what made the vision impossible? If your **beliefs** were somehow involved, what power did they carry? How far have you come in letting them go? What more is required?)

The emotional component of your third eye chakra back is much involved with your "self image." Although this is an egoic structure that expresses the many complexities of you as animal soul, there is a feeling/tone connected to the third eye back. It is this: as we gradually release our lovelessness towards ourselves, and open to receive the truth of what we are, we change our vision of ourselves and shift into self acceptance, regard and love. (If you are realizing that this is not yet the way you are feeling, you can assume that your third eye chakra back requires more healing. In this assumption, please note that the "redness" of your third eye is linked to the "redness" of your sacral chakra. (You will be given greater detail later in the lesson.) As your sacral chakra has healed, there has been a corresponding healing in your third eye back. The reverse is also possible. Ponder on these observations and bring in the Observer to help you. If more healing is required, trust that it shall be there. Stay in your heart awareness and on your path.)

Through the mental component of your third eye back you can receive the awareness of your **beliefs** about your true potential. There is in this a strong interaction with the self image of your animal soul mental body. With the "higher" chakra, however, Truth is paramount and will be revealed. With the ongoing healing of your solar plexus chakra and heart "bridge," you become increasingly aware of your incredible ignorance about who you truly are. (Please recall that your animal soul structures of mentality, under-girded and reinforced by your **beliefs**, are to a huge extent, "learned ignorance."[461] Thus, you will be "blind" to your true being and caught up in immature and even self-rejecting ideas, until after letting go, they are replaced by the truth about you. Then, ponder on the beliefs you already know have limited you. If

---

[461] For more detail. see A. H. Almaas, *The Unfolding Now*, pp. 114-118.

there still are in you vestiges of learned ignorance, focus your "light," do your "worm-hole" work and get to the truth.)

In the spiritual component of your third eye chakra back, you can open fully to the governance and guidance of the indwelling Spirit (your nucleus of divinity), so that you heal, create your life and finally come to the full realization of who you truly are. This has been your possibility from the onset of your journey. In these "higher" centers of consciousness, the realization is awaiting you. Although your quest is not yet completed, you can joyfully anticipate this **knowing** that becomes your true **being**. Herein is the vibration of expectancy in the empty/fullness of your heart awareness. Stay there and on your culminating path of "Finding Wisdom." You have arrived at the point where exploring the soul structures of spirituality generated by your throat and third eye chakras is possible. But, first, let us pause.

At this moment, there is likely an immense insight in-forming you. Please recall all the shaman's stories about you and about this spirit-filled universe. Recall that as an energy being, you are a microcosmic expression of the One Consciousness, Creative Energy. Recall that you **knew** when you started this journey that animal soul was only your starting position. Recall the kundalini "shifts" that have been happening while you traveled your paths. Note your glowing sense of inner empowerment with its feeling/tone of purity, simplicity and unity. Note the sense of an inner presence that is you and not-you. Note also, with gratitude, the continuous development of your emerging holarchy. Although there is quite possibly more healing "work" yet to be undertaken, you already have a **knowing** of something wonderful about your **being**. And it is this:

Your spirituality and your humanity are one and the same. On your quest for wholeness, you are not achieving something called "spirituality," while you are leaving behind something called your "humanity." As a microcosmic expression of the divine, you have undertaken a quest that, in truth, has been a process in which you have been gestating and preparing to birth what you truly are; a fully self-realized, androgynous, human being. In other words, you are an energy being, a soul field, that has been evolving into spiritual humanness.[462]

On your culminating path of "Finding Wisdom," while you have remained in your heart awareness, you have been opening to the highest vibratory frequencies of consciousness energies that you are. Accept them with gratitude, while you are slowly realizing that finding wisdom means journeying on all the paths and actualizing the powers of letting go/letting be, balancing, containing and revealing/concealing; that finding wisdom means journeying on all the paths and accepting and allowing the powers of the detachment/discernment, the dynamic equilibrium, the loving i-am/self and the translucent knowing; that finding wisdom means journeying on all the paths and tuning into the reality of your emerging holarchy. Herein you are discovering the key to your spiritual humanness.

---

[462] In other words: "[…] Spirit is *both* the highest *goal* of all development and evolution and the *ground* of the entire sequence […]." Ken Wilber, *The Eye of Spirit*, p. 39.

At this moment, let us clarify and augment that awareness by exploring the transcendent soul structures generated by your throat and third eye chakras. It is a necessary prelude on your journey – a necessary readiness. While doing so, you will be making the final preparations for experiencing your crown chakra.

Your Soul Structures of Spiritual Physicality and Emotionality

Now take in a Celtic myth that will help you to explore and discover what those transcendent soul structures are of themselves and how they relate to both your animal soul structures and your spiritual humanness. It is a myth that will also prepare you for birthing what you truly are. Entitled "Y (eye) Chadee," this story is from the Isle of Man, where even today there are energies that "call" to you from the Otherworld.[463]

There were once two handsome princes, sons of the aging king and queen of Ellan Vannin. The elder prince, whose name was Eshyn, was a worthy heir to the throne. He was fearless in battle, just in his judgments, truthful in his speaking and pure in his dealings with women. Despite many seductive glances from the ladies, he stayed steadfast in his desire only for true love. He knew that he would one day meet his only beloved.

In stark contrast, Eshyn's younger brother, Ny-Eshyn, fed all his appetites for women, drink and gambling. Yet nothing ever satisfied him. And he spent many hours angrily brooding about his brother. Indeed, Ny-Eshyn's jealousy "gnawed like a knife twisting in his stomach."

One night, while returning home, Ny-Eshyn encountered a wizened old man, who offered to help him "seek joy in this life." After Ny-Eshyn had blurted out his jealousy and hatred of his brother, the old man provided a solution to his problem. Ny-Eshyn could take home a poisonous snake enclosed in a wicker basket and place it under his brother's bed. In less than a day, his brother would be changed into an ugly, coarse-featured creature who would revolt all who saw him. Eagerly, Ny-Eshyn accepted the old man's solution and hurried home. When Eshyn left to go hunting, Ny-Eshyn placed the lethal basket under his brother's bed.

That evening there appeared at the gates of the castle, "a bent figure of a man, with coarse grey skin and a protruding nose like the beak of a bird." The guards immediately restrained him. When they saw that the horse the creature was riding was Eshyn's favorite mount, they dragged him before the king. When Eshyn (for that's who it was) pleaded with both his parents to recognize him, what emerged from his throat was a grating

---

[463] Excerpted from Peter Beresford-Ellis, "Y Chadee," in *Celtic Myths and Legends*, pp. 164-178.

and grunting voice that was barely human. In horror, they ordered him to be gone.

When Eshyn paused in his flight to drink from a clear stream, he saw his reflection in the water. "He screamed at what he saw." Then he turned his footsteps towards the dark mountains. After wandering for a day and a night, he came to a deep, black lake. In utter despair, he sat on a great granite stone.

While he sat, an old woman came along staggering under the weight of a huge load of sticks on her back. Immediately, Eshyn stood up and gently offered to carry the load for her. When she told him that she lived at the top of the mountain, Eshyn "did not even consider the difficulty." As they climbed, the old woman kindly asked what ailed him. And Eshyn, who spoke only the truth, revealed the pain in his heart. They arrived at her little cottage, where he built a fire and prepared a simple meal for them. While Eshyn worked, the old woman stood at the window and carefully observed the patterns of the stars in the northern night sky. Then she knew that he could be restored to his former appearance, but the tasks ahead would be arduous.

In the morning, she gave him the instructions for the first part of the coming journey. She directed him to the same wizened old man that Ny-Eshyn had encountered. The old woman was very clear: Eshyn was to tell him what ailed him but was to do the exact opposite of what the old man told him to do. Although Eshyn could not fathom any part of the instructions, he promised to do as the old woman directed.

It came about exactly as the old woman had said; Eshyn encountered the wizened old man and told him his sad story, Pretending great concern, the old man asked for time to go away and think about the help he could provide. Then he casually instructed Eshyn to be on the lookout for the Queen of the Fairies, who might come by. If she did, Eshyn was to hide himself and neither stop her nor speak to her. Then the old man disappeared.

In the black night, Eshyn sat and waited. Suddenly there appeared a company of tiny fairy folk and in their midst a beautiful woman, the Queen of the Fairies, who carried a basket of light on her arm. Eshyn, remembering the old woman's instructions, immediately stepped forward and spoke. Quite taken aback, the Queen of the Fairies paused and ordered him to explain his actions. He recounted his tale and asked her to tell him what he must do. She examined his face carefully and recognized the evil work of sorcery. Like the old woman on the mountain, the Fairy Queen assured Eshyn that he could be restored, but he would have to accompany her.

Then she led the entire group toward the western sea and across the waves to a place on a distant shore that was alien and strange. There on the beach, they watched an armada of approaching vessels. Ordering complete silence, the Fairy Queen pointed to the first ship and informed Eshyn that it carried the people of Orion the great hunter, the light of the Otherworld. In that ship there was also the daughter of Orion, who was the most beautiful princess in this world and in the Otherworld. Her name was Y Chadee, the Everlasting Pearl, and she was the only one who could restore Eshyn. She would also become his wife if he was strong and did not fear the tasks before him. But the tasks would require all his strength and courage. Then the Queen of the Fairies instructed him in what he had to do.

There would be three immense tasks: he had to enter the "cave of heroes," seize the great sword of Orion, the "Sword of Light" and hold fast to it no matter what happened; he had to find the symbol of Y Chadee, the Everlasting Pearl, which was a "pearl of great beauty," seize it and not give it up; finally, he had to remain undistracted while he was being seduced by a woman of surpassing beauty. Pointing down a cliff path to the sea shore, the Fairy Queen told Eshyn to follow it. She cautioned him not to let any obstacle stand in his way. Then she and her fairy host vanished.

Eshyn had scarcely started along the path, when he was confronted by a huge gate sealed with tall iron bars. Remembering his instructions, he summoned up all his strength; he pulled and tugged at the bars until he had made an opening large enough to squeeze through. Immediately, he found himself in a huge cave filled with warriors, sitting at large wooden tables. They were drinking from a cauldron and gaming with dice. At the far end of the cave high up near the ceiling there hung a great gold and silver sword that shone with "an ethereal light." Stepping boldly forward, Eshyn ignored the warriors. But they began to shout an invitation to him to come to drink and play. They knew that the sword was out of reach and laughed when Eshyn truthfully informed them that he had come for it. They again urged him to join them while telling him that "today we enjoy life, for who knows the cares of tomorrow." But Eshyn steadfastly refused the invitation. He silently waited while they drank themselves into "deep, snoring, drunken sleep."

Quickly, Eshyn piled several tables on top of each other until he could reach the Sword of Light. He lifted it off its hook and leaped down. At that moment a great black raven flew screaming an alarm into the hall. Instantly, the warriors were alert and sober. But while Eshyn held the sword, he was invincible and they could not touch him. Holding the weapon in both hands, he left the cave.

Immediately, he was in a passage. Peering down, he saw below him a large hall that had no windows or doors and was lit by an eerie light. From where he stood he could see only a rope that hung down into the hall. In the center was a great table around which many obese and indolent warriors sat feasting. Along the walls of the hall, lay the bones, bottles and other debris of many such feasts. Eshyn's eyes were drawn to the middle of the table on which sat a gold candle-holder. But instead of a candle, it held a pearl of great beauty. It was the pearl that was emitting the light. Eshyn recognized it. After sheathing the Sword of Light, he slid down the rope into the hall.

He was greeted with much good humor and offered a place at the table. But Eshyn refused and truthfully told the warriors that he had come for the pearl. They drunkenly informed him that he would not succeed because the only way out was up the rope. The instant he touched the pearl the light would be extinguished and he would not find the rope in the darkness. But Eshyn sat and waited. The feast continued until all the warriors were in a snoring sleep.

Then Eshyn arose and, keeping one hand on the end of the rope, he seized the pearl. The light went out and, again, the black screaming raven flew in to sound the alarm. Instantly, the warriors were on their feet, but in the darkness they could only attack each other. With the pearl safely tucked into his pocket, Eshyn climbed up the rope back to the passage.

Immediately, he was standing before a great palace on the sea shore. He entered a room blazing with light and decorated with splendid tapestries. There were fountains splashing and soft music playing. On tables there were bowls of fruit and other delicacies. And lying there on couches were seven gorgeous maidens, who shouted with joy to see him. They pleaded with him to lay aside his sword and clothing and make love with them. They promised him unimaginable delights. And Eshyn, exhausted by his efforts, would have surrendered. But he remembered the old woman's warning and left the palace.

Immediately, he was on the sea shore. There in front of him was a great ship beached "in the shadows." Then he saw before him a maiden of such surpassing beauty that he almost fell at her feet. At that very moment, he gave his heart to her and wanted her. She spoke to him and asked him why he was in the Otherworld. When he told her, she laughed and, arching her swan-like neck, said that he was beautiful. Then, she asked him to give her the Sword of Light and the pearl. Sorely tempted, Eshyn summoned all his strength and told her that he could not do that. He was obligated to keep them until the Queen of the Fairies had given him leave to release them. And then Eshyn asked the maiden for her name. The reply was: "I am Y Chadee, the daughter of Orion, the Everlasting Pearl." While Eshyn sadly remained unseduced, he spoke to her these words: "although he who holds should be ready to give, I cannot do so even to you. I must hold these objects, for my joy in the world is more important than the shadows of this one." Then she released him.

He closed his eyes . . . and he found himself snuggled into the corner of the old woman's cottage. At first he thought he had been dreaming. But there was the Sword of Light and in his pocket was the pearl. Then, deeply grieving, Eshyn told the old woman that he would gladly have exchanged the "baubles" for the love of the woman on the sea shore, for she had smiled at him despite his ugliness. Sternly the old woman informed him that if he had, he would have been condemned to eternal ugliness. Then she handed him a mirror. There, gazing back at Eshyn, was the handsome man he had been.

Delighted, he asked the old woman how he could repay her. Her answer was that he was to take the sword and the pearl back to his father's palace and there, before all the court and despite any objections, he was to cast them into the dark seas below the walls. After promising to obey, Eshyn bade her farewell.

He arrived home and was greeted with great rejoicing. The only exception was Ny-Eshyn, who stood sullenly behind the throne and cursed the wizened old man for failing to destroy his brother. Then, after recounting his adventures, Eshyn announced that he had a further task to perform. He led the entire court to the battlements overlooking the seas. He informed all present that he would cast the sword and pearl, as he had promised, into the dark waters. There was a huge outcry from all those present. He was admonished even by his mother for wanting to throw away such treasures. But Eshyn hurled them over the battlements. Just before they hit the waves, the great arm of the sea god, Mannanan, came out of the waves and caught them.

When Ny-Eshyn muttered that Eshyn had thrown away a great treasure, his reply was swift: "Not so. I have kept a treasure, for I have garnered wisdom in great store. I hold that wisdom is the greatest treasure."

His father, the king, gravely responded: "He who holds must first have discovered. He who has discovered must first have sought. He who has sought must first have braved all impediments. Thus did the Druids teach." In a rage, Ny-Eshyn stormed out of the castle never to be seen again.

At that moment, a horn sounded and a gold and silver coach arrived in the courtyard. Out stepped a woman of surpassing beauty and Eshyn's heart "missed a beat." There before him stood the woman of the sea shore, Y Chadee, the Everlasting Pearl. Smiling, she extended her hand to him as his beloved and his future wife.

And the words she spoke that will end this story were these: "You did not settle for treasure from the Otherworld but rather for love in this one. For the love of a man such as you, I am destined in this world and the Otherworld, for there are no barriers to true love."

Please ponder long on the message of this myth. It is, in many ways, a culmination of all the stories you have been told throughout these lessons. By immersing yourself in the stories, you have become increasingly aware of the special energies that they carry. They can take you deeply into what you are as an energy being. They can show you not only how your soul structures have been shaped but also the "forms" they have taken. With each succeeding story, you have obtained a clearer picture of your own incredibly complex multidimensionality; how it expresses as you. And that picture has also revealed how all these dimensions of you must relate to each other in a healthy balance that indicates wholeness. In this culminating myth, you have a multi-level presentation: at the literal level, there is an intriguing story about a "man" whose jealous "brother" triggers a painful heroic journey that includes several exciting and magical events but ends happily for everyone, except the "brother;" on the metaphoric and symbolic level, there is a complex and colorful tale about soul questing, animal soul consciousness, upward and downward causation, Truth that reveals and conceals and an increasingly aware spiritual humanness.

And this is a splendid story about rebirthing into androgyny.

While exploring this myth, you shall be discovering the meaning of "spiritual humanness" that is found in the expression; "as above; so below." You will also discover the grandeur of your soul structures of transcendent physicality and emotionality, including the egoic structures. And you will discover that the myth itself is a distillation, in metaphor and symbol of the process that is required of any soul searcher – the process of developing an emerging holarchy. All of it is a preparation for the discovery of your highest **knowing** and **being**; that which is inherent in the transcendent soul structures of spiritual mentality generated by your crown chakra. You are nearing the end of your rebirthing quest.

Now, let us discover.

In this Celtic myth, the archetypal warrior/hero is a metaphor for and a symbol of a masculine energy of a far different vibration than what you encountered in the archetypal Cuchulain. Eshyn, whose name simply means "he," is the symbol of a highly developed masculine energy expressed by a healthy solar plexus chakra. As this story begins, he demonstrates that the primitive energies of a masculine root chakra can be transmuted and can "dance" with the feminine. This is indicated in Eshyn's interactions not only with the local seductive young women (he treats them courteously while realizing that none of them are his "true" love) but also with the "old woman" of the mountain (he ministers unto her with gentleness and strength). The unhealthy sexuality and the sacral chakra imbalance, so evident in Cuchulain, do not exist in Eshyn. Here is the consciousness energy of an evolved masculinity that can "dance" well with the feminine energies of both the sacral and the heart chakras, present within that solar plexus center.

In your quest for wholeness, the achievement of "balance" on your ongoing path of "Coming into Being" can take you to the threshold of your rebirth into androgyny. (This you have already learned from the fairy tale of "Roland and May-Bird," but in this myth of Eshyn the balancing is more precise. Here, in metaphor is the inner empowerment with its glowing feeling/tone of purity, simplicity and unity.) The healing of root, sacral and solar plexus chakras that has opened you to the energies of your spiritual centers of consciousness, in downward causation, would bring this about.

In this myth there is, however, an expression of the archetypal "shadows" that can in-form you as an energy being, a soul field. That motif is Ny-Eshyn, whose name simply means "of him." In the story, he is "the brother." But at a deeper level of symbolic meaning, Ny-Eshyn is part of Eshyn. Thus, Ny-Eshyn is the shadow that indicates an out-of-balance and primitive root chakra expressing as an undercurrent of uninhibited (mainly sexual) appetites, accompanied by a Wheel of Samsara realm of hell sacral chakra expressing as rage and murderous jealousy. Ny-Eshyn is also a motif of a dysfunctional solar plexus chakra's Saboteur, which can be at work secretly creating havoc in a seemingly "healthy" and balanced energy system.

Thus, this myth can teach you a great deal about your archetypal shadows. On your inner journey home, you have likely experienced something like this: you have made progress and are feeling good about yourself, when you suddenly find yourself quite unexpectedly "back sliding" into some old patterns of thoughts, feelings and actions. The old animal soul structures appear not to have changed. You go through a period of discouragement and are perhaps tempted to give up. Your Saboteur (for that is what is at work) might start to gain considerable strength. But something keeps "calling" and you struggle on. Of course, you are being helped: you are being guided by the indwelling Spirit (the nucleus of divinity), expressing in the spiritual component of your animal soul centers. Thus, with your healing therapies (disciplines) and the disciplines/practices of letting go/letting be, balancing and containing and with the help of the Observer, you have raised the frequencies of your animal soul chakras and opened to receive, through your gradually restored heart "bridge" the energies of your "higher" centers of consciousness. But the feelings of discouragement can often be quite pervasive. You can be involved in a "roller coaster" experience of joy and despair. You must recognize the Saboteur at work and be aware of what is happening in you.

In the myth, it is Ny-Eshyn, the "shadow," who seeks "joy" by destroying "he" (Eshyn). You have already recognized the motif of the "wizened old man" as an agent of evil in the fairy tale of "The Maiden Without Hands." The imagery of the poisonous snake adds a greater depth to the idea of destructive energies at work. The snake symbol is that of a dysfunctional and poisonous feminine energy (the emotional component of a dysfunctional root chakra) turned against life. The imagery of under the bed is, you will recall from the tale of the "Twelve Worn-out Dancing Shoes," a motif of primitive sexuality. But what happens to Eshyn (the masculine energy expressing as the healthy solar plexus chakra) is not primarily the damaging of animal soul structures. Ny-Eshyn, the "shadow," (the unhealthy masculine energies of the root chakra) has attempted to cripple **the generative power of the throat and third eye chakras**.

Here is a clarification:

You have already been instructed about the functioning of those chakras. Their generative power, present since your conception, has been creating your soul structures of transcendent physicality and emotionality. Already you have encountered these structures expressing through the archetypes of your heart that are invoked through your throat and third eye chakras. Now you can become familiar with more of the soul structures they can generate out of your malleable, impressionable, receptive and vulnerable soul substance.

The soul structures generated by your throat chakra include not only the "embodiments" of your Teacher and Warrior archetypes and your "etheric double" but also **everything that expresses the physicality of your spiritual humanness**. With its prime directive and reinforcing "i-am" statement of consciousness; "I am an expresser of Truth," your throat chakra "matrix" is actually the generative center of your "highest" expression of masculine energies. Here is an energy consciousness that expresses as a deep **knowing** about your soul structures of physicality; a deep discernment of animal soul physicality with a loving detachment from them. (It is this level of discernment, connected with the protoplasmic consciousness of your physicality, you are using when you are "muscle testing.") And this spiritual physicality is "voiced" inwardly and outwardly by a commitment to expressing the truth about you and your situation. With an unwavering and loving adherence to the truth about your real safety, security and survival and with the power given to you by your Teacher and Warrior archetypes, you can, with the Observer, finally heal a dysfunctional root chakra. In your **holistic** energy system, expressing Truth changes the anatomy of beliefs around those primitive root chakra energies and the sacral chakra's fear energies that often surround them. Because **form follows consciousness**, your egoic soul structures that have been shaped in the "dance" of malfunctioning masculine and feminine root and sacral chakra consciousness energies can also be changed. You become increasingly aware of your true beliefs and increasingly capable of "voicing" them. Thus, you add to your sense of inner empowerment and its glowing feeling/tone of purity, simplicity and unity. And in this gradual change, you also discover that expressing your truth can both reveal you to those who can "see" who you are and conceal you from those who cannot. In this realization you are aware that you are perfectly "safe" and "secure." In the kundalini "shifts" that are occurring, your throat chakra's power of generating spiritual physicality has helped to heal the animal soul root and sacral centers of consciousness. As above; so below. (Please note, however, that the healing therapies (disciplines) you have been patiently using to deal with your root and sacral chakras have significantly contributed to the healing.)

In the symbolism of the myth, the attack on the throat chakra by means of poisonous, feminine energies damages the etheric matrix, generates a dysfunctional root chakra and promotes physical malfunction. Thus, Eshyn presents an outward physical appearance of repulsive, reptilian ugliness. But, in reality, the work of the "shadow" is a direct attack on spiritual physicality. To reinforce the imagery, the "voice" that issues out of Eshyn is one of an "apparition." He is so horrible and horrifying that he is rejected by all those with whom he has always had acceptance in a safe haven. Moreover, even his royal parents, motifs of a "higher" awareness, are unable to recognize him. He is rejected by all. He is reduced to despair, a condition that often precipitates a quest for wholeness. Eshyn enters upon his quest.

In the myth, the physical change in Eshyn also indicates an attack on the third eye chakra. In a person, skin vibrates at the frequency of the third eye chakra.[464] Hence, Eshyn, whose skin has become reptilian, is in serious trouble before he meets up with the "old woman" of the mountain. In this familiar motif, you again encounter "higher" nurturing feminine spiritual energies, the energies of the heart. But she is more. In this myth, she has a **knowing** not only in this dimension but also in the Otherworld. She can "read" the stars. Hence, the "old woman" might also be the "Queen of the Fairies." In the Queen, there is a very high level of third eye consciousness energies. These are symbolized by the "basket of light." They are also indicated by her insights into the cause of Eshyn's disfigurement and into the healing therapy that is necessary.

Here, in metaphor/symbol is the generative power of the third eye chakra. The soul structures generated by this chakra can both "embody" your Healer and Visionary archetypes and express **everything that encompasses the emotionality of your spiritual humanness**. The third eye consciousness energies are the "highest" dimension of your feminine energies. Here are generated your "celestial" structures of soul where only Light is present and where the "high" dimensions of visioning and "seeing" are produced. In-formed by its prime directive and reinforcing "i-am" statement of "I am a seer of the Truth," your third eye chakra generates the soul structures of your transcendent emotionality. Over the heart "bridge" these powers can descend. With love and the light of Truth, they can undertake the healing of dysfunctional root and sacral chakras. Because **form follows consciousness** the physicality of your anatomy of beliefs along with the emotionality will also undergo healing change. And included will be the egoic structures that have been manifesting the dysfunction. It is the revealing/concealing Truth expressed by you that helps to re-shape those soul structures. Although there likely will be intense resistance from the sacral chakra's soul structures of emotionality (remember the Wheel of Samsara), the healing changes can be wrought in a **holistic** energy system not only in the sacral and heart feminine energies but also in those of the third eye. There is a wonderful connection that can be made with the heart energies of love, so that you can "see" with the "eye" of the heart. You can increasingly express your transcendent emotionality. As above; so below.

---

[464] From a lecture by Rosalyn Bruyere.

In the myth, Eshyn is helped by the "old woman/Queen of the Fairies" but only after he reveals a tender and loving inner beingness (a "readiness") and only after he agrees to obey her instructions. He is required to willingly perform some arduous "recovery" tasks, while he does not know anything about them. Therein is a perfect metaphor/symbol for the onset of your rebirthing quest. In the symbolism of Eshyn, there is the masculinity of the solar plexus (and, possibly, the more primitive energies of the root) chakra that is intent upon its own thoughts and personhood. These must observed, acknowledged and thereafter, involved in a healing process in order for you to trust and obey the spiritual direction you receive. And there are particular paths that are to be followed.

Herein, the myth teaches you about a fundamental part of the quest for wholeness; that your inner guidance system (the indwelling Spirit), must be obeyed. In the myth, Eshyn is commanded by higher spiritual beings to follow instructions without hesitation. His obedience, courage and trust must not waver. Already prepared by his loving energies, he successfully performs his tasks and completes his journey. Because he obeys, he arrives at a great **knowing**. Herein is the motif of the **knowing** that a soul searcher achieves in the quest for wholeness. It is the actualized translucent knowing of the emerging holarchy.

He journeys into unfamiliar, dark and challenging dimensions (the "Otherworld"), and he carries with him the qualities he already expresses of Life, Light and Love. He encounters (as all soul searchers do) the animal soul energies, twice symbolized by the appetite-driven, live-for-today "warriors." They had been put there to safeguard the "treasures" that Eshyn has to recover. In this motif, you are given powerful reminders about how easily people can be misled by their ignorance of the spiritual treasures they carry; how these can be neglected, taken for granted and eventually "lost." The "warriors" are also motifs of the Saboteur that soul searchers often encounter. Eshyn withstands their blandishments by using the revealing/concealing power of Truth and recognizing that he carries a greater power than theirs; the power of trusting the "higher" guides.

But after successfully eluding the "warriors" and making off with the first two "treasures," Eshyn's encounters with primitive animal soul energies are not yet finished. The seductive advances by the reclining maidens, to be followed by the exhausting encounter with Y Chadee, are both motifs of the energies of the Saboteur. Despite his "heart" involvement, Eshyn must resist these archetypal energies, for they symbolize both a corruption of healthy human sexuality and a loss of trust. These energies are also indicative of the Prostitute archetypal energies that can trip up a soul searcher. When lovingly recognized for what they are and gently "let be," their power vanishes.

(You are likely wondering why Y Chadee, the Everlasting Pearl, initially presents herself as a seduction that has to be resisted. The answer is given in the myth: Eshyn's words are the declaration of an achievement of spiritual humanness: he tells her that he must both obey spiritual guidance and seek joy **while living on this Earth plane**. This was not what Y Chadee had initially offered to him. There is more detail later in the lesson.)

Now, let us look at the "treasures" of a quest for wholeness. In the myth, Eshyn's first task is to obtain the Sword of Light. The Sword is a multilayered symbol that requires deep exploration. At the first layer, the Sword is a metaphor/symbol for the human power of cutting away false beliefs and other hindrances to the spiritual quest. It is a masculine symbol of the throat chakra's power of expressing Truth. With the Sword in his possession, Eshyn is "invincible." Symbolically, when in possession of the Sword of Light, the evolved masculine energies are invincible in dealing with the primitive "warrior" root chakra energies that are expressing learned ignorance. With the cutting away and letting go, there is the opening to inner illumination, symbolized by the "light" emitted by the Sword. With the light, there is also the third eye symbolism of the "higher" feminine energies. Thus, with a successful accomplishment of the first task, Eshyn is starting to heal the damaged throat and third eye. But the presence of a shrieking "raven" that alerts the careless guardians of the "treasure" indicates that obtaining this power of spiritual humanness is not an easy matter. The soul searcher must always be alert to the presence of the Saboteur, who is often far from silent.

You will receive further explanation of the Sword motif in a moment. Now, more discussion is needed about Eshyn's other tasks.

Eshyn's second and third tasks, those of obtaining the "pearl of great beauty" and of resisting the seductive actions of beautiful women including Y Chadee, the living embodiment of the "pearl," are also multilayered symbols. You will explore only the first layer now and return later for the others.

In many of the world's legends and myths, (especially those of the East) and in shamanic "spirit journeying," a pearl is the feminine symbol of a "birthing" or emergence out of "water;" the motif of the deep dimensions of "unknowing." What is birthed after great "labor," is the pure consciousness energy of an awakened spirituality that constitutes a "clear vehicle for the advancing states of wisdom, as well as a clean channel for receipt of spiritual guidance."[465] Thus, the pearl, as was the Sword, is a symbol of inner illumination. Herein are both masculine (outward) and feminine (inward) energies of "light;" and a symbol of androgyny.

But even here there is paradox: in Y Chadee, the Everlasting Pearl, the motif of a great feminine spiritual power, there is a primitive feminine sacral chakra energy combined with the feminine energies of a loving heart center and with the "highest" feminine discernment energies of the third eye. (In your **holistic** energy system all of these feminine (and astral) energies could be present and perhaps causing you grief.) In resisting Y Chadee's seductive energies, Eshyn maintains his spiritual focus and, thereby, stays within the higher vibratory frequencies. In doing this, he knowingly sustains his spiritual humanness and unknowingly clears the way for the feminine "vehicle" of wisdom.

Herein you arrive at the deepest level of teaching in this myth. You have come to the teaching about wisdom . . . and you have arrived at the threshold of your greatest **knowing**.

*   *   *

---

[465] Melody, *Love Is In the Earth*, p. 474.

About wisdom; it belongs with the Sword, which the myth states is "the symbol of the sum of all knowledge" with the power to "put to flight every ignorance." The "light" of the Sword is what makes Eshyn, (a motif of healthy masculine energy) "invincible" and brings him into his highest achievement of spiritual humanness.

His last and greatest "task" is to "give back" to the spirit world the material evidence of the treasures he has so arduously gained. He does this in the power and strength of his spiritual humanness, despite the almost overwhelming objections of his royal parents. He knows, and his father (the motif of "higher" spiritual awareness) also knows that he has already gained a great prize. Eshyn knows that he has gained wisdom and that wisdom does not grasp at anything. At that moment, his shadow (symbolized by his "brother," Ny-Eshyn) finally disappears.

About wisdom; it also belongs with the "pearl." With the arrival of Y Chadee, the Everlasting Pearl, Eshyn's beloved and future "wife," you are given the final teaching in the myth. Herein lie more of your legacy of wisdom teachings and the revelation of how you can **know** and **be** them. Herein also lie the reasons for remaining in your heart awareness and on your culminating path of "Finding Wisdom." Your readiness preparations are almost complete.

You read in *The Book of Wisdom*:[466]

> "For wisdom is quicker to move than any motion;
> She is so pure she pervades and permeates all things.
> She is a breath of the power of God,
> Pure emanation of the glory of the almighty
> So that nothing impure can find its way into her.
> For she is a reflection of the eternal light
> untarnished mirror of God's active power
> And image of [God's] goodness."

Thus, the wisdom that Eshyn gains through possession of the Sword of Light is reinforced by Y Chadee, the Everlasting Pearl; the motif of the immense feminine power, the astral power, of emotionality. inherent in the human energy system and expressing at its highest vibratory frequency in the third eye chakra. She can be in this world because of the love Eshyn, a motif of highly evolved (and healed) human masculinity, has for her. The symbolism of this myth reveals in Eshyn's illumined awareness that the great treasure of wisdom is the essential purpose of the quest. Thus, while you are questing for wholeness, you are "finding," i.e., discovering and integrating the **knowing** and **being** that wisdom requires and, thereby, attaining the spiritual humanness that it exemplifies.

In the myth, the "wedding" (a symbol of a sacred connection) of Eshyn and Y Chadee is not described. But we know that it will happen quickly. This symbol provides a final "piece" in the study of a rebirthing process. It is this: when there is obedience to and trust in the guidance

---

[466] *The Book of Wisdom*, 7:24-26. Quoted in Cynthia Bourgeault, *The Wisdom Way of Knowing*, p. 12.

of the indwelling Spirit, while the required tasks are undertaken and completed, there has been an ongoing gestation of an androgynous human being. Thus, Eshyn the symbol of the masculine force "finds" wisdom and is immediately joined by Y Chadee, the symbol of the feminine force that is the intuitive "knowledge" that wisdom carries.

In the "wedding" of Eshyn and Y Chadee you receive the imagery of the onset of an eternal partnership that will express wisdom and take you into the heights of spiritual humanness. This "wedding," like the *hieros gamos* of ancient wisdom teachings, symbolizes the androgynous partnering of the archetypal, "dancing" masculine and feminine energies, the microcosmic opposites that are inherent in your soul substance, present in your centers of consciousness and vibrating as your soul structures. **"Dancing" together, Eshyn and Y Chadee are the motif of the androgynous human being ready to undertake the next "journey."**

This wonderful pairing has been described by a modern woman of wisdom in these words:[467]

> "I know you.
> Haven't I always known you?
> cellular memories
> from somewhere
> deep inside
> push up and through
> today's amorphous reality
> revealing a primal bond
> awakened by your presence.
>
> You know me.
> Haven't you always known me?
> this connection so deep and familiar
> binding us
> [. . .]
> must have had its birth
> in time before time
> how magnificent to have found you again."

The myth has ended. In the preparation for your great awareness, you have been given an image of the rebirthing process, with its great challenges to be overcome and its great treasure to be won. You have been made ready to receive the final "piece" in the teaching about your spiritual centers of consciousness.

Your Crown Chakra

It is this: your gestating androgyny carries a **knowing** that further indicates the wisdom required by your spiritual humanness. It is for that wisdom and into that wisdom that you

---

[467] Minx Boren, *Soul Notes, Too*, an untitled poem, p. 39.

have traveled so far and ventured so much. On your culminating path of "Finding Wisdom," after all the foregoing preparation, you are ready to explore your crown chakra; the center of the **knowing** and your "highest" soul structures of spirituality.

While you remain in your heart awareness, gently scan your crown chakra by quickly passing your left hand over it from mid-forehead to center neck. Although it is not in this dimension, you can sense its energies. Then let us return to Celtic lore and start with the qualities of that center of conscious.

Your Crown Chakra's Qualities

The color of your crown chakra is white; another color that has been traditionally regarded as sacred. It is the color of purity and transcendence[468] and of sacred occasions both happy and sad; as in the rituals of christenings, marriages and funerals. Thus, white which is neither masculine nor feminine, can be the color of both life and death. Although life and death can be carried in the heart chakra green, it is here at your crown chakra that you carry the ultimate paradox! In Celtic stories, white garments indicated the presence of spiritual beings, who could be harbingers of both life and death.

The element of the crown chakra is magnetum, an element known to the ancient Egyptians and to medieval alchemists, but unknown to modern science.[469] In Bruyere's formulation of the energy flow up the system, the original spark that had started its ascent in the elemental root chakra fire, passed through the sacral (not to be quenched by the water element), through the solar plexus (to receive a strengthening in the air element), through the heart (not to be smothered by the earth element), has grown to a flame, "which may now be transmuted into ether, radium and magnetum, respectively."[470] That final element is involved with electromagnetic power, the sacred magnetism of attraction. Thus, the Celtic warrior, bested by a great opponent, could "surrender" to the strength and presence of that other human being. With your crown chakra you discover the power of surrender **into** the indwelling Spirit.

Please remain in your heart awareness. (Remember that it is the empty/fullness that contains your glow of inner empowerment, with its feeling/tone of purity, simplicity and unity, along with the sense of a presence that is you and not-you.) Now, let us focus upward and, with reverence, seek to understand the function and generative power of your crown chakra.[471]

Your Crown Chakra's Function and Generative Power

Within the ketheric dimensions of the crown center of consciousness, there is little meaning to the words "function," "front," "back," and "components." There are very few words and they are inadequate to deal with this center of consciousness and its generative power. Please focus within a light-filled expanse and within your open heart awareness realize the following:

---

[468] David Fontana, *The Secret Language of Symbols*, p. 67.
[469] Rosalyn Bruyere, *Wheels of Light*, p. 56.
[470] *Ibid.* p.55.
[471] For more detail, see Cyndi Dale, *New Chakra Healing*, pp. 45-47; 101-102; 124-125 and 155-159.

that the consciousness energies of your crown chakra convey a feeling/tone of inspiration, "peak experience" and wholeness; that by opening to your divine purpose, you can achieve physical healing, emotions of quiet bliss and stillness, and mental self-empowerment; that by surrendering into that great vibration and releasing any lingering desire to control, you come "face to face" with your own divinity. (Understand now the significance of your inner power with its glowing feeling/tone of purity, simplicity and unity. And understand now the significance of the inner presence that is you and not-you.) All of it indicates the generative power of your crown center of consciousness.

Your Soul Structures of Spiritual Mentality

With its prime directive of generating and maintaining your spiritual, i.e., transcendent, mentality; a **knowing** that is beyond all "knowingness" and with the reinforcing "i-am" statement of consciousness; "I am a knower of Truth," your crown chakra has the capacity to generate, out of the consciousness energies of your soul substance, the soul structures of wisdom that constitute transcendent mentality and the pinnacle of your spiritual humanness. At that pinnacle there is the "dancing" androgyny. (Recall how Eshyn "found" wisdom, displayed its power and then was merged with it.) Soul Searcher, that great treasure is almost yours.

And it will be described as part of the "afterward" of your rebirthing. But your crown chakra and its generative capacity has, like your other centers of consciousness, required loving nurturing. Since that might not have been the case, there is yet more "work" relating to your throat, third eye and crown chakras that must be undertaken.

From the myth, you have learned that your throat and third eye chakras can sustain terrible damage. (You have likely recognized some of your own.) There can also be damage sustained by your crown chakra. (Please be aware that with your heart "work" you have made considerable headway in healing all those centers. But at this point you must deal with their remaining malfunction and practice the self-healing therapies (disciplines) for them. Because yours is a **holistic** energy system, please also be aware that you might be dealing with other centers of consciousness and that you will likely require the familiar disciplines/practices; the letting go/letting be, balancing, containing and revealing/concealing, whose actualized powers of detachment/discernment, dynamic equilibrium, loving i-am/self and translucent knowing will continue to produce the emerging holarchy.)

Let us start with some preliminary information about the malfunction and the healing therapies for all three chakras. Then we shall explore each in greater depth.

Your Throat, Third Eye and Crown Chakras' Malfunction

The generative power of the "higher" centers of consciousness can be damaged just as severely as the generative power of the "lower" ones. In an extreme case, if the pre-birth symbiotic relationship with the mother is one of lovelessness and rejection, (an indication of her malfunctioning "higher" centers), the damage to the gestating fetus's "higher" centers of consciousness can set the stage for major dysfunction in the "lower" centers. As above; so below. After advent, if the lovelessness is continued and expressed physically, emotionally, mentally and spiritually, the child's entire energy system will be in jeopardy. In this extreme situation there will be physical and psychological malfunction to be addressed and healed within all the chakras. Please keep in mind your earlier lessons dealing with the malfunctioning "lower" centers and the heart, while you focus on the "higher" centers. Please also recall that when the quest for wholeness gets underway, some of the damage to the "higher" centers can be healed because of the **holistic** nature of the energy system. At this point you are dealing with the damage that has required direct healing, after major repairs to the heart "bridge."

Your Throat, Third Eye and Crown Chakras' Self-Healing Therapies

At this stage in your journey, there is no need to remind you again about following the "guidelines" or about seeking other forms of therapy when they are needed. There is also no further need to remind you that **form follows consciousness** and how the healing of soul structures, including the egoic structures, follows the transmutation of the energies of the centers of consciousness. And at this point, you have likely internalized the power of trust-full intent, faith-full attention and daily meditation.

In dealing with the self-healing therapies (disciplines) for throat, third eye and crown chakras, there is nothing that can be said, in these lessons, about their element. Whether there is too much or too little ether (throat chakra), radium (third eye chakra), or magnetum (crown chakra), cannot be explored because they are still in the realm of mystery. Although there is a relationship to Light, how that translates into "too much" or "too little" can best be dealt with by reference to the color of the chakra in the self-healing therapies to be provided.

Now we shall separately address the remaining malfunction of and the healing disciplines for those spiritual centers of transcendent consciousness. Please stay in your heart awareness.

Your Throat Chakra's Malfunction

With throat chakra malfunction, the physical damage can involve the larynx, thyroid, upper respiratory tract, esophagus, tonsils, teeth, jaws and ears. The psychological disorders are expressed in an inability to "voice" one's own truth. There can also be a lack of boundaries, a sense of victimization and issues involving over—or under-responsibility. (Please note how closely these malfunctions relate to the wounded Teacher and Warrior archetypes.)

As indicated by the myth, with throat chakra malfunction there can also be damage to the etheric matrix. As a result, the etheric double, connected with the root chakra's prime directive of physicality, can be damaged. Hence, spiritual physicality carries a direct involvement with the physicality of animal soul. If there is dis-ease in the throat chakra, there will be dis-ease in the root chakra and its generated soul structures.

Self-Healing Therapies for Your Throat Chakra

When there is too much blue energy or too little there has often been, in both situations, a mis-use of your "voice."

When there is **too much blue energy**, there has probably been an attempt to by-pass the necessary work of healing the "lower" animal chakras. Instead, the focus has been on developing "spirituality." In extreme cases, this has been done by engaging in breath work to "pull" the energies in through the crown center of consciousness, by spending excessive hours in "spiritual" practices perhaps involving unfocused, repetitive sounds, and by speaking inauthentically about transcendent matters. The latter involves the production of words, spoken and written, that appear to be "inspirational" but are motivated primarily by a desire for fame and (perhaps) fortune. Since there has been no "opening the way" by the letting go of old crystallized patterns of **beliefs**, no "coming into being" by the balancing of Earth energies with those of other dimensions and no "entering within" by the containing of resisting energies that would be present, the pressure on the throat center would be immense. (Please recall the descriptions of the wounded Teacher and Warrior. In the modern world, they have often presented themselves as spiritual gurus. They must be recognized as the false prophets that they are.) If this is what you have sought to do, please realize, without making any judgments, that there has been a failure, on many levels, to express the incredible Truth about yourself. Then continue with your healing.

Although much healing of the throat chakra will be accomplished by healing the other chakras, (all of the therapies for the root chakra are especially effective), there are several additional therapies that can be used specifically for the throat chakra.

Body Work

You have already experienced the balancing effects of using the opposite color for healing your root chakra. When there is too much blue energy, the balancing color to bring in with breath work is red.

You begin by "scraping" very gently and "pulling off" the excess energies. (They will often feel sticky, like pulling away soft chewing gum.) You will follow this with **grounding** breath work, which you will maintain throughout the therapy.

Proceed with the familiar "Ida/Pingala" breath work, by drawing up colorless energies through the system.

With each exhalation, pucker your lips and blow out "black." (The untruths have created the toxicity.)

After several exhalations, continue the "Ida/Pingala" breath work, by pulling up clear red "balancing" energies. Exhale colorless.

With the help of the Observer, stay tuned into your entire system.

When you sense even a slight "shift" in your throat chakra area, resume pulling in the colorless energies.

After several more exhalations of "black," tune again into the chakra.

If you sense that more red is necessary, resume the red inhalations.

Again, with the Observer tune into your entire system.

When you sense that some "clearing" has been achieved, drink a large glass of pure water.

Continue this exercise, along with others you find effective, until your throat chakra's excess blue energies have been transmuted.

Earth Energies

There are three crystals that are effective in dispelling excess blue energies.

Colorless tourmaline aligns the energy centers of the physical body to those of the etheric. By doing this, the crystal will gently remove the excess blue.

Nuummit, the oldest living mineral, "grounds" your field to both Earth and etheric energies. It balances and aligns the chakras.

Cat's eye is effective in clearing excess energies from the etheric field and protecting it.

In Chinese medicine, there are herbs that are specifically blended to fortify the Spirit. One such herb is **angelica**. It must be prescribed and administered by a competent professional.

Spirit Energies

Until the excess blue has been transmuted and the "lower" animal soul chakras have undergone extensive healing, the spiritual focus must remain on connecting with the energies of Earth with **grounding** breath work. Any practices of meditation and vocalizing should be discontinued. However, your expressions of gratitude and spontaneous prayers along with your times of staying in the stillness will aid in the healing.

If the mis-use of your "voice" has been driven by primitive root chakra energies that are expressed in screaming and/or other loud vocalizations, there will be physical damage to the throat and **too little blue energy**. When there are blockages in the system and there are energies generated by loud quarreling, or by unrestrained vocalizing at sports events, for example, the blue can be completely overwhelmed by red energies.

Too little blue energies can also be the result of physical and or mental abuse that has rendered the person "voiceless." Again, there is an excess of red energies; those that are that are fear-based and survival oriented. The resulting constrictions around the throat are very damaging. With that sort of damage, the etheric matrix could be compromised. This would be indicated by physical dysfunction that has no apparent physical cause.

Body Work

At first it might be necessary to correct the rotation, direction and/or size of your throat chakra front. You will start by scanning the field. If you sense that the chakra is misshapen and/or spinning backwards and/or too small, you might want to practice some "Hands-on Healing." You can do this by lovingly focusing your attention on your throat area and stating your intent to restore the chakra to its normal rotation, spin and size. Without hesitation and with complete trust in the creative energies you embody, lovingly cup your hand about one inch from your throat and gently move your hand in a clock-wise motion. As you feel the chakra responding, gradually move your rotating hand out to about three inches and widen the circle until it is the size of a healthy throat chakra. Continue this motion for several minutes. Then gently remove your hand and drink a large glass of pure water.

You might have to do this restorative work several times before you venture into the work of restoring the blue energies.

The breath work most effective for restoring blue involves "Up the Sushumma," which you will undertake as follows:

After gently "scraping" the entire throat area front and back, take several deep **grounding** breaths. Call in the Observer for assistance.

On the inhalation, pull up a clear cobalt blue color, directly up the sushumma and into the throat chakra. "See" the blue enter into the chakra.

On the exhalation, pucker your lips and blow out "black."

If you sense malfunction in the rotation and/or size of the chakra, go back to the work of healing them.

When that restoration is complete, return to the breath work. (A lot of the healing has already been accomplished.)

After several inhalations of blue directly up the sushumma, note the intensity of the "black" exhalations.

When the "black" has virtually disappeared, change to "reinforcing" orange energies. (You might feel some deep emotions as the work progresses. Let them go by letting them be and continue to inhale the orange color.)

Exhale any remaining "black."

When you sense that a kundalini "shift" has occurred, stop and drink a large glass of pure water.

Continue to do this work until you **know** that you have a "voice" that expresses who you truly are. You are neither a root chakra-driven screaming animal nor a cringing one. (The self-healing therapies you are also practicing, especially those for your root and heart chakras, will vastly augment this throat chakra therapy.)

You can enhance your breath work by "toning" the sound of a healthy throat chakra. In the Ayurvedic tradition, the sound of the throat chakra is "HAM." Listen to the D above Middle C on the piano. "Tone" the sound by taking a deep "grounding" breath and releasing it slowly as your vocal cords generate HHHHH . . . AAAHHH . . . MMMMM. All this time, focus your attention and intent on your throat chakra. Create a strong, deep vibration that you feel in the entire throat area. Repeat this "toning" nine times for one "round." After some practice, add the "toning" for the root ("LAM"), the sacral ("VAM"), the solar plexus ("RAM") and the heart ("YAM") chakras. Do one "round" for each sound. This is very effective self-healing therapy. (As you progress, you will notice that you will be able to sustain the sound of a particular chakra for an ever-increasing length of time. This indicates that the blockages in that chakra have been released.)

As your blue energy builds, you can further enhance the power by body work such as tai chi.

Earth Energies

The crystals you can use to stimulate blue energies are

Blue lace agate, which activates not only the throat chakra but also the heart, third eye and crown. Thus, the crystal helps you to enter into high frequency states of awareness.

Smoky quartz, which is an excellent grounding stone, will strengthen the etheric "body" and refine vibratory energies for meditation.

Lapis lazuli, a stone of total awareness, energizes both the throat and the third eye chakras by clearing them, thus, providing for a unification of all the chakras. The purpose is to maintain the "perfection" within a person.

One of the earliest known medicinal herbs, **lemon balm** was called the "Elixir of Life" and has been used for centuries to strengthen and revive the vital spirit.

Spirit Energies

When there is too little blue energy, "The Ring of Color" guided meditation is a trustworthy practice. This time, you focus on the color blue. Since you are working in high dimensions, make careful preparation and ensure that you will be uninterrupted. Please journal your experience as part of the records you are maintaining with this guided meditation.

A new guided meditation you might want to undertake is entitled "Inside the Etheric Womb." It requires that you undergo age regression into the embryonic stage so that you can heal your throat chakra woundedness, while you remain aware.

Make preparation by setting up a quiet and comfortable space, free of any potential interruptions. Wear loose clothing and have the usual glass of pure water on hand. Dim the lighting. Lie down and start your **grounding** breaths. With the clear intent of healing your throat chakra's wounds, focus your attention on going deeper, deeper and ever deeper into your own beingness.

You have arrived at the deepest place. You are sitting cross-legged on nothing. You sense the thick darkness all around you. You stretch out your arms and your fingertips touch a slippery surface. Slowly, you reach out in all directions and make contact with the slippery surface. As you wait, there gradually appears before you a seated figure that you recognize as your own physical presence. It is naked and seems to be surrounded by dancing kaleidoscope of colors. You watch it as the figure that is you slowly merges into you. You happen to look down at your hands. As you focus your attention on them, they slowly start to change. Gradually they become younger and smaller. Then you realize that the rest of your physical presence is also getting younger and smaller. You feel no alarm or discomfort. Indeed, you watch with fascination as your physicality gradually changes from an adult, to a younger adult, to an adolescent, to a child, to a toddler and to an infant. And all that time, the dancing kaleidoscope of colors surrounding you continues Then you really start to shrink in size and age. Smaller and smaller and smaller you become. Now you are lying on your side in a fetal position. You look at your tiny body and realize that you are a fetus. Still you continue to shrink. Now you are barely formed and the colors dancing around you are very dim . . . except for blue. Then you realize that you have come into that part of your fetal development that requires your help. You cease shrinking. You lie there. Slowly, you begin to sense a loving energy enfolding your littleness.

Then you hear your own voice, as it is in the third dimension, speaking softly as you, the fetus: "I am in the loving environment I have always needed. I am in my own etheric womb. I can speak in the blueness and undo the damage that I sustained in my first gestation. I speak with love and I trust in my creative, generative power. My throat center of consciousness is fully healed. I am expressing who I am." You lie in your etheric womb and **know** that what you have experienced is true.

Then, you slowly resume your gestation. Now the dancing kaleidoscope of colors around you is bright. You look at your physicality as it undergoes the changes from infant, to toddler, to child, to adolescent and, finally, to your present form. You are sitting cross-legged in the container. Your blue throat chakra color is intense as it "dances" with the others. You place your hand gently on your throat. Slowly, you caress it.

Now, return to this time and dimension. Feel your clothed body lying down in your comfortable space. Drink your large glass of pure water. Journal your experience.

In addition to your meditative practices, the practice of vocalizing your prayers will be strong healing therapy. There are many chants connected to all the world's spiritual traditions. You might already have your favorites. If you are still seeking, you might like to try the prayers and chants developed out of the Old Testament *Book of Psalms*, that will connect you to an ancient spiritual practice.[472]

As you continue your practices, you will enhance your awareness of your true beingness and the strictures in your throat chakra will vanish.

In the meantime, trust that with the further healing of your throat chakra, the soul structures of ego/self that have been generated as the result of malfunctioning masculine energies are being transmuted.

---

[472] Try Cynthia Bourgeault, *Singing the Psalms*, an audiotape available from Sounds True.

Your Third Eye Chakra's Malfunction

As was the case with all the others, your third eye chakra malfunctions as the result of unhealthy energies in your inner and outer environments. The damage exhibited by emotionally dysfunctional energies can exist from your prenatal stage. If they continue after your advent, the result can be a malfunctioning sacral chakra (armor plated), and a damaged heart "bridge" as well as a malfunctioning third eye chakra. When "negative" karmic patterns from past lives are also present, the damage is reinforced. The malfunction essentially reveals that you have received too little nurturing both from you and from others.

The malfunction can express in physical dis-eases of the eyes, including astigmatism, cataracts and glaucoma (all related to s desire not to "see.") The psychological problems are those related to self-image. A low self-esteem is revealed in emotional depression and a low physical body image is revealed in anorexia and/or bulimia.

Since it is the third eye chakra consciousness that is a prime component in your choice of a life's career path, damage can result in an inability to "see" what that path truly is. Likely, you will be involved in a career that satisfies the requirements of animal soul consciousness but is not full-filling. In your **holistic** energy system, with the healing of your predominantly feminine sacral and heart centers underway, that situation has likely changed, but more healing could be needed. Remain within your heart awareness and, after recalling (and even repeating) the therapies for those chakras, please focus on the following:

Self-Healing Therapies for Your Third Eye Chakra

When there is **too much purple energy,** there is usually as overload related to intense "visioning" and other meditative practices that have placed too much strain on the pineal gland. As could be the case with your heart and throat chakras, there has been a commitment to "spiritual" practices without the necessary healing of the "lower" animal soul centers of consciousness. There could also be a great emphasis on the development of "otherworldly" connections involving out-of-body experiences and a reluctance to stay in this dimension. In many instances, intimate and other relationships are marked by artificiality and even melodrama. Although much healing can be achieved with the therapies for the sacral and heart centers, there is likely more to be done.

Body Work

When there is too much purple energy, the breath work that is most effective is the "Ida/ Pingala." It is undertaken in the same fashion as that for your malfunctioning sacral chakra. Simply set your attention and intent on transmuting the excess purple energies

After gently "scraping" your aura in the area of your third eye, and being deeply **grounded**, you will proceed to release the toxins that have accumulated and then you will "pull up" the colorless energies. This breath work will positively affect all your chakras. And in the balancing that ensues, your sense of inner empowerment that glows with its feeling/tone of purity, simplicity and unity will be enhanced. Always finish by drinking a large glass of pure water.

Maintain this discipline until you have the sense that your third eye is clear. You will have the help of the Observer to do this. With it you will further "embody" the power of your Healer and Visionary heart archetypes.

Earth Energies

There are two "stones" that help you to transmute too much purple energy.

Pearls, as indicated by the myth, symbolize purity and can stimulate that condition throughout your energy system. As you have already learned, pearls provide both a channel and a vehicle for the in-flowing of wisdom.

Purple fluorite is a third eye stone bringing rationality to the intuitive qualities and assisting in the healing of the physical, emotional, mental and spiritual dimensions of your being.

Spirit Energies

It will be necessary to discontinue the meditative practices that have resulted in the excess purple energies, until you sense a restoration of "balance" in your third eye chakra. By doing the other meditative practices for your sacral and heart centers of consciousness, you will be greatly assisting that process. Your commitment to authenticity in all areas of your life will also help heal your third eye. And again you are reminded that your times of simply doing nothing and resting in the inner stillness will bring healing.

When there is a deep-seated fear of what the future might hold and a reluctance to use your spiritual gifts, there is a stricture in your third eye which results in **too little purple energy**. In addition, the lack of nurturing already mentioned can play an enormous role in producing this situation. In a world where children are left orphaned by civil wars and often required to "raise" themselves, where they are abandoned or sold into sex slavery, or where they are "raised" in an opulent environment where the focus is entirely on animal soul needs and satisfactions, there is not the nurturing necessary to develop the third eye. In such circumstances, wholeness will require a loving commitment to healing the entire energy system. At this stage of your journey, you have already healed much of your third eye dysfunction. But there are several healing therapies that will augment the process.

Body Work

Remain in your heart awareness and begin with several **grounding** breaths. Gently scan the auric field of your third eye front. If there is malfunction in the rotation, direction of "spin" and shape of that chakra, you might want to do the hands-on healing work that has already been suggested for restoring the throat chakra. (At this point in your development, this is work that you can do. But, if you are hesitant, you can seek professional healing help.)

Your breath work again will be "Up the Sushumma." The color this time will be clear purple. Proceed as you did with your throat chakra deficiency. When you introduce the "reinforcing" color, it is clear yellow.

You can enhance this breath work by "toning" the sound of a healthy third eye chakra. In the Ayurvedic tradition the sound of the third eye chakra is "OM." Listen to the E above Middle C on the piano. "Tone" the sound by taking a deep "grounding" breath and releasing it slowly as your vocal cords generate AAAAHHHHH . . . OOOOOHHHHH . . . MMMMM. Focus your attention and intent on your third eye. Create a strong, deep vibration that you feel in the chakra and in your mouth. Repeat this "toning" nine times for one "round." After some practice, add this to the "toning" for those you have already done. Do one "round" for each chakra. As you expand your capacity to "tone," you will be healing all your chakras and expanding your multidimensionality. (Please note that this not a self-aggrandizement. Indeed, the opposite is true. As you expand with "toning," you merge with the sound and release all sense of separate personas. You realize that there is no need for them.)

Other effective body work are the yoga exercises already undertaken to stimulate your sacral and the heart chakras.

Earth Energies

There are three crystals that help to rejuvenate your third eye purple energies.

Rose-eye agate not only stimulates the "balancing" of your masculine and feminine forces, it also stimulates your third eye to enhance you capacity for visioning.

Dioptase has been described as one of the best healing stones of the age. It can be used to clear and stimulate all the chakras. Use of dioptase over your third eye enhances your capacity to "see" to the root of a problem and gain the wisdom to deal with it.

Electric-blue sheen obsidian is an excellent third eye stone which helps you to probe deeply within and to deal with the images that appear. It also helps you to "tune into" your own cellular structure.

Spirit Energies

Any of the meditative work you have received for your sacral and heart chakras has already helped to heal your third eye. The "Pool of Rejuvenation" meditation for your sacral chakra is wonderfully effective.

The "Ring of Color" guided mediation that has become a stand-by is also very effective for your third eye. When working at this high frequency of vibration, make thorough preparation. The color will be purple. When you record your experience this time, your journal will be complete.

A new guided meditation that helps to generate purple energies is entitled "On the Mountaintop." You prepare your space and clothing as you have for the "Seeker's Lamp" the "Ring of Color," the "Pool of Rejuvenation," and "Inside the Etheric Womb." As this is a lengthy meditation, ensure that you will remain uninterrupted. Remain in your heart awareness. With attention and the intent to increase the energies of a healthy third eye chakra, enter deeply within on your **grounding** breaths. Focus within. Focus within . . .

"See" yourself standing on a patch of grass at the foot of a high mountain. You are wearing hiking clothes, including sturdy boots. Lying on the ground at your feet is a knapsack. Pick it up. Look up and "see" the summit.

Then you sense a presence beside you. "See" a very ancient and wrinkled personage. In a gentle and kindly voice, the presence speaks to you:

"Welcome, Soul Searcher. You have traveled far. You are almost at your destination. You will climb the mountain to the summit and see what you have never seen before. But before you reach the mountaintop, you will encounter four huge obstacles. What they will be you do not know. They are the obstacles that still exist within you. I have with me the four things you will need to surmount those obstacles. Here is the first." (You take the object into your hands. Do not question what you receive. "See" the object and trust the process.) "Place it into the knapsack." (You open the knapsack and put in the first object.) "Here is the second." (Again you receive, "see" it and place the object into the knapsack.) "Here is the third." (You repeat the process.) "Here is the fourth." (You receive the final object, "see" it and put it with the others.) Before you can thank the ancient man, he has vanished.

Shouldering the knapsack, you stride forward on to the path that appears before you. The incline is gradual and you walk steadily. The sun is warm on your back and, despite the load within it, the knapsack is light.

Watch the ground in front of you. Suddenly, there is a bend in the trail. Walk around some thick bushes . . . and there is a huge obstacle in your path. "See" it quite clearly and allow your feelings to rise. Stand there and observe every aspect of it. Also observe how it seems to connect with you . . . . Then, pull the knapsack off your back, . . . lay it down, . . . open it . . . and take out the first object you had received from the old one. Now, use it in order to remove the obstacle . . . It vanishes. Shoulder the knapsack and resume climbing.

Now the path gets steeper and the vegetation gets thinner. You have to bend slightly in order to climb. Watch the ground before you very closely. Occasionally, look up and "see" the summit in the distance above you. You come to another bend in the path. Walk around a large outcropping of rock . . . and there before you is the second obstacle. "See" it clearly and allow your feelings to rise. Observe every aspect of it and how it seems to connect with you . . . . Then you again lay down the knapsack . . . open it . . . and take out the second object given to you. Now you use it in order to remove the obstacle . . . . It vanishes. Replace the knapsack on your back and continue your climb.

The path is getting really steep and your legs are starting to get weary. There is nothing around you but rock. You slip occasionally and start climbing slowly with stooped back. Carefully keep your eyes on the path and pause now and then for a "breather." Yet, there above you, the summit awaits. You push on.

Suddenly, there is another bend in the trail. Slowly walk around an outcropping . . . and there is the third obstacle. Again, "see" it clearly and allow your feelings to rise. Carefully observe it and sense its connection with you . . . . Then lay down the knapsack . . . open it . . . and remove the third object the ancient one had given to you. Now use it to remove the obstacle . . . . It vanishes. With a sigh, you shoulder the knapsack and resume your climb.

The path is very steep and slippery with loose pebbles. You are really bent over now and taking few steps before pausing. Your calves are aching and you want to stop. Then look up and there it is . . . the mountaintop appears to be very close. You drop to your knees and crawl. Your hands and knees are scraped . . . and on you go. You lose track of "time" and still you climb. Then, there's the now-familiar bend in the trail. You wearily stand up and walk to meet the final obstacle . . . . There it is! Again, "see" it clearly and allow your feelings to rise. Gently, place the knapsack on the ground . . . open it . . . and remove the last object it has contained. Now use it to remove the final obstacle . . . . It vanishes. And so does the knapsack.

All your tiredness falls away. You joyfully stride those last steps to the mountaintop. What you are feeling is gratitude and an indescribable sense of freedom. With arms raised in blessing and praise, gaze out and "see" such wonders. Slowly turn in a circle and "take in" all that there is to "see" in this splendid moment of accomplishment . . . . "See" it all now and allow the images to enter into your innermost being.

Softly, say to the mountain and the sky: "I am at the pinnacle. And I am ready for whatever will happen in my life."

Now, turn and start to descend . . . . Immediately, you are at the foot of the mountain. Look around for the ancient one. But there is no one in the space.

Then, slowly, return to this dimension. Drink a large glass of pure water. Journal your experience.

Begin your necessary pondering by summoning the Observer. Your established habit of introspection will stand you in good stead. First, please note that the "ancient one" you met at the foot of the mountain was a powerful spirit guide. Unlike the one encountered by both Ny-Eshyn and Eshyn, (and in several of the fairy tales of Lesson Four) this guide came bearing great healing gifts from your indwelling Spirit. Second, the "obstacles" you encountered as you made your ascent were those you have continued to carry as soul structures that impede you on your journey.

Review the entire experience. Then ponder the first gift together with the first obstacle images. Identify them as well as you can. Allow time for insights to rise. Remain in that place of pondering until you receive an insight. If this requires several attempts, be patient. Then proceed with all the others in the same fashion. This is necessary healing work and might take time. Be assured that the inner transmutations and transformations are happening. While the "work" continues, remember the moment on the mountaintop.

Your Crown Chakra's Malfunction

Let us pause briefly and return to the discussion of the energies that can afflict your throat and third eye chakras. When present in the environment prior to and/or after your advent, those energies can also afflict your crown center of consciousness. To be sure, there are varying degrees of affliction and resultant damage and malfunction. To deal with the worst case scenario; if your early years were spent in the appalling conditions of poverty, violence and bloodshed prevalent in many parts of this world, the damage to your crown chakra would be extensive. The dis-eases in your soul structures of physicality could include all or most of your physical "systems;" the glandular, immune system and central nervous system. Because you likely were a "voiceless" victim, this damage could also prevail in your etheric double. In a situation of brutality and lovelessness, there could also be extensive damage to the sacral, heart and third eye chakras. Thus, your soul structures of emotionality could be expressed in the maxim: "kill or be killed." As for your soul structures of mentality, the dis-eases could involve schizophrenia and other psychosis, multiple personality disorder, neurosis and learning disorders.

Although this rarely happens, there can be too much of the white energies in the crown chakra. This can occur when there is a premature kundalini awakening. In other cases of an "explosion" of the white light reported by people usually described as "saints," the experience is very fleeting and often leaves the person unable to communicate what happened. Because the kundalini has been equated with orgasmic sexuality, there are those who strive to awaken it, without the necessary clearing of the "lower" animal soul chakras. For that reason, this lesson includes the self-healing therapies (disciplines) for too much crown chakra energies.

What is usually the case is that there are too little (or no) white energies for the crown chakra. Essentially, there has not been enough because, for whatever the reason, you rejected your own divinity. Mainly, that has been the result of learned ignorance. But there are people who have done this deliberately. How is that possible? There are vulnerable souls who are subjected to such harsh treatment in the name of a particular religion, (for example, they had the "devil beaten out of them,") that in their adulthood they reject that religion and any other forms of "religiosity." But these souls are often soul searchers, whose Life Plan requires that they undertake the rigors of rebirthing.

Self-Healing Therapies for Your Crown Chakra

When there is **too much white energy**, there is the need for **grounding** and remaining closely connected to Earth's energies. The chances are that the "lower" animal soul chakras have required extensive healing. While you stay in your heart awareness, this ongoing healing of your "lower" centers will continue to be the focus of your "work." With the help of the Observer, always include the discipline/practices of letting go/letting be and balancing that will actualize the powers of detachment/discernment and dynamic equilibrium for the emerging holarchy. And into your heart "space" continue the discipline/practice of containing that will actualize the powers of the loving i-am/self. And the focus on the truth about you will invariably promote more translucent knowing. Of course, the "work" of healing your crown chakra will entail many moments of just staying in the inner stillness.

Body Work

All the **grounding** breath work of previous lessons can be undertaken. The "relaxation" breath work is also very helpful. While this is underway, the "scraping" and "pulling off" of the excess crown chakra energies can be undertaken but with **caution**. Within your **holistic** energy system, the "scraping" and "pulling off" can be focused on all of the other chakras, front and back, with only minimal work around the crown itself.

Earth Energies

There are quietening stones that work together.

    Apatite is a stone that can be used with other "grounding" stones to help transmute over-activity in any chakra. For the crown, the other "grounding" stones are **phenacite**, **rhonite**, and **scheelite**.

    By **stimulating** the "lower" chakras, with the crystals, herbs and aromas already given in previous lessons, healing can be achieved in the crown center.

Spirit Energies

    All the meditative work for healing by augmenting the depleted energies of wounded "lower" animal soul chakras and the heart "bridge," helps to heal the crown chakra.

    When there is **too little white energy** in the crown center, the chances are that the entire system is out of balance. The self-healing therapies that are required, first of all, are those that have already addressed the healing of the other chakras.

Body Work

All of the breath work given in previous lessons is effective. At this point, if you sense that more is required, the "pranayama" breath work of the yogic tradition can be undertaken.[473]

You can enhance the breath work by "toning" all the sounds of the chakras. Do this with focused attention and intent. Be aware of the kundalini "shifts" that will inevitably occur, as the vibratory frequency of your energy system is raised and the "dancing" masculine and feminine energies finally achieve dynamic equilibrium. The "tone" for the crown chakra is silence. Remain in your heart awareness and have a reverential sense of high ascension as you complete this "work."

Any of the yogic "poses" given in previous lessons will be effective in healing the crown chakra.

Earth Energies

There are many crystals and other "gifts" of Earth that can stimulate the crown chakra. The most precious ones are these:

The **diamond,** known as the "king of the crystals," has immense power, including that of inspiring creativity, imagination, ingenuity, inventiveness and brilliance. The diamond can stimulate the crown chakra and produce a connecting force between the intellect of the solar plexus chakra and the "higher knowledge" of transcendent spiritual mentality.

Gold, in even a small piece of gold quartz, also has immense power in that it can be used to clear the crown chakra and thereby attain and maintain communion with the Source of all being.

Spirit Energies

Any of the guided meditations given in previous lessons to augment the energies of your "lower" chakras helps to heal the crown. The "Ring of Color" guided meditation you have undertaken with the other chakras can be used for the crown. With reverence, "pull in" the color white. Complete the meditation as usual.

A new guided meditation for the healing of your crown chakra is entitled: "On Holy Ground." This meditation requires that you prepare your own "sacred space," bathe your physical body, wear clean clothing and have ready the Barbra Streisand song, "On Holy Ground."[474] Ensure at least one hour of uninterrupted time. Hold the remote control for your CD player.

Stand in the center of the space and begin your deep **grounding** breaths. After several breaths, start to "pull" the color white up your sushumma. As you do this, gradually "see" your space becoming empty. Then see it slowly filling with gentle, white light. See it enfolding

---

[473] For this you will require the help of specially trained professionals.

[474] The CD is entitled "Higher Ground."

you. When you sense that you are filled with white energies and enfolded in white light, start the music.

Surrender to the sound and to the light. If you want to kneel, please do so. If you feel yourself "dissolving," let it happen. You are completely safe. When the song ends, turn off the CD player and remain in the space. Stay there and savor the wholeness/holiness that you feel. If any thought of old wounds of any kind comes stealing into this precious moment, accept the energies and quietly state: "it's over; it's forgiven; it's released." Then stand, raise your arms and say "thank you." Drink a large glass of pure water. Journal your experiences.

Continue with the healing therapies (disciplines) and disciplines/practices until you have an inner sense of completion.

*   *   *

We have arrived at the culmination of these lessons and of your journey. When all is said and done, what is left is the mystery. Essentially, your rebirthing comes *of* water; the symbol/metaphor of your dark depths of unknowing, when what has been untrue and hidden becomes visible and is transformed by your awareness of the truth. Your rebirthing comes *of* the Spirit;[475] the nucleus of divinity that has guided the process by providing the undercurrents of Life, Light and Love and the upward and downward causation ("as above; so below"). Your rebirthing comes by means of your **holistic** energy system; the Spirit in microcosm, when the consciousness energies of the physical, emotional, mental and spiritual components of your "wheels of light" are healed enough to bring about the transformation of the soul structures they have generated. Above all else, these are the physical, emotional and mental egoic structures of soul (the microcosmic "i-am") that are transformed into the wholeness of self-realization and connection with the indwelling Spirit (the macrocosmic Self/"I-AM"). Your rebirthing comes when you, an energy being that is a soul field, are vibrating at the frequency of readiness. And you are vibrating at that frequency when you come into this realization:

From your first moment of readiness and intent, from your first encounter with the Observer, from your first attempts to "work" with your healing therapies (disciplines) and the disciplines/practices, from the first step of the journey until now, you have been gestating your fully self-realized androgynous being. It has been developing and forming as an emerging holarchy: an androgyny which is constituted of translucent knowing within which the actualized powers of detachment/discernment, dynamic equilibrium and the loving i-am/self are fully expressing; an androgyny, ready for birthing.

Then, there is a "coming-together" point, when all the energies that have been involved in transforming, liberating and regenerating you reach "critical mass." In a culmination (remember Eshyn!) you realize that you have become whole; that in truth you are "real," that your **knowing** has become your **being**. With that awareness, the miracle happens. Your heart awareness: that vast empty/fullness wherein the androgyny has been developing, wherein the

---

[475] Recall from the "Prologue" that "*of*" means "out of" and "part of" and refers to the teaching in *The Gospel of John*.3:1-12.

sense of empowerment has been glowing with purity, simplicity and unity and wherein there is the presence that is you and not-you, becomes a "cave."[476]

And in that cave you, the androgyny, a human energy being in-formed by spiritual humanness, are gently and silently birthed.

When that will happen for any soul searcher cannot be predetermined. You will know it by the sense of balanced centeredness in your heart awareness. You will know it by an inner sense of certainty and completion. What a journey it has been! Stay with it for yet a little while.

This lesson within the stone circle is finished.

With the loving eyes of familiarity, please look around you in this sacred space. You are timeless in a timeless connection that you have been acquiring since your quest began. In this place, that sense of always "now" has become part of the **knowing** and part of the deep vibration of expectancy.

You may leave the stone circle.

* * *

At this point, your culminating path of "Finding Wisdom" ends and has its new beginning. It is this: just as there were the great ones of the wisdom teachings, hereafter you can aspire to be "**moshel meshalim,**" a Master of Wisdom.[477] This is your great treasure and wondrous possibility.

At yet another opening of the way, coming into being and entering within you will continue finding wisdom, but as an androgynous human being. In that "journey," the substance of your final lesson, you will be living the paradox of being both in this third dimension realm of "materiality," and in the multidimensional realms you already **know**. And you will continue to develop your spiritual humanness; the **being** that is all that you really are as an energy being, as a soul field.

Please stay with this lesson in an "interlude" of assimilation. You may deal with all or part of the instruction in whatever manner you are guided. Continue in this, while the inner "shifts" happen. Trustingly await your miracle. It will be there. And when it is, you will be at the end of your quest. But you will also be at the next (and final) stage of your journey. It will be this:

Although your rebirthing quest has brought you into androgyny and, thereby, into another readiness — wisdom readiness — yours (unlike Eshyn's) are in their infancy. Thus, you will continue on your path of "Finding Wisdom," which includes the final interlude and the "afterward." In this journeying, you will find yourself again opening the way and traveling on those other familiar "paths." And you will be living the paradox of being both in this Earth dimension and in your multidimensionality. But having realized your spiritual humanness,

---

[476] There are many references in the Sufi and other Middle Eastern wisdom teachings to the cave of the heart. Also, in some Christmas stories, the stable of Bethlehem is described as a cave. In many spirit journeys, shamans go into the cave of the heart to obtain spiritual knowledge.

[477] For more detail, see Cynthia Bourgeault, *The Wisdom Way of Knowing*, pp.4-5, 13-14 and 84.

you will live that paradox with equanimity and joy. In your ongoing grand adventure, you will continue to evolve, while you become **moshel meshalim**, a Master of Wisdom.

Remain here, Soul Searcher, until you have come to the end of your quest. Then take a well-earned rest before continuing.

Peace and blessings

FOURTH INTERLUDE

Here in the North, in this place of transition, let us pause for another interlude. Unlike the other interludes, it will not be one of further assimilation (you are already vibrating at the frequency of wholeness). But, like the other interludes, it will provide the opportunity for developing yet more inner empowerment. Soul Searcher, although you have achieved so much, there are new attainments awaiting you. In this "work," you will expand and deepen your **knowing** and **being** in order to nurture the androgyny that you have birthed. In other words, you will be a self-nurturing, androgynous energy being living and learning in your spiritual humanness!

Without any fanfare or even a "blaze of glory," you have emerged. After having rested with gratitude, you who are the birther and the birthed are ready to receive further teaching. It will enhance your understanding about the developmental process you have come through and prepare you for what comes next.

You begin by adding insights about yet another undercurrent of the inner divinity. Although you have encountered this aspect of the divine in the myth about Eshyn and Y Chadee (in the "spiritual beings" who required total trust and obedience), you were not told what they symbolized. It had to be left until you were ready to learn more. That undercurrent of the inner divinity is the Law. In the North, on your culminating path of "Finding Wisdom," there has been all along the aspect of Law. In learning about the Law, you can acquire an even greater awareness of the Power that has in-formed you as a soul field.

As a preface, please note that in the shaman's story about your many lifetimes as animal soul, you were reminded about your eternal connection with the Spirit. In other words, in all the times and ways you have lived, the Life, Light and the Love aspects of the indwelling Spirit were always there. Those sustaining Powers were helping you on your chosen journey into wholeness in this lifetime, while you sought to bring about healing changes throughout your **holistic** energy system. Please remember that it is the indwelling Spirit (your nucleus of divinity) that has governed and guided all the functions of that system; all the generative, creative processes that you undertook with the healing therapies (disciplines) and the disciplines/ practices, all the alchemy of transmutation and transformation. Now, let us go deeper.

Eternally part of that governance and guidance is the aspect of Law.

When the poet, Robert Browning, wrote: "I spoke as I saw. I report, as a man may, of God's work: all's love, yet all's law. Now I lay down the judgeship he lent me,"[478] he was describing

---

[478] Robert Browning, "Saul." Verse XVII. Located in www.PoemHunter.com.

what a soul searcher must eventually realize. It is this: that "Love points the way and Law makes the way possible."[479] But there is the word "yet" to consider. It is this: the soul searcher must also realize that although animal soul structures can develop splendidly with nurturing love, a spiritual humanness requires a willing **surrender** to the guidance of the Spirit; a surrender that has been described in these words:[480]

> "Surrender is the way of freedom. It connects us to our
> Source and allows us to blossom as ecstatic beings."

Surrender is a paradox that has been the subject of much pondering throughout many centuries. In your own pondering, please recall the teaching about the covenant between God and people. It is part of the wisdom legacy of Judaism and Christianity and indelibly imprinted in Western culture. In the tradition, the covenant has indicated (as you have already learned) the aspect of Love that is both macrocosmic and microcosmic. Yet, in the wisdom teachings, this aspect of Love has been paired with the requirement of obedience. In the stories out of Judaism, especially, there have been accounts about terrible "punishments" inflicted by a wrathful Jehovah on the disobedient people, who had forgotten the covenant. Now, take your pondering into the **symbolic** meaning of those stories. Over the many centuries since they were first told, there has come the slowly dawning realization that Love and Law (both macrocosmic and microcosmic) are inextricably connected. Even now this connection is not clearly understood, (an animal soul's understanding of "Love/love" is not sufficient) but it has been demonstrated so often that it is impossible not to perceive it. Thus, it is essential that in your spiritual humanness you acknowledge, allow and accept the connection of the Love and Law aspects of the indwelling Spirit.

In anticipation of greater detail later in this interlude, please note that in your quest for wholeness, your connection with the Life, Light, Love and Law was manifested in the "upward causation" that took you "up" into rebirthing and in the "downward causation" that brought the healing energies "down" from your "higher" centers of consciousness. Then, over the heart "bridge" and into the "crucible," where the Love energies could do the "work" of alchemy, the Law of Causality promoted your rebirthing. In your present ponderings embrace your heart awareness of how the aspects of the indwelling Spirit have been sustaining you.

* * *

Then let us venture deeper. Here in the North, in this place of transition, we will explore the manner of your rebirthing.

---

479 Ernest Holmes, *The Science of Mind*, p. 43.
480 Margot Anand, *The Art of Everyday Ecstasy,* p. 214.

We will start with the final lines of a poem by W. B. Yeats. In "The Second Coming," he speaks about the collective animal soul consciousness, but his words also pertain to the individual:[481]

> ". . . a vast image out of *Spiritus Mundi*
> Troubles my sight: somewhere in sands of the desert
> A shape with lion body and the head of a man,
> A gaze blank and pitiless as the sun,
> Is moving its slow thighs . . .
> [. . .]
> And what rough Beast, its hour come round at last,
> Slouches towards Bethlehem to be born?

With that last image you, who are now deeply aware of animal soul consciousness energies, realize that animal soul itself **knows** when it is ready to undertake its inner journey home. Meanwhile, in the metaphor of Bethlehem **the infant androgyny** awaits.[482] And the rebirthing journey, the quest that will generate the holarchy of androgyny, of spiritual humanness and take you into heart awareness — into the cave of the heart symbolized by the Bethlehem stable — gets underway.

Throughout the entire journey, there are the "pangs" of birthing. By following the paths and accepting all the challenges, you are permitting the "labor" to progress. At first, the allowing takes all the spiritual courage you can muster, for your soul structures of emotionality, your very own Wheel of Samsara, carry on a determined "resistance." Those conflictual energies create your labor. Interacting closely with your root chakra's consciousness energies of survival drives and needs and dominating your **belief** structures, those emotional consciousness energies show you no mercy. In addition, the thought content of your soul structures of mentality, which include your "personality," is driven by those emotional energies. In your mental twistings and turnings, you can find yourself seriously doubting the wisdom and the real practicality of the soul "work" you are doing. In addition, your egoic structures; those soul structures that have come about as the result of the workings of the "i-am" consciousness of your animal soul chakras can be "torn." You can experience apparently schizoid ego/selves frequently expressing an agonizingly conflicted inner environment. As you persist along your paths, the emotional energies resist. That is the "labor pain" and there is no escape from it. This is what happens, especially in the beginning when your "lower" centers of consciousness are undergoing the alchemy of transmutation, your crystallized soul structures of emotionality are being transformed and your soul substance is being shaped anew. (This process has been compared to the metamorphosis endured by a caterpillar in its cocoon "container," in which

---

[481] W. B. Yeats, "The Second Coming," taken off the Internet at Poets.org (From the Academy of American Poets).

[482] Therein lies the immense paradox about animal soul, referred to in Lesson Three. Not only does animal soul **know** its own readiness but it also **chooses** to take its rebirthing journey home to its own inner being, the indwelling Spirit.

it is enclosed and completely dissolves. After every part of the caterpillar has been liquefied, it is reshaped **out of the original material but with a new design,** into a butterfly. During its alchemy of transformation, the caterpillar likely experiences terrible pain.)

In a different context, the beginning period of rebirthing can be described as the "dark night of the soul." It is marked by feelings of aloneness and even abandonment. Those animal soul energies in the darkest obscurities cannot even sense the indwelling Spirit. And, until there has been some healing of those centers of consciousness with the corresponding kundalini "shifts" in the soul structures of physicality, emotionality and mentality, your egoic structures will largely remain unchanged. In other words, in your "dark night" of aloneness and pain, your "i-am" self-identification, deriving from the "i-am" statements of your animal soul centers of consciousness, will continue to express their damage and to be in-formed (by and large) by your unhealed soul structures of emotionality. (Please recall that these multidimensional structures can be regarded as an "entity" and can be enormously powerful.)[483]

But, there has been from the beginning, a four-fold spiritual power, a gentle, persistent undercurrent promoting the transformation, liberation and regeneration of animal soul. The power has been emanating from your nucleus of divinity, the indwelling Spirit, your inner guidance system. Even in the darkest, blackest "night" you have endured, that Power has been constant. During your quest, you were accepting the Power in the times when you meditated (perhaps in tears) and when you simply stayed in the stillness. Although you have already learned a great deal about it, that Power can now be described in its deepest dimensions; as the "midwives" present throughout your rebirthing journey.[484]

First, there is the Life aspect of the Spirit; present in you and in the **grounding** energies of both your legacy of wisdom teachings and your connection with Earth consciousness. On the ongoing quest, as you "open the way," you gradually experience a deep feeling/tone of inner strength that sustains you. With this fortifying influx, there comes the will to persist. It is a quiet, uncontrolling will that carries the confidence synonymous with "faith." As the Life energies permeate your soul field, there comes a deepening sense of freedom. But it is a new kind of freedom, linked not to your root chakra's need for feeling safe, secure and "in charge," nor to your solar plexus chakra-generated "personas." It is the freedom expressed in an increasingly tangible "sensation" of inner empowerment. And this sensation is expressing the power of the emerging holarchy, which has its beginnings in your first encounters with the Observer and then, in the disciplines/practices of letting go/letting be. The power of discernment/detachment (the holon of the self-actualized androgyny) is being gestated. With each kundalini "shift," there emerge the many other Life qualities that add to that sense of inner empowerment; authenticity, vitality, purpose, focus, courage, confidence, self-esteem and openness, to mention a few. As you experience them, always with the steadfast assistance of the Observer, you **know** them and you identify with them, while your animal soul "i-am"

---

[483] On extremely rare occasions, the "entity" is a "killer" energy that has "possessed" the soul field. Often, during loving self-healing "work," that type of entity will leave on its own. If it does not, exorcism by a qualified spiritual healer will be necessary.

[484] This is a metaphor borrowed from the sermons of Meister Eckhart.

identifications of physicality, emotionality and mentality are slowly being re-formed. In other words, as **form follows consciousness**, your egoic structures of animal soul gradually transform into identification with the qualities of Life. And you are already shedding the impurities, excesses and complications of a survival-oriented animal soul. The qualities of Life are who you really are and you start to **know** this.

The second aspect of your indwelling Spirit undercurrent is that of Light. It is always there on your busy path of "Coming into Being," as you seek with your seeker's lamp of "ground" luminosity. Within the illumination provided by the Light energies, the truth about who you really are comes increasingly to the fore. In that illumination, the personas, especially the "shadows" that you have mistakenly believed were "you," are revealed as what they are. And those immense structures are gradually transformed. As the Light permeates your soul field, you add to the sense of inner empowerment the illuminated qualities of purity and simplicity. All this has been taking place while you gestated the powers of detachment and discernment and "worked" assiduously with the discipline/practice of balancing. Into the emerging holarchy there was added the power of dynamic equilibrium (the second holon of the self-actualized androgyny). This is directly related to your masculine and feminine energies of consciousness; the masculine and/or feminine forces in your chakras and inherent in the soul substance which has been crystallized into egoic soul structures. These are slowly healed and brought into balance. Thus, there is a slow but steady "invitation to the dance." And in the "dance" there is the expression of the new type of "self" that is developing while the animal soul egoic structures, that are the expressions of the "out-of-rhythm" masculine and feminine forces, are changed. Then, while **form follows consciousness**, your egoic structures of animal soul are transformed into identification with the qualities of Light. They are who you really are and you start to **know** this. While that happens, you experience the other side of "faith;" namely, "trust." That power, by mitigating the power of resistance, gently softens the labor of rebirthing. And in this development, you add to your inner empowerment and to its illuminated purity and simplicity.

The third aspect of your indwelling Spirit undercurrent is that of Love. It is already awaiting you on your path of "Entering Within." The incredible power of Love often appears as an energy gradually permeating your soul field **after** the Life and Light aspects have been expressing their Power. To explain: while "entering within," you begin the transformation of the soul structures of lovelessness that you have carried. In the great "work" of your heart crucible, the transmutation of your heart energies requires the Life and Light aspects as a **preparation** for the inflow of Love that heralds the last phase of rebirthing into androgyny. This preparation is implied in the great "love" message of Paul's letter to the Corinthians.[485] It reveals that along with the magnificent qualities that express Life and Light, your spiritual humanness requires the qualities of Love. And as Paul describes them, those qualities are immense. They include compassion, empathy, constancy, tolerance, fortitude and kindness. During the alchemy of transformation, they, too, in-form your sense of inner empowerment.

---

[485] See *I Corinthians* 13: 1-7.

And while this is happening, you have already added the third holon of your emerging holarchy with the discipline/practice of containing, which has been actualizing your power of the loving i-am/self. It has been emerging out of the powers of discernment/detachment and dynamic equilibrium, while the Love energies impacted upon your root, sacral and solar plexus chakras, and yet more of your egoic structures of animal soul underwent transformation.

Increasingly, you are becoming "real;" who you truly are.

As a brief aside: your entire process of rebirthing has been described as the spiritual form of alchemy that both the pre-Christian and the medieval alchemists knew was the real subject of alchemical exploration. Its prime purpose was to produce a "conscious integration of the human subject with its own transcendent nature."[486] This was (and still is) the "heart work" of alchemy.[487] It brings about the great empty/fullness that is your heart awareness.

And you start to discern you and another Presence in your expanding heart awareness. You start to embrace yourself (and others) with compassionate detachment and discernment. You are starting to **know** who you are . . . with love.

And so it is that animal soul/Beast starts its rebirthing journey into wholeness by heeding the inner "call." In this chosen obedience, animal soul surrenders to the Law, the fourth and the most mysterious aspect of your indwelling Spirit. The Law is eternally immutable, implacable and impersonal. It is the Law that undergirds the entire process. It is the Law that allows you to invoke the Life and the Light, which in turn prepare you for the inflow of Love. By heeding the call and by accepting the Law, animal soul enters into the "covenant" with the indwelling Spirit. The Law has been permeating the soul field that is you ever since your conception. Your animal soul centers of consciousness have been able to generate your soul structures, including your egoic structures, because the Law has been present. When the journey of rebirthing commences, there is the choice of surrendering into obeying and trusting. In order for wholeness to evolve, there is the accepting and the enduring of the birthing pangs. As the journey progresses, the obedience and trust become the commitment to the covenant and to the requirements of Truth. In consequence, you expand your great heart awareness, while the indwelling Spirit guides you along the culminating path of "Finding Wisdom." In the final stage of gestating your self-actualized androgyny, there is added the fourth holon; the translucent knowing that has been slowly actualizing with all the other disciplines/practices but especially with the discipline/practice of revealing/concealing (your commitment to Truth). In your ongoing gestation, because **form follows consciousness** your egoic structures are also transformed by the power of the Law into the fundamental qualities of what you are as an energy being, a soul field. In addition to those of Life, Light and Love already being developed, the qualities of the Law include equanimity, centeredness, patience and calmness. With that development, your experience of an inner empowerment of illumined purity, simplicity (and

---

[486] Joscelyn Godwin, *The Golden Thread: The Ageless Wisdom of the Western Mystery Traditions*, p. 119.
[487] For more detail, see Mark Stavish, *The Path of Alchemy*, pp.19, 37, 149 and 170. See also Julius Evola, *The Hermetic Tradition*, "The Centers of Life," pp.56-59, pp. 127 and 128.

now) unity nears completion. With it you also increasingly discern the great Presence that is you and not-you. It is the incalculable prize that awaits a questing animal soul.

* * *

There is more that you must understand about this rebirthing experience. It is this: you have not been merely the passive recipient of spiritual re-shaping. Indeed, while you have received the immense spiritual powers that have just been described, you have also been directly involved in an essential "work" of creativity. This was possible because you are the microcosmic creator, whose focused creative energies were "working" from the moment you set your intent and stepped into the circle of stones. Thereafter, you repeatedly summoned up and tapped into your creative energies. You did this by connecting with the shaman's spirit world, by taking in the shaman's stories and by immersing yourself in the myths and fairy tales. By using your creative energies, you increasingly became a multidimensional soul searcher in the "imaginal realm."

Now you can be given more insights into that "place" of creativity. By stepping inside the stone circle and outside the narrow "body/mind" context you had hitherto lived in, you were opening to the great awareness provided by your "awakened imagination."[488] This energy consciousness has been, all along, an essential component of the imaginal realm. While being involved with your imagination in the stone circle, you were directly triggering the energies of rebirthing. Then, at the conclusion of each lesson, after leaving the circle, you were required to live in this third dimension and to continue the quest by undertaking the self-healing therapies (disciplines) and the disciplines/practices. With the help of the Observer, these were exercises in focusing your imagination (and gestating your androgyny).

In short, while you struggled out of your darkest obscurities, you were slowly changing your soul structures by using your own creative power. Then, during the first, second and third interludes while you focused on assimilating the lessons, you expanded the **knowing** that was increasingly becoming your **being**. Please note that **your own efforts were required before anything could be accomplished. By "working" in this manner, you were triggering the awaiting spiritual undercurrents and connecting with the Law.**

Truly, you have been involved in both a grand adventure and a mystery!

Out of the mystery and the intensity of rebirthing, you the androgynous "image and likeness" have finally emerged. Your eternal covenant with the Creator/Spirit is providing a new beginning. And again there is paradox, for you as Little Soul have **known** all along who you were and where you were heading. It is in the **knowing** that you have become the **being**, although this was not part of your immediate awareness. It is an immense paradox that can

---

[488] The connection between human creative energy and imagination is discussed in Ernest Holmes' *The Science of Mind*, p. 600. For a detailed description of the creative process that requires the integration of "believing" and "knowing," see Neville, *Awakened Imagination*, pp. 11-33. For accounts of the relationship of imagination to the imaginal realm, see Cynthia Bourgeault, *The Wisdom Way of Knowing: Reclaiming an Ancient Tradition to Awaken the Heart*, pp. 79-90. For a discussion of the crucial difference between imagination and fantasy, see Joscelyn Godwin, *The Golden Thread: The Ageless Wisdom of the Western Mystery Traditions*, pp. 124-125.

be understood in this way: **since consciousness energies are both the energies of knowing and the energies of soul, and the energies of soul are both the energies of knowing and the energies of being, the knower and the known are one and the same. i.e., the knowing and the being are one and the same. In your rebirthing, there is the realization that in the knowing, you, the microcosm, are both actualizing and connecting with the being that you are. To go further; since you are an expression of the Divine and the divinity is the indwelling Spirit, when you realize your being, you are coming closer to connecting with the Spirit, the great "I-AM."**

There are some additional insights to "explain" what has happened with you . . .

As the old crystallized structures of soul are transmuted, you experience the kundalini "shifts" that are simultaneously those of energies and awareness. In all of this shifting you are shedding your ignorance and slowly entering into the **knowing.** In this learning, your perceptual filtering system, that has been in-formed by the inner and outer environmental energies impacting upon it, undergoes change. It starts to "filter" through the "fabric" of the Truth instead of the fear-based, ignorance-sustained beliefs that you have discovered (during your "worm-hole" and other explorations) to be predominantly untrue. Thus, with the healing of your root chakra's perceptual filtering system, your archetypal human energy system, of which the perceptual filtering system is an essential part, undergoes purification. And with that healing, there is an increasing simplicity and unity of perception. Thus, while you are shedding your learned ignorance, you are developing your sense of illumined inner empowerment and enshrining Truth.

So you have birthed into androgyny by undergoing a type of "gestation" in which you, a microcosmic, multidimensional energy being, both the creator and the receiver of inner empowerment, re-form your soul structures, by gestating and bringing forth the holarchy; the **knowing** of who you truly are. It is the **knowing** that is **your** spiritual humanness, It is the **knowing** that has become a **being** that is **your** "real" and androgynous self. Now you are ready to express that which is newborn and you declare with joyful relief, humility and gratitude: "I am the aware medium, the conscious medium itself."[489] It is your glorious statement about you as an energy being, a soul that "speaks" a wholeness that includes all your substance, all your centers of consciousness, all your soul structures and all your "i-am." It is your statement about you as an energy being of authentic empowerment and true humanness.[490]

* * *

---

[489] A.H. Almaas, *The Unfolding Now*, p. 136.

[490] If you have been working with the Abraham Maslow (and others) "needs hierarchies," you have likely acquired deep insights into your own rebirthing process.

Please remain in this interlude for as long as it is necessary for you to be centered in the **knowing**. While you stay here, you might want to heed these thoughts of a Christian **moshel meshalim**, who equated wholeness and holiness in these words:[491]

> *"What is the test that you have indeed undergone this holy birth?*
> *Listen carefully.*
> *If this birth has truly taken place within you,*
> *then no creature can any longer hinder you.*
> *Rather, every single creature points you toward God*
> *and toward this birth.*
> *You receive a rich potential for sensitivity,*
> *a magnificent vulnerability.*
> *In whatever you see or hear, no matter what it is,*
> *you can absorb therein nothing but this birth.*
> *In fact, everything becomes for you*
> *nothing but God.*
> *For in the midst of all things,*
> *you keep your eye only on God.*
> *To grasp God in all things,*
> *that is the sign*
> *of your new birth."*

And afterward . . . please pause and realize this; that you are likely entering into the grandest adventure you have undertaken thus far. You are an androgynous energy being; a unique, microcosmic anthropos, a multidimensionality who is looking forward to walking **with** the indwelling Spirit. But you are in a state of infancy that requires considerable nurturing and nourishing for all its ongoing development. Thus, while you continue your journeying, you will again set about opening the way, coming into being, entering within and all along you will be finding wisdom. There are exciting times ahead!

Peace and blessings

---

[491] Matthew Fox, *Meditations with Meister Eckhart*, p. 83. Please keep in mind that Meister Eckhart referred to the Spirit (the One Consciousness, the Creative Energy) as "God" and that you are God-like as the microcosmic creative energy.

Lesson Eight

AND AFTERWARD

Hello: at the end of such a long winter season . . . welcome again to the stone circle. This morning we celebrate the arrival of the springtime . . . in many ways. While there are still some snow patches along the pasture fences, here on the crest all is clear. See, in this light-filled enclosure the tender, new grass is appearing. And here you are, a seasoned soul searcher, returning to a much-loved place of nurturing. Into this sacred space, where transcendent Spirit dwells, please make your accustomed way. And in the early "springtime" of your life, in your newborn androgyny, welcome!

Come here to the center. Stand quietly for a moment while you **ground** with Earth's familiar energies and bask in the embrace of Long Meg and her Children.

Look around you. In this stone circle everything has changed (even the stones) and everywhere in both your outer and inner environment there is "newness." Yet, at the same moment, there is all-pervading "sameness." And you, who are well acquainted with paradox, are ready to explore this one. Here is your warm poncho to ward off any lingering wintry breezes and here's your ground cover. Please be seated . . . .

Look around you and experience, yet again, your connection with all the energies of this Earth plane. Now, prepare to expand your **knowing** and your **being** yet further.

In this stone circle and everywhere outside of it, you are surrounded by and you are included in "an unceasing process of disintegration and renewal."[492] In this constant beginning-ending-beginning cycle, the paradox that you will explore is both concealed and revealed. In other words, both the newness and the sameness are the eternal Truth inherent in the cycle.

In that ongoing process, there is the constant Presence of a transcendent, immanent and unchanging Spirit, the eternal sameness, in which you live, move and have your **being**. In this moment, you can tune into that Consciousness Energy. You have already done this many times in your moments of deep stillness and focused awareness, when you were experiencing the undercurrents of Life, Light, Love and Law. Now, please remember that these aspects of the indwelling Spirit, your nucleus of divinity, were constantly in attendance on your rebirthing journey. And they were constantly the same, while you labored through all your "endings" (all the letting go/letting be, all the kundalini "shifts") and all your "beginnings"

---

[492] For more detail, see Sri Aurobindo, *The Life Divine*, p. 190.

344

(all the balancing, all the containing, all the revealing/concealing.) Do you perceive how you are the microcosm of the macrocosmic unending sameness? Do you realize how you are a microcosmic anthropos?

And the sameness of you will continue after your rebirthing in two more essential ways. This is an awareness that you must carry with you.

First, although your quest for wholeness has resulted in a wondrous achievement (you are a newborn, self-actualized androgyny), you still embody the microcosmic, archetypal energy system that you had as animal soul. In other words, you are a soul field, a microcosmic creative consciousness energy being of whom the qualities, the prime directive, the "i-am" statement of consciousness, and the generative function and power of each center of your energy system have remained indelibly unchanged. That sameness will continue.

Second; as your "afterward" unfolds, you will require the sameness of a consciousness energy that has been with you all along. The Observer, your steadfast companion throughout your rebirthing quest, is there to assist you as you "grow up." At this point in your **knowing** and **being**, tune into the energies of the Observer. From within your deep sense of glowing inner empowerment, what is the feeling/tone you get about your relationship to the Observer? (Pause and ponder.) . . . Perhaps you require more time to come into further realizations. They will come. In the meantime, please be aware of the immanence[493] and unchanging sameness of the Observer.

And here is a word of caution for you to carry with you:

The chances are good that there will be, for a little while longer, traces of the old animal soul structures. As such, they are a sameness that can reappear in unexpected ways. Thus, your "shadow" energies of wounded Child, Victim, Prostitute and Saboteur could still present themselves. There might even be some vestiges of the shadows of your heart archetypes. And some old personas, such as the Critic or the Controller, might also be very slow in departing. All of them were well-established patterns that have left deep traces. But, now you have your heart awareness; the immense capacity both for recognizing them and for lovingly encouraging them to transform. Thus, this sameness will **not** continue as it has been. You are not the old "selves" you thought you were. You must not forget that you, the newborn androgyny, the anthropos in microcosm are the aware, conscious and creative medium.

And the newness will also continue.

It is there in the unceasing beginning-ending-beginning cycle, both in you and around you. In you, the newness is the vibratory frequency of wholeness, i.e., the healthy capacity of each one of your centers of consciousness to interact with the others and generate soul structures that express Life, Light, Love and Law. And as time goes by, the newness will continue, because you will constantly be generating the holarchy of wholeness. In this respect, you will always be complete and a "work in progress"! You, the paradox, will be both the sameness and the newness. And, in this moment, while you are experiencing the changes wrought by all

---

[493] To assist in your pondering, see Paul Brunton, "The Hidden Observer," in *The Wisdom of the Overself*, pp. 141-147. The teaching is that it is only the presence of the Observer that makes it possible for you to be a Self.

the unchanging spiritual energies that have brought you into your rebirthing, please be aware that in this place of springtime, those energies of sameness are being revealed everywhere in/ as the amazing newness. Take some time to assimilate this paradox . . . and prepare for the next one . . . .

Please know that your androgyny is both a newness that you have become and a sameness that you have always been. The Truth is that "we do not become androgynous; we already are. It is necessary only to let ourselves be ourselves."[494] Being your paradoxical, androgynous self, however, is not effortless. This newness requires that you consistently practice your capacity to "dance" the masculine and feminine "opposites within."[495] This, in turn, requires that you lovingly focus on how precious you are, while you experience your wholeness and your constantly expanding inner empowerment. And all of this is a manifestation of your evolving spiritual humanness. (It seems rather miraculous after your experiences as animal soul with all its permutations! But, there it is.) To describe it differently and to add some "finishing touches:" a newborn, androgynous human being, a self-realized energy being, soul field, is a quietly "joyful aliveness" marked by a commitment to Truth,[496] by compassion for oneself and others, and by the awareness that despite the ups-and-downs of an ordinary life, it can be lived in an extraordinary way.

You, the newborn androgyny, the anthropos in microcosm are heading out into uncharted territory. In your newness, you are venturing onto your simultaneous paths of "Opening the Way" and "Finding Wisdom" with nothing external, neither map nor manual, to guide you. But you have your inner guidance system And you have all that you have become and are still becoming. There is the constantly changing newness of your **knowing** and **being** as an ever-expanding, multidimensional, microcosmic wholeness and there is the unchanging sameness of your nucleus of divinity, the indwelling Spirit. That is sufficient.

Now take in a shaman's story that you will co-create. It will be about you in the "afterward" of your rebirthing. In that new journey, while you make your way in both this dimension and in the imaginal realm, you will be involved in a "parenting" experience that will greatly augment your spiritual humanness. Again, be prepared for paradox. On the one hand, you will be nurtured and nourished by caring others in this dimension, and you will be nurtured and nourished by caring spirit guides, in the imaginal realm. On the other hand, you will nurture and nourish yourself by co-creating and living this story. After all, it *is* all about you!

Come; take your first steps. Your story starts like this . . . .

Into this lifetime you, Little Soul,
Bringing your Life Plan . . . and your karma,
Incarnated as a human being.
As such, you were an androgynous soul field,

---

[494] June Singer, *Androgyny: The Opposites Within*, p, 199.
[495] If you want to hear the sound of that dance, please listen closely to Nicolo Paganini's Concerto in F for Guitar and Violin.
[496] A commitment to Truth involves not only seeking it but also living it in all ways.

A microcosmic energy being,
An immense creative power,
An anthropos,
But you didn't know that.

Although you were an expression of the Divine,
No one, including you, recognized you.

Throughout your "growing up" years
You made your way as animal soul;
A fear-based, instinctual, physical survival-oriented being,
In a state of ignorance and spiritual immaturity
Of which you were totally unaware.
And you did not discover who you really were
Because the other people in your life
Were also animal souls.

Your "knowing" was what you and the others believed,
Your "being" was what you and the others thought you were.

Although you were supposed to be "at home" on this Earth plane
There was deep within you an existential aloneness;
A feeling/tone of not-quite belonging.
While your Life Plan unfolded without your awareness,
You related to your sacred contracts, for better and for worse,
And you related, in your own way, to the rest of humanity.

As the years of this lifetime rolled on,
And you manifested the results of your soul shaping:
The soul structures; physical, emotional, mental and spiritual
That your energy system, your creative power, had generated.
There was no realization, except perhaps a dull ache,
That you were wounded and carried huge holes,
That you were animal soul in need of rebirthing into wholeness.

[Pause here and add your own thoughts to the account. If you prefer, you might even start an autobiographical "modern" myth or fairy tale. There is a great need in this world for that sort of "story." There are deep layers of symbolic meaning that could be developed. If you have already started your own "sacred story," however, please feel inspired to continue.]

Then one day, you heeded the "call" of your indwelling Spirit
Who had always been there "calling" to you
You finally paid attention to your "readiness messages,"
Because you really were a soul searcher.

And you started on your quest for wholeness;
Your inner journey "home,"
Whose first phase brought you
Toward the indwelling Spirit.

You became a pilgrim whose journey followed the shaman's "paths."

In the East, South, West and North
You opened the way, came into being, entered within
And found the beginnings of wisdom.

During your quest, your disciplines/practices involved
The letting go/letting be (the releasing),
And the balancing and containing (the collecting),
Of immense energies,
While you slowly expanded your capacity for revealing/concealing
The truth about you, your relationships and your "world."

During that quest you were actualizing the immense powers
Of detachment/discernment,
Of dynamic equilibrium,
Of the loving i-am/self
And of translucent knowing.

You were actualizing those powers
As an emerging holarchy;
The androgynous being that you really were.

Throughout your journey
In a "labor" that was intense, you struggled
To transmute your centers of consciousness
And transform your crystallized animal soul structures,
To heal all the wounding and damage you had carried for years,
Perhaps for lifetimes.

Then you, an androgynous human being, finally emerged.
The soul searcher had realized spiritual humanness
The soul searcher had become anthropos
Eagerly willing to evolve into greater knowing and being.
And the next phase of your inner journey home began.

You had stepped into the "now"
And decided to stay there.

[Pause here in the story and add your own experiences of "shifting." Explore and describe your developing sense of awareness and of empowerment. Use the context of holarchy, if you are comfortable with it]

You have a deep yearning to become *moshel meshalim*,
While you joyfully live in this world
Where troubles can abound and nothing is certain
Except the beginning-ending-beginning cycle
Of every living thing.

You sense the nearness of the indwelling Spirit,
Whose aspects of Life, Light, Love and Law
As undercurrents, flow within you.
And you rely on the ever-present Observer.
You know that you are a microcosmic anthropos,
An energy being, a soul field.
You embrace your multidimensionality
And you set your intent
To live in this third dimension and in the imaginal realm,
To recognize and continue on your paths,
To allow the indwelling Spirit to guide you,
To surrender to the process and
Continue to grow.

[Pause here and add your awareness about Life, Light, Love and Law and how those undercurrents sustain you. Them tell about the role of trust, faith and obedience in your process.]

As you step forth on your next grand adventure,
Here are four "instructions;"

First, from the Lakota wisdom teachings:[497]

> "Friend, do it this way,
> that is, whatever you do in life
> do the very best you can
> with both your heart and mind.
>
> And if you do it that way,
> The power of the Universe
> will come to your assistance,
> if your heart and mind are in Unity.

---

[497] "Lakota Instructions for Living" from *Lakota Wisdom and Other Related Texts*, found on the Internet.

When one sits in the Hoop of the People,
one must be responsible,
because all of Creation is related
and the hurt of one is the hurt of all,
and the honor of one is the honor of all
and whatever we do
affects everything in the Universe.

If you do it that way,
that is, if you truly join
your heart and mind as One,
whatever you ask for
that's the Way It's Going to Be."

The second "instruction" is from the Tao Te Ching:[498]

"I have just three things to teach:
simplicity, patience, compassion.
These three are your greatest treasures.
Simple in actions and in thoughts,
you return to the source of being.
Patient with both friends and enemies,
you accord with the way things are.
Compassionate toward yourself,
you reconcile all beings in the world."

The third instruction is from an outstanding scholar of the twentieth century;[499]

"[Follow your bliss] . . . if you follow your bliss, you put yourself on a kind of track that has been there all the while waiting for you, and the life that you ought to be living is the one you are living. Wherever you are if you are following your bliss, you are enjoying that refreshment, that life within you, all the time."

The fourth "instruction" is from a great modern spiritual teacher:[500]

"The Spirit [. . .] is reminding you
That you are an exquisite, precious and powerful being.
Shine! Sing!

---

[498] Quoted in Philip Novak, *The World's Wisdom: Sacred Texts of the World's Religions*, p. 164.
[499] Joseph Campbell, *The Power of Myth*, p. 113.
[500] Michael Bernard Beckwith, *Spiritual Liberation*, p. 219.

Be bold enough to articulate what you are sensing, feeling
and knowing.
Now is the time for you to partner with that
immense power.
Allow the tidal wave of the divine inspiration to
wash over you and express in, through and as you.
Consciously and confidently enter the sacred process
of co-creation,
Because That which expresses as you does not happen
through anyone else
in quite the same way.
Become a master of your own divine, radiant, creative
expression."

[If you resonate with these words, pause to reflect on the ways in which you are being asked to relate to yourself, to all other living things and to this Earth. Put this into your story. If you do not resonate with these words and you already respond to other teachers and teachings, please include them.]

While opening the way into further spiritual humanness
And into finding wisdom,
You are carrying a multidimensional awareness of
Your soul structures and how they are expressing themselves.
You discern their "forms" with loving detachment and
Recognize those that are still awaiting your healing attention.
And you realize that becoming *moshel meshalim* means relating
Truthfully, first of all to you.

And, here at the outset, you are gratefully aware that
The constant Presence — the you that is not-you
Is accompanying your tentative steps,
And that the Life, Light, Love and Law undercurrents
Are subtly sustaining and guiding you.

And you,
With the help of the Observer
And with focused intent, reverence and abiding trust
Embrace, first of all, your physicality.
For It is your connection to this Earth plane.

As you love this Earth, you love your soul structures of physicality
In all their manifestations, including your sexuality and gender.
Knowing your "maleness" or "femaleness," as what they really are
Not as what you maintained in your ignorance,

You relate to your physicality with Truth.
You treasure your unique characteristics.
And you "dance" the masculine and feminine,
While now, you allow for different orientations.
You explore your necessary "gender" choices and
Embrace a lifestyle that is both balanced and wise.

In all your awareness of your physicality
You are connecting with your glowing inner empowerment.
And you remain centered and grounded.

[Pause here to ponder the requirements of your soul structures of physicality. Be thoroughly aware of any karmic patterns. Welcome the ways in which you are being assisted by those around you and by the guides within. Again, explore the layers of symbolic meaning, while you maintain the narrative.]

And, your other soul structures are continuing to be re-shaped
In this expanding and deepening relationship you are cultivating
With all that you are.

In this there is both the sameness and newness.

The sameness is that your "subtle" bodies of consciousness
Are constantly being generated and regenerated,
While you continue opening the way.
And with your commitment to Truth
You joyfully embrace the power of your heart archetypes;
The Teacher, Healer Warrior and Visionary,
Who have become part of your heart awareness;
The guides ceaselessly working
In you, through you and as you.

And the newness is that all your bodies of consciousness
Are vibrating at the increasingly higher frequency of pure Light
In their interpenetrating "dance"
That enhances your relatedness with you,
While you expand your relatedness with others.
And you increasingly become aware that
Because you are connected in a web of life with others
Whose soul field has impacted, often intimately, on yours,
You are also opening the way
To, perhaps, different involvements with them.

In your Truth, your relationships with intimate others

Become new in different ways.
There might occur a "letting go."
There might occur a "letting be."
There might be new soul contracts and new intimacies in store.

And you become increasingly aware of the inner Love/Light/Being,
The wondrous Presence that you know is you and not-you.
Then, you realize, at last, that the inner Love/Light Being
Is the Beloved
And you journey toward that meeting;
First, in this dimension.

One day, the meeting happens
And you share the surprised delight of the poet
When his "soul mate" came along:[501]

> "One day in spring a woman came
> In my lonely woods,
> In the lovely form of the Beloved.
> Came, to give to my songs, melodies,
> To give to my dreams, sweetness.
> Suddenly a wild wave
> Broke over my heart's shores
> And drowned all language.
> To my lips no name came,
> She stood beneath the tree, turned,
> Glanced at my face, made sad with pain,
> And with quick steps, came and sat by me.
> Taking my hands in hers, she said:
> "You do not know me, nor I you.
> I wonder how this could be?"
> I said:
> "We two shall build, a bridge forever
> Between two beings, each to the other unknown,
> This eager wonder is at the heart of things."

Meanwhile, your connection with the "world" becomes clearer.
You start to welcome the stranger at your gate.
(Although you might note the vestiges of your "shadows,"
You walk in your Life strength, Light awareness and Love trust).
And you heed some wisdom teachings from the Arabs who say:[502]

---

[501] Aurobindo Bose (trans.), *The Later Poems of Rabindranath Tagore*, p. 62.
[502] Naomi Shihab Nye, "Red Brocade," in *19 Varieties of Gazelle* Copied from a greeting card created for KPFA Free Speech Radio, 2008.

"When a stranger appears at your door
feed him for three days
before asking who he is,
where he's from,
where he's headed.
That way, he'll have strength
enough to answer.
Or, by then you'll be such good friends
you don't care.

[. . .]

No, I was not busy when you came!
I was not preparing to be busy.
That's the armor everyone puts on
to pretend they have a purpose
in the world.

I refuse to be claimed.
Your plate is waiting.
We will snip fresh mint
Into your tea."

[At this point, you might choose to enrich your story with your own or others' poetry or prose.]

This shaman's story has shifted onto the path of "Coming into Being"
Where there is more and deeper "growth" to be experienced.
Yet, in this growing process, you will always be opening the way
As wondrous new possibilities arrive and
In your spiritual humanness, you live them with Truth, and
You live them with joy and
You live them with increasing wisdom.

As you come more into being, more of all that you are,
There is a further refining of all your structures of soul
And of your relationships to others.
At this point, you become yet more aware
(Perhaps, because of the beloved outer presence),
Yet more aware of the inner Beloved Presence.[503]

---

[503] The "Beloved" has also been referred to as the "Inner Christ," the "Buddha Within" and as "True Nature."
You probably have found others in various teachings.

And as you increasingly tune into the soul fields around you,
You also recognize that the "world" is becoming, for you,
The Beloved Community, which simply does not require
Warfare and other forms of enmity.[504]
How can it, when you increasingly sense your connectedness
With all those others . . . and with the inner Beloved?
Quite clearly, your heart archetypes have been on the job!

[Ponder on all the "tuning into" that you have been doing and how that has brought about a releasing of old relationships on the one hand and, on the other hand, has expanded your sense of connection with intimate "others" and with the world. How have your heart archetype "guides" entered into that process? How has this helped to dispel any lingering "shadows"? Explore the many layers of meaning that come to you.]

And always the path is one of "Finding Wisdom,"
Of becoming *moshel meshalim* and
Always you are "dancing."

You are opening the way and finding wisdom,
Coming into being and finding more wisdom.
There is within you a rising sense of joyful expectancy
Of a newness about-to-appear.
You sense another birthing, but without the darkness and pain.
Wisely, you just go on "dancing" and trusting that all is well.

[Pause again and consider the ways in which you are "dancing." Consider your own expectancy and what is nurturing it. Add your insights to the story as you are guided to do.]

And now, you are on the path of "Entering Within"
And you are held in a warm constraint,
While the qualities of Life, Light and Love pour through you.
You wait . . . while the Law is doing Its work.
You wait . . . and in that heart awareness, that sacred empty/fullness
You sense, (so close!) the immanent Presence . . . and you wait . . .
Then, in an all-enveloping sweetness and tenderness
You come face to face.
With joy, you realize that the inner Beloved is walking with you:
The inner Beloved is sharing your journey.
And you realize, with a mixture of feelings,
That the Observer seems gently to have disappeared.

---

[504] For a splendid treatment of this idea, see Michael Beckwith, *Spiritual Liberation*, various paging.

There is within you a feeling/tone of dancing stillness.[505]

You remain there, in the still point,
And you *know* that
You, who are the androgynous energy being
Are also the androgynous Self.
And you *know* that
You, the microcosmic anthropos, are the splendid embodiment of
An ever-developing *moshel meshalim,*
Whose wisdom is grounded in the trust
That the cosmic Law will remain unchanged and unchangeable.

And you *know* that
Your spiritual humanness is the glowing inner empowerment
That was fostered by you throughout your quest
And fostered by the indwelling Spirit,
And that you are your wholeness
Without any trace of the "self"-consciousness
Of animal soul.

[Here, you are invited to pause and ponder the meanings of your own story: your experience with the in-dwelling Spirit Presence. Yours is likely to be a unique expression and indicative of your creative gifts.]

You continue to live your ordinary life in an extraordinary way,
While you expand your soul field to encompass the world,
And you resonate with these words by a 14th century Persian poet: [506]

> *"I have come into this world to see this:*
> *the sword drop from men's hands even at the height*
> *of their arc of anger.*
>
> *because we have finally realized that there is just one flesh to*
> *wound and it is His – the Christ's, our Beloved's.*
>
> *I have come into this world to see this:*
> *all creatures hold hands as we pass through this miraculous*
> *existence we share on the way to an even greater being of soul,*

---

[505] In Canto II of "Burnt Norton" (*The Four Quartets*), T.S. Eliot writes: "At the still point of the turning world […] there the dance is, […] except for the point, the still point, there would be no dance, and there is only the dance." Taken off the Internet at allspirit.co.uk/Norton.
[506] Hafiz, "I Have Come Into This World To See This," in *Love Poems from God*, compiled by Daniel Ladinsky, pp. 159-160.

a being of just ecstatic light, forever entwined and at play
with Him.

I have come into this world to hear this:
every song the Earth has sung since it was conceived in
the Divine's womb and began spinning from
His wish,
every song by wing and fin and hoof,
every song by hill and field and tree and woman and child
every song of stream and rock,
every song of tool and lyre and flute,
and fire,
every song the heart should cry with magnificent dignity
to know itself as
God;
for all other knowledge will leave us again in want and aching—
only imbibing the glorious Sun
will complete us.

I have come into this world to experience this:
men so true to love
they would rather die before speaking
an unkind word,
men so true their lives are His covenant—
the promise of hope.

I have come into this world to see this:
the sword drop from men's hands
even at the height of their arc of
rage
because we have finally realized
there is just one flesh
we can wound."

[Pause here and tune into the longing and the spiritual humanness of this long-ago poet, whose words have echoed down through the many centuries. At this point, if you choose, you might want to add something that could start like this: "I have come into this world to . . ." And, if you are not ready yet to make this statement, stay with your unfolding story and let it be part of the process.]

There is nothing more to relate in this shaman's story,
For you have come to the "meeting point" where

You are with the indwelling Spirit
In your relatedness with you, with others and with the world.

Then, note that you are once again at an ending that is yet another
Beginning.

Your cycle of sameness has come into newness and
You are ready for the final phase
Of the inner journey home.

That ends the shaman's story. But yours has barely started. You will journey with the indwelling Spirit into yet more beginnings, endings and beginnings. You are a "work in progress" until such time as you and it are complete. Before you leave this sacred enclosure, please remain in its timeless energies and ponder on their presence in you.

When you are ready, you may leave the stone circle.

* * *

How wonderful it has been to have shared these lessons with you! Here is a parting gift:

May you walk with the indwelling Spirit
In all your beginnings and endings.
May you be given great peace and great turmoil
Great joy and great sadness
Great ease and great hardship.
For you are on this Earth to experience
All that spiritual humanness involves.
You are on this Earth to know
And to be what you really are—
A "dancing" expression of the Divine,
A precious embodiment of the timeless "I AM."
Amen

Until we meet again, wherever and whenever that happens,

Peace and blessings

EPILOGUE

Shamans know that the Cosmos yields up its treasures only gradually and only to those souls who search with intent and with trust. In other words, yours has been (and must continue to be) an ongoing focus (the masculine) "dancing" with an ongoing receptivity (the feminine). (The focusing and the receiving have always been the basic constituents of your journey.) Shamans also know that the process can neither be hastened nor made easier. Your rebirthing into an androgynous anthropos proceeded in its beginning-ending-beginning cycles in response to your **readiness**. While you gradually became ready and better able to focus and receive, your centers of consciousness were healed. Because form follows consciousness, you as soul substance were re-shaped and your crystallized soul structures were transformed — by you. In other words, you as a soul field, with a nucleus of divinity, raised your vibratory frequency and, thereby, changed your consciousness energies. In all this undertaking, your cyclical and spiraling "paths" constantly interacted with and paralleled each other. With each "new" turn, your being was regenerated and expanded. Like the seed planted in Earth, the old "you" ended, to be reborn into a new **knowing** that became more **being**. In the aftermath of that rebirthing process, you as a microcosmic anthropos continued your development, with unhurried grace. And your spiritual humanness continued to express its immense possibilities. You "parented" your androgynous being/self while it "grew up" from its animal soul infancy into what it became as **moshel meshalim**. In that new journey, you have gradually achieved a vibratory frequency high enough to bring you face-to-face with the inner Beloved. As an androgyny, in the eternal "now," you have lovingly **known** your true "calling;" to live your **being** while you have walked **with** the indwelling Spirit.

In-formed by spiritual humanness, you continue to live an ordinary life (whatever and wherever it is) in an extraordinary way. You focus on transcendent physicality, emotionality and mentality. Because you are constantly finding wisdom, you increase your ability to face life's challenges. You realize with joy and gratitude that when you arrive at every "ending" of your on-going "paths," you who are a "work in progress," arrive at the next "beginning." As you do this, always with the indwelling Spirit, your constant guide, you continue to raise the vibratory frequency of all that you are as a soul field.

Finally, the great being that you are merges into Being. Having always been the microcosm of the macrocosm, a vibrating particle/wave of the omnipresent One Consciousness, Creative Energy, you understand, at last, the final paradox: that you have always been in the Spirit; that what you learned in Lesson Two as "theory" was your Truth: what you as the soul searcher were looking for was what you were looking with and what you were looking at. And you realize that you can embrace all of this, (as the Teacher Jesus taught), while you live in this dimension as a multidimensional energy being, in truth and in love with yourself and with "others." In your spiritual humanness, you glory in your fullness of Being, in the immensity of who you are . . . in the Spirit.

You know, like the shamans, that your realms are vast and wonderful and that you can continue to explore and to experience them, with intent and with trust, for the rest of your days. And if this lifetime ends before all is accomplished, there will be the next one: you, Little Soul, have some amazing Life Plans in store and some incredible evolving to do!

With these words the lessons are ended.

**They
can be a great help—words.
They can become the Spirit's hands
and lift and
caress
you.**[507]

---

[507] Meister Eckhart, "The Spirit's Hands," in Daniel Ladinsky, *Love Poems from God*, p. 110.

BIBLIOGRAPHY

Almaas, A. H. *Essence* with *The Elixir of Enlightenment: The Diamond Approach to Inner Realization*. York Beach, Maine: Samuel Weiser, Inc., 1998. (Two Books in One Volume)

_____. *The Inner Journey Home: Soul's Realization of the Unity of Reality*. Boston: Shambhala, 2004.

_____. *The Pearl Beyond Price: Integration of Personality Into Being: An Object Relations Approach*. Berkeley, California: Diamond Books, 1988.

_____. *The Unfolding Now: Realizing Your True Nature Through the Practice of Presence*. Boston, Massachusetts: Shambhala Publications, 2008.

American Psychiatric Association. *Desk Reference to the Diagnostic Criteria from DSM-IV-TR*. Arlington, Virginia: American Psychiatric Association, 2000.

Anand, Margot. *The Art of Everyday Ecstasy*. New York: Broadway Books, 1998.

Arrien, Angeles. *The Four-Fold Way: Walking the Paths of the Warrior, Teacher, Healer and Visionary*. New York: HarperCollins Publishers, 1993.

Baring, Anne and Cashford, Jules. *The Myth of the Goddess: Evolution of an Image*. London, England: Penguin Book, Ltd., 1991.

Beckwith, Michael Bernard. *40 Day Mind Fast Soul Feast*. Culver City, California: Agape Publishing, 2000.

_____. *Spiritual Liberation: Fulfilling Your Soul's Potential*. New York: Atria Books, 2008.

Belenky, Mary Field, Clinchy, Blythe McVicker, Goldberger, Nancy Rule and Tarule, Jill Mattuck. *Women's Ways of Knowing: The Development of Self, Voice and Mind.* New York: Basic Books, 1997.

Berresford-Ellis, Peter. *Celtic Myths and Legends.* New York: Carroll and Graf, Publishers, 1999.

Bly, Robert. *A Little Book on the Human Shadow.* San Francisco: HarperCollins Publishers, 1988.

_____. *Iron John: A Book About Men.* New York: Addison-Wesley Publishing Company, Inc., 1990.

Boren, Minx. *Soul Notes Too.* Palm Beach Gardens, Florida: Fourfold Path, Inc., 2003.

Bose, Aurobindo (Translator). *Later Poems of Rabindranath Tagore.* New Delhi, India: Rupa & Co., 2002.

Bourgeault, Cynthia. *The Wisdom Way of Knowing: Reclaiming an Ancient Tradition to Awaken the Heart.* San Francisco: John Wiley and Sons, Inc., 2003.

Bowman, Catherine. *Crystal Awareness.* St. Paul, Minnesota: The Llewellyn New Times, 1994.

Breaux, Charles. *Journey Into Consciousness: The Chakras, Tantra and Jungian Psychology.* York Beach, Maine: Nicolas-Hays, Inc., 1989.

Brennan, Barbara Ann. *Hands of Light: A Guide to Healing Through the Human Energy Field.* New York: Bantam Books, 1987.

British and Foreign Bible Society. *The Holy Bible: Old and New Testaments.* London, England: Oxford University Press, 1907.

Brumet, Robert. *The Quest for Wholeness: Healing Ourselves, Healing Our World.* Unity Village, Missouri: Unity House, 2002.
Brunton, Paul, Dr. *The Hidden Teaching Beyond Yoga.* York Beach, Maine: Samuel Weiser, Inc., 1941 and 1984.

_____. *The Wisdom of the Overself.* York Beach, Maine: Samuel Weiser, Inc., 1941 and 1984.

Bruyere, Rosalyn L. *Wheels of Light: Chakras, Auras, and the Energy of the Body.* New York: Simon and Schuster, 1989, 1991, 1994.

Campbell, Joseph. *The Hero with a Thousand Faces.* 3rd Edition. Novato, California: New World Publishing, 2008.

_____. *Myths to Live By: How We Re-Create Ancient Legends in Our Daily Lives to Release Human Potential.* New York: The Penguin Group, 1972.

_____. *Pathways to Bliss: Mythology and Personal Transformation.* Novato, California: New World Library, 2004.

Campbell, Joseph (with Bill Moyers). *The Power of Myth.* New York: MJF Books, 1988.

Campbell, Joseph. *Thou Art That: Transforming Religious Metaphor.* Novato, California: New World Library, 2001.

Cashdan, Sheldon. *The Witch Must Die: The Hidden Meaning of Fairy Tales.* New York: Basic Books, 1999.

Chopra, Deepak. *Ageless Body, Timeless Mind.* New York: Harmony Books, 1993.

Churton, Tobias. *The Gnostics.* New York: Barnes and Noble Books, 1997.

Citro, Massimo and Laszlo, Ervin. *The Basic Code of the Universe: The Science of the Invisible in Physics, Medicine and Spirituality.* Rochester, Vermont: Park Street Press (published in e-book format), 2011.

Coghlan, Andy. "Gay Brains Structured Like Those of the Opposite Sex." *New Scientist*, June, 2008. Taken off the Internet, March 15, 2010.

Cohen, Alan. *The Peace That You Seek.* Des Moines, Washington: Alan Cohen Publications, 1985, 1991.

Cowan, Tom. *Fire in the Head: Shamanism and the Celtic Spirit.* New York: HarperCollins Publishers, 1993.

_____. *Shamanism as a Spiritual Practice for Daily Life.* Freedom, California: The Crossing Press, 1996.

Dale, Cyndi. *New Chakra Healing: The Revolutionary 32-Center Energy System.* St. Paul, Minnesota: Llewellyn Publications, 1997.

De Bertodano, Teresa. *Soul Searchers: An Anthology of Spiritual Journeys.* Grand Rapids, Michigan: Wm. B. Eerdman's Publishing Company, 2002.

De Mello, Anthony. *Wellsprings: A Book of Spiritual Exercises.* New York: Image Books, 1986.

Docter, Richard F. *Transvestites and Transsexuals: Toward a Theory of Cross-Gender Behavior.* New York: Plenum Press, 1988.

Dossey, Larry. *Healing Words The Power of Prayer and the Practice of Medicine.* San Francisco: HarperSanFrancisco, 1995.

Douglas-Klotz, Neil. *Desert Wisdom: Sacred Middle Eastern Writings from the Goddess through the Sufis.* New York: HarperCollins, 1995.

_____. *Prayers of the Cosmos: Meditations on the Aramaic Words of Jesus.* New York: HarperCollins, 1994.

_____. *The Sufi Book of Life: 99 Pathways of the Heart for the Modern Dervish.* New York: Penguin Group (USA), 2005.

Dyczkowski, Mark S.G. *The Doctrine of Vibration: An Analysis of the Doctrines and Practices of Kashmir Shaivism.* New York: State University of New York Press, 1987.

Eliade, Mircea. *Shamanism: Archaic Techniques of Ecstasy.* Princeton, New Jersey: Princeton University Press, 1964.

Eliot, T.S. "Burnt Norton," Canto II in *The Four Quartets.* Taken off the Internet web site allspirit.co.uk/norton.

Epstein, Mark. *Thoughts Without a Thinker: Psychotherapy From a Buddhist Perspective.* New York: MJF Books, 1995.

Evola, Julius. *The Hermetic Tradition: Symbols and Teachings of the Royal Art.* Rochester, Vermont: Inner Traditions International, 1995.

Evola, Julius and the UR Group. *Introduction to Magic: Rituals and Practical Techniques for the Magus*. Rochester, Vermont: Inner Traditions, 2001.

Fontana, David. *The Secret Language of Symbols: A Visual Key to Symbols and Their Meanings*. San Francisco: Chronicle Books, 1994.

Fox, Matthew. *Meditations With Meister Eckhart: A Centering Book*. Rochester, Vermont: Bear and Company, 1983.

_____. *Original Blessings*. Santa Fe, New Mexico: Bear and Company, Inc., 1983.

_____. *Passion for Creation: The Earth-Honoring Spirituality of Meister Eckhart*. Rochester, Vermont: Inner Traditions International, 2000.

Freke, Timothy and Gandy, Peter. *The Jesus Mysteries: Was the "Original Jesus" a Pagan God*? New York: Three Rivers Press, 1999.

_____. *The Laughing Jesus: Religious Lies and Gnostic Wisdom*. New York: Three Rivers Press, 2005.

Frenier, Carol and Hogan, Lois Sekerak. "Engaging the Imaginal Realm: Doorway to Collective Wisdom." *The Collective Wisdom Initiative, Seed Paper*. Printed off the Internet, August 1, 2009.

Friedman, Barton R. *Adventures in the Deeps of the Mind: The Cuchulain Cycle of W. B. Yeats*. Princeton, New Jersey: Princeton University Press, 1977.

Gibran, Kahlil. *Thoughts and Meditations*. London: William Heinemann, Ltd., 1961.

Gienger, Michael and Maier, Wolfgang. *Healing Stones for the Vital Organs: 83 Crystals With Traditional Chinese Medicine*. Rochester, Vermont: Healing Arts Press, 2007.

Gilligan, Carol. *In a Different Voice: Psychological Theory and Women's Development*. Cambridge, Massachusetts: Cambridge University Press, 1982.

Godwin, Gail. *Heart: The Story of Its Myths and Meanings*. London, England: Bloomsbury Publishing, 2001.

Godwin, Joscelyn. *The Golden Thread: The Ageless Wisdom of the Western Mystery Traditions*. Wheaton, Illinois: Theosophical Publishing House. 2007.

Goleman, Daniel. *Emotional Intelligence*. New York: Bantam Books, 1995.

Gregory, Lady. *Cuchulain of Muirthemne*. London, England: Billing and Sons Ltd., 1902.

Grimm, Jacob and Grimm, Wilhelm. *Grimm's Fairy Tales*. London, England: Thomas Nelson and Sons, c1904.

Griscom Chris. *Ecstasy Is a New Frequency*. Santa Fe, New Mexico: Bear and Company, 1987.

_____. *Feminine Fusion*. New York: Simon and Schuster, 1991.

Harris, Judith Rich. *No Two Alike: Human Nature and Human Individuality*. New York: W. W. Norton and Company, Inc., 2006.

Hoeller, Stephan A. *Gnosticism: New Light on the Ancient Tradition of Inner Knowing*. Wheaton, Illinois: Theosophical Publishing House, 2002.

Holmes, Ernest. *The Science of Mind*. New York: G. P. Putnam's Sons, 1988.

Houston, Jean. *The Search for the Beloved: Journeys in Mythology and Sacred Psychology*. New York: G.P. Putnam's Sons, 1987.

Hume, Robert Ernest. *The Thirteen Principal Upanishads*. Oxford. England: Oxford University Press, 1921.

Hunt, Valerie V. *Infinite Mind: Science of the Human Vibrations of Consciousness*. Malibu, California: Malibu Publishing Company, 1989, 1996.

Jacobi, Jolande (Ralph Manheim, Translator). *Complex, Archetype and Symbol in the Psychology of C. G. Jung*. Princeton, New Jersey: Princeton University Press, 1959.

Johnson, Luke Timothy. *Mystical Tradition: Judaism, Christianity, and Islam*. In Thirty-Six Lessons on DVD with Course Guidebook. Chantilly, Virginia: THE TEACHING COMPANY, 2008.

Judith, Anodea. *Wheels of Life: A User's Guide to the Chakra System*. St. Paul, Minnesota: Llewellyn Publications, 1999.

Jung, C. G. (R.F.C. Hull, Translator). *Aspects of the Feminine*. Princeton, New Jersey: Princeton University Press, 1982.

_____. *Aspects of the Masculine*. Princeton, New Jersey: Princeton University Press, 1989.

_____. *Four Archetypes*: Mother/Rebirth/Spirit/Trickster. Princeton, New Jersey: Princeton University Press. 1969.

Jung, Emma. *Animus and Anima*. Dallas, Texas: Spring Publications, Inc., 1957.

Kaji, Dhruv S. *Common Sense about Uncommon Wisdom: Ancient Teachings of the Vedanta*. Honesdale, Pennsylvania: The Himalayan Institute press, 2001.

Keen, Sam. *Fire in the Belly: On Being a Man*. New York: Bantam Books, 1991.

Kelly, Robin. *The Human Hologram: Living Your Life in Harmony with the Unified Field*. Santa Rosa, CA: Energy Psychology Press, 2011.

Klein, Doris. *Journey of the Soul*. Lanham, MD: Sheed and Ward, 2000.

Ladinsky, Daniel. *Love Poems from God: Twelve Sacred Voices from the East and West*. New York: Penguin Books, Ltd., 2002.

Lamsa, George M. (Translator). *Holy Bible: From the Ancient Eastern Text*. New York: HarperCollins Publishers, 1933.

Laszlo, Ervin and Currivan, Jude. *CosMos: A Co-creator's Guide to the Whole-World*. Carlsbad, California: Hay House, 2008.

Laszlo, Ervin. *The Akashic Experience: Science and the Cosmic Memory Field*. Rochester, Vermont: Inner Traditions, 2009.

_____. *Science and the Akashic Field: An Integral Theory of Everything*. Rochester, Vermont: Inner Traditions, 2004.

Lawless, Julia. *The Encyclopedia of Essential Oils: The Complete Guide to the Use of Aromatics in Aromatherapy, Herbalism, Health and Well-Being*. Rockport, Massachusetts: Element, Inc., 1992.

Le Brun, Annie. *The Reality Overload: The Modern World's Assault on the Imaginal Realm*. Rochester, Vermont: Inner Traditions, 2000.

LeLoup, Jean-Yves (Translator). *The Gospel of Philip: Jesus, Mary Magdalene and the Gnosis of Sacred Union*. Rochester, Vermont: Inner Traditions, 2003.

Levine, Peter A. *Waking the Tiger, Healing Trauma: The Innate Capacity to Transform Overwhelming Experience*. Berkeley, California: North Atlantic Books. 1997.

Lipton, Bruce H. *The Biology of Belief: Unleashing the Power of Consciousness, Matter and Miracles*. Santa Rosa, California: Mountain of Love/Elite Books, 2005.

Loehr James E. and Migdow, Jeffrey A. *Breathe In, Breathe Out: Inhale Energy and Exhale Stress by Guiding and Controlling Your Breathing*. Alexandria, Virginia: Time Life Books, 1999.

Mair, Victor H. (Translator). *Tao Te Ching*. New York: Bantam, Doubleday, Dell Publishing Group, 1990.

Mann, Mary Pat. "The Door to the Imaginal Realm." In *Mytholog*, Vol. 4, Number 3, Summer, 2006.

Maslow, Abraham. *Motivation and Personality*. New York: HarperCollins, Publishers, 1987.

_____. *Toward a Psychology of Being*. San Francisco: John Wiley and Sons, 1998.

Matt, Daniel C. *The Essential Kabbalah*. New York: HarperCollins, Publishers, 1998.

Matthews, Caitlin and Matthews, John. *The Encyclopedia of Celtic Wisdom: The Celtic Shaman's Sourcebook*. Shaftsbury, Dorset: Element Books, 1994.

_____. *Ladies of the Lake*. Northampton, England: Aquarian Press, 1992.

Matthews, John. *The Celtic Shaman: A Handbook*. Shaftesbury, Dorset: Element Books, 1991.

_____. *Taliesin: Shamanism and the Bardic Mysteries in Britain and Ireland*. Hammersmith, London: Aquarian Press, 1991.

McTaggart, Lynne. *The Field: The Quest for the Secret Force of the Universe*. New York: HarperCollins Publishers, 2001.

Meade, Michael. *Men and the Water of Life: Initiation and the Tempering of Men*. San Francisco: HarperCollins, 1993.

Melody. *Love Is in the Earth: A Kaleidoscope of Crystals*. Wheat Ridge, Colorado: Earth-Love Publishing House, 1995.

Mercatante, Anthony S. and Dow, James R. *The Facts on File Encyclopedia of World Mythology and Legend*. Vol. 1 (A-L). New York: Facts on File, 2004.

_____. *The Facts on File Encyclopedia of World Mythology and Legend*. Vol. 2 (M-Z). New York: Facts on File, 2004.

Meyer, Marvin W. (Editor). *The Ancient Mysteries: A Sourcebook of Sacred Texts*. Philadelphia: University of Pennsylvania Press, 1987.

Michell, John. *Secrets of the Stones: New Revelations of Astro-archaeology and the Mystical Sciences of Antiquity*. Rochester, Vermont: Inner Traditions International, 1989.

Miller, Jean Baker. *Toward a New Psychology of Women*. Boston: Beacon Press, 1978, 1986.

Millman, Dan. *The Life You Were Born to Live: A Guide to Finding Your Life Purpose*. Tiburon, California: H J Kramer, Inc., 1993.

Moir, Anne and Jessel, David. *Brain Sex: The Real Difference Between Men and Women*. New York: Dell Publishing, 1989, 1991.

Moss, Richard. *The Second Miracle: Intimacy, Spirituality and Conscious Relationships*. Berkeley, California: Celestial Arts, 1995.

Myss, Carolyn. *The Language of Archetypes*. CD #1, Sounds True Audio Learning Course, 2006.

_____. *Sacred Contracts: Awakening Your Divine Potential*. New York: Three Rivers Press, 2002, 2003.

Nettleton, John A. *Cumbria: Shire County Guide 25*. Princes Risborough, Buckinghamshire: Shire Publications, Ltd., 1996.

Neville. *Awakened Imagination* and *The Search*. Camarillo, California: DeVorss Publications, 1946, 1954, 2004. (Two Books in One Volume)

Novak, Philip. *The World's Wisdom: Sacred Texts of the World's Religions*. San Francisco: HarperCollins Publishers, 1994.

Pearson, Carol S. *Awakening the Heroes Within: Twelve Archetypes to Help Us Find Ourselves and Transform Our World*. San Francisco: HarperCollins, Publishers, 1991.

Pert, Candace B. *Molecules of Emotion: Why You Feel the Way You Feel*. New York: Scribner, 1997.

Piaget, Jean and Inhelder, Barbel. *The Psychology of the Child*. New York: Basic Books, Inc., 1969, 2000.

Piaget, Jean. *The Child's Conception of the World*. Boston: Rowman and Littlefield Publishers, Inc., 1929 and 1951.

Pierrakos, Eva. *The Pathwork of Self-Transformation*. New York: Bantam Books, 1990.

Pinkola-Estes, Clarissa. *Women Who Run With the Wolves: Myths and Stories of the Wild Woman Archetype*. New York: Ballantine Books, 1992.

Ritberger, Carol. *Your Personality, Your Health: Connecting Personality With the Human Energy System, Chakras and Wellness*. Carlsbad, California: Hay House, Inc., 1998.

Roche, Lorin. *The Radiance Sutras: Tantra Yoga Teachings for Opening Up to the Divine in Everyday Life*. Marina del Rey, California: Syzygy Creations, Inc., 2008.

Rolleston, T. W. *Celtic Myths and Legends*. Mineola, New York: Dover Publications, Inc., 1917 and 1990.

Schaef, Anne Wilson. *Beyond Therapy, Beyond Science*: *A New Model for Healing the Whole Person*. San Francisco: HarperCollins Publishers, 1992.

Shah, Idries. *The Sufis*. New York: Random House, 1964 and 1971.

Sherwood, Keith. *The Art of Spiritual Healing*. St. Paul, Minnesota: Llewellyn Publications, 1992.

_____. *Chakra Therapy: For Personal Growth and Healing*. St. Paul, Minnesota: Llewellyn Publications, 1993.

Singer, June. *Androgyny: The Opposites Within*. Boston: Sigo Press, 1989.

_____. *The Gnostic Book of Hours: Keys to Inner Wisdom*. Berwick, Maine: Nicolas-Hays, Inc., 2003.

Small, Jacquelyn. *Awakening in Time: The Journey from Co-Dependence to Co-Creation*. New York: Bantam Books, 1991.

_____. *Embodying Spirit: Coming Alive With Meaning and Purpose*. New York: HarperCollins Publishers, 1994.

Smart, Ninian and Hecht, Richard D. *Sacred Texts of the World: A Universal Anthology*. New York: Crossroad Publishing Company, 2001.

Smith, F. LaGard (Narrator). *The Narrated Bible, in Chronological Order*. Eugene, Oregon: Harvest House Publishers, 1984.

Smith, Huston. *The World's Religions: Our Great Wisdom Traditions*. San Francisco: HarperCollins Publishers, 1991.

Smoley, Richard and Kinney, Jay. *Hidden Wisdom: A Guide to the Western Inner Traditions*. Wheaton, Ill.: Theosophical Publishing House, 2006.

Sri Aurobindo. *The Life Divine*. Twin Lakes, Wisconsin: Lotus Press, 1990.

Stavish, Mark. *The Path of Alchemy: Energetic Healing and the World of Natural Magic*. Woodbury, Minnesota: Llewellyn Publications, 2007.

Stevens, Anthony. *Archetypes: A Natural History of the Self*. New York: William Morrow and Company, Inc., 1982.

_____. *Ariadne's Clue: A Guide to the Symbols of Humankind*. Princeton, New Jersey: Princeton University Press, 1998.

_____. *Private Myths: Dreams and Dreaming*. Cambridge, Massachusetts: Cambridge University Press, 1995.

_____. *The Two Million-Year-Old Self*. Texas: A&M University Press, 1993.

Stewart, R.J. *Earth Light: The Ancient Path to Transformation: Rediscovering the Wisdom of Celtic and Faery Lore*. Shaftesbury, Dorset: Element Books, Ltd., 1992.

_____. *Power Within the Land: The Roots of Celtic and Underworld Traditions; Awakening the Sleepers and Regenerating the Earth*. Shaftesbury, Dorset: Element Books, Ltd., 1992.

_____. *The Way of Merlin*. Hammersmith, London: The Aquarian Press, 1991.

Stone, Hal and Stone, Sidra L. *Partnering: A New Kind of Relationship*. Novato, California: Nataraj Publishing, 2000.

Stuart, Malcolm. *The Encyclopedia of Herbs and Herbalism*. Slovak Republic: Edgerton International Ltd., 1994.

Sviri, Sara. *The Taste of Hidden Things: Images on the Sufi Path*. Inverness, California: The Golden Sufi Center, 1997.

Talbot, Michael. *The Holographic Universe*. New York: HarperCollins Publishers, 1991.

Thompson, Keith (Editor). *To Be A Man: In Search of the Deep Masculine*. Los Angeles: Jeremy Tarcher, Inc., 1991.

Todeschi, Kevin J. *Edgar Cayce on the Akashic Records: The Book of Life*. Virginia Beach, Virginia: A.R.E. Press, 1998.

Tolle, Eckhart. *A New Earth: Awakening to Your Life's Purpose*. New York: Penguin Group, 2005.

Treben, Maria. *Health From God's Garden: Herbal Remedies for Glowing Health and Well-Being*. Rochester, Vermont: Healing Arts Press, 1986.

Ulanov, Ann and Barry. *Transforming Sexuality: The Archetypal World of Anima and Animus*. Boston: Shambhala, 1994.

Underhill, Evelyn. *Mysticism, A Study in the Nature and Development of Man's Spiritual Consciousness.* New York: Dutton, 1912.

Von Franz, Marie-Louise. *Animus and Anima in Fairy Tales.* Toronto: Inner City Books, 2002.

_____. *Archetypal Dimensions of the Psyche.* Boston: Shambhala Publications, Inc., 1997.

_____. *Archetypal Patterns in Fairy Tales.* Toronto: Inner City Books. 1997.

_____. *The Interpretation of Fairy Tales.* Boston and London: Shambhala Publications, Inc., 1996.

_____. *The Psychological Meaning of Redemption Motifs in Fairy Tales.* Toronto: Inner City Books, 1980.

Walker, Barbara G. *The Woman's Dictionary of Symbols and Sacred Objects.* Edison, New Jersey: Castle Books, 1988.

Washburn, Michael. *The Ego and the Dynamic Ground: A Transpersonal Theory of Human Development.* New York: State University of New York, 1995.

White, Ruth. *Working With Your Chakras: A Physical, Emotional and Spiritual Approach.* York Beach, Maine: Samuel Weiser Inc., 1994.

Wilber, Ken. *The Essential Ken Wilber: An Introductory Reader.* Boston: Shambhala, 1998.

_____. *The Eye of Spirit: An Integral Vision for a World Gone Slightly Mad.* Boston: Shambhala, 2001.

_____. *Integral Spirituality: A Startling New Role for Religion in the Modern and Postmodern World.* Boston and London: Integral Books, 2007.

Wolinsky, Stephen. *Trances People Live: Healing Approaches in Quantum Psychology.* Connecticut: The Bramble Company, 1991.

Worthington, Roger. *Finding the Hidden Self: A Study of the Siva Sutras.* Honesdale, Pennsylvania: Himalayan Institute Press, 2002.

Yeats, W. B. *Writings on Irish Folklore, Legends and Myth*. London, England: Penguin Books, 1953.

Yogananda, Paramahansa. *The Autobiography of a Yogi*. Los Angeles, California: Self-Realization Fellowship, 1946.

_____. *The Bhagavad Gita: The Immortal Dialog Between Soul and Spirit*. Volumes One and Two. Los Angeles, California: The Self-Realization Fellowship, 1995.

Young, Jacqueline. *The Healing Path: The Practical Guide to the Holistic Traditions of China, India, Tibet and Japan*. London, England: Duncan Baird Publishers, 2001.

Zipes, Jack (Translator). *The Complete Fairy Tales of the Brothers Grimm*. New York: Bantam Books, 2003.

INDEX

E

Earth (planet) 8, 10, 15, 16, 18, 26, 39, 43, 46, 51, 60, 63, 69, 71, 72, 74, 77, 85, 89, 103, 105, 107, 108, 113, 128, 130, 156, 173, 174, 180, 219, 220, 231, 233, 269, 271, 272, 283, 288, 296, 320, 331, 333, 344, 351, 357, 358, 359
   as a living being 22, 25, 39, 70, 167, 181
   as consciousness energies 18, 19, 20, 21, 36, 39, 43, 87, 107, 111, 112, 173, 175, 208, 220, 221, 222, 223, 234, 247, 269, 270, 273, 319, 320, 322, 325, 326, 330, 331, 338
   as Spirit 84, 85
East (shamanic direction). *See* path of the East
Ego/self 7, 78, 97, 161, 162, 195, 202, 203, 212, 221, 235, 238, 266, 295
   as consciousness energies 30, 119, 162, 203
   as structures of soul 60, 96, 169, 181, 199, 259
   development of 76, 94, 98, 150, 157, 183, 184, 199, 201, 203, 205, 216
   environmental impact on 97, 205
   purpose 95, 96
   transmutation of 110, 177, 323
Egyptian wisdom teachings 22, 47, 133, 238, 239
Electromagnetic energy field (human) 26, 30, 36, 59, 84, 87, 104, 113, 114, 172, 173, 174, 195, 295, 297, 300, 342
   experiencing and exploring 42
Emotional body. *See* soul structures of emotionality.
Energy being (human) 8, 53, 60, 63, 74, 80, 81, 86, 87, 90, 125, 183, 185, 199, 203, 209, 224, 234, 257, 302, 342, 347
   as soul 53, 58, 117, 169, 333, 342, 345, 346
   definition 8
Energy field (human)
   pulling 319
   scanning 321
   scraping 319, 321
Entering Within. *See* path of the West
Environment (inner) 51, 56, 59, 72, 85, 130, 140, 201, 342
   and belief 252
   and chakra malfunction 162, 167, 170
   and healing 168, 344
   wounds and wounding 155, 337
Environment (outer) 37, 51, 56, 59, 72, 80, 82, 83, 85, 86, 87, 94, 98, 99, 108, 122, 124, 126, 130, 140, 186, 188, 195, 201, 204, 205, 208, 247, 262, 296, 323, 342
   and belief 90, 127, 216, 252
   and chakra malfunction 102, 104, 167, 202, 253, 267, 329
   and healing 344
   shielding against 36

   wounds and wounding 97, 100, 129, 155, 170, 210
Ether 294, 316
Etheric body. *See* throat chakra – and etheric energies.
Etheric matrix 76, 81, 82, 84, 86, 91, 99, 101, 102, 129, 200, 294, 318, 320
Etheric womb 46, 99, 129, 291, 294, 323
Evolutionary holarchy. *See* holarchy, evolutionary
Evolutionary spirituality. *See* spirituality, evolutionary

F

Fairy tales 7, 69, 80, 133, 157, 170, 188, 202, 205, 209, 347
   origins 124, 133
   purpose 133, 188
Feminine energies 6, 118, 156, 157, 169, 192, 218, 227, 246, 247, 259
   and the ego/self 73, 96, 97, 131, 150, 157, 161, 184, 206, 266, 274, 339
   as a force 7, 10, 133, 140, 150, 205, 252, 266, 315
   as cosmic principles 6, 23, 58
   as spiritual energies 145, 150, 156, 161, 162, 168, 193, 194, 311, 313
   in soul substance 36, 47, 57, 97, 98, 99, 100, 101, 131, 188, 206, 339
   in the human energy system 9, 29, 30, 35, 36, 80, 96, 122, 143, 149, 150, 156, 169, 184, 185, 188, 191, 194, 203, 213, 217, 224, 248, 274, 310, 311, 326, 339, 346, 352, 359
Finding Wisdom. *See* path of the North.
Form follows consciousness 87, 103, 118, 133, 139, 144, 145, 155, 161, 171, 217, 218, 223, 268, 310, 318, 339, 340

G

Gender (human) 35, 97, 98, 99, 101, 104, 203, 205, 209, 211, 216
   and brain sex 101
Gnostic wisdom teachings 23, 24, 49
Gratitude. *See* healing practices described herein
Greek wisdom teachings 23, 47, 58, 128
Grimms' fairy tales excerpted herein
   "King Thrushbeard" 152
   "Roland and May-Bird" 191
   "The Blue Light" 141
   "The Fisherman and His Wife" 147
   "The Juniper Tree" 134
   "The Maiden Without Hands" 163
   "The Worn-Out Dancing Shoes 158
Gross body. *See* soul structures of physicality
Grounding (breath work). *See* breath work given herein - grounding

H

Healing practices described herein
  chanting 323
  gratitude 110, 173, 219, 320
  meditation 109, 173, 219, 220, 322
  prayer 110, 241, 242, 243, 295, 320, 323
  swinging 175
  undulating 112, 222, 269
Heart awareness 10, 286, 287, 290, 292, 295, 297,
    299, 301, 302, 314, 316, 318, 324, 326, 327,
    330, 331, 332, 333, 336, 337, 340, 345, 355
Heart "bridge"
  and dreams 241, 258
  bridging structures of soul 255, 261
  damage 246
  purpose 237, 338
Heart chakra 106, 128, 129, 194, 216, 218, 219, 223,
    232, 233, 242, 251, 252, 255, 257, 258
  color (green) 246, 247, 270, 271, 272, 273
  component, emotional 253, 254
  component, mental 253, 255
  component, physical 252, 254
  component, spiritual 254, 255
  damage 248, 255, 261, 267, 268, 329
  element (earth) 247, 248, 270, 271, 272, 273
  feminine energies 157, 248
  generative power 238, 244, 257, 272
  "i-am" consciousness 244, 258
  malfunction 248, 254, 255, 267, 268
  onset of function 244, 256
  prime directive 244, 253, 255, 258
  purpose 257
  self-healing therapies 274
Heart "crucible" 235
  alchemy (inner) 258, 335, 336, 337, 338, 339
Heredity. See root chakra - DNA.
Higher sensory perception 59, 300
Hindu wisdom teachings 26, 29, 50, 239, 240
Holarchy, evolutionary
  and holons
    detachment/discernment 245, 254, 257, 277,
      286, 287, 293, 295, 296, 298, 300, 301, 302,
      317, 330, 332
    dynamic equilibrium 245, 254, 257, 277, 286,
      293, 295, 298, 302, 317, 330, 332
    the loving i-am/self 286, 293, 298, 302, 317,
      330, 332
    translucent knowing 293, 298, 302, 317, 330, 332
  of androgyny 232, 245, 254, 257, 258, 274, 277,
    279, 283, 286, 291, 293, 298, 300, 302, 308,
    312, 317, 330, 332, 337, 338, 339, 340, 342, 345
  theory of 52
Holographic theory. See consciousness energies

(human) - and holographic theory; macrocosm
  - and holographic theory; microcosm - and
  holographic theory.
Homework 73, 177, 238
  review as assimilation 63, 172, 176, 225, 276, 329
Homosexuality 99
Human energy system 8, 11, 26, 80, 98, 102, 133,
    169, 186, 216, 217, 256, 268, 290
  archetypal nature 34, 91, 199, 215, 257
  as microcosm 32, 33, 91, 257, 342, 345
  channels 29
  generative power 33, 60, 95, 118, 150, 162, 207, 211
  holistic nature 30, 84, 120, 143, 145, 156, 162,
    194, 202, 246, 267, 274, 299

I

Ignorance 3, 132, 140, 151, 156, 236, 239, 299, 301,
    312, 313, 314, 329, 342, 347, 351
Imaginal realm 8, 77, 78, 119, 124, 133, 152, 188,
    248, 290, 341, 346, 349
Imagination 12, 129, 181, 262, 331, 341
Inner guidance system. See Spirit (indwelling)
Inner journey home. See rebirthing journey
Intuition 39, 262, 297
Islamic wisdom teachings 50, 241

J

Jesus, the Christ 3, 5, 50, 237, 240, 241, 246, 360
  as androgyny 7
Judaic wisdom teachings 23, 24, 48, 49, 239, 240,
    278, 336

K

Kabbalistic wisdom teachings 49, 128
Knowing 3, 5, 9, 10, 11, 16, 21, 38, 42, 49, 55, 58,
    60, 69, 115, 133, 150, 177, 188, 196, 216,
    224, 231, 232, 234, 240, 241, 242, 257, 284,
    302, 311, 312, 315, 317, 333, 335, 341, 342,
    344, 345, 359
Kundalini 29, 82, 84, 85, 91, 101, 102, 112, 129,
    144, 172, 200, 222, 273, 310, 329
Kundalini shifts. See Transformation (inner)—as
    kundalini "shifts

L

Law. See aspects of the Spirit - Law
Letting go 18, 57, 64, 114, 254, 271, 279, 313, 319
  and letting be 64, 181, 224, 231, 232, 344
  as power 16, 69, 70, 283
Liberation (inner) 7, 8, 64, 239, 338
  definition 7
Life Force 29, 81, 144, 213, 264

heretability 204
  theories 80, 122, 186, 208, 246, 247
Physical body. *See* soul structures of physicality
Piaget's theory 203, 208, 216
  and the human energy system 200, 201, 202, 203, 215, 216
  and the soul structures of mentality 201, 215
Pilgrims (ancient) 11, 181
  as soul searchers 18
  in the stone circle 18, 43, 181, 233, 285
  ring dance 233
Pilgrims (modern)
  as soul searchers 2, 3, 5, 54, 63, 64, 72, 114, 256, 275, 277, 313, 329, 335, 336, 341
    in the stone circle 43, 71, 180, 181, 233, 285, 344
Poetry excerpted herein
  Blake, William, "The Everlasting Gospel" 50
  Boren, Minx, "I Know You" 315
  DeMello, Anthony, "The Advent" 73
  Eckhart, Meister, "The Spirit's Hands" 360
  Gibran, Kahlil, "O Night" 115
  Hafiz, "I Have Come Into This World" 356
  Rumi, "The Chance of Humming" 182
  Tagore, Rabindranath, "One Day in Spring" 353
Power
  as spiritual knowledge 15
  definition 16
  of the East (shamanic direction) 16, 65
  of the North (shamanic direction) 283
  of the South (shamanic direction) 69, 70
  of the West (shamanic direction) 231
Power (macrocosmic) 15, 16, 51, 63, 95, 130, 193, 295, 338, 340
Power (microcosmic) 9, 12, 16, 21, 25, 36, 51, 72, 79, 102, 108, 109, 110, 119, 121, 144, 150, 176, 183, 196, 199, 205, 207, 212, 215, 217, 224, 241, 242, 246, 247, 248, 254, 257, 258, 264, 291, 292, 294, 299, 300, 301, 310, 311, 312, 313, 314, 339, 341
Power microcosmic) 5
Purity, simplicity and unity 225, 226, 245, 254, 276

Q

Quantum physics. *See* consciousness energies (human) - and quantum physics; macrocosm - as universal energy field; zero point field (ZPF)
Quest. *See* rebirthing journey - as a quest

R

Readiness 2, 65, 215, 223, 227, 259, 347, 359
Rebirthing journey
  as a developmental process 5, 47, 69, 117, 224, 246, 283, 284, 300, 314, 340, 341, 359

as an inner journey home 15, 38, 54, 75, 234, 237, 240, 242, 340, 341, 344, 346, 347
  as a quest 289, 337, 345
  as gestation 5, 168, 232, 342
  Biblical story 5
  definition 2
  midwives 338
Regeneration (inner) 7, 8, 64, 81, 157, 267, 338
  definition 7
Resistance 103, 171, 218, 261, 263, 265, 266, 271, 273, 295, 311, 337, 339
Revealing/concealing
  as power 283
  as Truth 311, 312
Root chakra 29, 76, 78
  and addictions 104, 299
  color (red) 78, 79, 80, 81, 85, 102, 103, 104, 105, 106, 107, 108, 109, 111, 112, 113, 114, 120, 121, 185, 268, 298, 320
  component, emotional 83, 84, 122
  component, mental 83, 85
  component, physical 82, 84
  component, spiritual 84, 85, 108
  damage 102, 104, 111
  DNA 83, 84, 86, 91, 99, 101, 104, 124, 198
  element (fire) 79, 81, 85, 102, 103, 104, 107, 109, 111, 114, 120, 121, 185
  generative power 76, 79, 87, 90, 94, 101, 104
  "i-am" consciousness 30, 76, 131, 150, 162, 201, 248
  malfunction 80, 86, 102, 191, 192, 197
  masculine energies 79, 80, 81, 82, 85, 145, 160, 188, 192, 251, 308
  onset of function 76
  prime directive 30, 76, 120, 150
  self-healing therapies 114

S

Sacral chakra 117, 118, 119, 217, 218, 264, 267, 301
  and astral energies 129, 130, 198
  and karma 130
  color (orange) 120, 121, 171, 172, 173, 175
  component, emotional 123, 125
  component, mental 124, 125, 139, 149
  component, physical 124, 143, 150
  component, spiritual 124, 125
  damage 139, 155, 156, 157, 161, 170, 171, 329
  element (water) 120, 121, 171, 172, 173, 176, 247
  feminine energies 121, 122, 134, 139, 144, 145, 146, 150, 155, 156, 160, 161, 167, 168, 188, 193, 208, 248, 251
  generative power 122, 125, 129, 139, 170
  "i-am" consciousness 119, 131, 162